Treasures

A Reading/Language Arts Program

Mc Graw Hill **Macmillan McGraw-Hill**

Contributors

Time Magazine, Accelerated Reader

Students with print disabilities may be eligible to obtain an accessible, audio version of the pupil edition of this textbook. Please call Recording for the Blind & Dyslexic at 1-800-221-4792 for complete information.

A

The **McGraw·Hill** Companies

Macmillan McGraw-Hill

Published by Macmillan/McGraw-Hill, of McGraw-Hill Education, a division of The McGraw-Hill Companies, Inc., Two Penn Plaza, New York, New York 10121.

Printed in the United States of America

ISBN-13: 978-0-02-198815-0/6
ISBN-10: 0-02-198815-3/6

3 4 5 6 7 8 9 (071/043) 11 10 09 08

Treasures

A Reading/Language Arts Program

Program Authors

Donald R. Bear
Janice A. Dole
Jana Echevarria
Jan E. Hasbrouck
Scott G. Paris
Timothy Shanahan
Josefina V. Tinajero

Macmillan McGraw-Hill

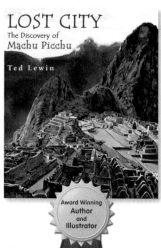

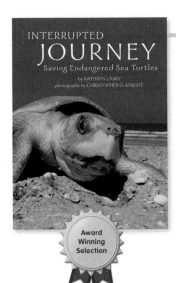

Unit 3

Great Ideas

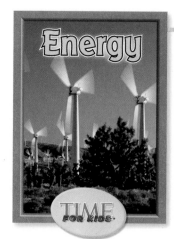

Unit 4 Achievements

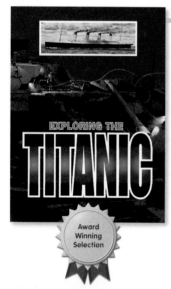

Award Winning Illustrator

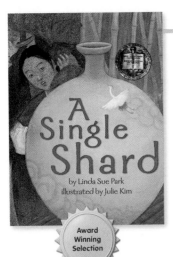

Award Winning Selection

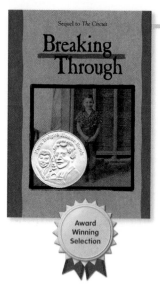

Award Winning Selection

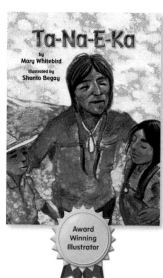

Award Winning Illustrator

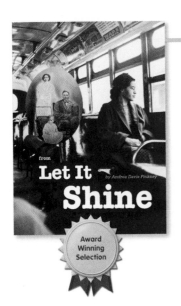

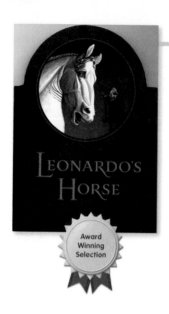

Award
Winning
Selection

Award
Winning
Author

RESCUE TEAMS

Talk About It

What do you think it would be like to be part of a rescue team?

LOG ON Find out more about rescue teams at
www.macmillanmh.com

Vocabulary

abruptly	engulf
anxiety	procedure
conscious	souvenir
intersection	cascade

Dictionary

Multiple-meaning Words have more than one definition.

conscious *adj.* knowing or realizing

conscious *adj.* awake

Sam's Summer Search

by Kristi McGee

Sam **abruptly** stopped swinging. He jumped off the swing without even slowing down. He yelled, "Mommmm, where's Champ?" He realized he hadn't seen his new puppy for over an hour.

Sam looked around the yard, behind the bushes, and under the picnic table. No Champ! His mother heard the **anxiety** and fear build in his voice as he called her a second time. "Mom, I can't find Champ!" She was **conscious** of the mounting fear in her son.

She came outside quickly. "Let's look around the yard first. I'm sure he has just gone to take a nap."

"Champ! Champ! Come here, boy!" shouted Sam and his mother over and over. But still no Champ. They did get other responses, though. José, the next-door neighbor, immediately agreed to help Sam and his mom search for the lost dog. Then Sam's friend Tasha joined in the search, along with her older brother, Jamal.

The group decided to split up to look for Champ. They scoured the neighborhood from the main **intersection** of the big streets to the smallest alley. Still no Champ. Sam felt sadness and fear **engulf** him. He was sure that his best friend was gone forever. He was overwhelmed by the thought it was his fault.

After an hour, Tasha suggested they go home and make posters with pictures of Champ. It was the **procedure**, or way of doing things, animal rescue had suggested when she had lost her cat. She explained, "Somebody called the next day. He found Boots in his backyard. Posters really work!"

REWARD!
Lost Puppy
His name is Champ.
Please call Sam: 555-2610

Sam agreed. When they got home, Sam made a poster with a picture of Champ. It was a **souvenir** photograph from doggie kindergarten that Sam received to remind him of Champ's progress. Then Sam heard a noise and opened his bedroom door. He was greeted with a **cascade** of wet kisses. Champ had been locked in the bedroom this whole time! Sam's mom was right. Champ had been napping. Sam had never been so happy in his entire life!

Reread for Comprehension

Story Structure
Character, Setting, Plot
A Story Map helps you figure out the characters, setting, and plot of a story. These are important parts of the story structure. The plot is often based on a problem that a character has. As the character tries to find a solution, the setting may have an influence on whether he or she is successful.

Use the Story Map as you reread "Sam's Summer Search."

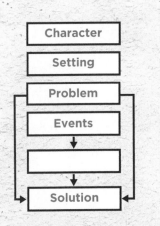

Character
Setting
Problem
Events
Solution

Comprehension

Genre

Realistic Fiction is an invented story that could have happened in real life.

Story Structure

Character, Setting, Plot
As you read, use your Story Map.

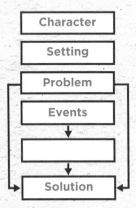

Character
Setting
Problem
Events
Solution

Read to Find Out

What does Sara learn about herself as she searches for Charlie?

THE SUMMER OF THE
SWANS

by Betsy Byars • illustrated by John Rowe

Sara and Joe must find Sara's little brother Charlie, a ten-year-old who suffered a brain injury as a small child and doesn't speak. Charlie leaves home during the night to find some swans he's seen on a nearby lake. After becoming lost in the woods near his home, Charlie doesn't know where to turn. In the morning Sara and her classmate Joe join the town's all-out search for the lost boy. But after frantically looking for hours, Sara and Joe have found only a slipper belonging to Charlie.

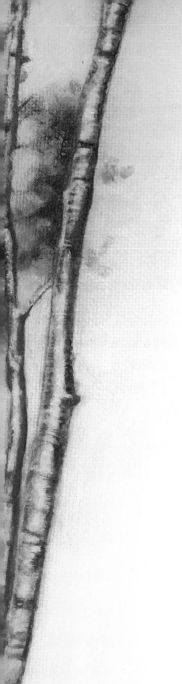

"**A**re you all right?"

"Yes, I just slipped."

She waited for a moment, bent over her knees, then she called, "Charlie! Charlie," without lifting her head.

"Oh, Charleeeeee," Joe shouted above her.

Sara knew Charlie would shout back if he heard her, the long wailing cry he gave sometimes when he was frightened during the night. It was such a familiar cry that for a moment she thought she heard it.

She waited, still touching the ground with one hand, until she was sure there was no answer.

"Come on," Joe said, holding out his hand.

He pulled her to her feet and she stood looking up at the top of the hill. Machines had cut away the earth there to get at the veins of coal, and the earth had been pushed down the hill to form a huge bank.

"I'll never get up that," she said. She leaned against a tree whose leaves were covered with the pale fine dirt which had filtered down when the machines had cut away the hill.

"Sure you will. I've been up it a dozen times."

He took her hand and she started after him, moving sideways up the steep bank. The dirt crumbled beneath her feet and she slid, skinned one knee, and then slipped again. When she had regained her balance she laughed wryly and said, "What's going to happen is that I'll end up pulling you all the way down the hill."

"No, I've got you. Keep coming."

She started again, putting one foot carefully above the other, picking her way over the stones. When she paused, he said, "Keep coming. We're almost there."

"I think it's a trick, like at the dentist's when he says, 'I'm almost through drilling.' Then he drills for another hour and says, 'Now, I'm really almost through drilling,' and he keeps on and then says, 'There's just one more spot and then I'll be practically really through.' "

"We must go to the same dentist."

"I don't think I can make it. There's no skin at all left on the sides of my legs."

"Well, we're really almost practically there now, in the words of your dentist."

She fell across the top of the dirt bank on her stomach, rested for a moment, and then turned and looked down the valley.

STRATEGY SKILL

Character
Describe Sara's emotions at this point. Support your answer.

She could not speak for a moment. There lay the whole valley in a way she had never imagined it, a tiny finger of civilization set in a sweeping expanse of dark forest. The black treetops seemed to crowd against the yards, the houses, the roads, giving the impression that at any moment the trees would close over the houses like waves and leave nothing but an unbroken line of black-green leaves waving in the sunlight.

Up the valley she could see the **intersection** where they shopped, the drugstore, the gas station where her mother had once won a set of twenty-four stemmed glasses which Aunt Willie would not allow them to use, the grocery store, the lot where the yellow school buses were parked for the summer. She could look over the valley and see another hill where white cows were all grouped together by a fence and beyond that another hill and then another.

She looked back at the valley and she saw the lake and for the first time since she had stood up on the hill she remembered Charlie.

Raising her hand to her mouth, she called, "Charlie! Charlie! Charlie!" There was a faint echo that seemed to waver in her ears.

"Charlie, oh, Charlie!" Her voice was so loud it seemed to ram into the valley.

Sara waited. She looked down at the forest, and everything was so quiet it seemed to her that the whole valley, the whole world was waiting with her.

"Charlie, hey, Charlie!" Joe shouted.

"Charleeeeee!" She made the sound of it last a long time. "Can you hear meeeeee?"

With her eyes she followed the trail she knew he must have taken—the house, the Akers' vacant lot, the old pasture, the forest. The forest that seemed powerful enough to **engulf** a whole valley, she thought with a sinking feeling, could certainly swallow up a young boy.

"Charlie! Charlie! Charlie!" There was a waver in the last syllable that betrayed how near she was to tears. She looked down at the Indian slipper she was still holding.

"Charlie, oh, Charlie." She waited. There was not a sound anywhere. "Charlie, where are you?"

"Hey, Charlie!" Joe shouted.

They waited in the same dense silence. A cloud passed in front of the sun and a breeze began to blow through the trees. Then there was silence again.

"Charlie, Charlie, Charlie, Charlie, Charlie."

She paused, listened, then bent **abruptly** and put Charlie's slipper to her eyes. She waited for the hot tears that had come so often this summer, the tears that had seemed so close only a moment before. Now her eyes remained dry.

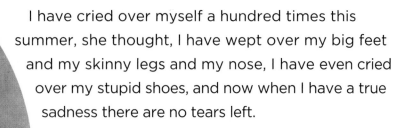

I have cried over myself a hundred times this summer, she thought, I have wept over my big feet and my skinny legs and my nose, I have even cried over my stupid shoes, and now when I have a true sadness there are no tears left.

She held the felt side of the slipper against her eyes like a blindfold and stood there, feeling the hot sun on her head and the wind wrapping around her legs, **conscious** of the height and the valley sweeping down from her feet.

"Listen, just because you can't hear him doesn't mean anything. He could be—"

"Wait a minute." She lowered the slipper and looked down the valley. A sudden wind blew dust into her face and she lifted her hand to shield her eyes.

"I thought I heard something. Charlie! Answer me right this minute."

She waited with the slipper held against her, one hand to her eyes, her whole body motionless, concentrating on her brother. Then she stiffened. She thought again she had heard something— Charlie's long high wail. Charlie could sound sadder than anyone when he cried.

In her **anxiety** she took the slipper and twisted it again and again as if she were wringing water out. She called, then stopped abruptly and listened. She looked at Joe and he shook his head slowly.

She looked away. A bird rose from the trees below and flew toward the hills in the distance. She waited until she could see it no longer and then slowly, still listening for the call that didn't come, she sank to the ground and sat with her head bent over her knees.

Beside her, Joe scuffed his foot in the dust and sent a **cascade** of rocks and dirt down the bank. When the sound of it faded, he began to call, "Charlie, hey, Charlie," again and again.

Charlie awoke, but he lay for a moment without opening his eyes. He did not remember where he was, but he had a certain dread of seeing it.

There were great parts of his life that were lost to Charlie, blank spaces that he could never fill in. He would find himself in a strange place and not know how he had got there. Like the time Sara had been hit in the nose with a baseball at the ice cream shop, and the blood and the sight of Sara kneeling on the ground in helpless pain had frightened him so much that he had turned and run without direction, in a frenzy, dashing headlong up the street, blind to cars and people.

By chance Mr. Weicek had seen him, put him in the car, and driven him home, and Aunt Willie had put him to bed, but later he remembered none of this. He had only awakened in bed and looked at the crumpled bit of ice-cream cone still clenched in his hand and wondered about it.

His whole life had been built on a strict routine, and as long as this routine was kept up, he felt safe and well. The same foods, the same bed, the same furniture in the same place, the same seat on the school bus, the same class **procedure** were all important to him. But always there could be the unexpected, the dreadful surprise that would topple his carefully constructed life in an instant.

The first thing he became aware of was the twigs pressing into his face, and he put his hand under his cheek. Still he did not open his eyes. Pictures began to drift into his mind; he saw Aunt Willie's box which was filled with old jewelry and buttons and knickknacks, and he found that he could remember every item in that box—the string of white beads without a clasp, the old earrings, the tiny book with **souvenir** fold-out pictures of New York, the plastic decorations from cakes, the turtle made of sea shells. Every item was so real that he opened his eyes and was surprised to see, instead of the glittering contents of the box, the dull and unfamiliar forest.

He raised his head and immediately felt the aching of his body. Slowly he sat up and looked down at his hands. His fingernails were black with earth, two of them broken below the quick, and he got up slowly and sat on the log behind him and inspected his fingers more closely.

Then he sat up straight. His hands dropped to his lap. His head cocked to the side like a bird listening. Slowly he straightened until he was standing. At his side his fingers twitched at the empty air as if to grasp something. He took a step forward, still with his head to the side. He remained absolutely still.

Then he began to cry out in a hoarse excited voice, again and again, screaming now, because he had just heard someone far away calling his name.

At the top of the hill Sara got slowly to her feet and stood looking down at the forest. She pushed the hair back from her forehead and moistened her lips. The wind dried them as she waited.

Joe started to say something but she reached out one hand and took his arm to stop him. Scarcely daring to believe her ears, she stepped closer to the edge of the bank. Now she heard it unmistakably—the sharp repeated cry—and she knew it was Charlie.

"Charlie!" she shouted with all her might.

She paused and listened, and his cries were louder and she knew he was not far away after all, just down the slope, in the direction of the ravine.

"It's Charlie, it's Charlie!"

A wild joy overtook her and she jumped up and down on the bare earth and she felt that she could crush the whole hill just by jumping if she wanted.

She sat and scooted down the bank, sending earth and pebbles in a cascade before her. She landed on the soft ground, ran a few steps, lost her balance, caught hold of the first tree trunk she could find, and swung around till she stopped.

She let out another whoop of pure joy, turned and ran down the hill in great strides, the puce tennis shoes slapping the ground like rubber paddles, the wind in her face, her hands grabbing one tree trunk after another for support. She felt like a wild creature who had traveled through the forest this way for a lifetime. Nothing could stop her now.

At the edge of the ravine she paused and stood gasping for breath. Her heart was beating so fast it pounded in her ears, and her throat was dry. She leaned against a tree, resting her cheek against the rough bark.

Character
How have Sara's emotions changed from the beginning of the story to when she hears Charlie?

She thought for a minute she was going to faint, a thing she had never done before, not even when she broke her nose. She hadn't even believed people really did faint until this minute when she clung to the tree because her legs were as useless as rubber bands.

There was a ringing in her ears and another sound, a wailing siren-like cry that was painfully familiar.

"Charlie?"

Charlie's crying, like the sound of a cricket, seemed everywhere and nowhere.

31

She walked along the edge of the ravine, circling the large boulders and trees. Then she looked down into the ravine where the shadows lay, and she felt as if something had turned over inside her because she saw Charlie.

He was standing in his torn pajamas, face turned upward, hands raised, shouting with all his might. His eyes were shut tight. His face was streaked with dirt and tears. His pajama jacket hung in shreds about his scratched chest.

He opened his eyes and as he saw Sara a strange expression came over his face, an expression of wonder and joy and disbelief, and Sara knew that if she lived to be a hundred no one would ever look at her quite that way again.

She paused, looked down at him, and then, sliding on the seat of her pants, went down the bank and took him in her arms.

"Oh, Charlie."

His arms gripped her like steel.

"Oh, Charlie."

She could feel his fingers digging into her back as he clutched her shirt. "It's all right now, Charlie, I'm here and we're going home." His face was buried in her shirt and she patted his head, said again, "It's all right now. Everything's fine."

She held him against her for a moment and now the hot tears were in her eyes and on her cheeks and she didn't even notice.

MEET THE AUTHOR

Betsy Byars's first book was rejected eleven times! But she kept reading (a book a day) and writing, and now she has many published books. *The Summer of the Swans* won the Newbery Medal, a distinguished honor. All of Byars's stories come from her life. She calls them scrapbooks because they bring back memories from her past. When Betsy is not reading or writing, she is flying in her plane, parked at the end of her airstrip outside her front door!

LOG ON Find out more about Betsy Byars at **www.macmillanmh.com**

Other books by Betsy Byars: *The Midnight Fox* and *The 18th Emergency*

Author's Purpose

Authors write to inform, persuade, entertain, or explain. In describing the longest day in Sara's life, Byars both entertains and informs. Give examples.

Comprehension Check

Summarize

STRATEGY SKILL

Use your Story Map to summarize *The Summer of the Swans*. Tell about the different emotions that Sara feels while searching for Charlie.

Character
Setting
Problem
Events
Solution

Think and Compare

STRATEGY SKILL

1. Reread page 32, paragraph 3. How do you think Charlie's reaction to seeing Sara changes how Sara feels about herself? **Story Structure: Character, Setting, Plot**

2. Why does Sara feel **anxiety** when she looks at the forest? Use evidence from the text to support your answer. **Analyze**

3. Reread the flashback section on page 27. If you saw the world like Charlie does, how would you handle being lost? **Evaluate**

4. The setting of the story presents many obstacles for Sara to overcome. If you were to plan a search for Charlie, what would you need in order to overcome these obstacles? **Synthesize**

5. Read "Sam's Summer Search" on pages 18–19. How do friends help in the two situations? **Reading/Writing Across Texts**

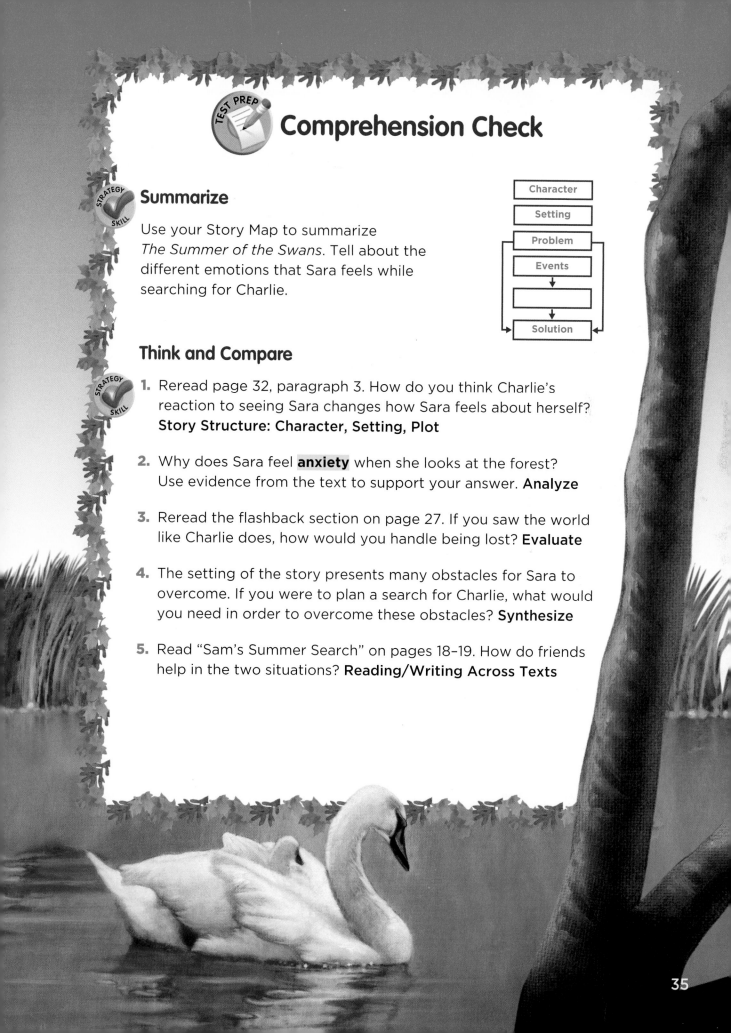

Caleb and Lisa Bryant, wearing snowshoes, headed up Route 113 in Stow, Maine, yesterday, in search of eight missing high school students and two teachers.

Storm Surprises Maine Students

By Brian MacQuarrie

SOUTH PARIS, Maine—For eight students in the Wilderness Leadership class at Oxford Hills High School, a three-day weekend hike in the White Mountain National Forest sounded like a fun, challenging course requirement.

But when a storm dumped up to 3 feet of snow on western Maine, a rugged learning experience turned into a crash course in winter survival.

After anxious night, all found cold, tired

Reported missing from their scheduled rendezvous in Gilead at 5:30 P.M. Sunday, the eight students and two teachers were not found until 11 A.M. yesterday [Monday], after a pilot spotted the group moving single-file in rugged snow-blanketed **terrain**. The discovery

Boston Globe, December 9

followed an unsuccessful ground search by volunteers on snowshoes.

After the group was reported missing Sunday, volunteers hiked 3 miles into the woods to look for the students. The five-hour effort turned up nothing, and the decision was made to wait until yesterday morning to also **canvass** the area by air.

A Maine Warden Service pilot lifted off and spotted the group close to their intended trail at about 11 A.M. Heavy **turbulence** prevented him from **descending** toward the hikers but the group clearly recognized the plane as part of a search team.

"They waved at the plane. They laid down, spread out, and waved," said Mark Latti, a spokesman for the Maine Warden Service. "The pilot then guided a [search] party in to their location."

Connect and Compare

1. Look at the picture and read the caption. What clues do they give you about the subject of the article? **Reading a Caption**

2. What can these hikers do differently next time to be safer? **Analyze**

3. How was the rescue team in this article and the rescue effort in *The Summer of the Swans* the same? In what ways were they different? **Reading/Writing Across Texts**

Social Studies Activity

Research how police officers or firefighters rescue people in trouble. Then write a news article about a police or fire rescue team. Read your article to the class as if you were a TV reporter broadcasting live from the scene.

 Find out more about rescue teams at **www.macmillanmh.com**

Writer's Craft

A Good Paragraph

A **good paragraph** includes a topic sentence that tells the reader what the subject of the paragraph will be. Supporting details add information about the topic.

Save Our Parks

by Kayla J.

My topic sentence tells about a problem in my neighborhood.

I used different types of supporting details to make my story interesting.

Our local parks were in bad shape. It was spring, and they needed to be cleaned up and to have new flowers planted. No one was doing anything, so I called the parks department. That's when I learned there was no money to take care of our parks. I talked to my friends, and then we decided to do something about it.

"Do you want to help fix up the park down the street on Saturday?" I asked over and over again. I called at least twenty adults and students in the neighborhood that week. Most people were happy to help.

Saturday morning came, and all my neighbors were at the park ready to work! They were waiting for me to give them directions. I asked, "Will you clean those leaves?" to the people who had rakes. I told others where to plant the flowers.

It was a fantastic day! The park became a true neighborhood place after we worked together.

Your Turn

Write a few paragraphs about a time you worked with others to achieve a goal. Perhaps you worked together to complete a school project or to play a game. Be sure to use a topic sentence and supporting details to organize your writing. Use the Writer's Checklist to evaluate your narrative.

Writer's Checklist

 Ideas and Content: Did I express the importance of cooperation in my narrative?

 Organization: Did I form **good paragraphs** by beginning each with a topic sentence and then giving details to back it up?

 Voice: What about my writing makes it obviously mine? What can I add to make it more interesting?

 Word Choice: Did I use vivid adjectives and verbs?

 Sentence Fluency: Did I use a variety of sentence types?

Conventions: Did I punctuate each sentence correctly? Did I check my spelling?

A LOST CITY

AN INCA CITY

by Miguel Rojas

Vocabulary

remote	undergrowth
escort	venomous
interpreter	withstood
vegetation	foretold

Word Parts

Compound Words are made up of two or more words. The meanings of the individual words provide clues to the compound word's meaning.

undergrowth = *under* + *growth* = small trees and bushes that grow under large trees

Dear Li,

I'm sorry I didn't write sooner. I was away for the last month. I went to Peru with my mom and dad. My mom's company sent her there on business. It was great! We flew into Cusco. One weekend we took a train to visit Machu Picchu.

"What is Machu Picchu?" you ask. Well, it is a **remote**—and I mean secluded—Inca city. Actually, it is the remains of that city. Machu Picchu is on top of a mountain peak that overlooks the Urubamba River. It is more than 7,000 feet above sea level!

Greetings from Machu Picchu

How did we get up that high? We could have hiked the Inca Trail for four days. Instead we decided to ride the train. It runs right along the river. It takes only a few hours. Our **escort** was a man from the area who is descended from the Inca. Not only did he provide information about the area, he also worked as our **interpreter**. Some of the people of Peru speak Quechua, which of course we don't understand.

As we rode the train, our escort pointed out unfamiliar **vegetation** that grows in the rain forest. The **undergrowth**, the plants that grow near the floor of the rain forest, was so thick I could hardly imagine trying to get through it back in 1911. That was when Hiram Bingham, the man who searched for the ruins, started his expedition. We also learned about the animals that inhabit the region. There are some **venomous** snakes that live there.

One bite can kill a person. It must have been quite a journey that Bingham took!

His trip was well worth it, in my opinion. Machu Picchu was so big and beautiful! The stones have **withstood** the test of time. They have been there since the 1400s. There were terraces cut into the sides of the mountain, and green was everywhere. To top it all off, we were in the clouds!

We saw where the people lived, where they worshipped, and where they farmed. The history is fascinating!

The travel brochure **foretold** we would have an amazing adventure, and it certainly didn't lie!

Yours truly,
Maria

Reread for **Comprehension**

Story Structure

Character, Setting, Plot
By analyzing the structure of a story readers can see how the characters, setting, and events are depicted and how they develop.

Use a Character, Setting, Plot Chart to help you note particular people, places, and events as you reread "An Inca City."

Character	Setting	Plot

Comprehension

Genre

Historical Fiction is set in a real time and place in the past. It may include real people and incidents that actually happened along with fictional characters and events.

Story Structure

Character, Setting, Plot

As you read, use your Character, Setting, Plot Chart.

Character	Setting	Plot

Read to Find Out

Why did Hiram Bingham embark on such a risky adventure?

Award Winning
Author
and
Illustrator

Lost City
The Discovery of
Machu Picchu
written and illustrated by Ted Lewin

In his first journey to South America, Yale professor
Hiram Bingham longed to explore the hidden
lands that lay beyond the snowcapped peaks of the
Andes. Legend had it that the lost city of the Inca,
Vilcapampa, lay there. Bingham was determined to
discover it. So in 1910 the Yale Peruvian Expedition
was organized. Finally, in July 1911, Bingham and his
fellow adventurers arrived in Cusco, the first capital
city of the Inca. What lay ahead for them was far from
what they had expected. And more amazing. Our
story begins high in the mountains of Peru . . . .

The boy looked out at the cloud-covered peaks all around him. Already his papa was working in the terraced fields. But last night he had dreamed of a tall stranger carrying a small black box. He could not get the dream out of his mind.

Suddenly, the clouds burned off and the mountains were bathed in glorious light. The dream **foretold** of something wonderful, he was sure.

Sixty miles south, in Cusco, Hiram Bingham gazed thoughtfully at the old Incan stone wall. He had come to Peru in search of Vilcapampa, the lost city of the Inca. But right here was the most beautiful stonework he had ever seen—huge stones cut so perfectly that not even a razor blade could be slipped between them.

The Inca had no iron tools to carve them, no wheel or draft animals to move them. The wall had **withstood** time and earthquakes. How had the Inca built them!

It was a mystery.

He walked through the cobbled streets of the old capital. The Spanish had come to this city, conquered the Inca, taken their gold, and built churches over their temples. Suddenly, he stopped. Before him was the famous Temple of the Sun. He placed his hands on the sun-warmed stones so beautifully carved, as if they had grown together.

Hidden in the mountains, the lost city would be built of stones like these. Would it hold gold and fabulous riches like the Spanish had found in Cusco?

More than ever he was determined to find that city.

The next day Bingham began his search. He would look for ruins—that might be the key.

He and his party, accompanied by military **escort** Sergeant Carrasco, left by mule train for the sacred valley of the Urubamba River.

They came to the sleepy old village of Ollantaytambo, long ago an important city. Its ancient stone terraces stepped up into the clouds.

"Are there any ruins nearby?" Bingham asked. He went door to door. He sat for hours in the cantina. "Are there any ruins near here?" he asked anyone who came in. "Do you know of the lost city of Vilcapampa?" No one knew of it.

Traveling north, the adventurers came upon a **remote** and wild canyon. Granite cliffs rose thousands of feet above the roaring rapids of the Urubamba River. In the distance were snowcapped mountains over three miles high. Bingham's determination to find the lost city grew with each turn of the increasingly wild trail.

Meanwhile, high on one of these granite ridges, the boy tried to help his papa on the terraces. But he couldn't shake the dream from his mind. Who was this stranger with the black box? When would he come? What was in the black box? Anxiously, he searched the mountains for a sign.

Far below in the valley, Bingham's party camped on a sandy beach alongside the thundering rapids of the Urubamba. Days had gone by. He was tired and discouraged. No one knew of any ruins.

But now the travelers aroused the curiosity of a local farmer named Arteaga.

"Are there ruins nearby?" Bingham asked when Arteaga ventured into camp.

This time, through the **interpreter**, the farmer said, "Yes. There are very good ruins on top of the mountain called Machu Picchu."

The farmer pointed straight up.

"Can you take us there?" Bingham asked.

"No," said Arteaga. "It is a very hard climb and there are many snakes." Bingham offered him coins. Arteaga nodded—he would show them the way.

Arteaga led them down the river trail. Suddenly, he plunged into the jungle. Bingham and the sergeant followed Arteaga through dense **undergrowth** down to the very edge of the river to a flimsy bridge made of slim logs. What was he getting himself into!

Sergeant Carrasco and Arteaga took off their shoes and crossed easily, gripping with their bare feet. Bingham was terrified—he crept across the bridge on hands and knees. One slip and he would be dashed to pieces in the roaring torrent below.

Setting and Plot
How does the dangerous setting contribute to the story's suspense?

They climbed the bank into dense jungle. Now the slopes were slippery and the heat terrible. Arteaga had warned them of the fer-de-lance, a very **venomous** snake. Bingham's eyes searched the jungle.

Up and up they climbed. The wide river was now but a silver thread, far below. Arteaga could think of nothing but the fer-de-lance; Sergeant Carrasco thought about his good, sturdy shoes; Bingham thought of nothing but the lost city. They cut their way through tangled thickets. Up and up they climbed.

Had an hour passed? Two? Three? Now they crept on all fours. They slipped and slid. In some places, they held on by their fingertips.

Finally, thirsty and exhausted, they broke through the jungle into sunlight. Above them stood a little Quechua boy beside a stone hut. What could he be doing at the top of this mountain?

"*Ama llulla, ama quella, ama su'a*" (Don't lie, don't be lazy, don't steal), the boy called out in the traditional Quechua greeting.

It was the tall stranger from his dream. Carrying the black box!

The boy's whole family crowded around to greet the exhausted travelers, then brought gourds of cool water and boiled sweet potatoes.

Bingham, still gasping for breath, asked, "Where are the ruins?"

The boy said, "*Amuy, amuy!*" (Come, come!)

Bingham and the sergeant left Arteaga behind and followed at the boy's urging. "*Amuy, amuy!*" he kept saying.

At first they saw only stone terraces like the ones they had seen at Ollantaytambo. They looked as if they had been recently cleared of jungle and the **vegetation** burned off in order to plant crops.

But there were no ruins. Just more jungle beyond. Bingham had climbed this mountain and found—no lost city.

"*Amuy, amuy!*" Still, the boy beckoned him into the jungle beyond. Weary and discouraged, Bingham followed. At first all he saw were bamboo thickets and more tangled vines. Then he looked closer. Through the vines, he saw—stones. Inca stones. Then walls, beautiful stone walls! They were covered with mosses. And trees.

"*Jaway, jaway!*" (See, see!) the boy whispered, pointing ahead to a curved stone wall. Bingham pushed his way to it and placed his hands on the fine granite stones. A sun temple. More beautiful even than the one in Cusco.

They came to a grand stone staircase. Where could this lead? What else was here?

"*Jaway, jaway,*" the boy called.

At the top of the staircase was a clearing. A small vegetable garden, and then . . . a temple built of enormous stones. Grander than any Bingham had ever seen. It stole his breath away.

Something was going on here, he could sense it. Something just beyond his eyes. What was it?

He followed the boy to another temple. As magnificent. This one had three windows. But now he looked across the countryside. He looked past the thickets, past the vines. He began to see the outlines of stone streets and stone cottages. He began to see the outlines of a city!

"Here, boy," he said as he opened the black box that he had been carrying, extended the bellows and focused his camera.

Character and Plot
Why does Bingham decide to stop and take the picture?

The first picture would be of the boy. The boy who had led him to Vilcapampa, lost city of the Incas.

But about this Bingham was wrong. When the vines were removed and the tales told, he had discovered not Vilcapampa, but a place even more amazing.

He had stumbled on Machu Picchu, a city lost in time, a city lost in the clouds.

Traveling with Ted Lewin

Ted Lewin grew up with a lion, an iguana, a chimpanzee, … oh, and a mom, a dad, a sister, and two brothers. He always wanted to be an illustrator and paid for art school by being a professional wrestler. Today he and his wife, Betsy, also an artist, travel the world finding stories. In Machu Picchu, Ted took thousands of pictures, which he used to sketch his illustrations. After that, the painting went very fast. Ted says it was more fun than anything he has ever done before.

Other books illustrated by Ted Lewin:
Peppe the Lamplighter and *Elephant Quest*

Author's Purpose

Ted Lewin's account of the discovery of Machu Picchu is both entertaining and informative. Describe three things that you enjoyed learning from this selection.

 Find out more about Ted Lewin at **www.macmillanmh.com**

Comprehension Check

Summarize

STRATEGY SKILL

Use your Character, Setting, Plot Chart to help you summarize *Lost City: The Discovery of Machu Picchu*. How does Professor Bingham find the lost city?

Character	Setting	Plot

Think and Compare

STRATEGY SKILL

1. Before he realizes what he has really discovered, what is Professor Bingham searching for? Use evidence from the text to support your answer. **Story Structure: Character, Setting, Plot**

2. Why is the boy's dream at the beginning of the story so important? **Analyze**

3. Think about a time when you discovered something that surprised you. What was it? Where did you find it? Why was it important to you? **Synthesize**

4. Why do you think it would be important to uncover something like these **remote** ruins? Explain your answer. **Evaluate**

5. Read Maria's letter to Li on pages 42-43. Pretend that Maria has written you a similar letter detailing her trip to Machu Picchu. Write her back and tell her about *Lost City*. Talk about a character or an event that she might find interesting. **Reading/Writing Across Texts**

Genre

Nonfiction: Textbooks present facts and ideas about nonfiction topics.

Text Features

Textbook segments often feature changes in print, such as key words in color and boldface or italicized type. Headings and subheadings help to organize information. Captions and labels provide more information for photos and graphic aids.

Content Vocabulary

maize
quipu
terracing
aqueducts
legacy

EMPIRE
IN THE ANDES

Once a great empire grew in the Andes mountains of South America. This civilization took its name from its ruler, the Inca. The empire stretched from what is today Ecuador to central Chile.

Like the Aztec, the Inca worshiped the sun, depended on **maize**, and organized a strong army.

FROM VILLAGE TO EMPIRE

The Inca Empire began around 1200 in Cuzco (KOOS koh), a small village in a fertile mountain valley in what is today Peru. A drought reduced their farmland, so the Inca took over their neighbors' land. During the 1300s, the Inca ruled most of the valley.

In 1438, a ruler called Pachakuti (pah chah KOO tee) Inca extended the Inca borders west to the Pacific Ocean and south to Lake Titicaca high in the central Andes.

SWEAT OF THE SUN

The Inca worked rich gold mines. They called the metal "sweat of the sun" and used it to decorate temples to their sun god. The sun god's temple in Cuzco had a huge sculpture of him decorated with precious stones. There was even a golden "garden" with flowers and birds made of gold.

THE INCA CAPITAL

Cuzco served as the center of government, religion, and trade. The temples and government buildings at the center of Cuzco were constructed of stone blocks. These blocks still fit together so well that it is impossible to put a knife between them. They can also withstand earthquakes.

Beyond the main plaza were the palaces of the emperor and wealthy nobles. The nobles wore special headbands and earrings. One of the Spanish soldiers who visited the city was impressed by Inca wealth and skill. He wrote the following description in the 1500s:

The interior of the temple [of the Sun] was . . . a mine of gold. On the western wall was . . . [the sun god] . . . engraved on a massive plate of gold of enormous [size], thickly powdered with emeralds and special stones . . . The morning sun fell directly upon it at its rising, lighting up the whole apartment.

The ruins of Machu Picchu, an ancient city of the Inca Empire, high in the Andes

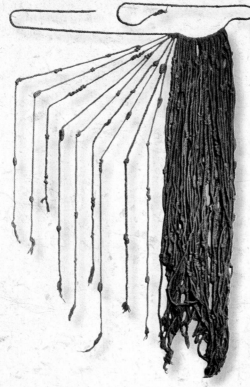

Peruvian quipu for counting and recording facts and events; of Inca workmanship.

TECHNOLOGY: SPEAKING WITH THREAD

The Inca used a special cord called a **quipu** (KEE poo). A quipu was about two feet long and had many threads of different colors hanging from it. For example, white threads stood for silver, yellow stood for gold, and red stood for war. By tying knots in the strings in a particular order, the Inca could send messages and keep records of battles, items traded, and births and deaths in a village.

PUTTING IT TOGETHER

Inca farmers began **terracing** and using fertilizer to increase the crops their land produced. In addition to many roads, Inca engineers built large **aqueducts**.

The Inca Empire controlled much of western South America until it was conquered by the Spanish in 1532. However, the Inca **legacy** remains. Millions of people still speak the Inca language, and many of the songs and poems of the Inca are still recited today.

A LOST CITY

The Inca built a vast network of highways over 19,000 miles in length. One road climbed into the Andes and ended at the city called Machu Picchu (MAHCH oo PEEK choo). This town was forgotten until an American explorer named Hiram Bingham came across it in 1911.

No one is sure why Machu Picchu was built or why it was abandoned. Machu Picchu is just one of many Inca mysteries. Although Spanish conquerors destroyed many Inca treasures in the 1500s, those remaining can give us a sense of the brilliant culture created by the "Children of the Sun."

The Inca built terraces on hillsides to hold rainwater for crops.

A stone wall (right) from Machu Picchu

Connect and Compare

1. How do the subheadings, photos, and captions help you understand the text better? **Reading Text Features**

2. How do we know the Inca were brilliant engineers? **Analyze**

3. Compare "Empire in the Andes" with *Lost City*. Give examples of two details in *Lost City* that are explained further here. **Reading/ Writing Across Texts**

 Social Studies Activity

If you were with Hiram Bingham in Machu Picchu in 1911, what would you include in a journal entry? Include some facts you have read about Machu Picchu.

 Find out more about Machu Picchu at **www.macmillanmh.com**

Writer's Craft

Topic Sentence and Details

Even when writing a letter, you should include a strong topic sentence and important details. Delete **unimportant details** that do not relate to your topic or improve your writing.

Write a Friendly Letter

October 16, 2008

Dear Aunt Becky,

> My topic sentence is about my visit to a science center.

How are you? Yesterday, Mom, Dad, my friend Nicole, and I went to COSI, Columbus's Center of Science and Industry.

COSI is enormous! We went to the planetarium and saw a show about our universe. We sat on benches around the edges of the room and leaned our heads back to look up at the stars.

> I remembered to make my letter interesting by including only the specific details about my special day.

My favorite part of the center was the Gadgets section. It had places where people can take things apart and put them back together again to see how they work. I actually lifted myself up off the floor with a pulley.

Do you remember how I told you that I wanted to be a scientist when I grow up? Well after visiting the Gadgets exhibit, I think I want to be an engineer.

Before we left, we got the calendar of events. I want to be sure to go back to see the dinosaur exhibit next month.

Love,

Jennifer

Your Turn

Write a letter to a friend or a relative. In your letter, describe an interesting place you visited. You might describe a visit to a local historical site or a trip to a local museum. Use details to capture the feeling of the place. Remember to use complete sentences and proper punctuation. Use the Writer's Checklist to review your letter.

Columbus's Center of Science and Industry Gadget Display

Writer's Checklist

☑ **Ideas and Content:** Did I delete **unimportant details** about the place I chose?

☑ **Organization:** What kind of order did I use? Why does it work well for this letter?

☑ **Voice:** Does the letter express my feelings about the place? Which words clearly express my opinions?

☑ **Word Choice:** Which words bring the description to life? Which words could be more vivid?

☑ **Sentence Fluency:** Did I write in complete sentences?

☑ **Conventions:** Did I punctuate the letter properly, using commas where needed? Did I capitalize the greeting and the first word in the closing? Did I check my spelling?

Talk About It

What is the role of science in people's daily lives?

LOG ON Find out more about scientists at
www.macmillanmh.com

SCIENCE FOR ALL

Vocabulary

altered

erode

absorb

concentrated

innovations

How LONG Will We LIVE?

In 1900 the average American lived to be 47 years old. By the end of the twentieth century, the average life span was 76 years. The U.S. government predicts that by the year 2100, 5 million Americans will be 100 or more years old. Many of today's kids will live to see the year 2100. Some may be around to ring in 2140!

FOREVER YOUNG

In the future, scientists may be able to more easily replace body parts that don't work well with new ones.

Cynthia Kenyon, a scientist who studies aging, believes it may be possible for humans to live twice as long and still look and feel half their age. Kenyon has proved that this is possible for tiny creatures called round worms. She **altered** some chemicals inside their bodies. This change allowed worms to live four times as long as they normally would. The change also turns back the effects of aging. The worms look as young as when they were babies!

No matter what the future may hold for us, one thing seems certain: we will have longer, healthier lives to look forward to!

Where did all that SALT come from?

Have you ever wondered why the ocean is salty? The short answer to that question is because sodium and chloride, the two ingredients in salt, flow into it.

Want a little more information? Here's the full answer: Rivers **erode,** or wear away, rocks containing sodium and carry it out to sea. Undersea volcanoes spit up chloride. Sea creatures **absorb** many of the other minerals found in the ocean, such as calcium and sulfur. They do not soak up sodium or chloride, however, so the salt gets **concentrated**. It stays in the sea water and accumulates.

Indian Ocean

Dorothea Lange with camera

Household Inventions Time Line

Here are a few of history's most amazing **innovations**, or inventions. Many seem almost magical, while others are tools to make life a little easier or more fun.

Alexander Graham Bell, inventor of the telephone

ca. 3800-3600 B.C.	Wheel
ca. A.D. 100	Paper
1870	Chewing gum
1876	Telephone
1885	Bicycle
1888	Hand-held camera
1891	Zipper
1893	Movies
1904	Ice-cream cone
1927	Television
1938	Ballpoint pen
1945	Microwave oven
1963	Home video recorder
1972	Compact disc
1983	Cell phones
1991	World Wide Web
1995	DVDs

LOG ON Find out more about inventions at www.macmillanmh.com

Gecko Glue, Cockroach Scouts, And Spider Silk Bridges

How can lizards, cockroaches, and spiders help make life better for humans?

How do product makers come up with big **innovations?** For some of their best new ideas, methods, and devices, scientists and researchers turn to designs found in nature for inspiration.

🐾 WHAT MAKES GECKOS STICK?

They run across ceilings. They zip up and down walls. What kind of crazy glue keeps geckos from tumbling down? Researchers at the University of California, Berkeley, and Lewis and Clark College in Portland, Oregon, have solved the mystery.

Scientists say that what makes geckos stick isn't tacky glue or suction, it's geometry. "We've solved the puzzle of how geckos use millions of tiny foot hairs to adhere to even smooth surfaces, such as polished glass," says scientist Kellar Autumn.

Gecko feet are covered with millions of tiny hairs called setae (SEE-tee), which split into hundreds of even tinier branches. Each gecko foot has as many as one billion of these split ends. Researchers

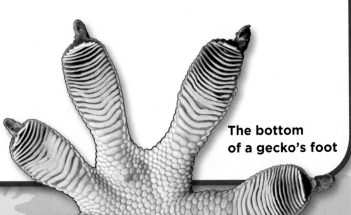

The bottom of a gecko's foot

found that the angle the toe hairs make with a surface allows them to stick. As scientists watched films of geckos in action, they noticed that geckos curl and uncurl their toes to get them to stick to surfaces.

Why the big interest in gecko "glue"? Researchers believe that a human-made version would be an ideal dry adhesive that could be useful underwater or in space. Researchers have already made artificial hair tips that stick almost as well as the geckos' own. "Now we've got to make billions of them to get significant adhesive force," says engineer Ron Fearing.

One thing is certain—it'll be a super glue. A million tiny setae, **concentrated** in an area the size of a dime, would be strong enough to lift a 45-pound child!

A gecko clings upside-down to glass.

🦎 COCKROACH SCOUTS

Think before you squish: The next roach you step on could save your life. That, at least, is the goal of Jeff Brinker, a scientist at Sandia National Laboratories in Albuquerque, New Mexico. Brinker and his team have thought of a way to use these insects to detect chemical or biological dangers.

The idea isn't as strange as it may sound. The government is already exploring how to use everything from bug-sized robots to live wasps for similar tasks. Brinker once worked on a project that tried to train honeybees to sniff out explosives.

Roaches were a natural next step. "It's a very durable beast," Brinker says. "Plus they tend to explore nooks and crannies." The key, Brinker says, is to use yeast that has been genetically **altered**. The yeast cells are glued to the bug's body and will glow when they come in contact with something harmful.

American cockroach

Living cells have several advantages over sensor machines, says Susan Brozik, a scientist working with Brinker. They're small, cheap, and very sensitive to their surroundings. Agent Roach reporting for duty!

The silk in a spider web is both flexible and strong.

THE ITSY-BITSY SPIDER IS A BIG BUILDER

Legend has it that when the mighty ruler Genghis Khan (JEN-gis KAHN) conquered Asia, his soldiers were protected from enemy arrows by very special clothing. These leather garments were interwoven with one of the strongest materials then known to humans—spider silk!

Eight hundred years later, scientists still can't make thread more durable than the stuff spiders use to make webs. But biologists trying to copy nature's strongest fiber are making great progress. The U.S. Army plans to use one of the Great Khan's tricks: making bulletproof vests woven with artificial spider silk.

What makes spider silk so remarkable is its unique combination of strength and stretch. Spider silk is as strong as the fiber now used to make bulletproof vests, but far more elastic. The web of a golden silk spider is strong enough to trap a bird. Researchers have figured out that a web woven of spider silk the thickness of a pencil could stop a jet in midair!

"When you think about the size and speed of a flying bee, the web that catches it has to be able to **absorb** a lot of energy," says Jean Herbert, an Army scientist in Natick, Massachusetts. Herbert is researching ways to use the tough fiber in everyday objects. Among the possibilities: jeans that don't wear out, car and truck bumpers that resist dents, and bridges whose structures will not easily **erode** and can withstand earthquakes.

Unlike silkworms, spiders cannot be raised on farms. (One reason: they tend to eat one another!) So scientists are inventing ways of making spider silk without spiders.

The ability to spin a web is controlled by certain genes inside the cells of spiders. Researchers at two chemical companies have made copies of these genes and put them into certain easy-to-grow bacteria. The scientists' goal: bacteria that can churn out spider silk. Transplanting spider genes is a sticky business. The genes don't always act exactly the way they would in a living spider, so the silk is not as strong or elastic as the real stuff.

For now, the surest silk-production method is the one that Genghis Khan supposedly used—spiders themselves. "I never step on spiders," says chemist John O'Brien. "I have too much respect for them."

Spider silk is strong enough to trap flies and bigger prey.

Think and Compare

1. What covers the feet of geckos and allows them to stick to walls?

2. Why are scientists interested in duplicating spider silk?

3. Of these three projects, which one will help the world the most? Explain your ideas.

4. How are the scientific innovations described in "How Long Will We Live?" on page 68 different from those in the gecko glue article?

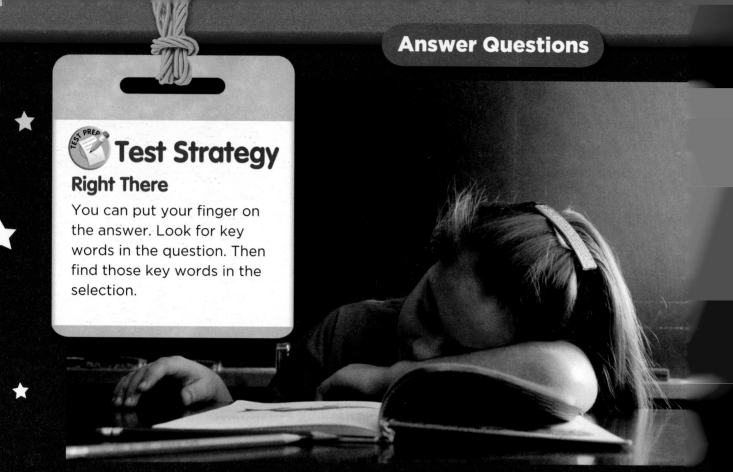

SLEEP IS GOOD FOR YOUR BRAIN

Tired of puzzling over a problem? Sleep on it! Research by a group of German scientists shows that getting enough sleep makes people better problem solvers. They found that people who sleep for at least eight hours each night are better at solving problems and thinking creatively. For their research study, the scientists divided 106 people into groups. The group that got eight hours of sleep was more than twice as likely to find a shortcut for solving a math problem than the group that had stayed awake all night.

Skimping on sleep has become a bad habit for many American kids. According to a survey by the National Sleep Foundation, 51% of kids ages 10 to 18 go to bed at 10 P.M. or later on school nights. The foundation reported that nearly 60% of 7- to 12-year-olds admitted that they felt tired during the day.

This is important information for parents and for kids. Getting enough sleep can improve a kid's performance

Directions: Answer the questions.

1. **The research by a group of German scientists shows that**

   A people who sleep enough are better problem solvers.

   B school administrators and parents should sleep more hours each night.

   C good math students do not require eight hours of sleep.

   D the National Sleep Foundation has 106 members.

Tip

Look for key words.

2. **According to the selection, how did the study group that got eight hours of sleep demonstrate that sleep improves performance?**

   A They demonstrated more factual knowledge.

   B They found a quicker way to solve a math problem.

   C They scored much higher on standardized tests.

   D They did not doze off while taking the test.

3. **Why is skimping on sleep bad for you?**

   A American kids require more sleep.

   B Kids fail in school if they are not in bed by 8:00 P.M.

   C When you feel tired, you can't perform well at school.

   D Not getting enough sleep is good for your brain.

4. **What is the main idea of this article?**

5. **Why do you think so many kids skimp on sleep?**

Write to a Prompt

"Sleep Is Good for Your Brain" reports on the benefits of getting a good night's sleep. Do you think people are getting enough sleep? What might be the benefits of getting more sleep? Use details from the article to support your answer.

I used details from the article in my answer.

In Praise of Sleep

Scientific research says that sleep is good for us. People who get enough sleep think better and do better work. Research also shows that most of us don't get enough sleep and that a lot of kids feel tired during the day at school.

Getting enough sleep is like eating healthful foods or getting enough exercise. It is an important part of our daily life and something we all need to do.

It isn't always easy to go to bed early enough to get 8 hours of sleep. We have to make adjustments in our daily routines. One thing we can do is find ways to get our homework done earlier. It will only take a few nights to prove that it is worth it. Not only will kids do better in school, but they will also feel better.

A good night's sleep is an important part of our daily lives.

Writing Prompt

Getting enough sleep is important, as the selection "Sleep Is Good for Your Brain" points out. The article describes the short-term effects of lack of sleep. But what might the long-term effects be? How important is sleep? Explain what the long-term consequences of not getting enough sleep could be for young people. Use research to support your answer.

Writer's Checklist

☑   Ask yourself, who is my audience?

☑   Think about your purpose for writing.

☑   Choose the correct form for your writing.

☑   Plan your writing before beginning.

☑   Be sure your ideas are clear and organized.

☑   Use your best spelling, grammar, and punctuation.

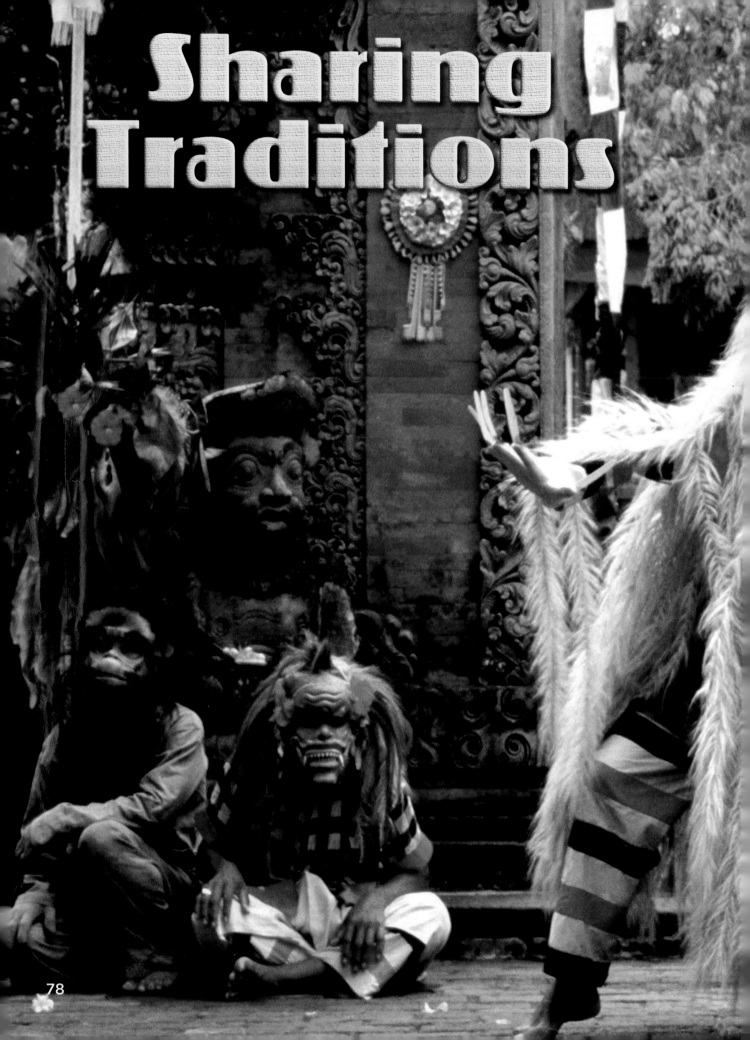

Sharing Traditions

Talk About It

Story telling is entertaining. Why do you think traditional stories are important to a culture?

LOG ON Find out more about sharing traditions at **www.macmillanmh.com**

Vocabulary

rummaged	pathetic
undetected	ricocheting
chameleon	famine
generosity	scrounging

Context Clues

STRATEGY SKILL

Context Clues provide hints to help readers figure out the meaning of an unfamiliar word. Restatement is a kind of context clue that gives a definition of the unfamiliar word.

"Her great-grandmother left her village because of a famine, a time of extreme scarcity of food."

Keira's Magical Moment

by Leonora Halvi

As Keira climbed into bed, she thought about tomorrow's field trip. Her class was going to a presentation by a West African traditional storyteller. Keira was excited because she was of West African descent. Her great-grandmother had come to the United States from Senegal. Until now, Keira hadn't thought much about her roots.

When her alarm went off, Keira **rummaged** through her closet. She was looking for something that showed her West African roots. She dug through every drawer, but she couldn't find anything that really stood out. Finally, she put on a white shirt and jeans. Despite her plain clothes, she hoped that her interest in her heritage would not go **undetected**.

At the community center, Keira was lucky enough to get a front-row seat. The first speaker talked about African writers and how they often use traditional stories with traditional characters, such as the Tortoise and the Spider. The speaker mentioned writers her mother and grandmother liked! Also, Tortoise was a favorite character in Keira's bedtime stories. Finally, the speaker mentioned Doudou N'Diaye Rose. He was Keira's favorite drummer. He was from Senegal. She began to realize just how much her West African heritage influenced her American life.

Finally, the griot, or storyteller, took the stage. He told a story that explained how the **chameleon**, a small lizard, changed its colors. Then he introduced the tricksters Spider and Tortoise. They were known to fake **generosity** while actually looking for a handout. Some of the stories made these characters seem **pathetic** as they fought for every last scrap. However, they were simply naughty. They certainly did learn their lessons!

Keira couldn't keep her mind from **ricocheting** through all the different stories her mother had told. Her memory was bouncing around like a ball! She knew about everything the griot said.

After the presentation, the class talked to the griot. Keira told about how her great-grandmother had moved to the United States from Senegal. Her great-grandmother left her village because of a **famine**, a time of extreme scarcity of food. She had explained to Keira's grandmother that the villagers spent days **scrounging** for food. Her great-grandmother eventually came to the United States. Keira told the griot about the familiar bedtime stories.

When Keira was finished, the griot pointed out that she had just taken on his job. She had described her family and the stories they told. Keira could hardly wait to tell her mother and grandmother the news!

Reread for **Comprehension**

STRATEGY SKILL

Make Inferences and Analyze

Cause and Effect

In a story, the actions of the characters often cause a series of events to unfold. Making inferences about a character's actions can help you identify cause-and-effect relationships between events in the story.

Use your Cause-and-Effect Chart to record important causes of events as you reread "Keira's Magical Moment."

Cause → Effect		
	→	
	→	
	→	
	→	

Comprehension

Genre

A **Folk Tale** is a story based on the traditions of a people or region which is handed down from one generation to the next and becomes legendary.

Make Inferences and Analyze

Cause and Effect

As you read, use your Cause and Effect Chart.

Cause	→	Effect
	→	
	→	
	→	
	→	

Read to Find Out

What is the cause of Chameleon's generosity?

The Magic Gourd

by Baba Wagué Diakité

Award Winning
Author
and
Illustrator

It all began

when the sun refused to allow the
clouds to gather, and there was
no rain. First came drought. Then
came **famine**. Everyone was hungry.
And it was then that Brother Rabbit
wandered around the parched
countryside searching for wild roots
to feed his starving family. As he
walked, he sang . . .

Feeyeh ku, feeyeh ku.
Waara sa kun tay.
Luck will come. Life will be good.

Suddenly, Rabbit was interrupted by a sweet little voice that called out, "Dogo Zan! Dogo Zan! Rescue me from this thorny bush! My arms are being poked and scratched! Help me, and I will pay you well."

Rabbit was busy, but still he stopped. "I will help simply to avoid seeing my brother suffer," said Rabbit. Gently he lowered his hand between the thorny branches and saved the green **chameleon**. As Rabbit turned to leave, Chameleon called out to him once again.

"Dogo Zan! Don't go yet! Would you mind getting my gourd from the bush, too?"

"A gourd?" cried Brother Rabbit. "You want me to scratch myself again for a little gourd?"

"Please, Dogo Zan," begged Chameleon. "I will reward you well."

Again, Rabbit's kind nature got the best of him, and he bent into the thorny bush and **rummaged** around.

Rabbit brought out a beautifully decorated gourd and handed it to Chameleon. But Chameleon just said, "Keep it. It's your reward."

"It's just an empty gourd," Rabbit cried.

"It's not *just* an empty gourd," Chameleon replied. "It's MAGIC!"

"*Ee ko dee!*" cried Rabbit. "A magic gourd?"

"Oh, yes!" said Chameleon. "Watch this: Magic Gourd, fill yourself up with insects!"

Brother Rabbit watched in amazement as Chameleon licked up a bowl full of insects.

"Why are you giving me such a valuable gift?" Rabbit asked.

"You were kind to me, Brother Rabbit," Chameleon said. "Besides, I have my own secret for catching insects," and he quickly unrolled his lo-o-o-o-o-ong tongue for Rabbit to admire.

Rabbit thanked Brother Chameleon and rushed home with his gourd.

STRATEGY SKILL

Cause and Effect
What happened as a result of Rabbit's kindness?

As soon as he arrived home, his entire family eagerly gathered around.

"An empty gourd?" they all gasped in disbelief.

"It's not *just* an empty gourd," said Brother Rabbit. "It's a magic gourd! Watch this: Magic Gourd!" he said. "Fill yourself up with carrots!"

To their astonishment, the gourd magically filled with carrots. Happily, they ate them all.

"Magic Gourd! Fill yourself up with couscous!" he said.

Again they ate until they were satisfied.

"Magic Gourd! Fill yourself up with water!" he said, and they drank deeply.

From that day on, Brother Rabbit's family drank and ate well.

But as much as they wanted to keep the magic gourd a family secret, they also could not sit and watch friends and neighbors suffer. So they invited them to share their meals every day.

And this is how word floated around from one to the other until it came to the house of Mansa Jugu, the greedy king.

One day, the greedy king and his soldiers broke into Rabbit's compound and forced the little gourd away from him. Now, with the magic gourd in his possession, Mansa Jugu sat day and night commanding the little gourd to fill and refill with more and more gold.

Meanwhile, unable to get the magic gourd back, Rabbit returned once again to his poor life, **scrounging** for wild roots to feed his hungry family. Despite the hardships of the moment, he still had courage to sing . . .

*Feeyeh ku, feeyeh ku. Waara
sa kun tay.*

Luck will come. Life will be good.

Cause and Effect
What happened when Rabbit decided to share the gourd with his neighbors?

88

One day, while hunting for roots, Rabbit heard his name being called again.

"Dogo Zan, Dogo Zan!"

Recognizing the sweet little voice, he turned and looked in all directions. Slowly the chameleon came into view right next to him on a sparkling green rock.

"Dogo Zan! What has happened to you?" cried Chameleon. "You look skinny and **pathetic**!"

Rabbit told him all about the greedy king who stole the gourd. Again, Brother Chameleon offered a gift to Brother Rabbit. This time, it was the beautiful crystal rock he had been standing on.

"What is this, Brother Chameleon?" asked Rabbit.

"This is just a *fara*, a little rock!" As soon as the words came out of his mouth, the rock leaped into the air and bounced off his head.

"*Eee-heeeee! Fara!*" cried Rabbit. "Stop! Stop!"

Again, the rock knocked his head.

"Excuse me, Dogo Zan," said the chameleon. "You must call him by his name, *Fara-Ba!*" With that, the rock dropped silently to the ground. Rabbit thanked Chameleon for this unusual gift and returned home.

The next day, Brother Rabbit rolled the rock in a fresh *sheeyo* leaf and walked to the king's palace. "I have brought you a mysterious gift, your Majesty," said Brother Rabbit.

"*Aaa ha! Moondon!* What is it?" asked the king anxiously. Rabbit slowly unrolled the rock from the *sheeyo* leaf and showed it to Mansa Jugu.

"*Eeeeeeh! Fara doron?*" exclaimed the king. "A simple rock?"

And with that, the little rock began **ricocheting** off the head of the king.

"*A toh! A toh!* Stop this rock!" cried the king, but no one could capture it. All day and all night the little rock played music on the heads of the king and his soldiers. The annoyance continued and the king became troubled. Mansa Jugu was finally forced to call on Rabbit for help.

Cleverly, Brother Rabbit demanded his little gourd back first.

"You may take all the gold, but leave me the gourd," said the greedy king.

"But the gourd was a gift to me," replied Rabbit.

"Then take all my food from my royal storage bins, but leave me the gourd," cried the annoyed king.

"*Ee dusu dah*. Let us bargain," countered Rabbit. "My little gourd is my prize."

The king angrily shouted, "*U-TAH, U-TAH*—TAKE IT ALL! Take the gold, the food, and the little gourd!"

Rabbit took the gourd, but left the gold and the food behind. And before he turned to flee, he shouted, "*Fara-Ba!*"

Calmly, the little rock dropped into Rabbit's hand.

Fearing revenge from the king, Rabbit's family escaped to the country to join their faithful friend Chameleon. From Chameleon's great lessons in disguises, Brother Rabbit learned the skill of hiding in the bush. Today Dogo Zan and his family are masters at going **undetected**. One could be hiding in your backyard right now.

Mansa Jugu, the greedy king, and his soldiers felt embarrassed by their defeat at the hand of a rabbit and a small rock. The king could not believe that in his moment of weakness, he had given away the wealth of his kingdom. Exhausted and hungry, the king sat down to eat before pursuing Brother Rabbit for revenge. Upon opening his storage bins, he was surprised to discover that all of his wealth and food remained.

"Come eat!" he called to his soldiers and servants. "Let us appreciate what we have been given."

From this final kind act of Rabbit, the greedy king, Mansa Jugu, began to learn the importance of **generosity** and friendship.

As for Rabbit and Chameleon, they have always understood that loyal friendships are the true treasures that make one rich.

And for their many good deeds, all sang a song of praise to Rabbit and Chameleon.

Glossary

Here are some words from the story that are in Bambara, the national language of Mali.

Dogo Zan (DOE-go ZAHN) - Brother Rabbit

Mansa Jugu (MAHN-sah JOO-goo) – greedy king (mansa means ruler; jugu means greedy)

* **Ee dusu dah** (ee du-SU dah) – Let us bargain; calm down

* **Ee ko dee** (EE ko DEE) – exclamation of surprise when a person doesn't believe what they have just heard (What did you say?)

Fara (FAH-rah) – rock

* **Fara-ba** (FAH-rah BAH) – Mr. Rock (title of respect)

Fara doron (FAH-rah DOH-ron) – a simple rock

Moondon (MOON-don) – What is it?

Sheeyo (SHEE-yoh) – a bush with large leaves found in Mali

A toh! (ah TOH) – Stop!

U-tah (OO-tah) – Take it all!

* **Feeyeh ku, feeyeh ku**. (FEE-yeh koo) **Waara sa kun tay**. (WA-rah sah KOON-teh) – This is a chant of encouragement to give hope for survival in difficult times.

(Note: Bambara is a metaphorical language, so the English translation is not always literal.)

* Not a literal translation

Meet the Storyteller

Baba Wagué Diakité with his daughters, Penda and Amina

Baba Wagué Diakité grew up in Mali, West Africa. During the evening meal, his whole family told stories, often about the rabbit Zozani [Zoh-Zah-NEE]. Zozani was clever and could always find a way to solve a problem. In the end, Zozani sings a song of praise, something storytellers in Mali have been doing for centuries.

In addition to ceramic art, Baba Wagué Diakité used mud cloth designs to illustrate this story. These are traditional designs painted with dark mud on cotton cloth. Each design means something special. For example, a flower means family happiness.

Other books by Baba Wagué Diakité: *The Hatseller and the Monkeys* and *The Hunterman and the Crocodile*

 Find out more about Baba Wagué Diakité at **www.macmillanmh.com**

Author's Purpose

The main purpose of this tale is to entertain. It also teaches that kindness pays and gives a fictional origin for rabbits' ability to hide. Why do rabbits need to hide in the real world?

Comprehension Check

Summarize

Use your Cause and Effect Chart to help you summarize *The Magic Gourd*. What causes Brother Chameleon to give Brother Rabbit the gourd? What effect does the gourd have on Brother Rabbit and the King?

Cause → Effect
→
→
→
→

Think and Compare

1. Something unexpected takes place at the end of *The Magic Gourd.* What is it? What causes this event to happen? How does this event help you understand the moral of the story? **Make Inferences and Analyze: Cause and Effect**

2. How does the weather affect the characters in the story? Use examples from the text to support your answers. **Synthesize**

3. Think of a time when you did a good deed for someone. What happened? How did your **generosity** help? How did it make you feel? **Evaluate**

4. Who gets the bigger reward from the gourd: the King or Brother Rabbit? Explain why. **Analyze**

5. In "Keira's Magical Moment" on pages 80-81, Keira says her great-grandmother left Senegal because of a famine. What do you think the role of a folk tale such as *The Magic Gourd* would have in Keira's great-grandmother's native culture? **Reading/Writing Across Texts**

By the 700s, the empire of Ghana was already a major power in Africa. It grew rich and powerful as a source of gold for the Mediterranean world.

THE ORIGIN OF GHANA

by Patricia and Fredrick McKissack

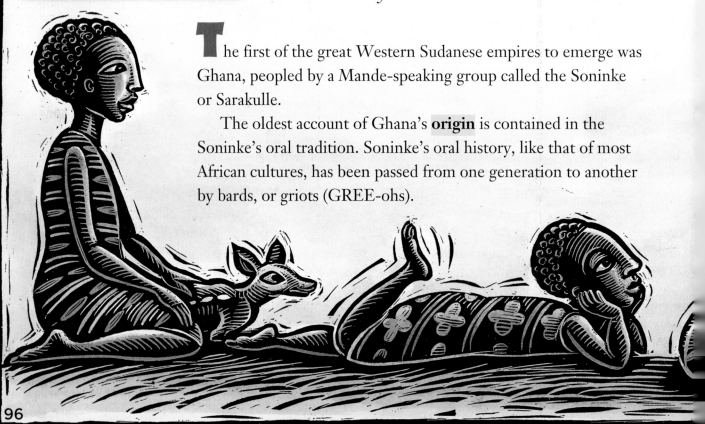

The first of the great Western Sudanese empires to emerge was Ghana, peopled by a Mande-speaking group called the Soninke or Sarakulle.

The oldest account of Ghana's **origin** is contained in the Soninke's oral tradition. Soninke's oral history, like that of most African cultures, has been passed from one generation to another by bards, or griots (GREE-ohs).

96

For centuries the griots have combined history, music, poetry, dance, and drama to entertain and teach their audiences. They can be compared with ancient Greek bards, like Homer, who were fascinating storytellers but so much more. Before the Soninke had a written language, the griots were the historians, the keepers of memories. Every village had a griot, and so did every clan. The royal family and other important families sometimes hired a personal griot to record their actions. Griots kept mental records of all memorable events—feasts and ceremonies, royal coronations, births, deaths, marriages, victories, and defeats. Some of their presentations were as long and artful as *The Iliad* and *The Odyssey*.

According to legend, Gassire was the first griot from whom all other Soninke griots are descended. He invented the *pui*, which is a poem about a hero, also called a praise-song.

One of the first stories a Soninke griot learns is the pui of Gassire. The story tells of a guinea hen who laid several large and beautiful eggs. While she was away, a fat snake came and ate her eggs. The hen was so angry, she declared war on the snake. To **bolster** her courage, she sang a song about what she was going to do. The hen defeated the snake, then flew to a tree to sing about her deeds. People say that Gassire heard the hen's victory song and learned it.

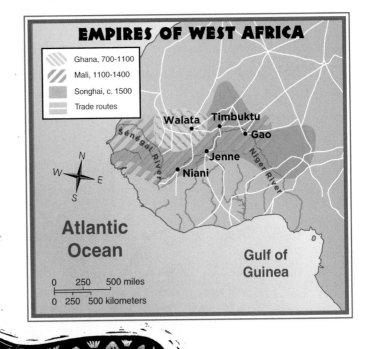

EMPIRES OF WEST AFRICA

Ghana, 700-1100
Mali, 1100-1400
Songhai, c. 1500
Trade routes

Walata
Timbuktu
Gao
Sénégal River
Jenne
Niani
Niger River

N
W E
S

Atlantic
Ocean

Gulf of
Guinea

0   250   500 miles
0   250   500 kilometers

SKILL ✔ READING A TIME LINE

A time line is a diagram showing the order in which events took place. This time line shows dates important to the early history of Ghana, Mali, and Songhai.

1000	1100	1200	1300	1400	1500	1600

1067
Al-Bakri, a Muslim writer, was writing of Ghana's great wealth

1235
Battle of Kirina was important in the rise of the Mali Empire

1312
Mansa Musa, great ruler of Mali, came to power

1464
Sunni Ali, powerful ruler of Songhai, began reign

1591
Songhai army defeated by an army from Morocco

Historians believe this pui is a **mythological** retelling of Ghana's origin. The hen represents the early Soninke people who overthrew an enemy who was more powerful.

By the middle of the 1000s, Ghana had attracted many rivals who sought to share in the wealth of the gold trade. The new empire Mali (MAH lee) had great influence by about 1250. After 1337 the rulers of Mali grew weaker. They were unable to control the empire and its gold trade. Mali was replaced by an even stronger empire, the Songhai (SOHNG hī). By the late 1490s, Songhai included Mali and parts of present-day Benin, Niger, and Nigeria.

This West African brass weight was used with a scale to measure the weight of gold.

Connect and Compare

1. Use the time line to find the year the Songhai army lost power. **Reading a Time Line**

2. Why do you think that the griots are still important today? **Analyze**

3. Why did the pui of Gassire and the narrator in *The Magic Gourd* use animal characters? **Reading/Writing Across Texts**

Social Studies Activity

Research one of the early West African kingdoms. Write and illustrate a fact card using the interesting facts you discovered during your research.

 Find out more about griots at **www.macmillanmh.com**

Writer's Craft

Precise Words

Choose **precise words** to describe your topic and to show how you feel about it. Using colorful words can help bring a poem or other writing to life.

Write a Poem

My Best Buddy

by Jaycee L.

I met you seven years ago at a
    stranger's house.
When I looked at you,
I knew we would be friends forever.

Quickly, I ran across the room
And gathered you in my arms.
I petted your long, floppy ears.
I tickled your round, pink belly.
I smelled your sweet puppy breath.

After eight long weeks passed,
You came to live with me.
We ran through the green grass.
We played hide-and-seek.
We swam in the cool stream.

Now you are older and slower,
But you are still there for all I do.
I share my secrets with you.
I spend my happiest days with you.
I will love you forever,
My best buddy.

I used the words *friends forever* to appeal to my readers' emotions.

I used words like *long, floppy ears* and *round, pink belly* to help readers imagine what my puppy looked like.

100

Your Turn

Write a poem about a lesson you learned or an important friendship. You might write a narrative poem that tells a story. Or you might choose to write a lyric poem that captures the feeling of a friendship or presents a lesson you learned. Be sure to include precise and colorful words to bring your poem to life for readers. Remember to punctuate sentences within the poem. Use the Writer's Checklist to review your poem.

Writer's Checklist

 Ideas and Content: Did I precisely describe a lesson I learned or an important friendship?

 Organization: Did I divide my poem into stanzas? Did I use logical line breaks?

Voice: Does my poem capture the emotion I feel about my topic?

Word Choice: Did I use colorful and **precise words** to bring the poem to life?

 Sentence Fluency: Did I include complete sentences and a variety of sentence lengths?

  Conventions: Did I punctuate within the poem properly? Did I check my spelling?

Talk About It

In what ways do people protect wildlife? What kinds of things can harm wildlife?

LOG ON Find out more about protecting wildlife at **www.macmillanmh.com**

Protecting Wildlife

Comprehension

Genre

Informational Nonfiction is a detailed account of real situations or people using verifiable facts.

Make Inferences and Analyze

Main Idea and Details
As you read, use your Main Idea Web.

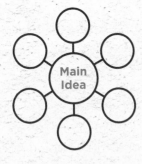

Read to Find Out

How did volunteers help save the endangered sea turtles?

INTERRUPTED JOURNEY

Saving Endangered Sea Turtles

by KATHRYN LASKY

photographs by CHRISTOPHER G. KNIGHT

Award Winning Selection

Stranded

The young turtle has been swimming for three months now in the same warm shallow bay, grazing on small crabs and plankton, basking in an endless dream of calm water and plentiful food. But as the days begin to shorten and the light drains out of the sky earlier and earlier, the water grows colder. It drops to fifty degrees Fahrenheit. The turtle is confused. Swimming is harder. Its heartbeat slows— and almost stops.

Ten days before Thanksgiving, on a beach where Pilgrims once walked, Max Nolan, a ten-year-old boy, and his mother begin their patrol. The Nolans are among volunteers who walk Cape Cod's beaches during November and December to search for turtles who are often cold and stunned and seem dead—turtles whose lives they may be able to save.

It is a blustery day on Ellis Landing Beach. At twenty-five knots the bitter northwest wind stings Max's face like sharp needles. It makes his eyes water but he keeps looking—looking above the high-water mark through the clumps of seaweed, looking below the tide line where the sand is hard and sleek and lapped by surf— looking for a dark greenish-brown mound about the size of a pie plate, looking for a Kemp's ridley turtle that is dying and perhaps can be saved.

Max and his mother and the other volunteers work for a **vital** cause. All sea turtles are threatened or endangered; Kemp's ridleys are the most endangered of all. Right now on our planet there are fewer than eight thousand Kemp's ridley turtles left. They are a vanishing species.

On Ellis Landing Beach, snow squalls begin to whirl down. The waves are building, and as they begin to break, the white froth whips across their steep faces. So far there is no sign of a turtle.

Max is far ahead of his mother when he sees the hump in the sand being washed by the surf. He runs up to it and shouts to his mom, "Got one!" The turtle is cold. Its flippers are floppy. Its eyes are open, but the turtle is not moving at all. It might be dead, but then again, it might not.

Main Idea

What is the main idea on pages 108–109? What details support it?

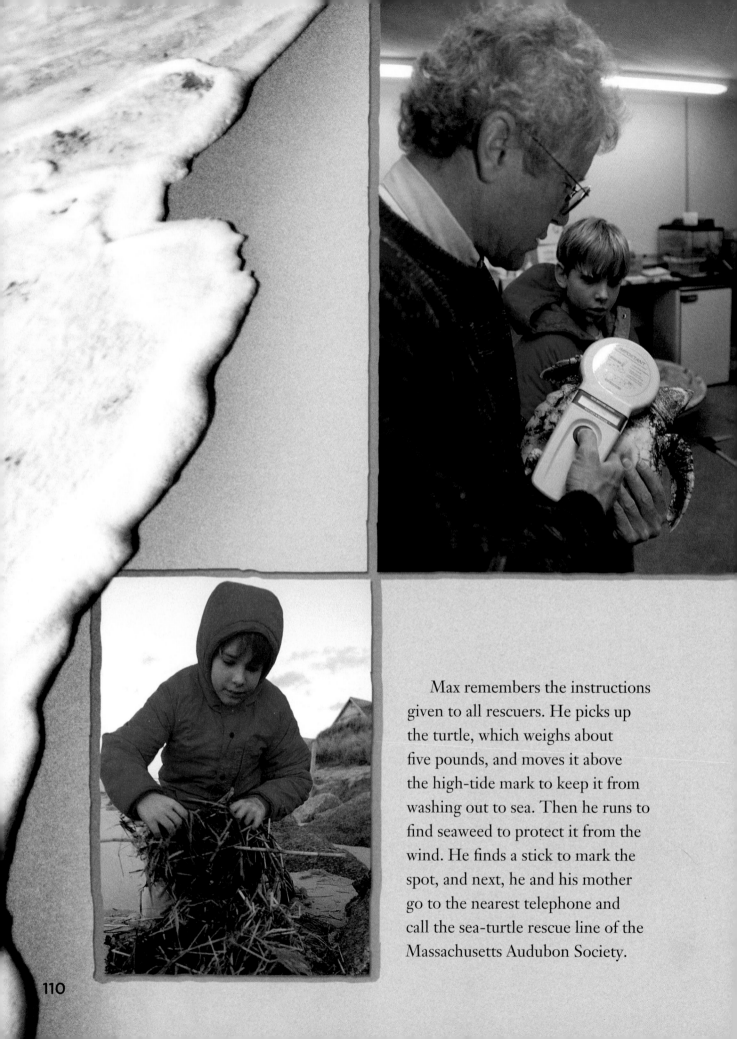

Max remembers the instructions given to all rescuers. He picks up the turtle, which weighs about five pounds, and moves it above the high-tide mark to keep it from washing out to sea. Then he runs to find seaweed to protect it from the wind. He finds a stick to mark the spot, and next, he and his mother go to the nearest telephone and call the sea-turtle rescue line of the Massachusetts Audubon Society.

Within an hour the turtle has been picked up and taken to the Wellfleet Bay Wildlife Sanctuary on Cape Cod. Robert Prescott, the director of the Sanctuary, examines the turtle. "It sure does look dead," he says softly. "But you never can tell." If the turtle is really alive, it must be brought out of its cold, stunned condition. That is a task for the New England Aquarium with its medical team who, over the years, have made a specialty of treating turtles.

Robert puts the new turtle in a plastic wading pool with another turtle that is quite lively. Max crouches by the edge and watches his turtle. It is as still as a stone. He gently touches a flipper. Nothing moves. Then after about twenty minutes, he thinks he might see a flicker in the turtle's left eyelid. He leans closer. "Hey, it's moving!" It wasn't just the eyelid. He saw the right rear flipper move a fraction of an inch. Over the next five minutes, he sees the turtle make three or four microscopically small motions with its right rear flipper. Soon, the rescue team from the New England Aquarium arrives.

Emergency

Beth Chittick is a vet at the New England Aquarium. When the turtles arrive she is ready for them. The turtles are taken immediately into the examination room. Beth is joined by head veterinarian, Howard Crum. They insert a thermometer into the cloaca, the opening under the turtle's tail. The temperature of the turtle Max found is fifty degrees Fahrenheit. Normal temperature for a turtle is usually about seventy-five degrees. Howard next tries to find a heartbeat. He listens intently. "I think I can hear a faint sound . . . " He holds the stiff turtle against his ear as one might hold a seashell. "Why, gee whiz, I can hear the ocean," he jokes.

Main Idea

What is the main idea of this paragraph? Find two details to support your answer.

Howard is still not convinced that the turtle is dead. "With turtles," Howard says, "death is a relative term." Turtles can operate, can survive, even when their hearts slow down for periods of time. Events that might damage the larger, more complicated brains of other animals will not always prove fatal to turtles.

In fact, a turtle's heartbeat naturally slows down at times to just one or two beats per minute in order to **conserve** oxygen and keep vital organs like the brain working. So Howard won't give up on this turtle yet. The turtle does not seem **dehydrated**. The skin on its limbs is not wrinkled—a good sign.

An assistant swabs down an area on the turtle's neck, from which a blood sample will be taken. By **analyzing** the blood, Howard and Beth will be able to see how the turtle's kidneys and other organs are functioning.

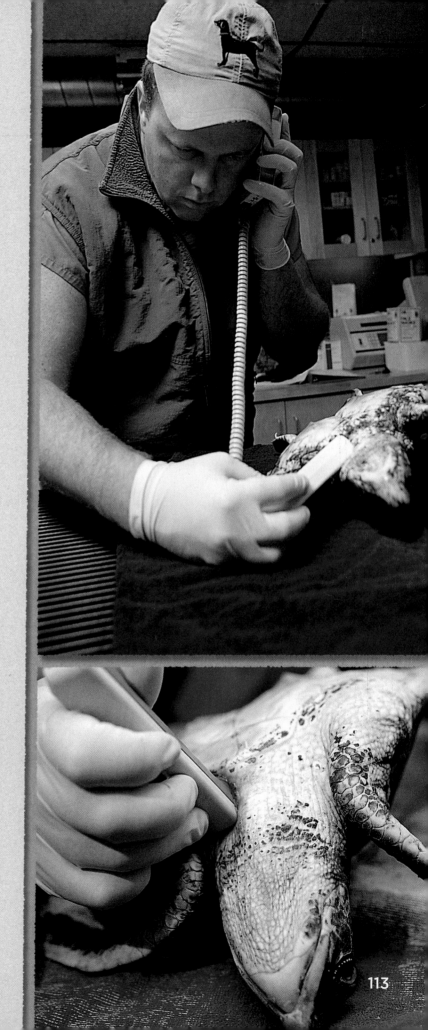

Next the turtle is cleaned. The algae are washed and wiped from its shell. The doctors detect movement in its tail and then see some of the same movements that Max saw in its flippers. They are the motions a turtle makes when it swims. They do not necessarily mean that it is alive, though. It has been **speculated** that these movements could be what are sometimes called vestigial motions, echoes of long-ago actions, fossil behaviors **embedded** in the brain of an ancient creature. The turtle could be swimming in death or swimming toward life.

Nonetheless, the vets hook up the turtle to an intravenous needle through which fluids will be pumped very slowly at a temperature slightly higher than the turtle's body. Beth and Howard have learned much about the condition of this turtle but they are still not sure if it is really alive or dead.

Finally the turtle is tagged with a yellow-blue
band. It will be known as Yellow-Blue. It is put
in the Intensive Care Unit, a large temperature-
controlled stainless steel box with a glass window.
Inside, the turtle is placed on a soft pile of towels
so its shell is supported and it will not have to
rest on its ventrum, or bottom shell.

Then the team turn their attention to
another turtle, which is definitely alive.
Howard picks up the turtle and talks to
it as its flippers thrash madly. "Okay, little
man!" This turtle's temperature is
sixty-two degrees. When they take
its blood, the sample appears much
redder than the nearly brownish
blood of Yellow-Blue, which indicates
that there is more oxygen in it.

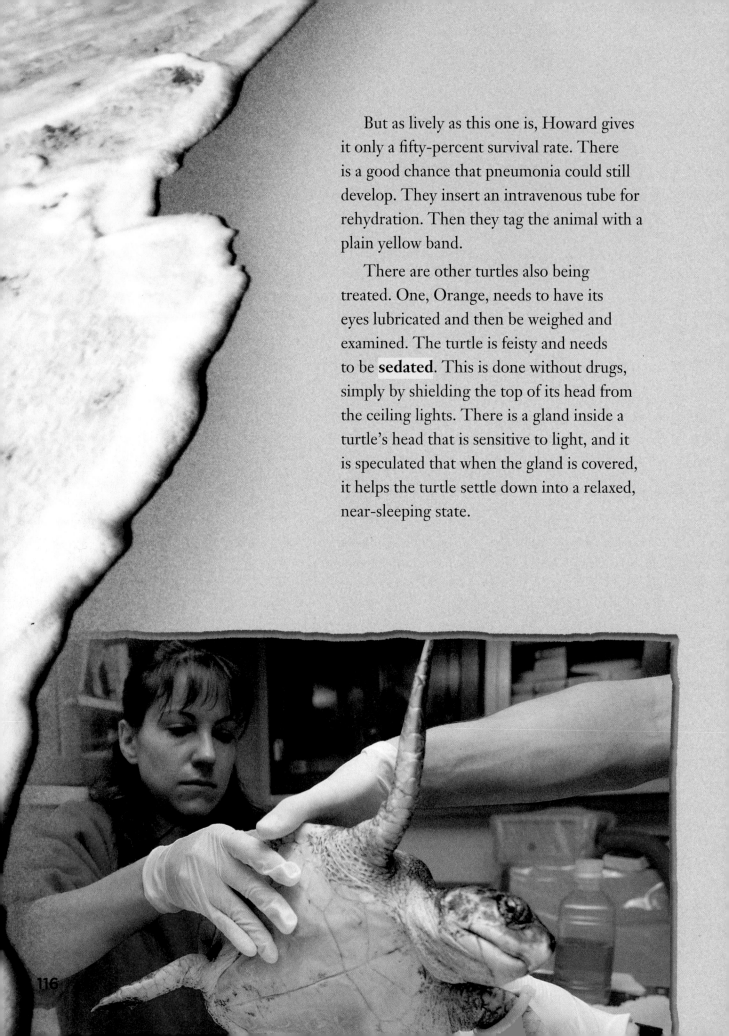

But as lively as this one is, Howard gives it only a fifty-percent survival rate. There is a good chance that pneumonia could still develop. They insert an intravenous tube for rehydration. Then they tag the animal with a plain yellow band.

There are other turtles also being treated. One, Orange, needs to have its eyes lubricated and then be weighed and examined. The turtle is feisty and needs to be **sedated**. This is done without drugs, simply by shielding the top of its head from the ceiling lights. There is a gland inside a turtle's head that is sensitive to light, and it is speculated that when the gland is covered, it helps the turtle settle down into a relaxed, near-sleeping state.

In this peaceful state, Orange begins to "swim" on the table, its flippers making the paddling motions that have since birth **propelled** it through thousands of miles of sea. Its heart rate, at thirty-six beats a minute, is good. Its respiration rate is still slow. It takes only one breath every minute. Its temperature is near seventy degrees. Orange is x-rayed for signs of pneumonia. The lungs are clear.

Whatever the outcome for these three turtles, Beth, Howard, Robert, Max, and his mother all know they are doing their part to help return the turtles to health, to help return them to the sea.

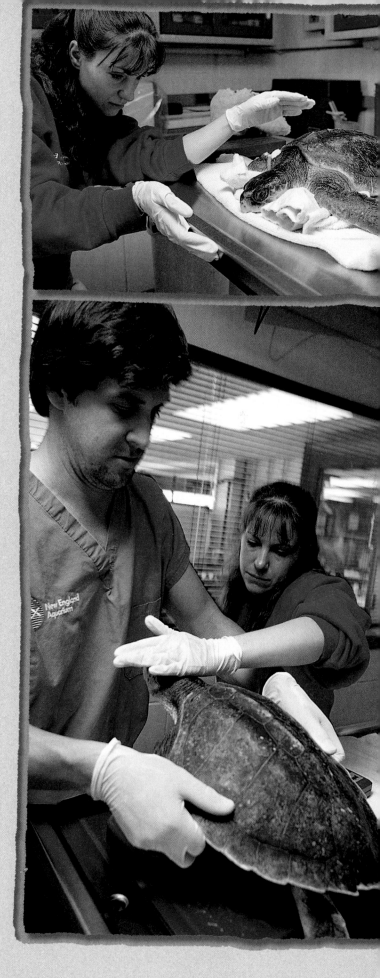

Take a Journey with Kathryn Lasky and Christopher G. Knight

Kathryn Lasky has written more than 100 books in all genres. You would think she wouldn't have time for anything else, but twice she has sailed with her husband across the Atlantic Ocean in a small sailboat. Even when she was seasick, Kathryn loved watching the birds and the dolphins . . . and maybe she even saw a sea turtle!

Christopher G. Knight is Kathryn Lasky's husband. He is also a photographer and an adventurer. He has paddled a kayak from Alaska to Seattle and canoed through seven countries in Europe. Then he met Kathryn. They have two children and have done seventeen books together.

Other books by Kathryn Lasky:
The Man Who Made Time Travel and
A Voice of Her Own

LOG ON Find out more about Kathryn Lasky and Christopher G. Knight at **www.macmillanmh.com**

Author's Purpose

Kathryn Lasky's purpose here is to inform. She tells about real people doing real things and documents those acts with photographs. How do the photos add to the text?

Comprehension Check

Summarize

Use your Main Idea Web to help you summarize *Interrupted Journey*. State the main idea in one or two sentences.

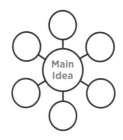

Think and Compare

1. What are some important details that Kathryn Lasky includes to explain why the sea turtles need assistance? **Make Inferences and Analyze: Main Idea and Details**

2. Do you think the yellow-blue turtle will live? Explain why or why not. Use information from the text to support your answer. **Evaluate**

3. Max and his mother are volunteers. What kind of volunteer work would you like to do? Are volunteers **vital** to your community? Why or why not? **Synthesize**

4. What facts from *Interrupted Journey* would you choose to show if you were to give a presentation about conservation? Explain your choices. **Apply**

5. Read "Protecting the Clouded Leopard" on pages 104-105. Compare and contrast the conservation project detailed in this selection with the one in *Interrupted Journey*. How are the two projects similar? How are their methods different? **Reading/Writing Across Texts**

Poetry

Free Verse has irregular lines and lacks a metrical pattern and rhyme scheme.

Song Lyrics are the written words of a song. Long ago poems were not just recited but were often sung.

Literary Elements

Alliteration is the repetition of initial consonant sounds.

Imagery is the use of words to create a picture in the reader's mind.

Birdfoot's Grampa

by Joseph Bruchac

The old man
must have stopped our car
two dozen times to climb out
and gather into his hands
the small toads blinded
by our lights and leaping,
live drops of rain.

The rain was falling,
a mist about his white hair
and I kept saying
you can't save them all,
accept it, get back in
we've got places to go.

But, leathery hands full
of wet brown life,
knee deep in the summer
roadside grass,
he just smiled and said
*they have places to go to
too.*

The words *lights, leaping,* and *live* all begin with *l* to create alliteration.

The poet creates a picture when he describes the toads as "live drops of rain."

This Land Is Your Land

lyrics by Woody Guthrie

This land is your land, this land is my land
From California to the New York island;
From the redwood forest to the Gulf Stream waters,
This land was made for you and me.

As I was walking that ribbon of highway,
I saw above me that endless skyway;
I saw below me that golden valley,
This land was made for you and me.

The lyricist uses imagery when he compares a highway to a ribbon.

Connect and Compare

SKILL

1. Find another example of imagery in "Birdfoot's Grampa" or "This Land Is Your Land." How does the image appeal to one of your senses? **Imagery**

2. What kind of person is Birdfoot's grandfather? Give examples from the poem. **Analyze**

3. How are Max Nolan's attitudes toward wildlife in *Interrupted Journey* and the grampa's attitudes in "Birdfoot's Grampa" similar? **Reading/Writing Across Texts**

LOG ON Find out more about poetry at **www.macmillanmh.com**

Writer's Craft

Transition Words

Use **transition words** in sentences to show cause and effect. Words such as *because* and *as a result* can make your writing clearer.

"As a result" explains why it was cold in July.

I included the word *because* here to explain why we stopped during the hike.

July 15

Dear Diary,

My hike to Black Lake in the Rocky Mountains was incredible and a unique experience! I went with a group from the parks department last Saturday.

We met early on Saturday morning and took a bus to the Glacier Gorge Trail Head. Even though it's July, it was pretty cool. This was as a result of being so high up, more than 9,000 feet above sea level. We decided to climb a lot higher! In fact, we climbed 1,000 feet more.

First, we stopped at Mills Lake. It was really quiet in the middle of the mountains. I have never felt so small in my life! From Mills Lake, we kept going up. Because the climb became harder and harder, the guide let us stop every few minutes to rest. During the last part of the hike, we actually walked through snow! Black Lake was beautiful! It was well worth the trip.

Your Turn

Write a diary entry about a personal experience with nature or a conservation group. You can describe a real experience or one you would like to have. Remember that this writing is about how you feel. Include transition words to show cause and effect. Use the Writer's Checklist to review your diary entry.

Writer's Checklist

 Ideas and Content: Did I clearly describe my experience and my reactions to it?

 Organization: Did I organize my ideas logically?

 Voice: Does my diary entry capture my feelings about the experience?

 Word Choice: Did I use **transition words** to show cause and effect?

 Sentence Fluency: Did I avoid using run-on sentences? Did I vary the length of my sentences?

 Conventions: Did I correct run-on sentences by combining them with commas and conjunctions, or by writing them as two separate sentences? Did I check my spelling?

Test Strategy

Think and Search

The answer is in more than one place. Keep reading to find the answer.

EDDIE: *(voiceover)* It was midnight. Just when I was expecting to get some shut-eye, I got the call instead about a stolen ruby, a museum, and a four thousand-year-old mummy. My name is Eddie Grimes, and I solve crimes.

(Sounds: Crowds, cameras snapping.)

EDDIE: *(voiceover)* I showed up at the crime scene and found my good friend Sergeant Tommy Drake of the Victory City Police Department. The museum had reporters crawling all over it.

DRAKE: What can I do for you, Grimes?

EDDIE: Tell me what you know about this ruby business.

DRAKE: It's the Isis Ruby. It's been stolen. The ruby is a rare gem on loan from a London museum. The place was locked. There are guards on every door. Nobody could get in or out after closing.

EDDIE: You're wrong, Tommy. Nobody was supposed to get in or out, but someone did. Hey, this coffin looks interesting.

(Sounds: Footsteps on a marble floor, then a creaky door.)

DR. BLOOM: What do you think you are doing? That's a priceless artifact. I am Dr. Donald Bloom, head curator of the Victory City Museum.

DRAKE: Sorry, Dr. Bloom. This is Eddie Grimes, private investigator.

Go On ▶

DR. BLOOM: No one opens the sarcophagus except to restore it. The coffin stays shut. The precious paintings on the inside must not be exposed to light. Their green pigment is already flaking off.

EDDIE: So this coffin thing is part of the same exhibit as the ruby?

DR. BLOOM: Yes. We just got it back from the restoration department, and I haven't even seen the inside of the sarcophagus yet.

EDDIE: Restoration, eh? Who does the restoring?

DR. BLOOM: Why, that's Dr. Peterson. Her office is across the street.

EDDIE: Thanks, Doc. It was nice to meet you.

(Sounds: Two pairs of footsteps.)

DRAKE: What's up, Eddie?

EDDIE: I want to talk to this art restorer.

(Sounds: Street sounds, a knock, then the door opens.)

EDDIE: You must be Dr. Peterson. My name is Eddie Grimes, private investigator.

DR. PETERSON: You must be looking into the missing ruby.

EDDIE: What do you know about it?

DR. PETERSON: I know that its value is beyond measure. But I don't know how the thief got into and out of the museum.

EDDIE: *(voiceover)* I took a stroll around the place. There were books on mummies, and jewels, and magic tricks. Magic tricks? A pair of old boots sat under her desk. There were flecks of green paint on the side of one boot. That was strange. But what was even stranger was that these were men's boots. Then, right in the middle of a work bench, I spotted the largest ruby I had ever seen.

DRAKE: The Isis Ruby!

DR. PETERSON: No, just a glass copy. I was preparing to replace the real ruby until it is found. Excuse me, sir. I really have a lot to do before the exhibit opens.

EDDIE: Don't let me keep you. Besides, my mummy's waiting.

EDDIE: *(voiceover)* I went back to my office to check my messages. I thought about what Dr. Bloom had said when I was messing with his creaky old coffin. Then it hit me.

(Sound: Bells to indicate a flashback.)

Go On   125

DR. BLOOM: No one opens the sarcophagus except to restore it. The coffin stays shut. The precious paintings on the inside must not be exposed to light. Their green pigment is already flaking off.

EDDIE: *(voiceover)* And then. . .

DR. BLOOM: We just got it back from the restoration department, and I haven't even seen the inside of the sarcophagus yet.

(Sound: Bells to indicate end of flashback.)

EDDIE: *(voiceover)* That was it! I had the answer. I called Drake and told him to round up the good doctors and meet me at Dr. Peterson's office and to have the sarcophagus moved there.

DR. BLOOM: What's the meaning of this? I was sleeping soundly.

EDDIE: You'll sleep in prison, Dr. Bloom. You stole the ruby.

DR. BLOOM: This is outrageous. Where's your proof?

(Sounds: Harsh squeal of hinges, a thump.)

EDDIE: This Egyptian sarcophagus has a false back wall.

DR. PETERSON: That's a lie.

EDDIE: The magic books tipped me off. Doing a little research into disappearing tricks, Doc?

DR. BLOOM: I knew she did it!

EDDIE: Not so fast, Dr. Bloom. You said you hadn't seen the inside of the sarcophagus yet, but you also said that the paintings inside were flaking. How would you know unless you had seen the inside? You snuck out of the museum with the ruby hidden inside this coffin when it was sent for restoration. Those size-thirteen boots under her desk aren't Dr. Peterson's. They're yours! Drake, stop Dr. Peterson, that ruby isn't glass, it's the real thing.

DR. PETERSON: Let me go!

DRAKE: Good work, Grimes.

(Music: Dramatic climax.)

EDDIE: *(voiceover)* It was just another night in the big city. I'm Eddie Grimes, and I solve crimes.

THE END

Go On ▶

Tip

Keep reading. The answer may be in more than one place.

Directions: Answer the questions.

1. **Which word BEST describes the author's tone in the play?**

   A grim
   B light-hearted
   C sad
   D serious

2. **How was the Isis Ruby smuggled out of the museum?**

   A in Dr. Peterson's pocket
   B in Dr. Bloom's boots
   C in a false compartment inside the sarcophagus
   D in Dr. Peterson's work bench

3. **To whom do the boots in Dr. Peterson's office belong?**

   A Dr. Peterson
   B Dr. Bloom
   C Eddie Grimes
   D Isis

4. **Why does Eddie call Drake and ask him to "round up the good doctors"?**

5. **What is the most likely reason the author included a flashback in the play? Write two paragraphs, and include examples from the selection.**

Writing Prompt

Think of a problem or mystery in your own life. Write a friendly letter to someone asking for help in solving your problem. Your letter should be at least two paragraphs.

STOP

Team Spirit

Talk About It

Think of a time when you were on a team. What did you enjoy about being part of a team?

Find out more about team spirit at **www.macmillanmh.com**

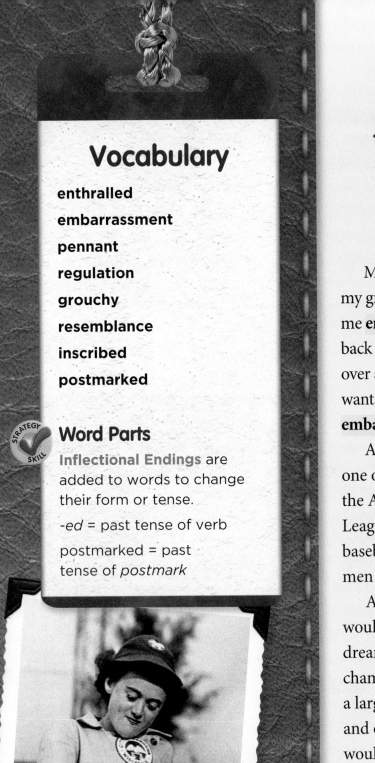

Kenosha Comets

1946 YEAR BOOK

An Aunt's Baseball Dreams

by Danielle Martin

Maybe it's my love of baseball that connects my great-aunt Helen and me. She has always kept me **enthralled** with her stories of playing baseball back in the 1940s. I would listen to these stories over and over. She used to say, "Go after what you want, Sarah. Don't be ashamed of failing. Real **embarrassment** comes from never trying."

Aunt Helen should know. In 1943, she was one of the young women who tried out for the All-American Girls Professional Baseball League. This league was created to entertain baseball fans because many of America's young men were fighting in World War II.

Aunt Helen had heard rumors that a team would play right in South Bend, Indiana. She dreamed of what it would be like to win a championship for her hometown! She imagined a large **pennant** hanging at the baseball field, and on this banner the name Helen Baker would be there for all to see.

On the day of the tryouts, Aunt Helen played baseball for hours with many young women. For this new league, some of the rules were different from the rules for regular softball. They still used a standard **regulation** softball, but the bases and pitcher's mound were placed at longer distances, for example.

All the rules were explained by a **grouchy** man in a suit. Aunt Helen said that wearing a suit in the hot sun was what put him in a bad mood. But he had a **resemblance** to Aunt Helen's father. And if he looked like her father, she thought, he couldn't be bad.

About a week later, Aunt Helen collected the mail and found an envelope with her name **inscribed** in blue ink. The envelope was **postmarked** from Chicago. The letter was from the leaders of the girls' baseball league, who were located in Chicago! Aunt Helen tore it open and learned that she had been invited to the league's main tryouts!

But as the days went by, Aunt Helen became worried about traveling to Chicago alone. What if she went all that way and failed? When the day of the tryouts came, she was too afraid to go.

Team members go over the play book.

Aunt Helen has spent the rest of her life wondering what would have happened if she had gone to those tryouts. Because of this, she never missed another opportunity in her life. She learned that every dream is worth chasing, even if you catch only a few of them.

Reread for **Comprehension**

Generate Questions

Make Inferences

As you read, ask yourself what is happening. Sometimes a writer does not tell you everything. When you make inferences, you use clues from the story plus your own knowledge to understand what is not directly stated.

Use the Inferences Chart as you reread "An Aunt's Baseball Dreams."

Text Clues and Prior Knowledge	Inference

Comprehension

Genre

Realistic Fiction is an invented story that could have happened in real life.

Generate Questions

Make Inferences

As you read, use your Inferences Chart.

Text Clues and Prior Knowledge	Inference

Read to Find Out

Why does Tía Lola's plan succeed?

How Tía Lola Came to Visit Stay

by **Julia Alvarez**
illustrated by **Lester Coloma**

Award Winning Author

Miguel and Juanita Guzmán have moved to Vermont from New York City because their mother has taken a job at a local college. Their mother's aunt, Tía Lola, arrives for a visit from the Dominican Republic. Tía Lola soon impresses Miguel's friends and Rudy, the owner of a local restaurant and the coach of Miguel's baseball team. At the restaurant, Tía Lola also charms the difficult Colonel Charlebois who owns the farmhouse that Miguel's family rents.

 he long, sweet, sunny days of summer come one after another after another. Each one is like a piece of fancy candy in a gold-and-blue wrapper.

Most nights, now that school is out, Tía Lola tells stories, sometimes until very late. The beautiful cousin who never cut her hair and carried it around in a wheelbarrow. The grandfather whose eyes turned blue when he saw his first grandchild.

Some nights, for a break, they explore the old house. In the attic, behind their own boxes, they find dusty trunks full of yellowing letters and photographs. Miguel discovers several faded photos of a group of boys all lined up in old-fashioned baseball uniforms. Except for the funny caps and knickers and knee socks, the boys in the photos could be any of the boys on Miguel's team. One photo of a boy with a baseball glove in his hand is **inscribed**, *Charlebois, '34.*

Miguel tries to imagine the **grouchy** old man at Rudy's Restaurant as the young boy with the friendly smile in the photograph.

But he can't see even a faint **resemblance**.

* * *

Since the team doesn't have a good place for daily practice, Miguel's mother suggests they use the back pasture behind the house. "But let me write Colonel Charlebois first, just in case."

134

Their landlord lives in a big white house in the center of town. He has already written them once this summer, complaining about "the unseemly shape of the vegetation," after Tía Lola trimmed the hedges in front of the house in the shapes of pineapples and parrots and palm trees.

"Can't you just call him and ask him, Mami?" Miguel asks. After all, the team is impatient to get started with practice. A letter will take several days to be answered.

"You try calling him," Miguel's mother says, holding out the phone. Miguel dials the number his mother reads from a card tacked on the kitchen bulletin board. The phone rings once, twice. A machine clicks on, and a cranky old voice speaks up: "This is Colonel Charles Charlebois. I can't be bothered coming to the phone every time it rings. If you have a message, you can write me."

"Let's write that letter, shall we?" Mami says, taking the phone back from Miguel.

Make Inferences
What inferences can you make about Colonel Charlebois based on his pre-recorded message?

135

Two days later, Colonel Charlebois's answer is in their mailbox. It has not been **postmarked**. He must have driven out and delivered it himself.

"I would be honored to have the team practice in my back pasture," he replies in a shaky hand as if he'd written the letter while riding in a car over a bumpy road.

"Honored!" Miguel's mother says, lifting her eyebrows. She translates the letter for Tía Lola, who merely nods as if she'd known all along that Colonel Charlebois is really a nice man.

And so every day Miguel's friends come over, and the team plays ball in the back field where only six months ago, Miguel wrote a great big welcome to Tía Lola. Twice a week, Rudy drops by to coach. They play all afternoon, and afterward when they are hot and sweaty, Tía Lola invites them inside for cool, refreshing smoothies, which she calls *frío-fríos*. As they slurp and lick, she practices her English by telling them wonderful stories about Dominican baseball players like Sammy Sosa and the Alou brothers and Juan Marichal and Pedro and Ramón Martínez. The way she tells the stories, it's as if she knows these players personally. Miguel and his friends are **enthralled**.

After a couple of weeks of practice, the team votes to make Miguel the captain. José, who is visiting from New York, substitutes for whoever is missing that day. Tía Lola is named manager.

"*¿Y qué hace el manager?*" Tía Lola wants to know what a manager does.

"A manager makes us *frío-fríos*," Captain Miguel says.

Every day, after practice, there are *frío-fríos* in a tall pitcher in the icebox.

It is a happy summer—

Until Tía Lola decides to paint the house purple.

* * *

Miguel and his friends have been playing ball in the back field—their view of the house shielded by the maple trees. As they walk back from practice, they look up.

"Holy cow!" Miguel cries out.

The front porch is the color of a bright bruise. Miguel can't help thinking of the deep, rich purple whose name he recently learned from his father in New York. "Dioxazine," he mutters to himself. The rest of the house is still the same color as almost every other house in town. "**Regulation** white," Papi calls it whenever he comes up to visit and drives through town.

In her high heels and a dress with flowers whose petals match the color of the porch stands Tía Lola, painting broad purple strokes.

For a brief second, Miguel feels a flash of that old **embarrassment** he used to feel about his crazy aunt.

"Awesome," his friend Dean is saying.

"Cool!" Sam agrees.

They wave at Tía Lola, who waves back.

"¡Frío-fríos!" she calls out. Today she has chosen grape flavor in honor of the new color of the house.

137

By the time Miguel's mother comes home from work, he and his friends look like they have helped Tía Lola paint the house: their mouths are purple smudges. When they open their mouths to say hello, their tongues are a pinkish purple.

"Okay, what is going on?" Mami asks, glancing from Miguel to Tía Lola. She looks as if she is about to cry, something she has not done in a long time.

Tía Lola speaks up. Don't the colors remind her of the island? *"La casita de tu niñez."* The house where Mami spent her childhood.

Miguel can see his mother's face softening. Her eyes have a faraway look. Suddenly, Mami is shaking her head and trying not to laugh. "Colonel Charlebois is going to throw a fit. Actually, he's going to throw us out."

"El coronel, no hay problema," Tía Lola says, pointing to herself and Miguel and his friends. Miguel's mother looks from face to face as if she doesn't understand. Miguel and his friends nod as if they understand exactly what Tía Lola is up to.

* * *

The next afternoon, when Miguel's friends come inside from practice, Tía Lola takes their measurements. She has bought fabric with the money the team has collected and is making them their uniforms.

When it is Miguel's turn, he stands next to the mark that his mother made on the door frame back in January. He is already an inch taller!

"Tía Lola, what are you up to?" the team keeps asking. "Are we going to lose our playing field if Colonel Charlebois takes back his house?"

"No hay problema," Tía Lola keeps saying. Her mouth curls up like a fish hook that has caught a big smile.

* * *

"Are you going to work magic on him?" Miguel asks his aunt that night.

"The magic of understanding," Tía Lola says, winking. She can look into a face and see straight to the heart.

She looks into Miguel's eyes and smiles her special smile.

As the house painting continues, several neighbors call. "What's happening to your house?" farmer Tom asks Miguel. "I don't believe I've ever seen a purple house. Is that a New York style or something?"

Their farming neighbors think of New York as a foreign country. Whenever Miguel and his family do something odd, Tom and Becky believe it is due to their having come from "the city."

"I've never seen a purple house in my life," Miguel admits.

"Neither have I," José adds, "and I live in the city!"

"I've seen one!" Juanita speaks up, showing off.

"Where?" Miguel challenges.

"In my imagination." She grins.

Miguel has been trying to imitate Tía Lola, looking for the best in people. He stares straight into Juanita's eyes, but all he can see is his smart-alecky little sister.

One afternoon, soon after José has returned to the city, Miguel is coming down the stairs to join his teammates in the back field. He pauses at the landing. The large window affords a view of the surrounding farms and the quaint New England town beyond.

A silver car Miguel doesn't recognize is coming down the dirt road to their house. Just before arriving at the farmhouse, it turns in to an old logging road at the back of the property. Behind a clump of ash trees, the car stops and the door opens.

Later, as he stands to bat, Miguel can make out a glint of silver among the trees. Who could it be? he wonders. He thinks of telling his mother about the stranger, but decides against it. She would probably think an escaped convict was lurking in the woods and not allow the team to practice in the back field anymore.

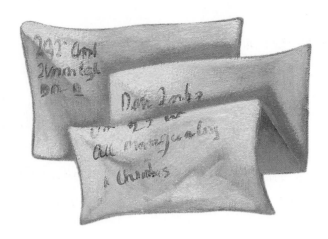

The next afternoon, Miguel watches from behind the curtain as the same silver car he saw in the woods yesterday comes slowly up the drive. His friends have already left after their baseball practice, and his mother is not home from work yet. He can hear Tía Lola's sewing machine humming away upstairs.

"Who is it?" Juanita is standing beside him, holding on to her brother's arm. All her smart-alecky confidence is gone.

"I think it's him—Colonel Charlebois," Miguel whispers. Now that the car is so close, he can make out the old man behind the wheel. The hood has a striking ornament: a little silver batter, crouched, ready to swing. "I'm going to pretend no one is home," Miguel adds.

But Colonel Charlebois doesn't come up to the door. He sits in his car, gazing up at the purple-and-white house for a few minutes, and then he drives away. Later that day, a letter appears in the mailbox. "Unless the house is back to its original white by the end of the month, you are welcome to move out."

"*Welcome* to move out?" Miguel repeats. He wrote ¡BIENVENIDA! to his Tía Lola when she moved in. It doesn't sound right to *welcome* someone to move out.

"We've got three weeks to paint the house back or move," their mother says in a teary voice at dinner. "I'm disappointed, too," she admits to Tía Lola. After all, she really loves the new color. That flaking white paint made the place look so blah and run-down. "But still, I don't want to have to move again," Mami sighs.

Tía Lola pats her niece's hand. There is something else they can try first.

"What's that?" her niece asks.

They can invite *el coronel* over on Saturday.

"But that's the day of our big game," Miguel reminds his aunt. They'll be playing against another local team from the next county over.

Tía Lola winks. She knows. *"Pero tengo un plan."* She has a plan. Miguel should tell his friends to come a little early so they can change.

"Change what?" Miguel's mother asks. "Change the color of the house?"

Tía Lola shakes her head. Change a hard heart. She'll need more grape juice from the store.

Make Inferences
What can you infer about Tía Lola's character? Support your answer.

The day dawns sunny and warm. The cloudless sky stretches on and on and on, endlessly blue with the glint of an airplane, like a needle sewing a tiny tear in it. Every tree seems filled to capacity with dark green rustling leaves. On the neighboring farms, the corn is as tall as the boys who play baseball in the fallow field nearby. Tía Lola's garden looks like one of Papi's palettes. But now, after living in the country for seven months, Miguel has his own new names for colors: zucchini green, squash yellow, chili-pepper red, raspberry crimson. The eggplants are as purple as the newly painted house. It is the full of summer. In a few weeks, up in the mountains, the maples will begin to turn.

Miguel's friends and their parents arrive early. The boys head upstairs behind Tía Lola and Rudy. Their parents stay downstairs, drinking grape smoothies and talking about how their gardens are doing. At last, the silver car rolls into the driveway.

Slowly, Colonel Charlebois climbs out. He stands, a cane in one hand, looking up at the house. One quarter of the house is purple. The other three-quarters is still white. Which color will the whole house end up being?

Miguel looks down at the old man from an upstairs window. Suddenly, he feels a sense of panic. What if Tía Lola's plan doesn't work? He doesn't want to move from the house that has finally become a home to him.

He feels his aunt's hand on his shoulder. *"No hay problema, Miguelito,"* she reassures him as if she can read his thoughts even without looking into his eyes.

Colonel Charlebois is still staring up at the house when the front door opens. Out file nine boys in purple-and-white-striped uniforms and purple baseball caps. They look as if the house itself has sprouted them! Miguel leads the way, a baseball in his hand. Behind them, Tía Lola and Rudy each hold the corner of a **pennant** that reads: CHARLIE'S BOYS.

Colonel Charlebois gazes at each boy. It is difficult to tell what is going through his mind. Suddenly, he drops his cane on the front lawn and calls out, "Let's play ball!" He stands, wobbly and waiting and smiling. Miguel looks into the old man's eyes and sees a boy, legs apart, body bent forward, a gloved hand held out in front of him.

He lifts his arm and throws the ball at that young boy—and the old man catches it.

Visiting With Julia Alvarez

Julia Alvarez wrote this story for her ten-year-old nephew. Julia thought back to when she was ten—the year her family moved from the Dominican Republic to the United States. What did she remember about growing up? Of course, she remembered the tías—her wonderful aunts, who had told her endless stories about their childhood. The story is set in Vermont, where Julia now lives. She said moving to the United States made her a writer, but the memory of her tías kept her first home alive.

LOG ON Find out more about Julia Alvarez at **www.macmillanmh.com**

Author's Purpose
Julia Alvarez wrote this selection to entertain. What makes her character Tía Lola so enjoyable to read about?

Comprehension Check

Summarize

Summarize *How Tía Lola Came to Visit Stay*. Think about how baseball is important to all the different elements of the story.

Think and Compare

Text Clues and Prior Knowledge	Inference

1. What does Tía Lola know about Colonel Charlebois that leads her to believe that he will not evict Miguel's family? Use your Inferences Chart to help you answer the question. **Generate Questions: Make Inferences**

2. Miguel sometimes feels brief **embarrassment** about the things Tía Lola says and does. Why, however, do you think Miguel so quickly realizes that Tía Lola has good solutions for problems? Explain your answer. **Evaluate**

3. Tía Lola is extremely helpful to Miguel and his family. Do you have a friend or relative who is helpful to you or your family? Compare that person with Tía Lola. **Synthesize**

4. Tía Lola used baseball to bring people together. How do you think sports can help bring a community together? **Analyze**

5. Read "An Aunt's Baseball Dreams" on pages 130-131. How is the author's great-aunt Helen like Tía Lola? If Tía Lola were to be offered a baseball tryout, do you think she would react the same way Helen did? Why or why not? **Reading/Writing Across Texts**

Math

Genre

Nonfiction Articles present facts and information about different subjects.

Text Feature

Almanacs are reference books compiled annually. **Charts** in almanacs present information, such as statistics, in a clear manner.

Content Vocabulary

statistics   triples
data

Babe Ruth

ROGER MARIS

Baseball
By the Numbers

Baseball fans love to read and discuss **statistics**. Statistics are individual facts, or **data**, expressed as numbers. You can compare these numbers to find out all kinds of interesting information: who had the most hits in a particular world series or who pitched the most strikeouts in a lifetime career.

The most hits by a player in a single season was 262 by Ichiro Suzuki of the Seattle Mariners in 2004. He broke a record of 257 set by George Sisler way back in 1920.

Who hit the most **triples** in one season? A Pittsburgh Pirate named Owen Wilson set that record in 1912. In 1927 Babe Ruth earned the one-season home run crown by hitting 60. That record lasted until the end of the 1961 season, when Roger Maris rounded the bases after hitting his sixty-first homer. Maris's record has been broken a number of times since then, but that is the nature of records; they are challenges to be broken. Who will be the next to challenge the home run record?

Pos.	GP	St	AB	Run	Hits	2B	3B	HR	RBI	SF	SH
30	25	25	82	21	32	5	1	8	11	2	

Fact Finding

Reading an Almanac

Look at this segment of an almanac entry to discover who won the National League's Most Valuable Player (MVP) Award from the years 1997-2000. When did Sammy Sosa win? On what team did he play that year? In the year that Chipper Jones won MVP, how many home runs did he hit?

National League's Most Valuable Player Award Winners					
Year	Name	Team	Home Runs	RBIs	Avg.
1997	Larry Walker	Colorado Rockies	49	130	.366
1998	Sammy Sosa	Chicago Cubs	66	158	.308
1999	Chipper Jones	Atlanta Braves	45	110	.319
2000	Jeff Kent	San Francisco Giants	33	125	.334

Almanacs provide statistics on many different subjects.

Connect and Compare

1. Look at the chart in the almanac entry. Find the player who hit the fewest home runs during the year he was awarded the National League's Most Valuable Player Award. **Reading a Chart**

2. What are some ways that you like to present information? Why are charts a useful way to present information? **Evaluate**

3. If Miguel in *How Tía Lola Came to Visit Stay* gave Colonel Charlebois a baseball almanac, how do you think the Colonel would respond? **Reading/Writing Across Texts**

Math Activity

Research a major league baseball pitcher. Make a baseball card that includes statistics showing wins versus losses over his career.

 Find out more about baseball at **www.macmillanmh.com**

Writer's Craft

Denotation and Connotation

A word's **denotation** is its meaning. A word's **connotation** is the feeling attached to the word. The words *smile* and *smirk* have similar definitions, but *smirk* implies a negative connotation.

526 Sunbury Street
Columbus, OH 43201
April 27, 2008

Mr. Stephen Merton
Merton's Dry Cleaning
1132 Canfield Avenue
Columbus, OH 43201

Dear Mr. Merton:

> I stated exactly why I am writing to Mr. Merton.

I am the captain of my sixth-grade baseball team, and I am writing to ask for your support. For $500, you can sponsor our team. This money will pay for our uniforms, equipment, and a banner to hang at the league's field. The banner and all our uniforms will say Merton's Dry Cleaning. This is a great opportunity to advertise your business and help out the community.

My team chose Merton's Dry Cleaning because we would like to be called the Merton White Sox. Then, everyone who sees us play will think of clean socks!

> I used words with good connotations like "show off" to persuade Mr. Merton.

My teammates and I want to show off the name and photos of a local business at all of our games. We hope that name will be Merton's Dry Cleaning.

Yours truly,

Amar Nandra

Amar Nandra

Your Turn

Imagine that you are on an athletic team and your team needs money for uniforms and equipment. Write a business letter to persuade a local business to help support your team. As you choose persuasive words for your letter, remember to keep in mind the connotations of the words. Also remember to capitalize proper nouns. Use the Writer's Checklist to check your writing.

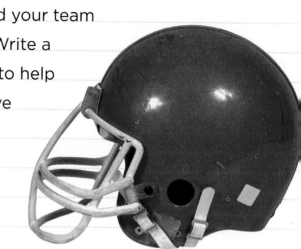

Writer's Checklist

 Ideas and Content: Did I clearly explain my reason for writing the letter?

 Organization: Did I organize my writing in a logical way?

Voice: Does my letter show that a real person wrote it? Have I included words and phrases that reveal my personality?

Word Choice: Did I use persuasive words effectively? Do the persuasive words carry the proper **connotations**?

 Sentence Fluency: Do my sentences blend together in a way that makes my letter pleasant to read?

 Conventions: Did I capitalize all proper nouns? Did I include all of the important parts of a business letter? Did I check my spelling?

THE SOLAR SYSTEM

Talk About It

Why do you think people want to learn more about what they see in the night sky?

LOG ON Find out more about the solar system at **www.macmillanmh.com**

Vocabulary

spicy	broadcast
unsatisfactory	calculations
undone	vigil
ravaged	marveled

Dictionary

A **Pronunciation Key** is a list of letters and symbols that helps you figure out how to say words correctly.

vigil (vij´əl)

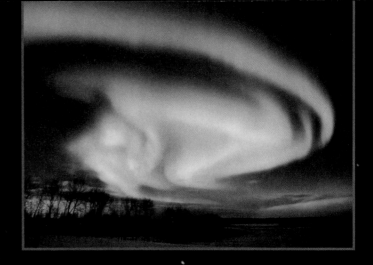

The Night of the Northern Lights

by Ayisha Johnson

Tyrell was grumpy. He didn't want to go, and he told his parents that. But now he was packing his suitcase. His family was traveling to Minnesota to visit his grandma. He would miss school and football practice for a few days. But that wasn't the worst of it. He would miss a chance to go somewhere new.

Tyrell had been to Minnesota before. It was a fine state, but it wasn't very different from his home state of Indiana. Tyrell dreamed of seeing the world. He wanted to touch the white, sandy beaches of the Caribbean. He wanted to taste the hot and spicy foods of Mexico. He wanted to ski in the Swiss Alps. To fulfill Tyrell's big dreams, a drive to Minnesota was unsatisfactory, not good enough.

To make matters worse, the drive was a disaster. The straps holding the family's luggage to the car roof came undone. Luckily, only one suitcase flew loose before Tyrell's dad stopped the car. They retrieved the suitcase, but it and the items inside of it were ravaged from the fall. What wasn't destroyed was very dirty.

It was almost dark when Tyrell's family finally reached his grandmother's house. When they walked in, she was watching a television news broadcast. She greeted each of them and said, "You picked a great day to visit Minnesota!" Then she pointed to the television.

"Scientists have made some calculations," the announcer explained. "The results say that the northern lights will be brighter this week than they have been in years!"

"Some people are holding a vigil down the road at the Johnston farm," Tyrell's grandma said. "I would love to stay up all night to see those beautiful lights!"

The family drove to the farm and joined a group of people in an open field. Tyrell looked up to where everyone was pointing. There were strange waves of red and green light in the sky! The waves seemed to be dancing to the beat of a silent song. Tyrell marveled at the northern lights for a long time. He was amazed by what he saw!

Tyrell's dad came next to him. He winked and said, "I bet you couldn't see this in the Caribbean."

And that's when Tyrell understood that he could find something amazing no matter where he was on Earth. All he had to do was give it a chance.

Reread for **Comprehension**

Generate Questions

Make Inferences

Generating questions as you read can help you make inferences. You make inferences when you combine your prior knowledge with evidence in the text in order to understand what the author does not state directly.

Use an Inferences Diagram to make inferences as you reread "The Night of the Northern Lights."

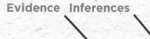

Evidence   Inferences

Comprehension

Genre

A **Short Story** is a brief work of fiction that describes a limited number of characters and a central event.

Generate Questions

Make Inferences

As you read, use your Inference Diagram.

Read to Find Out

How does Harriet feel about Mars?

The Night of the Pomegranate

by Tim Wynne-Jones

illustrated by Elizabeth Sayles

Award Winning Author

Harriet's solar system was a mess. She had made it—the sun and its nine planets—out of rolled-up balls of the morning newspaper. It was mounted on a sheet of green bristol board. The bristol board had a project about Austria on the other side. Harriet wished the background were black. Green was all wrong.

Everything about her project was wrong. The crumpled paper was coming **undone**. Because she had used the last of the tape on Saturn's rings, the three remaining planets had nothing to keep them scrunched up. Tiny Pluto was already bigger than Jupiter and growing by the minute. She had also run out of glue, so part of her solar system was stuck together with grape chewing gum.

Harriet's big brother, Tom, was annoyed at her because Mom had made him drive her to school early with her stupid project. Dad was annoyed at her for using part of the business section. Mostly she had stuck to the want ads, but then an advertisement printed in red ink in the business section caught her eye, and she just had to have it for Mars. Harriet had a crush on Mars; that's what Tom said. She didn't even mind his saying it.

Mars was near the earth this month. The nights had been November cold but clear as glass, and Harriet had been out to see Mars every night, which was why she hadn't gotten her solar system finished, why she was so tired, why Mom made Tom drive her to school. It was all Mars's fault.

She was using the tape on Ms. Krensky's desk when Clayton Beemer arrived with his dad. His solar system came from the hobby store. The planets were Styrofoam balls, all different sizes and painted the right colors. Saturn's rings were clear plastic painted over as delicately as insect wings.

Harriet looked at her own Saturn. Her rings were drooping despite all the tape. They looked like a limp skirt on a . . . on a ball of scrunched-up newspaper.

Harriet sighed. The wires that supported Clayton's planets in their black box were almost invisible. The planets seemed to float.

"What d'ya think?" Clayton asked. He beamed. Mr. Beemer beamed. Harriet guessed that *he* had made the black box with its glittery smears of stars.

She had rolled up her own project protectively when Clayton entered the classroom. Suddenly one of the planets came unstuck and fell on the floor. Clayton and Mr. Beemer looked at it.

"What's that?" asked Clayton.

"Pluto, I think," said Harriet, picking it up. She popped it in her mouth. It tasted of grape gum. "Yes, Pluto," she said. Clayton and Mr. Beemer walked away to find the best place to show off their project.

Darjit arrived next. "Hi, Harriet," she said. The project under her arm had the planets' names done in bold gold lettering. Harriet's heart sank. Pluto tasted stale and cold.

Make Inferences
Why is Harriet discouraged?

But last night Harriet had tasted pomegranates. Old Mrs. Pond had given her one while she busied herself putting on layer after layer of warm clothing and gathering the things they would need for their Mars watch.

Mrs. Pond lived in the country. She lived on the edge of the woods by a meadow that sloped down to a marsh through rough frost-licked grass and prickly ash and juniper. It was so much darker than town; good for stargazing.

By 11:00 P.M. Mars was directly above the marsh, which was where Harriet and Mrs. Pond set themselves up for their vigil. They found it just where they had left it the night before: in the constellation Taurus between the Pleiades and the Hyades. But you didn't need a map to find Mars these nights. It shone like rust, neither trembling nor twinkling as the fragile stars did.

Mrs. Pond smiled and handed Harriet two folding chairs. "Ready?" she asked.

Make Inferences
What is special about the Mars watch for Harriet and Mrs. Pond?

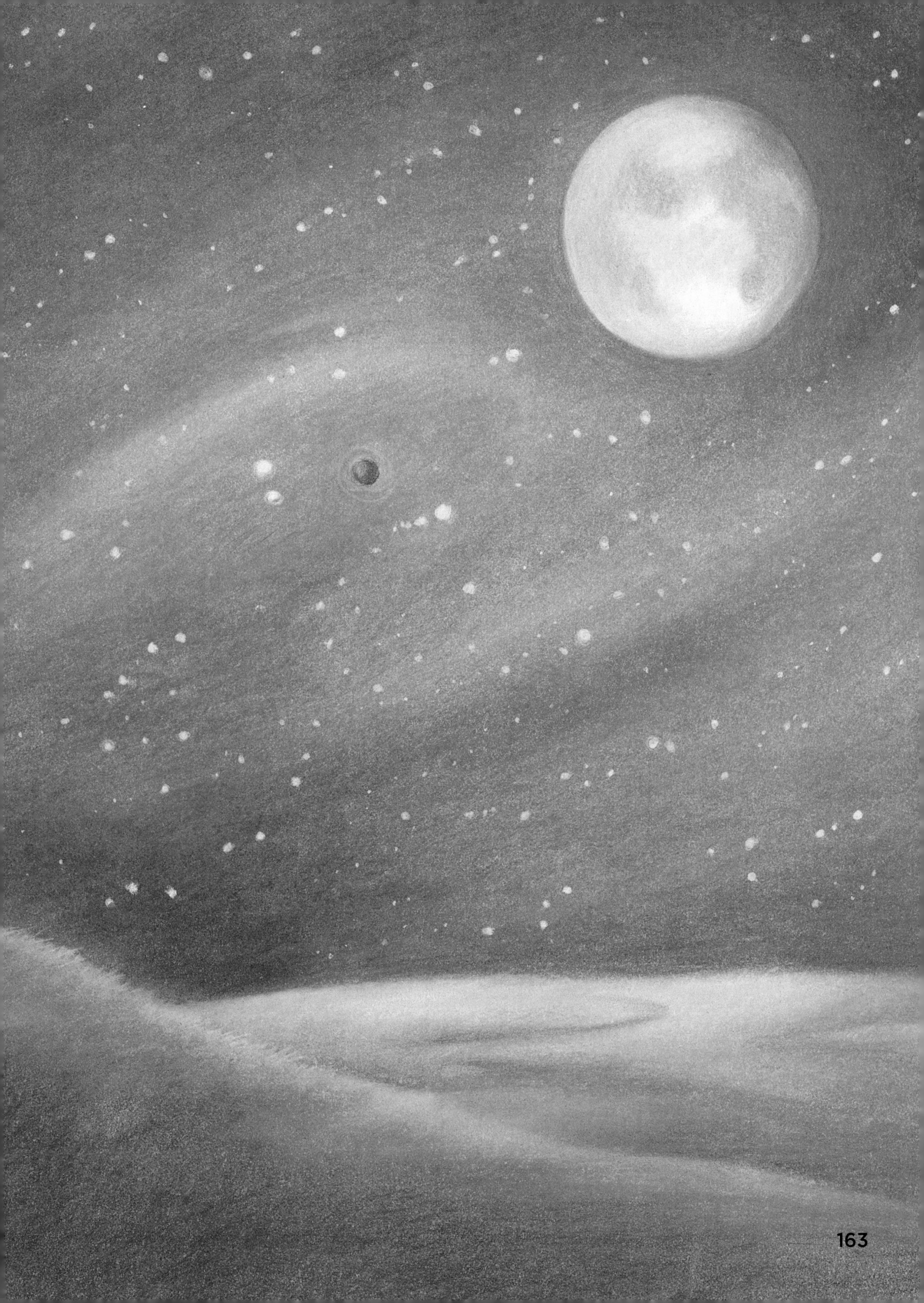

"Ready, class?" said Ms. Krensky. Everyone took their seats. Harriet placed the green bristol board universe in front of her. It was an even worse mess than it had been when she arrived. Her solar system was **ravaged**.

It had started off with Pluto and then, as a joke to make Darjit laugh, she had eaten Neptune. Then Karen had come in, and Jodi and Nick and Scott.

"The planet taste test," Harriet had said, ripping off a bit of Mercury. "Umm, very **spicy.**" By the time the bell rang, there wasn't much of her project left.

Kevin started. He stood at the back of the classroom holding a green and blue marble.

"If this was earth," he said, "then the sun would be this big—" He put the earth in his pocket and pulled a fat squishy yellow beach ball from a garbage bag. Everybody hooted and clapped. "And it would be at the crosswalk," he added. Everyone looked confused, so Ms. Krensky helped Kevin explain the relative distances between the earth and the sun. "And Pluto would be fifty miles away from here," said Kevin. But then he wasn't sure about that, so Ms. Krensky worked it out at the board with him.

Meanwhile, using Kevin's example, the class was supposed to figure out where other planets in the solar system would be relative to the green and blue marble in Kevin's pocket. Harriet sighed.

Until last night, Harriet had never seen the inside of a pomegranate before. As she opened the hard rind, she **marveled** at the bright red seeds in their cream-colored fleshy pouches.

"It's like a little secret universe all folded in on itself," said Mrs. Pond.

Harriet tasted it. With her tongue, she popped a little red bud against the roof of her mouth. The taste startled her, made her laugh.

"Tonight," Mrs. Pond said, "Mars is only forty-five million miles away." They drank a cocoa toast to that. Then she told Harriet about another time when Mars had been even closer on its orbit around the sun. She had been a girl then, and had heard on the radio the famous **broadcast** of *The War of the Worlds*. An actor named Orson Welles had made a radio drama based on a story about Martians attacking the world, but he had presented it in a series of news bulletins and reports, and a lot of people had believed it was true.

Harriet listened to Mrs. Pond and sipped her cocoa and stared at the earth's closest neighbor and felt deliciously chilly and warm at the same time. Mars was wonderfully clear in the telescope, but even with the naked eye she could imagine canals and raging storms. She knew there weren't really Martians, but she allowed herself to imagine them, anyway. She imagined one of them preparing for his invasion of the earth, packing his laser, a thermos of cocoa, and a folding chair.

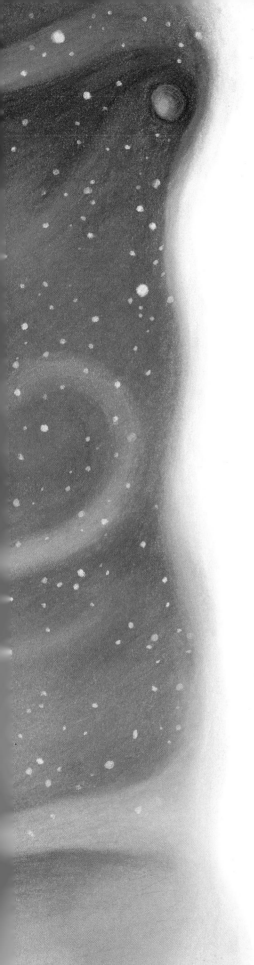

"What in heaven's name is this?" Ms. Krensky was standing at Harriet's chair, staring down at the green bristol board. There was only one planet left.

"Harriet says it's Mars," Darjit started giggling.

"And how big is Mars?" asked Ms. Krensky. Her eyes said **Unsatisfactory**.

"Compared to Kevin's marble earth, Mars would be the size of a pomegranate seed, including the juicy red pulp," said Harriet. Ms. Krensky walked to the front of the class. She turned at her desk. Was there the hint of a smile on her face?

"And where is it?" she asked, raising an eyebrow.

Harriet looked at the **calculations** she had done on a corner of the green bristol board. "If the sun was at the crosswalk," said Harriet, "then Mars would be much closer. Over there." She pointed out the window at the slide in the kindergarten playground. Some of the class actually looked out the window to see if they could see it.

"You *can* see Mars," said Harriet. "Sometimes." Now she was sure she saw Ms. Krensky smile.

"How many of you have seen Mars?" the teacher asked. Only Harriet and Randy Pilcher put up their hands. But Randy had only seen it on a movie.

"Last night was a special night, I believe," said Ms. Krensky, crossing her arms and leaning against her desk. Harriet nodded. "Tell us about it, Harriet," said the teacher.

So Harriet did. She told them all about Mrs. Pond and the Mars watch. She started with the pomegranate.

Out of This World with Tim Wynne-Jones

Tim Wynne-Jones was first an artist, but he was always thinking of the story behind the picture. He knew he was a writer, too, when he began to write in the margins of pictures he was drawing. For the volume in which this story appears, Tim won an award in Canada, where he lives. He wrote it for middle-grades, which he considers an "extraordinary age group." Tim enjoys mixing images with stories; he has even written the libretto, or words, for an opera, as well as a musical for children.

LOG ON Find out more about Tim Wynne-Jones at **www.macmillanmh.com**

Author's Purpose

Tim Wynne-Jones's purpose for this short story was to entertain. Does having Mrs. Pond unexpectedly assist Harriet help the author achieve his purpose? Explain.

Comprehension Check

Summarize

Summarize "The Night of the Pomegranate."
Why is Harriet's project initially such a mess?
How do the flashback sections help you to
understand Harriet's fascination with Mars?

Think and Compare

1. What evidence in the text can you find that
   Ms. Krensky will excuse the poor quality
   of Harriet's project? Use your Inferences
   Diagram to help answer the question.
   Generate Questions: Make Inferences

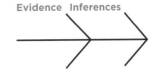

Evidence   Inferences

2. Harriet blames the "Mars watch" **vigil** for the fact that her
   project is unfinished and poorly done. Do you think her
   excuse is valid? Explain. **Analyze**

3. Think about a time when you had to do a project for school.
   What made it successful? Compare and contrast your
   experience with Harriet's. **Evaluate**

4. Do you think space exploration is important? Explain your
   answer. **Evaluate**

5. Read "The Night of the Northern Lights" on pages 154–155.
   How does Tyrell experience a turning point similar to Harriet's
   in "The Night of the Pomegranate?" Compare the lessons that
   each of the characters learned. **Reading/Writing Across Texts**

Science

Genre

Informational Nonfiction explains facts about real persons, places, or events.

Text Feature

Graphs are visual representations of numbers or quantities. Graphs make it easy to compare data.

Content Vocabulary

axis	**equator**
satellites	**revolution**

How Do We Know Earth Is Rotating?

We talk about the sun rising in the morning and setting at dusk, but in reality the sun isn't moving—we are! Earth rotates, or spins on its **axis**, just like a spinning top. The axis is an imaginary line through Earth from the North Pole to the South Pole.

It takes about 24 hours for Earth to make one rotation, or complete spin, on the axis. As each part of Earth rotates toward and away from the sun, we experience periods of daylight and darkness. As the day begins, the sun appears to "rise" in the east. By midday, the sun reaches its highest point in the sky. In the afternoon, as Earth keeps rotating, the sun appears to get lower in the sky, until it "sets" in the west. Earth makes this rotation about 365 times each year.

and the Sun

How do we know that Earth is spinning? One way is data from **satellites**. Satellites can observe the rotation of Earth from space.

An early piece of evidence was discovered by a French scientist named Jean Foucault (foo-KOH). A pendulum, or suspended weight, was hung by a long string. It was made to swing back and forth, north to south. As hours passed, the direction the pendulum was swinging moved around in a clockwise direction. After a while, it was swinging northeast-southwest; after a bit, it was

swinging east-west, then southeast-northwest, then finally north-south again. What caused this change in the pendulum's direction of swing was that Earth was rotating under it.

The shape of Earth is also a clue that it is rotating. Earth is not a perfect sphere. It is slightly flattened at the North and South Poles and bulges slightly at the **equator**. It is similar to what happens in a washing machine. As the clothes spin around, they get thrown to the edge. As Earth spins, its matter also gets shifted to the "edge," creating a slightly bulging equator.

Foucault's pendulum showed that Earth rotated.

 A line graph uses one or more line segments to show changes in data. This line graph shows the number of hours of daylight for three latitudes during a year.

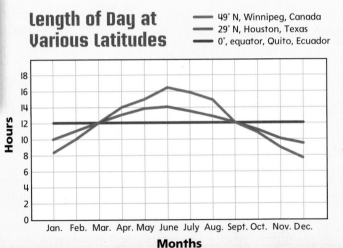

Length of Day at Various Latitudes

— 49° N, Winnipeg, Canada
— 29° N, Houston, Texas
— 0°, equator, Quito, Ecuador

Hours: 18, 16, 14, 12, 10, 8, 6, 4, 2, 0

Months: Jan. Feb. Mar. Apr. May June July Aug. Sept. Oct. Nov. Dec.

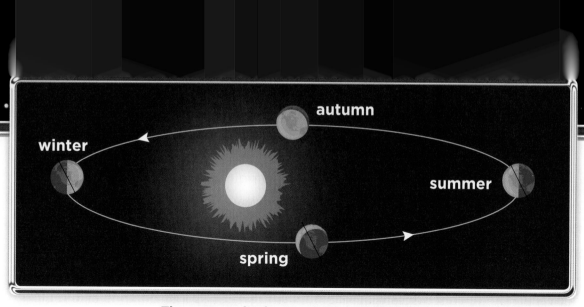

The seasons in the Northern Hemisphere

The Reason for Seasons

In many parts of the United States, as you switch from a bathing suit to a sweater to a winter coat to a T-shirt, you have certainly noticed that seasons change every year. The two biggest signs of change are temperature and length of day. Do you know what causes these changes?

Earth takes 365 1/4 days to revolve, or travel in its orbit, once around the sun. One complete trip around the sun is called a **revolution**. Remember that while Earth is revolving, it is also rotating on its axis. However, the axis is not vertical. It is tilted at an angle of 23 1/2° and always points in the same general direction. This means that as Earth goes around its orbit, the Northern Hemisphere (places north of the equator such as

the United States, Europe, and China) is at times leaning more toward or more away from the sun.

When it is summer in the United States, the Northern Hemisphere is tilted more toward the sun. As spring turns into summer, the sun climbs higher in the sky, it is above the horizon longer, and its rays strike the ground more directly. As fall turns into winter, the Northern Hemisphere tilts away from the sun. The sun is lower in the sky, it is above the horizon for a shorter period, and the rays of the sun strike the ground less directly.

The summer solstice, which happens around June 21, is the longest day of the year in the Northern Hemisphere. The sun appears to be at its highest in the sky and stays above the horizon for more than 12 hours, causing more hours of daylight and fewer hours of darkness. The summer solstice marks the first day of summer.

In contrast, the winter solstice, which occurs around December 21, is the shortest day of the year north of the equator. The sun doesn't appear to get very high in the sky and is above the horizon for fewer than 12 hours. This results in less daylight and more darkness. The winter solstice marks the first day of winter.

In the Southern Hemisphere, the winter and summer solstices are reversed. This means that when it is summer in North America, it is winter in parts of South America.

Connect and Compare

1. Look at the graph on page 173. When are days in Houston, Texas, longest? Why? When are they shortest? Why? **Reading a Graph**

2. How does Earth's rotation cause day and night? **Analyze**

3. Think about what you learned in this science article. If you were a character in "The Night of the Pomegranate," what information could you add to Kevin's and Harriet's presentations? **Reading/ Writing Across Texts**

 Science Activity

Research the number of moons each of the eight planets has. Then draw a graph to display the data.

 Find out more about the solar system at **www.macmillanmh.com**

Writer's Craft

A Good Topic

A **good topic** is one that you enjoy writing about and that is narrow in focus. Near the beginning of your editorial write a thesis statement that summarizes the topic.

My topic is my opinion on *space exploration*.

I put my thesis statement in the first paragraph.

Understand Our Earth First

by Pang C.

Some countries' leaders spend millions of dollars to help scientists explore the solar system. Is this money spent wisely? I do not think so. Most of the money spent on space exploration should instead be spent to help people here on Earth.

Scientists have helped humans live better lives in many ways. However, I believe that there is still more to do. Scientists should focus more on answering questions about humans and Earth. Then maybe we wouldn't have diseases, disasters, or endangered animals.

And think about the millions (or billions!) of dollars spent on space exploration. Governments should use that money to feed the hungry. Wouldn't that be a wonderful experiment to try?

Your Turn

Write an editorial on whether or not space exploration is important. Be sure to include your topic in a clearly written thesis statement. Then use facts and examples to support your main idea. Use the Writer's Checklist to check your writing.

Writer's Checklist

☑ **Ideas and Content:** Did I explain my opinion clearly?

☑ **Organization:** Did I include a thesis statement that clearly explains my **topic**? Did the ideas, facts, and examples I included support my main idea?

☑ **Voice:** Did I successfully share my opinion on the subject? Did I share my opinion in a way that only I can?

☑ **Word Choice:** Did I use interesting language to express my opinion?

☑ **Sentence Fluency:** Did I read my editorial aloud to check the flow of language? Did I include sentences of different lengths?

☑ **Conventions:** Did I properly use commas with words in a series? Did I check my spelling, including all plural nouns?

Talk About It

When a natural disaster occurs, what are some ways people can help one another?

LOG ON Find out more about natural disasters at **www.macmillanmh.com**

Helping Hands

BE PREPARED
When Disaster Strikes

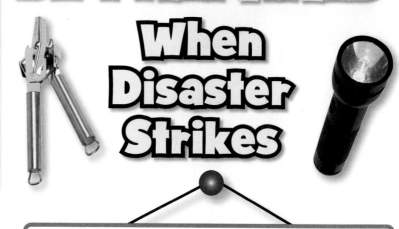

Vocabulary

calamities

mitigate

devastating

evacuate

administer

When disasters occur in the U.S., the Federal Emergency Management Agency (FEMA) always springs into action. Its mission is to help the victims of hurricanes, tornadoes, floods, earthquakes, and other **calamities**. FEMA uses many methods to help people. Education is one method FEMA uses to help **mitigate** the potentially **devastating** effects of a natural disaster. One thing it teaches is the importance of being prepared by having a disaster kit ready in case it's ever needed.

According to the American Red Cross, a disaster kit should include:

✓ First-aid kit and essential medications

✓ Canned food and a can opener

✓ At least three gallons of water for each person in the house

✓ Warm clothing, rainwear, and bedding or sleeping bags

✓ At least one flashlight and extra batteries

✓ A battery-powered radio

✓ Special items for babies, the elderly, or disabled family members

✓ Written instructions for how to turn off the electricity, gas, and water in your home

In addition to these items, it's always important to know what to do in case there is an order to **evacuate**. Everyone should know how to get out of harm's way and to a safe place.

LOG ON Find out more about organizations that help at **www.macmillanmh.com**

Volunteers check on Kokomo in the pool.

A Whale in a Pool

It was their last resort! For two weeks, workers from a dolphin hospital in Key Largo, Florida, visited a hotel swimming pool to **administer** aid to a sick whale. Kokomo, a 1,200-pound pygmy sperm whale, had been moved to the pool at the Islander Resort hotel in Islamorada after being rescued by the Coast Guard. It's the only heated seawater pool in the area. Although Kokomo was still weak, "he's beaten a lot of odds," said the hospital's Rick Trout. Later, Kokomo was moved to the hospital's lagoon.

TOP 5 HURRICANE STATES

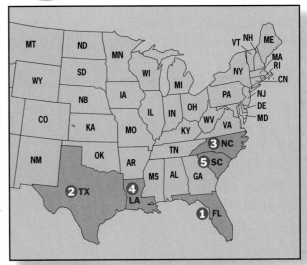

From 1900 to 2004, 173 hurricanes struck the continental United States. The states that hug the Atlantic Ocean and the Gulf of Mexico get hit most often. Here are the states where the most hurricanes have blown ashore.

STATE	NUMBER OF HURRICANES
1. Florida	62
2. Texas	38
3. North Carolina	30
4. Louisiana	25
5. South Carolina	15

Sources: National Hurricane Center and National Climatic Data Center

Comprehension

Genre

A **Nonfiction Article** in a newspaper or magazine presents facts and information.

Generate Questions

Make Generalizations

A generalization is a way of describing a subject or situation in broad statements, without giving a lot of details or specifics.

Zoo Story

What happens when a fierce hurricane nearly destroys a zoo?

Hurricane Andrew was a **devastating** natural disaster for South Florida. In terms of property damage, it is one of the worst **calamities** ever to hit the United States. When Andrew swept ashore with wind gusts of 175 miles per hour, thousands of people lost their homes. The storm also nearly destroyed Miami's Metrozoo, home to thousands of wild animals. Setting their own losses aside, 100 dedicated men and women worked frantically to take care of the needs of the dazed and helpless animals roaming through the wreckage of the zoo. For some creatures whose habitats were destroyed, survival was a race against time.

SAVING THE KOALAS

The zoo's three koalas lost their only source of food—a eucalyptus grove—and the roof of their air-conditioned enclosure. They were suffering in dangerously high heat and humidity.

Metrozoo worker Ron McGill surveys the damage to the zoo by Hurricane Andrew.

"It was very important to get them to another facility immediately," said Ron McGill, a zoo employee. "We called Busch Gardens in Tampa, the closest zoo that has koalas, but we had the problem of getting them there fast."

After he made a radio appeal, a private pilot came to the rescue. He got permission from the National Guard to have a runway cleared of debris at Tamiami Airport. Then he loaded the koalas into his small plane and was able to **evacuate** them to a temporary and safe new home. "You shouldn't have to wait for a natural catastrophe for these things to happen," said McGill. "But it shows that a lot of good will come of this."

A COMMUNITY COMES TOGETHER

After Andrew hit, the area had to deal with looting, food and water shortages, and the misery of 250,000 people left homeless. The hasty cleanup of Metrozoo emerged as one of the brightest examples of public generosity in the face of a disaster. With its soaring aviary and sleek monorail, Metrozoo had been a source of civic pride for Miamians.

Zoo staff took steps in advance to try to **mitigate** damage the hurricane might cause. These efforts included drastically trimming trees to reduce the number of broken limbs. They sheltered all flamingos, storks, and cranes in the

Ron McGill tries to recapture some of the exotic birds that escaped during the storm.

zoo's concrete restrooms. Despite these measures, Andrew would not be denied. Exhibit roofs peeled off while uprooted trees and trailers tore through the air like missiles. They demolished chain-link fences and freed an antelope herd, a gibbon, a tapir, hundreds of birds, and several 500-pound Galapagos tortoises. "We had to get a forklift to put the tortoises back," said McGill.

Another casualty was the zoo's spectacular aviary, containing 320 birds of 80 different species. The 60-foot-high netting roof collapsed, crushing many of the birds and leaving others at the mercy of 150-mph winds. Fortunately, the rhino and giraffes were uninjured and stayed in their torn enclosures. They probably "felt more secure in a familiar place," explains McGill. The animals that might have posed a threat to humans—lions, tigers, bears, and gorillas—rode out Andrew's high winds behind the steel grates and poured concrete of their night houses. The zoo's fatality list was miraculously short: three antelope, an ostrich that was hit by flying debris, a small gibbon, and many birds.

"When I first got here," said McGill, "I sat down and cried. I wondered if we would ever be able to rebuild."

ANSWERING THE CALL FOR HELP

Reacting to calls for help, other zoos started sending specialized foods for the animals. Veterinarians offered to **administer** care, and many people donated chain saws to cut fallen trees.

McGill checks to see if this elephant has been injured.

Zoos also delivered meat for the big cats and fish for the birds. An hour after McGill appealed on TV for refrigeration help, a man lent the zoo two large refrigerated trucks. "We've gotten such an overwhelming response to our requests," McGill said. "I don't know if I got more emotional over the tragedy of the loss or over the outpouring of support." Still, he said, "while we all love animals, we need to take care of people first. I don't want anyone to bring us water if it takes away from a family that needs it."

McGill was hopeful about the animals' future. He told the story of the workers who came across a tiny miracle in the wreckage. There lay a baby yellow-backed duiker (DIGH•kur), a small, now motherless antelope born during the storm and still alive. They promptly dubbed it Andrew. "In the midst of the destruction, here was this new life," said McGill. "It was like a ray of hope. And we knew as long as we didn't lose hope, we'd be okay."

Think and Compare

1. What generalization can you make about the people in the article?

2. Give three examples of how community members were able to help save the zoo.

3. If you had to evacuate because of an oncoming hurricane, what would you take with you, and why?

4. "Be Prepared When Disaster Strikes" on page 180 offers steps to take in emergencies. What steps did the staff at Miami's Metrozoo take to protect the animals?

Test Strategy

Author and Me

The answer is not directly stated. You have to think about what you know and link it to the text.

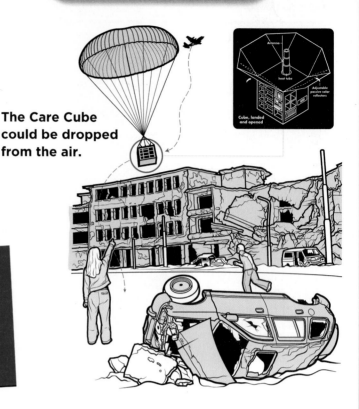

The Care Cube could be dropped from the air.

A CARE PACKAGE OF TECHNOLOGY FOR THE 21ST CENTURY

For its 2004 design competition, *Popular Science* magazine used the theme of a twenty-first century care package. Entrants were asked to consider this question: How could emerging technology help a community in need? They were to identify a community, define a need, and imagine a way that technology could fix it.

Alexander Rose and Danny Hillis took the grand prize with their "Care Cube." The pair thought that infrastructure was the key to a community's recovery after a disaster. They identified clean water, communications, and power as the most fundamental needs to be restored first. Therefore, their idea featured a six-foot-square box, weighing about a ton, stocked with these basics:

✓ Solar-powered cell phone/personal digital assistants that automatically signal other units until users' messages are picked up or make it to the Internet.

✓ LCD screens and software-driven keyboards that shift easily between alphabets of different languages.

✓ Retractable sinks and water purification filters.

✓ An engine fueled by solar reflectors or a combustion box that would store energy. (The box would also contain a stationary bicycle as an alternative way to generate electricity should the engine fail.)

For a community devastated by a crisis, the "Care Cube" could literally be a lifesaver!

Go On ▶

Directions: Answer the questions.

1. The BEST meaning for infrastructure is

- **A** construction materials.
- **B** basic services and resources.
- **C** power source.
- **D** interior design.

2. What goal did *Popular Science* most likely want to achieve with this contest?

- **A** to find ways technology can help communities in an emergency
- **B** to select new technologies that should become profitable
- **C** to showcase America's technological expertise
- **D** to increase interest in water treatment systems

3. What generalization can be made about the grand prize winner of the contest?

- **A** The Care Cube efficiently answers the needs of a community in crisis.
- **B** The Care Cube allows people to learn different languages.
- **C** The Care Cube could save lives by purifying contaminated water.
- **D** The Care Cube is a flawed concept because it does not provide a source of food.

4. What three options does the Care Cube offer for generating power? Which one seems most practical, and why?

5. Explain how a community could use the Care Cube after suffering a natural disaster. Be sure to include details and examples to support your ideas.

> **Tip**
> You have to think about the entire passage to choose the best answer.

Write to a Prompt

You just read about one idea for helping people in need. People help each other in many ways. Write a story about a time when you helped someone in need. Include details about what happened, what you did to help, and how you felt.

Finding a Way to Help

I won't ever say I'm starving again. Two weeks ago, our class read about hunger in the world. I learned that millions of people really are starving.

That night after dinner, I looked at the plates. We were actually throwing out food! Right then, I decided to do something. First, I talked to community leaders about how to help people in need. The best thing to do, they agreed, was raise money to buy food.

I talked with my friends and we went to Ms. Rogers, our teacher. She agreed to let us organize a Bike for Hunger day. Next, we signed up sponsors. They agreed to donate so much for each mile we rode. The local paper even did a story about our project.

Yesterday, we had our ride. We rode 30 miles in all—the most I've ever done! I was so tired, I could hardly stand. Then my dad said, "You raised over a thousand dollars today." I could have jumped over the moon! Next year, we will do it again.

I wrote my story in chronological order and finished with a strong ending.

Writing Prompt

Cell phones are one form of technology that has helped people in many ways. Think of an emergency when you used a cell phone or other form of technology to help solve a problem or to get someone out of a dangerous situation. Write a one-page story about what happened, and put events in a logical order.

Writer's Checklist

☑ Ask yourself, who is my audience?

☑ Think about your purpose for writing.

☑ Plan your writing before beginning.

☑ Use details to support your story.

☑ Be sure your story has a beginning, a middle, and an ending.

☑ Use your best spelling, grammar, and punctuation.

Tales of Old

Talk About It

Why do you think people still read fairy tales today?

LOG ON Find out more about tales of old at **www.macmillanmh.com**

From Daughter to Daughter

by Ramón Pérez

It was a tradition. Every Delgado mother taught her daughter how to make "the famous Delgado empanadas." Empanada is a Spanish word that means "pie" or "meat pie." But the Delgados were not famous for meat pies. They were famous for their dessert empanadas.

Today Lucy Delgado would learn the recipe. She wanted to ask about her family's past, but she was feeling shy. She looked **sheepishly** at her grandmother. "Abuelita, how did we become famous for our empanadas? How did you start a bakery?" she asked.

Abuelita said, "I was making empanadas the way my mother did and the way her mother did. Then I started trying new things. I put rice pudding or chocolate inside an empanada. Some of my friends thought they tasted so good that they asked me to make the sweet pies for them. I wanted to start my own business but I did not have the money."

"So how did you get the money?" Lucy asked.

"By a series of strange **coincidences**. A businessman at a friend's party tasted my empanadas. He thought the **sumptuous** pies were wonderful. My friend had a space for rent so the businessman offered to help me start my bakery. To **sweeten** the pot, he said that he would give me a year's contract to supply his company's cafeteria with empanadas."

"Abuelita had the money and the space, but we still had **phase** three of our problems to face," Lucy's mom said.

"There was so little heat in the space we rented that our fingers were too numb to work," laughed Abuelita. "Sometimes it was so cold in the building that we had to wear gloves on our hands and **mufflers** around our necks while we made the dough!"

"I worked so hard some days that I **hobbled** home at night because my legs were so tired," Abuelita continued. "But soon the business **prospered**. We were making enough money to hire workers. And that's how the bakery still runs today."

Lucy smiled at Abuelita with pride. After hearing that story, the empanadas seemed to taste sweeter than before.

Reread for **Comprehension**

Summarize
Problem and Solution
A Problem and Solution Chart can help you summarize the events of a story. Identify a story's problem and solution to help you capture its most important details in your summary.

Use a Problem and Solution Chart to help you identify the important parts of the story as you reread "From Daughter to Daughter."

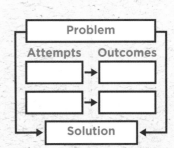

Comprehension

Genre

A **Fairy Tale** features imaginary characters and takes place long ago. It has a plot with a conflict between good and evil. A parody is a humorous imitation of another recognizable work.

Summarize

Problem and Solution

As you read, use your Problem and Solution Chart.

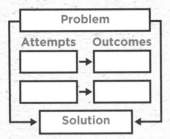

Read to Find Out

How does Rumpelstiltskin's daughter use the king's greed to solve her problem?

Rumpelstiltskin's Daughter

Award Winning Selection

written & illustrated by Diane Stanley

Once there was a miller's daughter who got into a heap of trouble. It was all because her father liked to make up stories and pass them off as truth. Unfortunately, the story he told was that his daughter could spin straw into gold, which, of course, she could not. Even more unfortunately, he told this whopper in the hearing of a palace servant who rushed right off to tell the king. Since the king loved nothing in this world more than gold, he had the miller's daughter hauled up to the palace immediately and made her an offer she couldn't refuse. He put her in a room full of straw and ordered her to spin it into gold by morning, or die.

By one of those unlikely **coincidences** so common in fairy tales, no sooner had the king closed and bolted the door than a very small gentleman showed up and revealed that he really *could* spin straw into gold. Furthermore, he offered to do it in exchange for her necklace, which was made of gold-tone metal and wasn't worth ten cents. Naturally, she agreed.

The next morning, the king was so overjoyed with his room full of gold that he rewarded the miller's daughter by doubling the amount of straw and repeating his threat. Once again, Rumpelstiltskin (for that was his name) arrived to help her out. This time she gave him her paper-band pinkie ring.

After this second success, the king was practically apoplectic with greed. He proceeded to empty every barn in the neighborhood of straw and to fill the room with it. This time, he added a little sugar to **sweeten** the pot: If she turned it all into gold, he would make her his queen. You can just imagine how the miller's daughter was feeling when Rumpelstiltskin popped in for the third time.

"That's quite a pile," he said. "I suppose you want me to spin it into gold."

"Well, the situation has changed just a bit," said the miller's daughter (who also had a name—it was Meredith). "If you *don't*, I will die. If you *do*, I marry the king."

Now *that*, thought Rumpelstiltskin, has possibilities. After all, getting to be the queen was a big step up for a miller's daughter. She would surely pay him anything. And there was only one thing in the world he really wanted—a little child to love and care for.

"Okay, here's the deal," he said. "I will spin the straw into gold, just like before. In return, once you become queen, you must let me adopt your firstborn child. I promise I'll be an excellent father. I know all the lullabies. I'll read to the child every day. I'll even coach Little League."

"You've got to be kidding," Meredith said. "I'd rather marry *you* than that jerk!"

"*Really?*" said Rumpelstiltskin, and he blushed all the way from the top of his head to the tip of his toes (which admittedly wasn't very far, because he was so short).

"Sure," she said. "I like your ideas on parenting, you'd make a good provider, and I have a weakness for short men."

So Rumpelstiltskin spun a golden ladder, and they escaped out the window. They were married the very next day and lived happily together far, far away from the palace.

Meredith and Rumpelstiltskin lived a quiet country life, raising chickens and growing vegetables. Every now and then, when they needed something they couldn't make or grow, Rumpelstiltskin would spin up a little gold to buy it with.

Now, they had a daughter, and she was just as sunny and clever as you would expect her to be, having such devoted parents. When she was sixteen, they decided she ought to see more of the world, so every now and then they allowed her to take the gold into town to exchange it for coins and to do a little shopping.

The goldsmith grew curious about the pretty country girl who came in with those odd coils of gold. He mentioned it to his friend the baker, who mentioned it to the blacksmith, who mentioned it to the tax collector, who hurried to the palace and told the king.

It may not surprise you to learn that the king hadn't changed a bit. If anything, he was greedier than before. As he listened, his eyes glittered. "I once knew a miller's daughter who could make gold like that," he said. "Unfortunately, she got away. Let's make sure *this* one doesn't."

So the next time Rumpelstiltskin's daughter went to see the goldsmith, two of the king's guards were waiting for her. In a red-hot minute, she was in a carriage and speeding toward the palace. And what she saw on the way broke her heart. Everywhere the fields lay barren. Sickly children stood begging beside the road. Nobody in the kingdom had anything anymore, because the king had it all.

Finally they reached the palace. There were high walls around it and a moat full of crocodiles. Armed guards were everywhere, gnashing their teeth, clutching their swords, and peering about with shifty eyes. As the carriage went over the bridge and under the portcullis, the hungry people shook their fists at them. It was not a pretty sight.

Rumpelstiltskin's daughter was taken at once to the grand chamber where the king sat on his golden throne. He didn't waste time on idle pleasantries.

"Where did you get *this*?" he asked, showing her the gold.

"Uh . . . ," said Rumpelstiltskin's daughter.

"I thought so," said the king. "Guards, take her to the tower and see what she can do with all that straw."

Rumpelstiltskin's daughter looked around. She saw a pile of straw the size of a bus. She saw a locked door and high windows. She gave a big sigh and began to think. She knew her father could get her out of this pickle. But she had heard stories about the king all her life. One room full of gold would never satisfy him. Her father would be stuck here, spinning, until there was not an iota of straw left in the kingdom.

After a while she climbed the pile of straw and thought some more. She thought about the poor farmers and about the hungry children with their thin faces and sad eyes. She put the two thoughts together and cooked up a plan. Then Rumpelstiltskin's daughter curled up and went to sleep.

Problem and Solution

Identify the main problem Rumpelstiltskin's daughter faces. Look for actions she takes to solve the problem.

The next day, the king was very disappointed.

"Where's my gold?" he wanted to know.

"I'm sure you have rooms full of it upstairs," said Rumpelstiltskin's daughter. And she was right. He did.

"But I want *more!*" he said. "And I want *you* to make it for me."

"Alas," she said, "I never made gold in my life. But"—and here she paused for effect—"I saw my grandfather make it." When the king's face brightened, she added, "He died years ago."

"Surely you remember how he did it," cried the king. "Think! Think!"

"Well," she said slowly, "there is one thing I'm sure of. He didn't spin it, he *grew* it."

The next morning the king and Rumpelstiltskin's daughter got into his glittering coach, with two guards up front and two guards behind and a huge bag of gold inside. They drove under the portcullis, over the bridge, and out into the countryside. At the first farm they came to, they stopped and sent for the farmer. He was thin and ragged and barefoot. So were his wife and children.

"Now tell the farmer he must plant this gold coin in his field, and you will come back in the fall to collect everything it has grown. Tell him you will give him another gold coin for his pains," she whispered.

"Do I *have* to?" the king whined.

"Well, I don't know," she said. "That's how my grandfather always did it."

"Okay," said the king. "But this better work." He gave the farmer two gold coins, and they hurried on to the next farm. By the end of the week they had covered the entire kingdom.

All through the summer the king was restless. "Is it time yet?" he would ask. "Is the gold ripe?"

"Wait," said Rumpelstiltskin's daughter.

Finally August came and went.

"Now," she said. "Now you can go and see what has grown in the fields."

So once again they piled into the glittering coach (with two guards up front and two guards behind) and brought along wagons to carry the gold and a lot more guards to protect it.

As they neared the first farm, the king gasped with joy. The field shone golden in the morning sun.

"Gold!" he cried.

"No," said Rumpelstiltskin's daughter, "something better than gold."

"How can anything be better than gold?" said the king.

"It's wheat," she said. "You can eat it. You can't eat gold."

Before the king could start turning purple, the farmer and his family came running toward the carriage. In their arms they carried baskets of wheat and barley and apples and green beans and pumpkins and corn and I don't know what all. They piled it into the wagon and kissed the king's hand, grinning ear to ear. I can promise you that nothing like that had ever happened to the king before.

"Well," he said **sheepishly**, "maybe there will be gold at the next place."

But everywhere it was the same. The land **prospered**, the children looked healthy, and the king was a hero. At the end of the week they returned to the palace with all the food the wagons could carry.

The cook was so overjoyed, he put on a **sumptuous** feast to celebrate. Unfortunately, there was no one to invite except Rumpelstiltskin's daughter and the guards, who spent the whole meal gnashing their teeth, clutching their swords, and peering about with shifty eyes.

"I wish they'd quit that," said Rumpelstiltskin's daughter.

After dinner, the king spoke. "That was all very nice, my dear," he said, "but you must have been mistaken. That was how your grandfather grew *food*, not how he made gold."

"Right," she said as she pulled her shawl tightly around her shoulders and gazed longingly at the fire. Even in the palace she could feel the chill of autumn. *Time for* **phase** *two*, she thought.

"Of course you're right," she said. "I told you it was long ago. But I think I remember now. He didn't grow gold. He *knitted* it with golden knitting needles."

Problem and Solution

What related problem has arisen as the story unfolds? Look for ways Rumpelstiltskin's daughter solves this problem.

205

So the next day they loaded the coach with knitting needles, a bag of gold, and lots and lots of yellow wool. Then they headed off under the portcullis, over the bridge (with two guards up front and two guards behind), and out into the countryside.

At the first cottage they came to, they asked to see the granny. She **hobbled** to the door in her rags and curtsied to the king.

"Now," whispered Rumpelstiltskin's daughter, "give her a bag of wool and a pair of needles. Tell her to knit it all up and you will come back in a month to collect your riches. Give her a gold coin for her pains."

"Do I *have* to?" the king whined.

"My grandfather always did," she said. "I would, if I were you."

And so they went all over the kingdom, hiring every granny they could find.

At the end of the month, the king ordered his coach and wagons, rounded up his guards, and went to see the grannies. As he neared the first cottage, he heard the sound of singing. Looking out the window, the king saw crowds of happy villagers waiting there to greet him, cheering wildly as he passed. And every one of them was warm as toast in yellow woolly clothes.

"Gold!" cried the king.

"Something better than gold," said Rumpelstiltskin's daughter. "Your people will be warm all winter."

Everyone brought presents for the king. By the time he got back to his palace, he had seventeen sweaters, forty-two **mufflers**, eight vests, one pair of knickers, one hundred and thirty-five pairs of socks, twelve nightcaps, and a tam-o'-shanter. All the color of gold.

"Do they suit me?" asked the king as he tried them on.

"Absolutely," said Rumpelstiltskin's daughter.

The guards just stood there, gnashing their teeth, clutching their swords, and peering about with shifty eyes.

"Don't you think it's time you got rid of them?" she suggested. "And the walls and the moat and the crocodiles, too. You don't need them anymore—your people love you now."

She was right, as always, so the king set the guards to work tearing down the walls. And with the stones, they built a zoo for the crocodiles and houses for the poor.

"Are you sure you don't remember how your grandfather made gold?" asked the king one day.

"I'm afraid not," she said.

"It's a terrible pity," he sighed. "But you did try. And as a reward, I have decided to make you my queen."

"Why don't you make me prime minister instead," suggested Rumpelstiltskin's daughter.

And so the king did just that. He built her a nice house near the palace, and once a month she took time off to visit her parents. The people of the kingdom never went cold or hungry again. And whenever the king started worrying about gold, she sent him on a goodwill tour throughout the countryside, which cheered him right up.

Oh, and I forgot to tell you—Rumpelstiltskin's daughter had a name, too. It was Hope.

Once Upon a Time with Diane Stanley

Diane Stanley researches everything about her topic before she starts writing and illustrating a book. For this story, she even investigated different types of food from the days when the characters might have lived. Maybe she pays such close attention to detail because she used to illustrate medical books. She always chooses a subject she loves—someone she considers the most interesting person or character in the world—and then reads everything she can on her subject. This helps her create the right setting, which is on top of Diane's how-to-write list.

 LOG ON Find out more about Diane Stanley at **www.macmillanmh.com**

Another book by Diane Stanley:
Leonardo da Vinci

Author's Purpose
Diane Stanley's main purpose is to entertain, but she is also informing by teaching that kindness is more valuable than gold. What makes this story entertaining?

Comprehension Check

Summarize

Use your Problem and Solution Chart to help you summarize *Rumpelstiltskin's Daughter*. What is the main problem that Rumpelstiltskin's daughter encounters? How does she solve it?

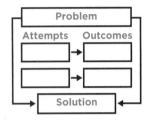

Think and Compare

1. How is the problem that Meredith and Rumpelstiltskin solve different from the problem that Hope solves? **Summarize: Problem and Solution**

2. What kind of a person is Rumpelstiltskin's daughter? Do you think she **prospered** in the end? Support your answer with story details. **Analyze**

3. The king's guards are always "gnashing their teeth, clutching their swords, and peering about with shifty eyes." If you were Hope, what might you do to change how the guards act? **Synthesize**

4. Rumpelstiltskin's daughter is named Hope. Why do you think the writer chose to end the story with that fact? Why is hope so important? **Evaluate**

5. Read "From Daughter to Daughter" on pages 192–193. What are the similarities between the way Lucy's grandmother makes special empanadas and the way Hope solves her problems in *Rumpelstiltskin's Daughter*? **Reading/Writing Across Texts**

The Golden Touch

retold by Mary Pope Osborne

Bacchus, the merry god, raised his goblet. "To you, King Midas," he said, "and because you have been so hospitable to me—ask for anything you wish, and I will grant it to you."

"What an idea!" said Midas. "Anything I wish?"

"Indeed, anything," said Bacchus.

"Anything?"

"Yes! Yes!"

212

"Ah, well," said the king, chuckling. "Of course, there's only one thing: I wish that everything I touch would turn to gold!" Midas looked sideways at Bacchus, for he couldn't believe such a gift could really be his.

"My friend, you already have all the gold you could possibly want," said Bacchus, looking disappointed.

"Oh, no! I don't!" said Midas. "One never has enough gold!"

"Well, if that's what you wish for, I suppose I will have to grant it," said Bacchus.

Bacchus soon took his leave. As Midas waved good-bye to him, his hand brushed an oak twig hanging from a tree—and the twig turned to gold!

The king screamed with joy, then shouted after Bacchus, "My wish has come true! Thank you! Thank you!"

The god turned and waved, then disappeared down the road.

Midas looked around excitedly. He leaned over and picked a stone up from the ground—and the stone turned into a golden nugget! He kicked the sand—and the sand turned to golden grains!

King Midas threw back his head and shouted, "I'm the richest man in the world!" Then he rushed about his grounds, touching everything. And everything, *everything* turned to gold: ears of corn in his fields! Apples plucked from trees! The pillars of his mansion!

When the king's servants heard him shouting, they rushed to see what was happening. They found their king dancing wildly on his lawn, turning the grass to glittering blades of gold. Everyone laughed and clapped as Midas washed his hands in his fountain and turned the water to a gleaming spray!

Finally, exhausted but overjoyed, King Midas called for his dinner. His servants placed a huge banquet meal before him on his lawn. "Oh, I'm so hungry!" he said as he speared a piece of meat and brought it to his mouth.

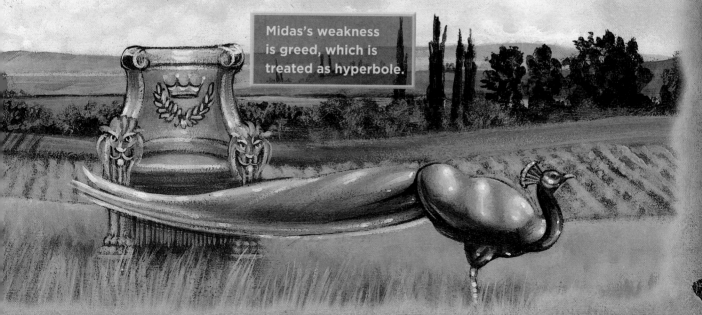

Midas's weakness is greed, which is treated as hyperbole.

But suddenly King Midas realized his wish may not have been as wonderful as he thought—for the moment he bit down on the meat, it, too, turned to gold.

Midas laughed uneasily, then reached for a piece of bread. But as soon as his hands touched the bread, it also became a hard, golden nugget! Weak with dread, Midas reached for his goblet of water. But alas! His lips touched only hard, cold metal. The water had also turned to gold.

Covering his head and moaning, King Midas realized his great wish was going to kill him. He would starve to death or die of thirst!

"Bacchus!" he cried, throwing his hands toward heaven. "I've been a greedy fool! Take away your gift! Free me from my golden touch! Help me, Bacchus!"

The sobbing king fell off his chair to his knees. He beat his fists against the ground, turning even the little anthills to gold. His servants grieved for him, but

none dared go near him, for they feared he might accidentally turn them to gold, too!

As everyone wailed with sorrow, Bacchus suddenly appeared on the palace lawn. The merry god stood before the sobbing king for a moment, then said, "Rise, Midas."

Stumbling to his feet, King Midas begged Bacchus to forgive him and to take away the curse of the golden touch.

"You were greedy and foolish, my friend," said Bacchus. "But I will forgive you. Now go and wash yourself in the Pactolus River that runs by Sardis, and you'll be cleansed of this desire to have more gold than anyone else!"

King Midas did as Bacchus said. He washed in the Pactolus, leaving behind streams of gold in the river's sands. Then he returned home and happily ate his dinner.

And that is why the sands of the Pactolus River were golden.

> The moral is not to wish for more than you need.

Modern Words with Greek Origins

arachnid term for spider groups; from Arachne, the girl whom Athena turned into a spider

iridescent like the colors in a rainbow; from Iris, the rainbow goddess

mnemonic a way to remember something; from Mnemosyne, goddess of memory

---

Connect and Compare

1. What lessons does the myth teach? **Moral**

2. Think of another unwise wish that Midas might have made. What would be the unfortunate results of that wish? **Synthesize**

3. Compare the king in *Rumpelstiltskin's Daughter* with Midas at the beginning of the selections and at the end. **Reading/Writing Across Texts**

 Find out more about myths at **www.macmillanmh.com**

A Strong Opening

When you write to express your ideas on a topic, it is important to start with a **strong opening**. You may want to lead with an interesting question or quotation.

Write a Point-of-View Essay

Money and People

by Donald R.

I included this question and quotation in my opening.

Did you ever hear people say, "Money is the root of all evil"? Do you agree? I disagree. Sometimes people do bad things when they have too much money. People also do bad things because they want more money, but the money itself is not a bad thing.

Think about all of the good things money can buy. Money can buy a home. Money can buy food. You probably take these things for granted, but think about someone who is in need. A little bit of money can help a hungry person get a good meal. Money can help a homeless person get an apartment to live in.

I gave examples to emphasize my ideas.

But some people do not try to help anyone but themselves with the extra money they have. It's not the money's fault. It is the fault of the person who uses the money. The same money in a kind person's hands might be used to help people. So let's not blame money for money problems. Let's blame some insensitive people.

Your Turn

Write a point-of-view essay about the good or bad aspects of money. You might use your own experiences with money, or you might use your ideas about others' experiences with money. Make sure you open with a strong statement. Perhaps you can include at least one familiar saying that relates to money. Use the Writer's Checklist to review your essay.

Writer's Checklist

☑ **Ideas and Content:** Did I use a **strong opening** to explain my point of view? Did I support my viewpoint with facts and examples?

✓ **Organization:** Did I organize my paper in a logical way? Do my ideas flow smoothly from one to another?

✓ **Voice:** Does my essay sound like me? Have I shared my point of view in a way that only I can?

✓ **Word Choice:** Did I use strong verbs to express my ideas? Did I include persuasive language?

✓ **Sentence Fluency:** Do my sentences work together to help me achieve my purpose for writing?

✓ **Conventions:** Did I check my spelling? Did I place apostrophes in the right places for possessive nouns?

Talk About It

What do you know about sled dogs? How could a sled dog become a hero?

LOG ON Find out more about dogs at **www.macmillanmh.com**

SLED DOGS AS HEROES

Vocabulary

pedestrians	**intercept**
outskirts	**quarantine**
unbearable	**epidemic**
rendezvous	**plight**

Thesaurus

A thesaurus lists **Synonyms**, words that have the same or nearly the same meaning.

intercept = *catch; stop; block; take away*

THE LAST
GREAT
RACE
ON EARTH

by David Goldberg

Life is different in Anchorage, Alaska, at the beginning of March. Every year at this time, the downtown streets become crowded with people. But these are not just regular **pedestrians**. In addition to the people walking through the streets, there are hundreds of dogs. It is time for the Iditarod—the famous dogsled race of Alaska.

The name of the race comes from the name of an Alaska gold rush town, Iditarod. It means "distant" or "distant place." It comes from one of the languages of native Alaskans.

More than sixty sled teams begin the race in Anchorage. When the teams reach the **outskirts** of town, they get a taste of Alaska's wilderness. For about two weeks, they will fight the **unbearable** cold, wind, snow, and ice to finish the race. The temperature on the trail is often well below zero degrees.

The Iditarod trail stretches for about a thousand miles. It has many **rendezvous** points. At these meeting places, race teams "check in" to let officials know how they are doing. Some teams get into trouble along the way. Officials will **intercept** them on the trail and give them the help they need. For example, officials might stop a team's progress to give first aid or to collect an injured or tired dog. These dogs are cared for and reunited with their owners after the race.

The Iditarod trail is an important part of Alaska's history. A part of the trail was used by some heroic dogs and humans in 1925. In Nome, Alaska, many people were catching the deadly disease diphtheria. The whole town was in **quarantine**, or isolation, in order to stop this **epidemic**. The only way to get medicine to Nome was by dogsled. About twenty "mushers," or dogsled drivers, offered to help. They wanted to save the people of Nome from this terrible **plight**.

Today the Iditarod race honors this heroic journey and all of the journeys on the famous trail. As the race organizers say, the Iditarod is "the last great race on Earth."

Reread for Comprehension

Summarize

Sequence
A Sequence Chart can help you summarize the events in a selection. Understanding the sequence will help you better understand what you read.

A flow chart can help you organize the events in a selection or the steps in a process. Use a Sequence Chart as you reread "The Last Great Race on Earth."

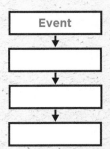

Event

↓

↓

↓

Comprehension

Genre

Nonfiction is a detailed account of real people or situations using verifiable facts.

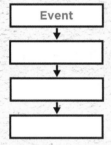

Summarize

Sequence

As you read, use your Sequence Chart.

Event

↓

↓

↓

Read to Find Out

What role did the sled dogs play in the sequence of events?

THE GREAT SERUM RACE

Nome

Anchorage

BLAZING THE IDITAROD TRAIL

Award
Winning
Selection

BY DEBBIE S. MILLER

ILLUSTRATIONS BY JON VAN ZYLE

*I*n March every year, dog sled teams and drivers from all over the world compete in the *Iditarod Trail Sled Dog Race*. This race, over a thousand miles from Anchorage to Nome, Alaska, commemorates the famous serum run of 1925. It is the longest sled dog race in the world. In this selection, you will read about how it all began.

On a dusky January afternoon in 1925, Dr. Welch walked quickly toward the **outskirts** of Nome. Sled dogs howled from their yards. Outside a small cabin, a worried Inupiat Eskimo mother greeted the doctor. She led him into her home where two small children lay in bed, struggling to breathe.

"Can you open your mouth?" Dr. Welch asked the three-year-old boy.

The weak child tried to open his mouth, but it was too painful for his swollen throat. His fever was extremely high. Dr. Welch comforted the mother and children, but there was little he could do. The next day, both children died.

Soon after, another girl, Bessie Stanley, was miserable with the same symptoms. But this time, Dr. Welch could examine Bessie's throat. He immediately recognized the symptoms of diphtheria. Poor Bessie would not live through the night.

Diphtheria. Dr. Welch had not seen a case in twenty years. This fast-spreading disease could wipe out the entire community of more than 1,400 people. Dr. Welch immediately met with the city council and recommended a **quarantine**. The schools and other public places were closed. Community leaders told people to stay in their homes.

There was only one way to fight diphtheria. The town needed a supply of antitoxin serum. Dr. Welch sent out a desperate plea for help by radio telegraph. The message soon reached Governor Bone in Juneau and other important officials. Newspapers across the nation picked up word that the historic gold rush town needed emergency help.

The nearest supply of serum was at a hospital in Anchorage, 1,000 miles away, across a snowbound wilderness. Officials considered flying the serum to Nome, but it was too dangerous to operate open cockpit planes in extreme cold temperatures. In those days, planes were used only during the summer. Nome was an icebound port, so boats were not an option. The serum could travel partway by train, and then the only safe means of transport was by sled dog team.

On January 26, an Anchorage doctor carefully packed the glass bottles of serum for the long journey. The bottles had to be protected to keep the serum from freezing. He gave the twenty-pound bundle to the conductor at the train station.

STRATEGY SKILL

Sequence
What event started the great serum race? When did it take place?

Soon, steam engine 66 began to chug its way north to Nenana, the closest railroad link to Nome. Nenana lay nearly 300 miles away, beyond the tallest mountains of North America.

On the frozen Tanana River, five-year-old Alfred John could hear the distant roar of the steam engine. His Athabaskan Indian family lived in a cabin near the train station in Nenana. Although it was late at night and nearly fifty degrees below zero, Alfred and his mother bundled up in their warmest caribou legskin boots and fur-lined parkas and walked to the station to greet the train.

As they waited by the tracks in the moonlight, Alfred watched the huge locomotive hiss steam into the frozen sky and slow to a screeching halt. He saw men unload the freight, and the conductor hand the serum package to Bill Shannon. Bill was the first of twenty mushers to carry the serum in a dog team relay to Nome. These brave men and their best dogs would travel nearly 700 miles on a snow-packed mail trail.

Bill covered the serum with a bear hide and lashed it to the sled. His strongest team of nine malamutes barked and were anxious to move. Just before midnight on January 27, Bill waved good-bye to Alfred and shouted to his dogs. *Swoosh!* Into the winter night, the dog team sped toward Tolovana, the first relay stop some fifty-two miles away.

Bill knew every turn of the trail. Like many of the mushers, his regular job was to transport mail and freight with his dog team. Traveling long distances in the extreme cold was a dangerous challenge. If the dogs ran too fast and breathed too deeply, they could frost their lungs. When the team reached bitter-cold stretches along the river, Bill slowed his dogs to protect them. He often ran behind the sled to keep himself warm.

Hundreds of miles away, Togo leaned into his harness and waited patiently for Leonhard Seppala to position Scotty and the other huskies. Togo, now twelve years old, was a proven leader for one of the strongest dog teams in the world. Leonhard, dressed in his warmest squirrel parka, sealskin pants, and reindeer mukluks, had carefully chosen twenty of his best dogs. Officials had asked the famed Norwegian musher to **intercept** the serum at Nulato, a village located halfway between Nome and Nenana.

Jingle, jangle—the bells on Leonhard's sled rang as the team rounded the corner. There were so many dog teams in Nome that mushers were required to carry bells to warn **pedestrians**. Togo led the team down Front Street while friends wished them good luck.

In Tolovana, Edgar Kalland, the twenty-year-old Athabaskan Indian mail driver, ate breakfast and waited anxiously for Bill Shannon. The Tolovana Roadhouse was a favorite rest stop for Edgar. Outside the roadhouse, Edgar's dogs pricked up their ears, and some began to howl. Bill's team drew closer.

The team looked exhausted when their frosted faces came into view. Two of the dogs would later die from frozen lungs. Following the doctor's instructions, Bill carefully removed the serum. He hurried into the roadhouse to warm the container and prevent the serum from freezing. As the two men talked about the weather, Edgar put on three pairs of socks and his boots.

Once the serum warmed, Edgar took off for Manley Hot Springs with his team of seven dogs. The thirty-one-mile trip to the next relay point was brutally cold. Temperatures fell to fifty-six degrees below zero. At one point the dogs had to wade through slushy overflow, a place where the river seeped through a crack in the ice. When the team reached Manley Hot Springs, the dogs could barely lift their ice-crusted legs. Edgar's mitts were frozen stiff to the sled handle. A roadhouse worker poured a kettle of hot water over the mitts to melt the ice and free Edgar's hands.

The relay continued from musher to musher, roadhouse to roadhouse, with teams pushing west through the biting cold. At each relay point, the mushers warmed the serum over wood-fired stoves. Following the winding rivers, the teams covered an average of thirty miles each, at a speed of six or seven miles per hour. The mushers traveled around the clock, usually by moonlight or twilight. In the middle of Alaska's winter, only a few hours of sunshine fell on the teams each day.

When the twelfth dog team headed for the village of Nulato, waves of northern lights flowed across the sky. Musher Charlie Evans faced the coldest temperatures at sixty-four degrees below zero. He wrapped the serum in a rabbit skin robe for extra protection. Charlie's nine-dog team moved slowly. Near open stretches of water on the Yukon River, a layer of eerie ice fog blanketed the valley. The ice fog, a mist of ice particles, was so dense that Charlie could barely see his wheel dogs, the ones closest to the sled. The experienced dogs followed the trail by scent rather than sight.

Nearing Nulato, two of the dogs moved stiffly and dragged their paws. The skin was beginning to freeze. Charlie stopped the team and gently loaded the poor dogs into the sled. In their struggle to save the lives of Nome's residents, these two dogs would fall victim to the deadly weather.

When the team reached the halfway point, conditions in Nome had grown worse. Five people had died from the disease, and more than twenty cases had been diagnosed. Another thirty people were suspected of having diphtheria. Newspapers across the country reported Nome's **plight** and the progress of the serum run.

The relay teams pressed onward. Togo and team worked their way east to intercept the serum. When Leonhard passed villages, he told residents about the **epidemic** and advised them to stay away from Nome. As the team approached the village of Shaktoolik, Togo picked up the scent of another dog team and sprinted forward. Leonhard could see a musher in the distance trying to untangle his string of dogs.

"On by!" Leonhard shouted to Togo.

Togo followed the familiar directions and steered the team away from the confusion.

"Serum—turn back!" shouted Henry Ivanoff, one of the relay mushers.

In the howling wind Leonhard barely heard the words. Luckily, he looked over his shoulder to see the musher waving frantically at him. Leonhard was surprised to see the relay team. After he set out for Nulato, twenty more mushers were chosen to travel short relays to speed up the serum run. Out in the wilderness, Leonhard had no idea that his **rendezvous** point was now 130 miles closer.

"Gee!" Leonhard yelled to Togo.

Togo gradually turned right and the swing dogs helped pull the sled toward the waiting team. The two men greeted each other briefly, shouting in the gale. Within minutes Leonhard had secured the serum package to his sled and instructed Togo to head home.

Togo and his teammate had traveled more than forty miles that day with the wind at their backs. Now the fierce gale blew in their faces with thirty below zero temperatures. Blowing snow plastered the team as they approached Norton Bay. Leonhard considered the risks. If they crossed the frozen bay, the sea ice might break up in the powerful gale. They could be stranded from shore on drifting ice. If they skirted the bay on land, the trip would take much longer. Leonhard thought of the children in Nome who were suffering from the disease. He decided to take the shorter route and cross the treacherous sea ice.

Leonhard believed that Togo could lead the team across twenty miles of frozen sea. As they pressed into the wind the dogs hit slick stretches of glare ice. They slipped, fell, and struggled to move forward. But mile after mile, Togo kept his course through the wall of wind. At day's end, Togo picked up the scent of food that drifted from the Inupiat sod house at Isaac's Point. After traveling eighty-four miles, they rested for the night. The dogs devoured their rations of salmon and seal blubber.

The following morning, Leonhard discovered that the previous day's trail had vanished. The ice had broken up and drifted out to sea. Worried about the unstable conditions, Leonhard decided to hug the shoreline for safety.

Togo led the way toward Dexter's Roadhouse in Golovin, about fifty miles away. Along the coast, the wind's force became **unbearable**. Blowing snow blasted the dogs' faces like buckshot. Some of the dogs began to stiffen up. Leonhard stopped the sled and gently massaged the freezing muscles of Togo, Scotty, and the others. When they finally reached Golovin, the dogs collapsed and buried their ice-coated faces beneath their tails. Togo and team had traveled farther than any other relay team.

Now it was another dog's turn to lead a fresh team of seventeen malamutes to Bluff, the final relay point. With a shout from musher Charlie Olson, lead dog Jack charged off into the blowing snow. After struggling through four hours of whiteout conditions, the experienced leader faintly heard a dog barking through the gale. It was Balto.

At Bluff, Balto and Fox waited for Gunnar Kaasen to adjust the leather harnesses and secure the serum package. Then the pair of leaders heard their musher's shout through the raging wind. Balto and Fox led the strong team of thirteen huskies into the swirling snow. Mile after mile, they trotted steadily toward Nome. During the final leg of the run, the wind assaulted them. A violent gust flipped the sled over, and the dogs went flying.

STRATEGY SKILL

Sequence
What happened after Gunnar Kaasen received the serum?

Gunnar struggled to his feet against the might of the wind. After he fought to untangle the dogs, he checked the sled to make sure the serum was securely fastened. Gunnar felt the bottom of the sled in disbelief. The serum package was gone!

In the dark, he crawled around the sled. Since he couldn't see his surroundings, he took off his mitts and felt through the snow with his bare hands. After more than 600 hard-won miles and twenty teams risking their lives, could it be that the serum was lost forever?

Panicked, Gunnar ran his numb hands across the windswept bumps of snow. All he could do was hope. Suddenly, he felt something hard. It was the serum! His frostbitten fingers struggled to tie the package onto the sled. Then the wind-battered team ran off.

They struggled on through the night. With less than twenty miles remaining, two of the dogs ran stiffly and appeared to be freezing. Gunnar anchored the sled and put rabbit-skin covers on the dogs to protect their undersides from frostbite.

Through the darkness, Balto and Fox smelled familiar scents. At last the exhausted team reached Nome. They drove into town as most people slept through the blizzard. When Gunnar knocked on the door, Dr. Welch greeted him with a stunned face. How could a musher and team have fought their way through such a storm?

With stiff hands, Gunnar gave the shocked but thankful doctor the life-saving serum.

Twenty brave mushers and more than 160 strong dogs traveled hundreds of miles in the worst conditions. The incredible relay took less than six days. Four dogs perished and several others grew lame because of the lethal weather. Yet their struggle saved many lives in Nome.

One month after the epidemic first began, the quarantine was lifted. The schools reopened and children hugged their old friends. The whole town celebrated by holding a dance and watching a movie at the theater. Togo, Scotty, Balto, Fox, Jack, and all the other dogs were true heroes.

ON THE TRAIL WITH

Debbie

Jon

Debbie S. Miller can look out her window and see a moose, a fox, and piles of snow. She lives in Alaska and used to teach school in an arctic village in the Brooks Mountain Range, near the Arctic Circle. Ideas for her books are all around her—the ice and snow, the polar bears, and, of course, those amazing husky dogs.

Jon Van Zyle and his wife live with twenty husky dogs and a black cat named Dickens near Eagle River, Alaska. Jon is the official artist for the Iditarod Trail Sled Dog Race. He has even competed twice in the race himself—all 1,049 miles of it!

Other books by Debbie S. Miller:
Disappearing Lake and *Flight of the Golden Plover*

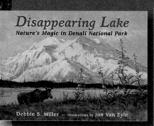

Author's Purpose

Debbie Miller is informing the reader about the origins of the Iditarod. The text is full of verifiable facts such as dates and distances. What are some examples?

 Find out more about Debbie S. Miller and Jon Van Zyle at **www.macmillanmh.com**

Comprehension Check

Summarize

Use your Sequence Chart to help you summarize *The Great Serum Race*. What were the series of events that led to the serum getting safely to Nome?

Event
↓
↓
↓

Think and Compare

1. When the serum traveled to Nome during the **epidemic**, what was the sequence in which the mushers handed off the serum? **Summarize: Sequence**

2. In your opinion, who made the biggest contribution to the successful delivery of the serum to the people of Nome? Use specific examples from the text to support your answer. **Synthesize**

3. Think about a time when you had to work with a team of people to get something important done. How was working as a team important to achieving your goal? **Analyze**

4. The mushers and dog sled teams involved in the serum race are heroes. What do you think makes a hero? Compare the heroes in *The Great Serum Race* to other heroes you know or have read about. What do they have in common? **Evaluate**

5. Read "The Last Great Race on Earth" on pages 220–221. Why is it important that the Iditarod feature the checkpoints and medical assistance described in this selection? Use specific evidence from *The Great Serum Race* to support your answer. **Reading/Writing Across Texts**

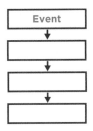

Poetry

Haiku is an unrhymed form of Japanese poetry that is three lines long. The first line often has five syllables; the second line, seven syllables; the third line, five syllables. Haiku often describes something in nature.

Literary Elements

SKILL

Symbolism is the use of an everyday thing to stand for something more meaningful.

Metaphor is a comparison of two essentially unlike things.

Haiku

Snow-swallowed valley,
Only the winding river . . .
Black fluent brush stroke.
—Boncho

The winding river is compared to a painting's single brush stroke.

A storm-wind blows—
out from among the grasses
the full moon grows.
—Chora

238

The sound of water symbolizes renewal and the coming of spring.

A mountain village:
Under piled-up snow
the sound of water.
—Shiki

Connect and Compare

1. What else might Shiki have used to symbolize the coming of spring? **Symbolism**

2. How does the choice of season help convey the mood of these poems? How do the poems make you feel? **Evaluate**

3. Compare and contrast the weather and feelings of isolation described in these poems with that portrayed in *The Great Serum Race*. **Reading/Writing Across Texts**

LOG ON Find out more about haiku at **www.macmillanmh.com**

Writer's Craft

Vary Sentences

Good writers use different kinds of sentences. **Sentence variety** prevents your writing from becoming dull. If you have too many simple sentences, combine some into compound sentences.

I wanted to persuade people reading my essay to think about physical challenges.

I used different kinds of sentences. Some are long and some are short. Some sentences are simple, while others are compound.

Challenging Sports
by Tracy M.

What do you think about people who climb the world's tallest mountains or who ride their bikes for three weeks straight? Do you see these people as heroes? Or do you think they are wasting energy?

Challenges help us learn who we really are and how much discipline we have. You can learn a lot about yourself when you push yourself to the limit.

People might say that these sports are silly. Some might say that they are too dangerous, and others might say that you can fail. I say that the goal is not winning. The goal is learning.

Jesse Owens, the famous African American Olympic gold-medal winner, said, "In order to make dreams into reality, it takes an awful lot of determination, dedication, self-discipline, and effort." Striving after these kinds of physical challenges can teach you about yourself.

Your Turn

Write a persuasive essay about why it is or isn't valuable to participate in physically challenging events, such as a marathon. Take time to learn more about the event you choose and to identify the details that support your viewpoint. If possible, use an appositive to give more information about a person, word, or concept in your essay. When you edit your essay, check to see that you have used different kinds of sentences. Also use the Writer's Checklist to check your writing.

Writer's Checklist

✓ **Ideas and Content:** Did I state my opinion clearly? Did I use supporting facts and details effectively?

✓ **Organization:** Did I organize my paper in a logical way? Did I connect my ideas?

✓ **Voice:** Did I write my essay with confidence? Will readers feel that I am talking directly to them?

✓ **Word Choice:** Did I choose persuasive words to support my opinion?

✓ **Sentence Fluency:** Did I use **sentence variety** to add interest to my writing?

✓ **Conventions:** Did I properly use commas with appositives? Did I check my spelling?

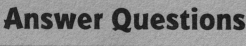

FLYING INTO FIRE

Test Strategy

Author and Me
The answer is not always directly stated. Connect the clues to figure it out.

Standing at the Door

You stand at the door as the wind whistles past. Engines roar just behind your head, and the pilot yells to the co-pilot, but no one can hear a word he is saying. Smoke from the trees below rises up to meet the airplane's propeller. As the pilot makes a slow turn over the smoldering forest, the spotter yells, "On final!" over the noise. You look for the markers thrown down only minutes before. They are the only way you'll know where to fall.

Your heart speeds up. Your head tingles. Your sweaty fingers slip on the edges of the door. And then it's time. You jump, first in line, out of the airplane and over the burning forest.

You've just chosen to jump from 3,000 feet in the air into the mouth of a raging forest fire. You are a smoke jumper.

A Different Kind of Courage

Most people agree that firefighters are heroes. But of all those American heroes, 450 have a very special responsibility and a special courage all their own. Smoke jumpers are a different kind of firefighter. They have their own history, their own training, and their own culture. They are the men and women to call when all other options have failed. When a fire burns out of control far from

Go On ▶

where cars and trucks can reach it, firefighters must find another way in. In times like these, the smoke jumpers drop in to lend a hand.

The first "fire jumps" took place in 1940 in the state of Washington. The jumpers thought that using parachutes to get closer to remote fires could help keep these small blazes from spreading. It was a good idea but a deadly one. Ever since its early beginnings, smoke jumping has been a very dangerous job. It takes training, discipline, and an adventurous spirit to join this special group of individuals. Do you have what it takes to be a smoke jumper?

The Fire Inside

First of all, people who want to be smoke jumpers must already have experience fighting wilderness fires. They must also be in top physical condition. During their training they are required to run for long distances while carrying heavy equipment. The intense heat adds another challenge. Even people who think they are in great shape suffer when exposed to the heat of a blazing forest fire. Then on top of that, add a heavy, padded jumpsuit and a helmet. It just keeps getting hotter!

As they get their bodies into peak condition, rookies also brush up on other skills, such as map and compass reading. During a jump, they might get caught dangling from a tall tree, so jumpers learn to cut themselves loose and climb safely to the bottom. In classes they learn to pack boxes of supplies, and then how to use those supplies to fight fires. Vital rations of food and water are included in this cargo, because even smoke jumpers can't save the day without the needed health and energy.

Learning to Fly

Parachute training is an important part of smoke jumper training. The use of parachutes is what separates the group from all other firefighters. As if battling an out-of-control blaze isn't scary enough, these brave people leap from a plane to do it! Special simulators give rookie jumpers a feel for what to expect during the fall. These simulators teach them how to steer their parachutes and make sure they open safely. The jumpers practice landing by jumping off towers that are built a short distance from the ground. Hitting the hard earth at top speed is no easy trick. It can be painful.

Many rookie jumpers limp away from their first landing, hoping that practice really does make perfect.

There are many ways to learn how to parachute, but no lesson takes the place of experience. After several weeks of preparation, rookie jumpers are ready for the real thing and make their first jump from an airplane. They jump over and over again. They land on hills. They land in open areas and densely wooded areas. They land in forests with high tree lines and forests with low tree lines. They even go to a swimming pool to learn how to survive if they ever experience an unexpected water landing.

Making the "Jump List"

Then training is over. After every test, some rookies stay and some quit. The people who pass graduate to the position of smoke jumper. They earn the right to be included on the "jump list," a special team of firefighters who are qualified to parachute into fires and act as the first line of defense. Then the rookies split up, and each member of the class goes his or her own way. They join different organizations, such as the U.S. Forest Service or the Bureau of Land Management, and scatter all across the country.

When a fire breaks out, wherever they are, smoke jumpers spring into action. The call goes out and the smoke jumpers are there. They fight fires when no one else can.

Go On ▶

Directions: Answer the questions.

Tip

Connect the clues or the ideas from the selection to choose the best answer.

1. **What kind of person is a smoke jumper?**

   A timid
   B fearless
   C inexperienced
   D frivolous

2. **Why is training important for dangerous jobs?**

   A to find out if the job is boring
   B to increase your heartbeat
   C because problems can occur without warning
   D because it's exciting to work as a team

3. **What is the BEST reason for parachuting into a fire?**

   A The smoke jumpers love to jump from planes.
   B It's too hot for firetrucks to operate.
   C The fire is at a low altitude.
   D Firefighters on the ground can't get to the fire.

4. **Based on the information in the selection, what might inspire someone to become a smoke jumper?**

5. **Who would make a better smoke jumper: a city firefighter or a member of the Air Force trained in parachuting? Write two paragraphs and include details from the selection.**

Writing Prompt

To save money, the government plans to cut the smoke jumper training program. Do you agree with this decision? Write an essay stating your opinion, and support it with details from the selection.

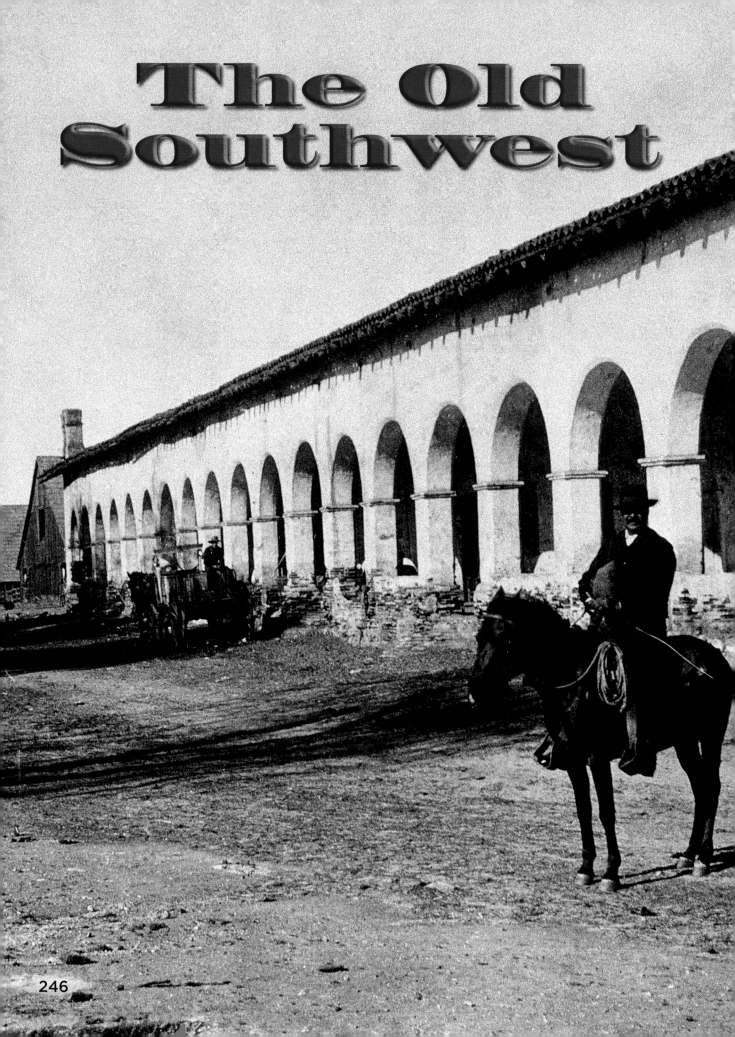

The Old Southwest

Talk About It

Many settlers came to the Southwest during the 18th and 19th centuries. What do you know about these settlers?

LOG ON Find out more about the Old Southwest at **www.macmillanmh.com**

247

Anasazi bowl

A Win-Win Week

by Victor Sanchez

A Challenge

Maria's family had just arrived in Greensboro, North Carolina. Her father was going to take over as **foreman** in charge of a big building project. As an **employee** who worked for a large construction company, Maria's dad was sent to many places. This time his family had moved, too. Maria missed her life and friends back home.

Maria sighed and **gritted** her teeth. She bit down so hard it hurt. Then she entered the classroom. The first day of school was not easy for someone who was shy.

A Team Player

Mr. Hall, the teacher, greeted the students with an announcement. They would research how different parts of the nation had changed over time. The group with the best report would win a prize.

Maria felt hopeful when she got her assignment. Her group was to learn about the Old Southwest. Maria and her family were from New Mexico. Perhaps she would be able to **fulfill** her role and be a real member of this team.

Maria's team met and made a list of the groups who had lived in the Old Southwest. The list included Native Americans, Spanish, Mexicans, and settlers from other parts of the United States and the world. The team also made notes about resources to use. "This is useful," said Keith. "We also need some interesting information about the customs and the influence of these different groups."

Maria spoke up. "My grandfather still lives in New Mexico," she said. "He has collected many stories and examples of folk art of the region. We could e-mail him with questions."

"Way to go, Maria!" **gloated** Sara with a big grin. "Now we have a real chance of winning."

A Wonderful Week

A week later, Maria's team was ready. The result was a winning presentation about the Old Southwest. They showed slides of the old ranches, of the fiestas held there, and of Native American artifacts. Since the area was always known for abundant crops, they showed pictures of the ones that still **flourish** today. They even had a tape recording of a Mexican folk tale. The class applauded **vigorously** as the team finished the presentation. They clapped loudly and cheered.

For Maria it was fun to be in touch with her grandfather, and she was proud of their presentation.

"We couldn't have done it without you," Sara and Keith told Maria.

Maria smiled **gleefully**. She was very happy. "I enjoyed working with you too."

Reread for **Comprehension**

Story Structure

Character, Plot, Setting
A Character, Plot and Setting Chart helps you understand the structure of a story. Recording key events in a story will help you recall what you have read. Take note of the narrator, the characters, the setting, and the events of the story.

Use the chart as you reread "A Win-Win Week."

Character	Plot	Setting

Comprehension

Genre

A **Folk Tale** is a story based on the traditions of a people or region which is handed down from one generation to the next and becomes legendary.

Story Structure

Character, Plot, Setting
As you read, use your Character, Plot and Setting Chart.

Character	Plot	Setting

Read to Find Out

How does Juan prove to be honest?

Juan Verdades
The Man Who Couldn't Tell a Lie

Award
Winning
Author

retold by Joe Hayes
illustrated by Joseph Daniel Fiedler

ONE LATE SUMMER DAY a group of wealthy rancheros was gathered on the village plaza, joking and laughing and discussing events on their ranches.

One of the men, whose name was don Ignacio, had a fine apple tree on his land. The rancher called the apple tree *el manzano real*—the royal apple tree—and was extremely proud of it. It had been planted by his great-grandfather, and there was something about the soil it grew in and the way the afternoon sun struck it that made the apple tree **flourish**. It gave sweeter and more flavorful fruit than any other tree in the country round about.

Every rancher for miles around knew about *el manzano real*, and each year they all hoped don Ignacio would give them a small basket of its sweet fruit. And so each of the ranchers asked don Ignacio how the fruit of the apple tree was doing. To each one don Ignacio replied, "It's doing beautifully, amigo, beautifully. My **foreman** takes perfect care of the tree, and every evening he reports how the fruit is ripening."

When don Ignacio said this to his friend don Arturo, the other man replied, "Do you mean to say, don Ignacio, that you don't tend your magnificent tree yourself? How can you have such faith in your **employee**? Maybe he's not doing all he says he is. Maybe he's not telling you the truth."

Don Ignacio wagged a finger at his friend. "*Mi capataz* has never failed me in any way," he insisted. "He has never told me a lie."

"Are you sure, *compadre*?" said don Arturo. "Are you sure that he has never lied to you?"

"Absolutely certain, *compadre*, absolutely certain. The young man doesn't know how to tell a lie. His name is Juan Valdez, but everyone calls him Juan Verdades because he is so truthful."

"I don't believe it. There never was an employee who didn't lie to his boss. I'm sure I can make him tell you a lie."

"Never," replied the proud employer.

The two friends went on arguing good-naturedly, but little by little they began to raise their voices and attract the attention of the other men on the plaza.

Finally don Arturo declared loudly, "I'll bet you whatever you want that within two weeks at the most I'll make this Juan Verdades tell you a lie."

"All right," replied don Ignacio. "It's a deal. I'll bet my ranch against yours that you can't make my foreman lie to me."

The other ranchers laughed when they heard that. "Ho-ho, don Arturo," they said, "now we'll see just how sure you are that you're right."

"As sure as I am of my own name," said don Arturo. "I accept the bet, don Ignacio. But you must allow me the freedom to try anything I wish." The two friends shook hands, and the other men in the group agreed to serve as witnesses to the bet.

The gathering broke up, and don Arturo and don Ignacio rode confidently away toward their ranches. But as don Arturo rode along thinking of what he had just done, he no longer felt so sure of himself. When he arrived home and told his wife and daughter about the bet, his wife began to cry. "What will we do when we lose our ranch?" she sobbed. And don Arturo began to think he had made a terrible mistake.

But his daughter, whose name was Araceli and who was a very bright and lively young woman, just laughed and said, "Don't worry, *Mamá*. We're not going to lose our ranch."

Araceli suggested to her father that he make up some excuse for them all to spend the next two weeks at don Ignacio's house. "If we're staying on don Ignacio's ranch," she said, "we'll surely discover a way to come out the winners."

Plot

What is the challenge facing don Arturo and his family?

The next day don Arturo rode to don Ignacio's ranch and told his friend, "My men are mending the walls of my house and giving them a fresh coat of whitewash. It would be more convenient for my family to be away. Could my wife and daughter and I stay at your house for a while?"

"Of course, my friend," don Ignacio answered. "Feel perfectly free."

That afternoon don Arturo and his family moved into don Ignacio's house, and the next morning Araceli rose at dawn, as she always did at home, and went to the ranch kitchen to prepare coffee. The foreman, Juan Verdades, was already there, drinking a cup of coffee he had made for himself and eating a breakfast of leftover tortillas. She smiled at him, and he greeted her politely: *"Buenos días, señorita."* And then he finished his simple breakfast and went off to begin his day's work.

That night don Arturo and his daughter made up a plan. Araceli rose before dawn the next day and went to the kitchen to prepare coffee and fresh tortillas for the foreman. She smiled sweetly as she offered them to Juan. He returned her smile and thanked her very kindly. Each morning she did the same thing, and Juan Verdades began to fall in love with Araceli, which was just what the girl and her father expected.

What Araceli hadn't expected was that she began to fall in love with Juan Verdades too and looked forward to getting up early every morning just to be alone with him. She even began to wish she might end up marrying the handsome young foreman. Araceli continued to work on the plan she and her father had made—but she now had a plan of her own as well.

Of course, Juan knew that he was just a worker and Araceli was the daughter of a wealthy ranchero, so he didn't even dream of asking her to marry him. Still, he couldn't help trying to please her in every way. So one morning when they were talking, Juan said to Araceli, "You're very kind to have fresh coffee and warm food ready for me every morning and to honor me with the pleasure of your company. Ask me for whatever you want from this ranch. I'll speak to don Ignacio and see that it's given to you."

This is exactly what the girl and her father thought would happen. And she replied just as they had planned. It was the last thing Juan expected to hear.

"There's only one thing on this ranch I want," she said. "I'd like to have all the apples from *el manzano real*."

The young man was very surprised, and very distressed as well, because he knew he couldn't **fulfill** her wish.

"I could never give you that," Juan said. "You know how don Ignacio treasures the fruit of that tree. He might agree to give you a basket of apples, but no more. I would have to take the fruit without permission, and then what would I say to don Ignacio? I can give you anything else from the ranch, but not what you're asking for."

With that the conversation ended and they separated for the day. In the evening Juan reported to don Ignacio, and they exchanged the exact words they said every evening:

"Good evening, *mi capataz*," the rancher said.

"Good evening, *mi patrón*," replied the foreman.

"How goes it with my cattle and land?"

"Your cattle are healthy, your pastures are green."

"And the fruit of *el manzano real*?"

"The fruit is fat and ripening well."

The next morning Juan and Araceli met again. As they sipped their coffee together, Juan said, "I truly would like to repay you for the kindness you've shown me. There must be something on this ranch you would like. Tell me what it is. I'll see that it's given to you,"

But again Araceli replied, "There's only one thing on this ranch I want: the apples from *el manzano real*."

Each day they repeated the conversation. Araceli asked for the same thing, and Juan said he couldn't give it to her. But each day Juan was falling more hopelessly in love with Araceli. Finally, just the day before the two weeks of the bet would have ended, the foreman gave in. He said he would go pick the apples right then and bring them to the girl.

Juan hitched up a wagon and drove to the apple tree. He picked every single apple and delivered the wagonload of fruit to Araceli. She thanked him very warmly, and his spirits rose for a moment. But as he mounted his horse to leave, they sank once again. Juan rode away alone, lost in his thoughts, and Araceli hurried off to tell her father the news and then to wait for a chance to talk to don Ignacio too.

Juan rode until he came to a place where there were several dead trees. He dismounted and walked up to one of them. Then he took off his hat and jacket and put them on the dead tree and pretended it was don Ignacio. He started talking to it to see if he could tell it a lie.

"Good evening, *mi capataz*," he pretended he heard the tree say.

"Good evening, *mi patrón*."

"How goes it with my cattle and land?"

"Your cattle are healthy, your pastures are green."

"And the fruit of *el manzano real*? "

"The . . . the crows have carried the fruit away. . . ."

But the words were hardly out of his mouth when he heard himself say, "No, that's not true, *mi patrón*, I picked the fruit. . . ." And then he stopped himself.

He took a deep breath and started over again with, "Good evening, *mi capataz*."

And when he reached the end, he sputtered, "The . . . the wind shook the apples to the ground, and the cows came and ate them. . . . No, they didn't, *mi patrón*. I . . . "

He tried over and over, until he realized there was no way he could tell a lie. But he knew he could never come right out and say what he had done either. He had to think of another way to tell don Ignacio. He took his hat and coat from the stump and sadly set out for the ranch.

All day long Juan worried about what he would say to don Ignacio. And all day long don Ignacio wondered what he would hear from his foreman, because as soon as Araceli had shown the apples to her father he had run **gleefully** to tell don Ignacio what had happened.

"Now you'll see, *compadre*," don Arturo **gloated**, "You're about to hear a lie from Juan Verdades."

Don Ignacio was heartsick to think that all his apples had been picked, but he had agreed that don Arturo could try whatever he wanted. He sighed and said, "Very well, *compadre*, we'll see what happens this evening."

Don Arturo rode off to gather the other ranchers who were witnesses to the bet, leaving don Ignacio to pace nervously up and down in his house. And then, after don Ignacio received a visit from Araceli and she made a request that he couldn't deny, he paced even more nervously.

All the while, Juan went about his work, thinking of what he would say to his don Ignacio. That evening the foreman went as usual to make his report to his employer, but he walked slowly and his head hung down. The other ranchers were behind the bushes listening, and Araceli and her mother were watching anxiously from a window of the house.

Character
How do you think Juan will account for the missing apples? Support your answer.

The conversation began as it always did:

"Good evening, *mi capataz*."

"Good evening, *mi patrón*."

"How goes it with my cattle and land?"

"Your cattle are healthy, your pastures are green."

"And the fruit of *el manzano real*?"

Juan took a deep breath and replied:

"Oh, *patron*, something terrible happened today.

Some fool picked your apples and gave them away."

Don Ignacio pretended to be shocked and confused. "Some fool picked them?" he said. "Who would do such a thing?"

Juan turned his face aside. He couldn't look at don Ignacio. The rancher asked again, "Who would do such a thing? Do I know this person?"

Finally the foreman answered:

"The father of the fool is my father's father's son.

The fool has no sister and no brother.

His child would call my father 'grandfather.'

He's ashamed that he did what was done."

Don Ignacio paused for a moment to think about Juan's answer. And then, to Juan's surprise, don Ignacio grabbed his hand and started shaking it excitedly.

The other ranchers ran laughing from their hiding places. "Don Arturo," they all said, "you lose the bet. You must sign your ranch over to don Ignacio."

"No," said don Ignacio, still **vigorously** shaking Juan's hand. He glanced toward the window where Araceli was watching and went on: "Sign it over to don Juan Verdades. He has proved that he truly deserves that name, and he deserves to be the owner of his own ranch as well."

Everyone cheered and began to congratulate Juan. Don Arturo's face turned white, but he **gritted** his teeth and forced a smile. He shook Juan's hand and then turned to walk away from the group, his shoulders drooping and his head bowed down.

But Araceli came running from the house and put her arm through her father's, *"Papá,"* she said, "what if Juan Verdades were to marry a relative of yours? Then the ranch would stay in the family, wouldn't it?"

Everyone heard her and turned to look at the girl and her father. And then Juan spoke up confidently, *"Señorita* Araceli, I am the owner of a ranch and many cattle. Will you marry me?"

Of course she said she would, and don Arturo heaved a great sigh. "Don Juan Verdades," he said, "I'll be proud to have such an honest man for a son-in-law." He beckoned his wife to come from the house, and they both hugged Juan and Araceli.

The other ranchers hurried off to fetch their families, and a big celebration began. It lasted all through the night, with music and dancing and many toasts to Juan and Araceli. And in the morning everyone went home with a big basket of delicious apples from *el manzano real*.

Storytelling with Joe and Joseph

Joe Hayes loves stories. When he is not writing, Joe is a professional storyteller. He recreates traditional stories, such as this one, and then crisscrosses the country, telling them to kids in schools and at festivals. How did he get started? By telling stories to his own children!

Joseph Daniel Fiedler lives in Talpa, a small village in the Hispanic Highlands of New Mexico. He is an award-winning artist of children's books and his paintings hang in art shows and galleries, too. He's a busy artist, but he has help—two cats named Iko and Obeah.

Other books by Joe Hayes: *¡El Cucuy!* and *Watch Out for Clever Women!*

LOG ON Find out more about Joe Hayes and Joseph Daniel Fiedler at www.macmillanmh.com

Author's Purpose
Joe Hayes entertains the reader with this traditional folk tale. What makes *Juan Verdades* informative, too?

Comprehension Check

Summarize

Use your Character, Plot and Setting Chart to summarize *Juan Verdades*. How do plot events lead to a satisfactory conclusion?

Character	Plot	Setting

Think and Compare

1. What plot developments ruin don Arturo's plan to get don Ignacio's loyal **employee** to tell a lie? **Story Structure: Character, Plot, Setting**

2. If the entire story were told from Araceli's point of view, what would be different? What would be the same? **Synthesize**

3. If you were Araceli and your father asked you to help trap Juan Verdades in a lie, what would you do? **Evaluate**

4. If Juan Verdades did lie about the apples, how would that affect the entire community? **Evaluate**

5. Read "A Win-Win Week" on pages 248–249. Pretend you are in Maria's group and have to complete the presentation on the Old Southwest. Think of *Juan Verdades* as a folk tale that Maria's grandfather has e-mailed. What information from the story would you include in the presentation? **Reading/ Writing Across Texts**

IN THE DAYS OF THE VAQUEROS:

America's First True Cowboys

by Russell Freedman

Social Studies

Genre

Informational Nonfiction gives facts about real things, people, or events.

Text Feature

A **Map** typically shows the relative position and size of the places represented.

Content Vocabulary

ranchos
feat
conquistadores

*Introduction: In the early days of the American Southwest, private landowners found many Native American vaqueros, or herders, to help in the rounding up of animals on the **ranchos**. Author Russell Freedman describes what went into the work of the vaqueros.*

Tools of the Trade

Over the centuries, ranching changed very little in New Spain. The most important tools for working cattle on the open range continued to be the vaquero's horse and his lariat.

He looked upon his lariat as his good right arm, and it was seldom out of reach of his nimble fingers. With it, he was ready for almost any task that came along.

He made his lariat himself, cutting long strips of untanned cowhide, which he soaked and stretched until they were pliable. Then he braided the leather strips into a rope, which he stretched again, oiled, and softened, working it over with loving care until he was satisfied that it was ready to use.

A typical lariat was about 60 feet long and as thick around as a man's little finger. There were longer ropes, *reatas largas*, which ran to 110 feet or more. Children had their own pint-sized lariats. It seemed that everyone was always roping for practice, and that every target was fair game. Dogs, pigs, and chickens became as expert at dodging the rope as the vaqueros were at throwing it.

Coyotes were considered the toughest wild animals to rope, and a man who managed to snare one was greatly admired. While he took pride in his **feat**, he would say with modesty, *"Ese fue un supo,"* "That was a lucky throw."

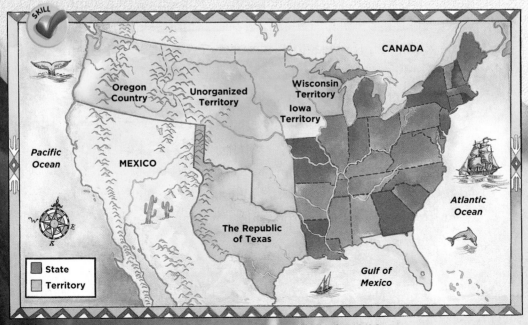

This map shows the Southwest in 1840.

A Vaquero by Frederic Remington circa 1881–1909

Vaqueros also made fine horsehair ropes, *mecates*, which were used for reins and halters. Different colors of hair were blended together, forming ropes that were not only strong but beautiful.

In the early days, vaqueros made their own saddles as well. They took as a model the old Spanish war saddle on which the **conquistadores** had ridden into Mexico, and they gradually transformed it to meet the special needs of cowhands working in cattle country.

They added a large round-topped saddle horn as a sturdy anchor to which their lariats could be secured when they roped a steer. They made the saddle's stirrup straps longer, allowing the rider to get a better knee grip. The stirrups themselves were carved out of wood. They were big enough to let a man stand upright while riding down a steep slope or trotting along the trail.

Saddles became stronger and more compact. At first, vaqueros placed a blanket, a piece of leather, or an animal skin over the seat of the saddle to provide a little comfort. Later they devised the *mochila*, a removable leather covering that fit snugly over the entire saddle and often had built-in saddlebags.

Vaqueros working in brush country covered their stirrups with leather casings called *tapaderas*, or taps, which shielded the rider's feet from cactus thorns. In the deserts of northwestern Mexico, saddles were rigged with *armas*, huge slabs of cowhide that hung down from the saddle on either side, covering and protecting the rider's thighs and lower legs.

Later, vaqueros attached smaller, lightweight *armitas* directly to their legs. These in turn developed into seatless leather leggings called *chaparreras*, or chaps, for protection while riding through mesquite and chaparral thickets. Chaps also protected a rider against rope burns, abrasions from trees and corral posts, and horse bites. They were made of smooth buckskin, or of goat, sheep, wolf, bear, or lion pelts with the wool or fur left on the outside of the chaps.

Since the vaquero often spent his days from sunrise to sunset in the saddle, no single piece of equipment was more important. A well-made saddle, lovingly maintained, was important to his horse, too. A rider with a gentle hand and a good rig could travel for hours and still have a healthy horse, but a poorly made saddle could make a horse sore in no time at all.

Connect and Compare

1. Study the map on page 269. What are some of the differences between this map and the United States today? **Reading a Map**

2. What would happen to a vaquero if his saddle was lost or damaged? **Analyze**

3. Think about this selection and *Juan Verdades.* How is Juan's life the same as and different from that of a vaquero? **Reading/Writing Across Texts**

 Social Studies Activity

Research information about vaqueros. Then imagine that you are a vaquero living on a California rancho. Write a journal entry that describes your day. Include information that you learned from your research.

 Find out more about vaqueros at **www.macmillanmh.com**

Write a Character Sketch

Writer's Craft

Voice

A writer's individual **voice** is important when describing someone. Voice can also tell something about the narrator. Choose words that make your writing more interesting.

The Storyteller

by Manny R.

Mando is quite the storyteller. He can capture the attention of any audience. With his wild, curly hair and his huge, sparkly eyes, Mando never seems to stop moving.

Mando spins tales about the most amazing subjects. He describes a family with a pet elephant in their home. He jokes about a wind that blows a steak off a barbecue and onto a neighbor's plate two houses away. He describes all of these scenes with a lot of elaborate hand waving.

He always has a crowd around him. No matter where we go, people always end up talking to Mando. Maybe it's because even though he likes talking, Mando is a good listener, too.

People often question the things Mando says. When he is asked if his stories are true, Mando always insists they are, with a wink. So we never know if he really believes them or not. Mando always keeps us guessing.

I wanted readers to understand how I feel about Mando. I used descriptive language in my sketch.

I used a specific voice to help bring Mando to life.

Your Turn

Write a few paragraphs about an interesting fictional person or animal. Be sure that readers can tell what your view of this character is through your use of a specific voice and descriptive words. Use the Writer's Checklist to check your writing.

Writer's Checklist

✓ **Ideas and Content:** Is my character sketch clear?

✓ **Organization:** Did I develop my character sketch around a central theme?

 Voice: Do the details and the voice tell how I feel? Do they make my writing more interesting?

✓ **Word Choice:** Did I choose strong action verbs to tell what happens?

✓ **Sentence Fluency:** Did I vary my sentence structures and lengths?

✓ **Conventions:** Do my subjects and verbs agree? Did I check my spelling?

PUTTING IT IN WRITING

The Mysterious Limousine

by Linda Ward Beech

There it was again! Luke turned to look as the **limousine** came slowly down the block.

"Isn't that a **sensational** car?" he said to his friend Eric. "It's big and shiny and beautiful. I see it around here a lot."

Eric came to a **precarious** stop on his skateboard. He put one unsteady foot on the ground so he wouldn't fall. "Me too," he said.

"Did you see that?" asked Polly, joining them by the tree. "That is one **extravagant** vehicle. It is so long. I bet it cost a lot of money. But when I get my own, it will be black."

The boys laughed. "Just how are you getting a car like that?" Luke asked. It would be as if something **unimaginable** happened in everyday life. How could they or their friends ever ride in such a car? They didn't even dream about it.

Polly asked, "Who do you think owns that one?"

Luke shrugged. "Who around here can afford it?" he **lamented.** He regretted he'd never have that kind of money.

"Well, someone must," said Polly, "or else it wouldn't be here so much. I think I'll take a quick **promenade** around the neighborhood to check things out. Maybe I can write a story for the block's newsletter. Want to walk with me?"

Eric looked at Luke. "Might as well." So they set off down Franklin Street on their boards.

A while later Luke stopped. "Let's go home. We're not going to find it. That car is gone."

But Polly had **embarked** on a mission. Once she started something, she liked to finish it. So she walked on as Luke and Eric turned back.

The next day Polly joined the boys again.

"So?" said Luke. "Did you learn anything?"

"I did. I talked to a lot of our neighbors," Polly said. "Do you remember Mr. Gomez? He used to be our school bus driver. His wife works in that diner on Allen Street. She's a real chef."

"But what does Mr. Gomez have to do with the limo?" asked Luke.

Polly smiled. "You'll see," she said.

A few minutes later, the white limousine appeared down the street. Polly waved. Much to the boys' surprise, the car stopped in front of them. It was Mr. Gomez. He explained that he drove for a limousine company. Even better, Mr. Gomez said he had permission to give them and their parents a ride on his day off.

"Way to go, Polly!" said Eric.

Polly was already on the way to her computer. "This is such a great story," she said. "I know it will get published in the newsletter!"

Reread for **Comprehension**

Monitor Comprehension

Draw Conclusions
To draw conclusions you think about various pieces of information and what you already know to arrive at a new understanding about the characters or story events. This will help you monitor your comprehension as you read.

Use the Conclusions Chart as you reread "The Mysterious Limousine."

What I Know	Text Evidence	Conclusions

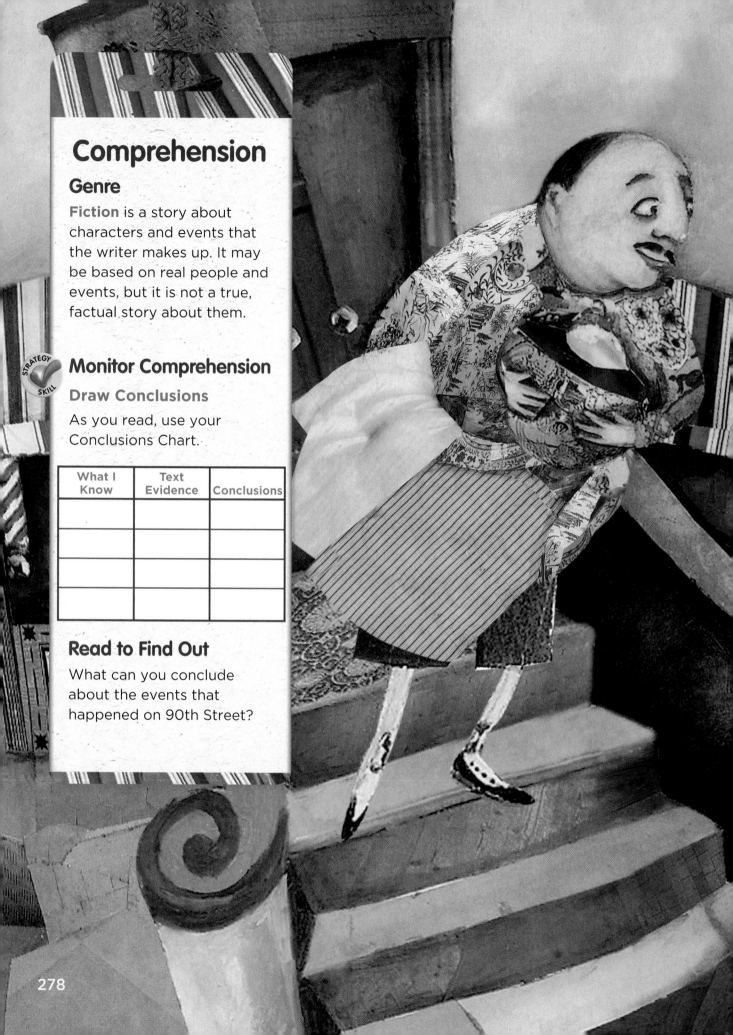

Comprehension

Genre

Fiction is a story about characters and events that the writer makes up. It may be based on real people and events, but it is not a true, factual story about them.

Monitor Comprehension

Draw Conclusions

As you read, use your Conclusions Chart.

What I Know	Text Evidence	Conclusions

Read to Find Out

What can you conclude about the events that happened on 90th Street?

NOTHING EVER HAPPENS ON 90TH STREET

BY RONI SCHOTTER

ILLUSTRATED BY KYRSTEN BROOKER

Award Winning Selection

FOR RENT

SEAFOOD

Eva unwrapped a cinnamon Danish, opened her notebook, and stared helplessly at the wide, white pages. "Write about what you know," her teacher, Mrs. DeMarco, had told her. So Eva sat high on the stoop and looked out over 90th Street waiting for something to happen. A horn honked. A radio rapped. A kid cried. The usual. "Nothing ever happens on 90th Street," Eva scribbled in her notebook.

A few doors down, Mr. Chang was arranging fish fillets in his newly opened Seafood Emporium. No one was buying, and his shop looked as empty and ignored as the tiny, boarded-up store next door to it. He nodded to a woman passing by and called hello to Eva.

Out the door of Eva's building came Mr. Sims, the actor, carrying his enormous cat, Olivier. Mr. Sims was "on hiatus again," which meant out of work, in between shows, and so, every day, dressed in his finest, he **embarked** on a daily **promenade** with Olivier under his arm. "Writing?" he asked.

"Trying to," Eva answered, "but nothing ever happens on 90th Street!"

"You are mistaken, my dear," Mr. Sims said. "The whole world's a stage—even 90th Street—and each of us plays a part. Watch the stage, observe the players carefully, and don't neglect the details," he said, stroking Olivier. "Follow an old actor's advice and you will find you have plenty to write about."

"Thanks," Eva said, and fast as she could, using as many details as she could recall, Eva described Mr. Sims in her notebook—his felt fedora hat, his curly gray hair, his shiny button shoes. When she looked up, he was halfway down the street and Mr. Morley, the mousse maker, was at his window.

Just as he did every day, Mr. Morley set his chocolate pot and coffee urn out on his ledge with a sign. Mr. Morley dreamed of having a catering business where the fanciest people demanded his dessert. But the trouble was . . . Mr. Morley's mousse was missing something. No matter how he tried, his mousse never had much taste, and Mr. Morley never had many customers.

"Writing?" he asked.

"Um. Hmmm," Eva answered, chewing on her pencil.

"Try to find the poetry in your pudding," Mr. Morley said softly. "There's always a new way with old words."

"You're right," Eva said, wishing Mr. Morley would one day find the poetry in *his* pudding. Taking his advice, she tried to think up a new way to describe the look of Mr. Morley's mousse. Smooth and dark as midnight. Or maybe more like mink! Yes, that was it! Eva thought, writing in her notebook.

The door to the building slammed and a gust of wind sent dead leaves soaring and dipping like crazy kites. Alexis Leora nodded to Eva and stepped gracefully down the steps to do her warm-up exercises. Alexis was a dancer. When she wanted to, she could hold an extremely long leg straight up against her ear like a one-legged woman with three arms. But she couldn't smile. Eva decided it was because Alexis Leora was lonely.

"Writing?" Alexis Leora asked Eva.

"Yes," Eva answered.

Alexis Leora did six deep knee bends and then sighed. "Stretch," she said sadly. "Use your imagination. If your story doesn't go the way you want it to, you can always stretch the truth. You can ask, 'What if?' and make up a better story."

"You're right," Eva said, thinking "What if?" What if Alexis Leora met someone? Would she smile then? What would that look like? Eva closed her eyes to try to picture it, but all she could picture was soup—Spanish soup—rich and brown and so spicy it seemed as if she could actually smell it.

She could! When Eva opened her eyes, Mrs. Martinez was standing beside her. She nodded to Alexis Leora as she handed Eva a bowl of soup. "Have some," she said. "Writers *need* soup. What's your story about?"

"Nothing much." Eva sighed. "Nothing ever happens on 90th Street."

"Add a little action," Mrs. Martinez said. "Like soup. A little this. A little that. And don't forget the spice. Mix it. Stir it. Make something happen. Surprise yourself!" She nodded again to Alexis Leora and went inside.

Eva put down her pencil and tasted Mrs. Martinez's wonderful, surprising soup. She thought about her story. It wasn't wonderful. It wasn't surprising. But what could she do? Nothing ever happened on 90th Street. How could she possibly "add a little action" and "make something happen"? Eva had no ideas. She was stuck!

Draw Conclusions
What conclusions can you draw about Eva's neighbors? Support your answer.

284

Then Mrs. Friedman from up the block came wheeling Baby Joshua in his stroller. He was holding a bright red ball in two tiny, fat hands. "Bird!" he called out to a pigeon hunting for something to eat. "Bird. Hungry!"

"Pigeon," Mrs. Friedman told him.

Eva sighed and looked down at her half-eaten Danish, then at her notebook. She looked at Baby Joshua, then at the pigeon. She remembered Alexis Leora's words of advice. "What if?" Eva thought. Suddenly she had an idea.

What if she stood up, broke her Danish into dozens of tiny pieces, and scattered them wide and wild into the street? What would happen? Eva laughed to think of it. . . .

From lampposts and ledges dozens of pigeons swooped down to dine on Danish. Eva eagerly picked up her pencil and began to write again. "Bird!" Baby Joshua called out, pointing. "More bird!" he cried, panting. The bright red ball dropped out of his tiny, fat hands and bounced onto the sidewalk. "Bye, bye, ball!" Baby Joshua screamed.

The ball rolled off the curb, into the street, and straight into the path of a pizza delivery man on his bicycle!

Everyone gasped in horror. Alexis Leora paused in mid-plié and leaped to the rescue. She got there just as the pizza delivery man landed, right side up, at her feet. Alexis Leora looked down at the pizza man and he looked up at her. And then something almost **unimaginable** happened: Alexis Leora smiled! "Are y-y-you all right?" she asked, shyly. Her smile was sweet and bright. Her teeth were straight and white. (It was the first time Eva or anyone on 90th Street had seen them!)

"Yes," said the pizza man, smiling up at her. It was love at first sight. Pepperoni and peppers rained down on the happy couple. The pizza man pulled a pepper out of his hair as horns began to honk.

Eva added this to her notebook and wondered what could possibly happen next. . . .

A long, white **limousine** was honking its horn loudest of all. The limo driver rolled down his window. "Whad'ya wanna block traffic for?" he called out. The back door of the limo opened and out stepped a woman in sunglasses, wearing a turban and a coat the color of a taxi.

"There seems to be a problem, Henry," she said in a fake English accent. "There's some sort of accident here. Perhaps—"

"It's *Sondra*!" someone suddenly screamed, interrupting her. "Sondra! Can I have your autograph?" Mrs. Martinez called out.

"Sondra Saunderson!" Mr. Morley blushed.

Was Eva dreaming? There, in the middle of 90th Street, larger than life, stood Sondra Saunderson, star of stage, screen, and the **sensational** soap opera "One World To Live In."

"Darlings, what's happening here? I'm sure I . . . *Lar*-ry!" she called out suddenly, and stretched her arms toward Mr. Sims, who had just returned from his promenade. "It's been an age since we saw each other!"

Mr. Sims' cat, about to be crushed in an **extravagant** embrace, leaped out of Mr. Sims' arms to chase after Baby Joshua's ball.

"Olivier!" Mr. Sims called out. "Come back!"

Everyone raced into the street after the ball, but it was the limo driver who, in the right place at the right time, leaned into the gutter and picked it up.

STRATEGY SKILL

Draw Conclusions
How does the action so far prove that things do happen on 90th Street?

With a flick of the wrist, he tossed the ball to Mrs. Friedman, who presented it to a drooling but grateful Baby Joshua.

"How's that for a throw?" the limo driver proudly asked the crowd.

No one, not even Baby Joshua, had a chance to answer. Olivier, frightened by so many people, raced past Eva, scrambled onto Mr. Morley's ledge, where he knocked over his coffee urn, spilling all the coffee into his mousse pot.

"Ruined!" Mr. Morley cried, wringing his hands.

At that, Olivier bounded to the top of a ginkgo tree, where he swayed dangerously like a heavy, white balloon.

"Now he'll *never* come down!" Mr. Sims lamented. "He's terribly stubborn."

"There, there, Larry," Sondra Saunderson comforted him. "I'm sure someone on 90th Street will have a solution."

Eva tried to imagine who that could possibly be. . . .

"I have one!" she heard Mr. Chang call out. Generously, he offered trout, fresh from his store, to Olivier.

High up in the tree, Olivier barely blinked.

"Raw trout?" Mr. Sims sighed. "My regrets, Mr. Chang. He won't eat it. He's a *gourmet* cat. I'm afraid I've spoiled him. Whatever will I do?"

"What if?" Eva asked herself for the second time that day, and suddenly she had another idea. A truly great one! She whispered it to Mr. Morley, Mrs. Martinez, and Mr. Chang.

"Brilliant!" Mr. Morley exclaimed. And with that he, Mrs. Martinez, and Mr. Chang, still clutching his trout, vanished into the building.

Eva righted Mr. Morley's coffee urn and stuck her finger into his ruined mousse, then into her mouth to determine the degree of damage. "Mocha!" she called out in surprise. "Mr. Morley's mousse is mocha now and . . . " She paused, trying to find the perfect word. "*Magnificent!*" she announced to the assembled throng. And, giving the pot a stir, she dished out samples to all assembled.

"Delicious!" Alexis Leora said, spooning some into the pizza man's mouth.

"Poetry!" Sondra Saunderson pronounced.

Now on 90th Street, people who had never spoken to one another before were speaking at last. The pizza delivery man and the limo driver shook hands, and everyone tried to tempt Olivier down from his **precarious** perch.

And then . . . Mr. Morley appeared on the steps, followed by Mrs. Martinez and Mr. Chang. Mrs. Martinez carried a large pot of her surprising soup, while Mr. Morley carried a platter of Mr. Chang's trout, now surrounded by many tiny vegetables and cooked to perfection. With the addition of a cup of Mr. Morley's cat-created mocha mousse— it was a meal worthy of the finest culinary establishment.

"Do you smell that, Olivier?" Mr. Sims called, fanning the steam so it rose up the ginkgo tree.

Olivier took one deep sniff and bolted down the tree to dine!

Everyone on 90th Street sampled each course and everyone on 90th Street sighed with delight. "Superb!" *"Fantastico!"* "Yum!"

Eva smiled and glanced up from her notebook. For the third time that day she asked herself, "What if?"

"Mr. Chang," she began, "you and Mr. Morley and Mrs. Martinez are such great cooks. The boarded-up store next to your Seafood Emporium, what if all of you used it for a restaurant?"

"A restaurant?" The three chefs looked at one another. "What a wonderful idea," they said, shaking Eva's hand. "Everyone on 90th Street could be our customers. You too, Sondra."

"Everyone but me," Mr. Sims said regretfully. "Just now, I'm between jobs and a bit low on cash."

"No longer!" Sondra called out. "You'll be on my show! I'll arrange it."

Mr. Sims kissed Sondra's hand, and everyone cheered.

"What an amazing day!" Mrs. Martinez said. "Who would believe it? If only someone had written it all down."

"I did," Eva announced, and she opened her notebook and began to read her story (the same story you're reading now) about how *nothing* ever happened on 90th Street.

"What a story!" Sondra exclaimed. "Full of detail. Dialogue. Suspense. A bit of poetry. A hint of romance. Even a happy ending. Why, you'd almost think some of it was made up!"

Eva smiled mysteriously. "Thanks," she said proudly. "But just wait. It'll be even better . . . after I rewrite it."

WHAT'S HAPPENING WITH RONI

Roni Schotter writes because she loves words. Words are powerful. Words can start people thinking. Words give people courage to reach out to the world. Roni also wants to help people use their imaginations. Don't ever tell Roni that "nothing ever happens!" When Roni uses her imagination, anything can happen! She hopes her books will help her readers imagine their own stories, too.

Other books by Roni Schotter: *F Is for Freedom* and *Dreamland*

 Find out more about Roni Schotter at **www.macmillanmh.com**

Author's Purpose

For what purpose does Roni Schotter use humor, dialect, and unexpected situations? Explain.

Comprehension Check

Summarize

Use your Conclusions Chart to help you summarize *Nothing Ever Happens on 90th Street*. Tell about what the people on 90th Street were like at the beginning of the story and what they are like at the end.

What I Know	Text Evidence	Conclusions

Think and Compare

1. How have the **sensational** events in the story changed the way Eva feels about her own writing abilities? **Monitor Comprehension: Draw Conclusions**

2. Why did Mr. Chang cook the trout? Support your answer with evidence from the story. **Analyze**

3. Eva engages in many dialogues throughout the story. In your opinion, what is the best piece of advice Eva gets? How is it helpful? Support your opinion. **Evaluate**

4. Eva is surrounded by different types of people who have different talents. Why do you think it is important for a writer to understand people with various jobs and abilities? **Evaluate**

5. Read "The Mysterious Limousine" on pages 276-277. How is what Polly and her friends find out similar to what Eva learns in *Nothing Ever Happens on 90th Street*? **Reading/ Writing Across Texts**

Social Studies

Genre

An **Interview** is a nonfiction account of questions asked by one person and answered by another.

Text Features

Questions and Answers are set off by using a different typeface or by shortening the words to **Q** and **A**.

Content Vocabulary

preferences   aspiring

spontaneous

Student Interview with Author

Karen Odom

by Perry Faulkner

Question: When and how did you get into writing?

Answer: I've been writing for as long as I can remember, starting with letters and my diary, where I faithfully wrote down my feelings almost every day. But I really became hooked when I became a reporter for my school newspaper when I was in third grade. I also remember writing a play called *The Silver Locket* in sixth grade.

Question: What kind of unique training do you need to be a writer?

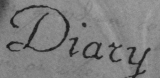

Answer: Many writers have been known to say the best training for a writer is living. I agree with that to a point. I think good writers also need discipline, creative talent, and a little bit of luck too. Writers are natural readers. Reading what others have written helps you not only appreciate good writing but also helps you understand different writing styles and how they affect you as a reader. If you're serious about being a writer, it's also important when you have the opportunity, whether it's in school or through special workshops, to take formal writing courses.

Question: What gives you ideas? What are your **preferences** when writing: people, places, things, or all of them?

Answer: You probably guessed it—I get ideas from all of them! I get ideas all the time, even when I'm not consciously thinking about it—when I'm driving to the store, in a meeting, watching TV, cooking, relaxing on the beach—you name it!

Question: What is your writing process? Do you write all at once or in fragments?

Answer: It all depends on what I'm writing. If I'm writing a nonfiction article that requires a lot of research and interviews, I do the research first, taking notes along the way. I organize my notes, but I also write a word or phrase by different sections of my notes so I can easily know what topic each section covers. Then I start writing. At this stage, I'm not concerned about sentence structure or how it reads or even how long the piece is running. Making sure it reads well, grabs the reader's attention, makes sense, and is the right length will come later when I begin editing and rewriting. And, believe me, there will be plenty of editing and rewriting!

Question: How do you organize your thoughts before writing? Do you create an outline? Or are you **spontaneous?**

Answer: I believe in outlines, but I'm also flexible. If the ideas are rushing in, I'll write down my thoughts (usually on my computer if I'm in my office) so I don't lose them, and then edit and rearrange them later. Otherwise I write out an outline.

Question: How have you changed the way you write over time?

Answer: Rewriting many times over has become second nature to me now. Luckily, it's a lesson I learned when I was very young. Some writers learn that in a much more painful way when they first begin writing professionally. There's ALWAYS a great deal of rewriting and editing that occurs before the final version that the reader sees. It's also much easier for me to let the material go now than it used to be. I'm less concerned about making the work "perfect."

Question: What is your favorite part of writing?

Answer: Actually I have two favorite things that I like about writing. The first is the excitement I feel when I'm brainstorming for a new project. The thoughts come almost faster than I can write them. My second favorite thing is finishing. There's something so satisfying about looking over the finished piece, liking the end result, and knowing that you've created it yourself.

Question: What are your plans for future writing? Are you going to write a book?

Answer: I plan to continue writing for both children and adults. There are many ways to earn a living as a writer. I've chosen writing for magazines, publishing companies, and business writing. It's interesting that you asked the question about writing a book. I have several books in mind, both fiction and nonfiction, but the first one—a children's picture book—is ready for publishing. I have been approaching different publishers to see if they are interested. I even entered it into a contest and was so excited when it won honorable mention in the *2003 Writer's Digest Annual Writing Competition.* I'll let you know what happens!

Question: What advice would you give a young, **aspiring** writer?

Answer: I have four main pieces of advice:

- Write, write, write, write, write, and write some more! Nothing beats just doing it.
- The life of a writer can be tough sometimes, and you have to be prepared for rejection along the way. You have to learn not to take it personally or dwell on it when something you've written is criticized or not accepted.
- Stick with it and never give up!
- And, remember, while you're writing the "Great American Novel," you may need to write some less exciting material to pay the bills!

Connect and Compare

1. Reread the questions in the interview. What kind of organizational plan do they show? Explain. **Reading an Interview**

2. How can Karen Odom's advice help you become a better writer? **Evaluate**

3. What writing advice do you think Karen Odom would give Eva in *Nothing Ever Happens on 90th Street*? **Reading/Writing Across Texts**

Social Studies Activity

Choose somebody to interview about his or her career. Ask at least five questions. Write your completed interview in a question-and-answer format.

 Find out more about interviews at **www.macmillanmh.com**

Writer's Craft

Dialogue

Good, well-chosen **dialogue** makes characters sound natural and believable. Forced or bland word choice can make characters sound unnatural or unbelievable.

Write Dialogue

Everyone in the Neighborhood

by Sabrena B.

I used specific language in dialogue to convey Mr. Mang's personality.

Details help convey a lot about Jill both in dialogue and in narrative.

It was Saturday morning. The doorbell rang.

"Coming! Hold on! One second!" called Mr. Mang, nervously. He opened the door. It was Jill, the mail carrier.

"Hi," she said. "This package is too big for your mailbox. I am so tired from climbing 10 flights of stairs!" Jill was panting and patting her face with a handkerchief.

Mr. Mang sighed, took the package, and went inside. The doorbell rang again. "I will be right there!" he called.

It was Joe from the dry cleaner's. "Here are your suits," said Joe. "We did a good job if I do say so myself."

Mr. Mang took the suits and went inside. The bell rang. "Okay, okay! Not again! One second!" he yelled.

It was Arnie, the newspaper boy. "Mr. Mang," he said. "It's collection day, old pal, old buddy."

Mr. Mang rolled his eyes, paid Arnie, and took the newspaper inside. The doorbell did not ring.

"Good," said Mr. Mang to himself. "Everyone in the neighborhood has been here. I'm tired of answering the door. I think I'll take a nap with some earplugs in!"

Your Turn

Write dialogue between two or more characters. Choose words that the characters would really say. Be sure language that is not in dialogue is also interesting and informative. Choosing to write about people you know can help make your dialogue sound more natural. Use the Writer's Checklist to check your writing.

Writer's Checklist

 Ideas and Content: Does my dialogue make sense?

 Organization: Do the events and dialogue proceed naturally?

 Voice: Do the voices of my characters come through and sound natural?

 Word Choice: Did I choose words in my dialogue that my characters would really use?

 Sentence Fluency: Does my dialogue flow well?

Conventions: Did I punctuate my dialogue correctly? Did I check my spelling?

Talk About It

Why are people around the world working hard to find new, renewable sources of energy?

LOG ON Find out more about energy at **www.macmillanmh.com**

302

Energy

SOURCES OF ENERGY

Vocabulary

nonrenewable

renewable

adverse

generate

apparatus

The energy we use in just about all aspects of our daily lives comes from two types of sources: nonrenewable and renewable.

Solar collectors

NONRENEWABLE Sources of Energy

Most of the energy we use comes from deposits of fossil fuels in the earth. These include coal, natural gas, and petroleum. Once these natural resources are used up, they are gone forever. Getting fossil fuels out of the earth involves drilling, mining, building pipelines, and other processes that can have **adverse** effects on the environment. Releasing the energy in fossil fuels requires combustion. This burning process releases pollutants that can contribute to acid rain and global warming.

Oil-drilling platform

RENEWABLE Sources of Energy

Renewable sources of energy are everlasting. Using them does not use them up. They generate much less pollution—both in gathering and production—than nonrenewable sources.

* Solar energy comes from the sun. Solar panels on buildings convert sunlight to electricity.

* Wind can **generate** electricity by turning a turbine, an **apparatus** with blades similar to a giant windmill.

* Geothermal energy comes from heat in Earth's core. Engineers use the heat to create steam to generate electricity.

* Dams and rivers generate hydropower. Water flowing through a dam activates a turbine that runs an electric generator.

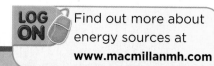

LOG ON Find out more about energy sources at **www.macmillanmh.com**

ENERGY PRODUCERS AND CONSUMERS

Here's a look at the world's top 10 energy consumers and producers.

TOP 10 ENERGY PRODUCERS	TOP 10 ENERGY CONSUMERS
1. United States	1. United States
2. Russia	2. China
3. China	3. Russia
4. Saudi Arabia	4. Japan
5. Canada	5. Germany
6. United Kingdom	6. India
7. Iran	7. Canada
8. Norway	8. France
9. Australia	9. United Kingdom
10. Mexico	10. Brazil

(**Source:** *Energy Information Administration, U.S. Dept. of Energy*)

WIND POWER

Wind exists because the sun warms Earth's surface air unevenly. Warm air expands and rises. Cool air rushes in to take its place. The resulting air movement is wind. Technology can turn this wind—and the sun—into pollution-free energy.

Wind "farm"

✳ The wind that blows through North Dakota, South Dakota, and Texas could create enough electricity to meet the needs of the entire country.

✳ More than 10,000 U.S. homes are totally powered by solar energy.

✳ The largest wind farm in the world is in Altamont Pass, California. It has 6,500 windmills!

✳ If every shopping mall in the U.S. had solar panels on its roof, the panels would produce enough power for every house in the country!

(Sources: Solar Energy Research and Education Foundation; *The Wind at Work* by Gretchen Woelfle)

BUILDING GREEN

Water-filled drums in a south-facing glass wall absorb heat from the sun and release it slowly at night to warm this New Mexico home in winter.

How can homes be made more environmentally friendly?

If Earth could talk, it might not call everyone's house "home sweet home." Instead, it would probably point out that many of our houses are not so "sweet." They can actually have an **adverse** effect on the health of the planet. Imaginative builders are out to change that by dreaming up new ways to make our homes more "green," a term that means "ecologically friendly."

HOME, GREEN HOME

Recently, a new house built near Houston, Texas, was so efficient that it didn't need a furnace. The hot-water heater kept the house warm enough in the relatively mild Texas winter. This, combined with reduced air-conditioning costs, saved enough money to offset the cost of the house's extra-thick insulation and high-performance windows.

This solar-powered house in Germany has transparent insulation and solar panels facing south to collect and store solar energy for everyday use.

Unfortunately the successful project, part of a Department of Energy program, hasn't much changed the habits of many homebuilders. "It's hard for big companies to change their way of doing things," says Bill Zoeller. He works with the firm that designed the Houston home.

But some builders are changing. For instance, Habitat for Humanity is building energy-efficient homes that rely less on **nonrenewable** sources of energy. It is working with the Environmental Protection Agency to clean up former industrial sites for affordable housing. Improved insulation and construction techniques are part of the plan. Zoeller sees significant gains in all this. He says, "In some parts of the country, even average homes are now 30 percent more efficient than a few years ago."

DRIVING HOME CHANGE

Many Californians claim they practically live in their cars. John Picard, 34, goes a step further: He lives in a lot of cars, literally.

"These are cars from the '60s that were in the junkyard," he says, indicating his 2,400-square-foot ultramodern home in Marina del Rey, California. "Now they are my house."

Picard's walls aren't made from hubcaps and fenders. They are made by a company that manufactures recycled-steel framing material from junked cars and discarded cans and washing machines. In fact, Picard's entire house—a space-age, two-story metal cube—was built using recycled material and modern technology. The result is a home that's environmentally correct and comfortable, too. The woodless construction alone, Picard estimates, "saved about 100 trees."

Other "ecohouse" features include filtered air and an **apparatus** that monitors the interior temperature and energy-efficient lighting. Plus there is a roof-mounted solar panel that can **generate** most of his home's energy needs. "My house," he notes proudly, "has the potential for zero utility bills."

Designing Picard's ecohouse took a year. Construction took four months. "I wanted to do an energy-efficient house that everybody could construct," Picard explains. He hopes that his ecohouse will inspire similar construction in the future. "I know it changes people when they see and understand it," he says. "It brings quality back into building, and it's good for the environment."

THE LATEST STRAW (NOT THE LAST!)

Straw seems like an improbable home-building material. After all, there is that story about the three pigs. And there's another story about a straw house that was eaten by cows.

Judy Knox, 50, and her husband Matts Myhrman, 54, have a different view. They are spreading the news that straw-bale construction, once used on the tree-barren American prairie, is ripe for a comeback. In this building technique, straw is stacked in bales, often bound by

John Picard's "metal cube" home

Charcoal-color flooring absorbs heat and helps warm the house.

chicken wire, and sealed with stucco or adobe. Straw is a cheap, energy-efficient resource, say Knox and Myhrman. Plus, new straw grows every year—so it is a **renewable** resource.

In 1990, the two launched their Tucson-based company, Out On Bale, to conduct workshops for straw builders. They've overseen construction of 20 straw structures, from a sauna to a bunkhouse. "It's an annually renewable

waste product," says Myhrman, that's "right for the planet."

Knox is a longtime environmental activist from New Hampshire. Myhrman is a Maine native and former ecology teacher. They became excited about straw houses after visiting two of them in New Mexico in the 1980s. With their two-foot-thick walls, the houses provided "a quiet restful kind of feeling," says Knox. "It felt friendly." Walls can be raised in a day or two. Quick-to-erect straw houses could, say Knox and Myhrman, shelter disaster victims or homeless people.

Straw, however, does have one drawback: When wet, it attracts fungi, so builders must take care to keep bales dry. And sometimes during construction "the straw bales break up, like shredded wheat," notes local architect Tom Greenwood, who recently designed a straw cabin. What then? Greenwood jokes, "Don't add milk."

Think and Compare

1. What does the term "building green" mean?

2. What makes the building techniques described in this article environmentally friendly?

3. If you were building a "green" house, which building technique would you want to use? Why?

4. "Sources of Energy" on page 304 outlines the consequences of relying on nonrenewable energy sources. How do the people in "Building Green" avoid these drawbacks?

Building a straw house

Test Strategy

Think and Search

Read on to find the answer. Look for information in more than one place.

LEARNING TO GO WITH THE FLOW

The Kennebec River flows freely now.

Dams are a source of energy in the United States and around the world. But damming rivers also causes environmental damage. In 1887, the Edwards Dam was built across the Kennebec River near Augusta, Maine, to generate electricity. Even back then, there was concern that the dam would interfere with the life cycle of fish in the area.

The concern was justified. It wasn't long after the dam was built that salmon, herring, shad, and other fish pretty much disappeared from the river. The dam blocked the fish from swimming to the upstream areas where they reproduce.

In 1997 the government concluded that the benefits the dam provided were outweighed by the environmental damage it caused. In 1999 the old dam was destroyed and the Kennebec came roaring back to life. Within weeks, native fish species returned by the hundreds. Edwards was the first U.S. hydroelectric dam ordered destroyed against its owners' wishes. It signaled the start of a successful campaign to remove other river dams around the country that were causing environmental damage.

Restoring rivers to their natural paths is hard work. But environmentalists say the effort always pays off—in expected as well as surprising ways, it turns out. The Edwards Dam had trapped hundreds of logs at its base that were salvaged and recycled into musical instruments, furniture, and other products.

Go On ▶

Directions: Answer the questions.

1 . What environmental damage did the Edwards Dam cause?

   A   The dam changed the water temperature in the river.

   B   Fish were unable to swim upstream, which affected their life cycle.

   C   The electricity produced by the dam killed the fish.

   D   The dam was a source of pollution that killed the fish.

> **Tip**
> Look for information in more than one place.

2. For how long did the Edwards Dam exist?

   A   just over 100 years

   B   two years

   C   two decades

   D   more than 150 years

3. What were the benefits of removing the Edwards Dam?

   A   Fish returned, and logs were retrieved and reused.

   B   Tourism and fishing increased in the Augusta, Maine area.

   C   The local electric utility received an increase in revenues.

   D   The Kennebec River became a source of energy again.

4. What was the significance of the decision to tear down the Edwards Dam for other hydroelectric dams over rivers in the U.S.?

5. The article refers to the benefits of the Edwards Dam as well as the damage it caused. Explain what you think the benefits were and why the government decided to tear down the dam. Use details from the article in your answer.

Write to a Prompt

In "Learning to Go with the Flow" you read about the government's decision to tear down the Edwards Dam because of the environmental damage it caused. Do you agree or disagree that preventing environmental damage is more important than projects designed to help people? Write a persuasive essay stating your opinion and supporting it with details and reasons.

The Good Side of a Dam

Sometimes people do things to the environment that are just wrong. But sometimes scientists make demands that are unreasonable. Tearing down a dam is an example of what I'm referring to.

People have protested and done all kinds of things to prevent damage to wildlife in certain areas. The reason? They want to protect a fish or a wild plant.

I'm all for protecting the environment, but I'm not for letting a fish cause the destruction of a dam. In this case, people's rights are "righter" than animals' rights. A hydroelectric dam generates much needed electricity for an area. We need electricity to keep people working and help the economy.

So I say, yes, let's take care of the environment. But I say no, let's not sacrifice dams and our economy to help plants and animals.

I used details to support my opinion.

Writing Prompt

Some environmentalists believe the government should ban certain kinds of cars that use a lot of gas because they increase air pollution as well as our dependence on oil, a nonrenewable resource. Other people think the government should not restrict the kind of cars people buy. Write a persuasive essay on this topic. State your opinion and support it with details and reasons.

Writer's Checklist

☑ Ask yourself, who is my audience?

☑ Think about your purpose for writing.

☑ Choose the correct form for your writing.

☑ Form an opinion about the topic.

☑ Use reasons to support your opinion.

☑ Be sure your ideas are logical and organized.

☑ Use your best spelling, grammar, and punctuation.

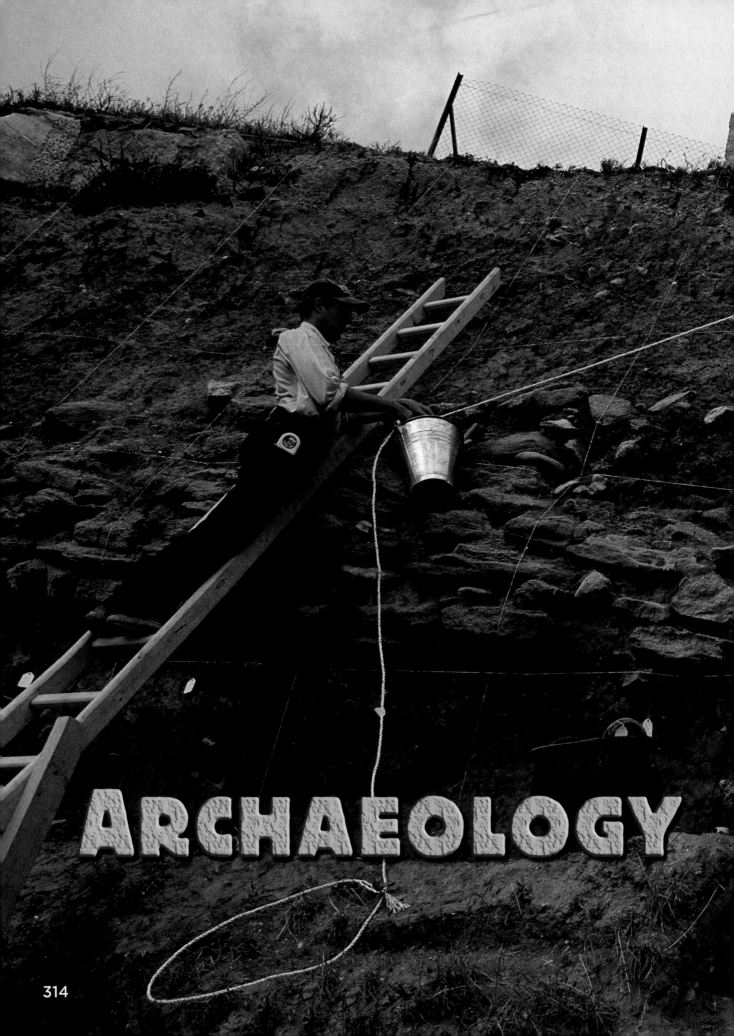

ARCHAEOLOGY

Talk About It

Think what it would be like to be an archaeologist. What do you think the archaeologists in the photo are doing?

LOG ON Find out more about archaeology at **www.macmillanmh.com**

BRINGING THE

by Sam Ames

An archaeologist is a kind of science detective. By studying objects from the past, an archaeologist can find clues about what life was like long ago.

An archaeologist can learn about the food people ate and the **utensils** they used to eat with. An archaeologist can learn from the weapons, art, and tools a people left behind. These objects help archaeologists figure out what a group's customs and beliefs were and if they were **superstitious**, holding unreasonable fears. They can help an archaeologist determine the **civilized**, or advanced group, versus the primitive.

Gathering Information

Archaeologists **excavate** in places where long-ago people once lived. Digging to uncover these places is exacting work. First, the scientists take surveys and make maps of the site. They dig long **trenches** around tombs or buildings. They try not to disturb any evidence buried in the earth.

Archaeologists work carefully and **steadfastly** for long hours to recover small objects. With patient determination, they often use paintbrushes to clean dirt off pieces of pottery

An archaeologist dusts off his discovery.

Vocabulary

utensils	trenches
superstitious	steadfastly
civilized	precede
excavate	prolong

STRATEGY SKILL

Word Parts

Prefixes are added to the beginning of words and change the meanings of words.

pro + = "extending out"

prolong = "to lengthen," "to take a longer time"

PAST TO THE PRESENT

or other delicate things. As an item is uncovered, the archaeologists photograph it and describe it.

Understanding the Findings

Archaeologists follow several steps to learn from what they find. First, they sort the items and look for patterns. Then they determine how old something is, a process known as dating. Besides the exact age of an object, the scientists want to know how old something is in relation to other things. Did a certain object **precede** others that were found, or did it come after?

Finally, archaeologists try to answer these questions: How did this culture develop? When and why did it change?

A Big Job

Work at a dig takes many years. One reason is that most archaeologists have jobs in museums or as teachers. Bad weather can also **prolong** the time it takes to excavate. Then, too, some archaeological sites are underwater or beneath existing cities.

Archaeologists have a big job in bringing the past to the present!

Reread for **Comprehension**

STRATEGY SKILL

Monitor Comprehension

Summarize

One way to monitor your understanding of a selection is to summarize events in a selection. As you summarize, look for major points and for the details that support them. Always use your own words.

Use the Summary Chart as you reread "Bringing the Past to the Present."

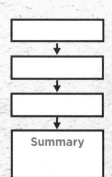

Summary

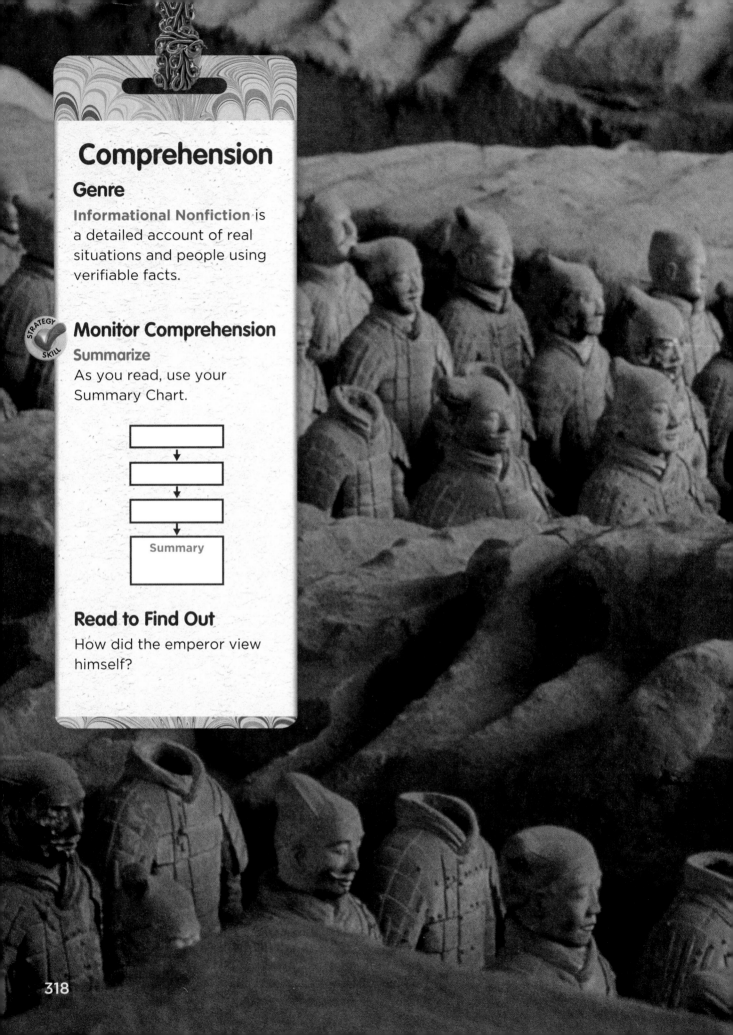

Comprehension

Genre

Informational Nonfiction is a detailed account of real situations and people using verifiable facts.

Monitor Comprehension

Summarize

As you read, use your Summary Chart.

```
┌──────────────┐
│              │
└──────────────┘
       ↓
┌──────────────┐
│              │
└──────────────┘
       ↓
┌──────────────┐
│              │
└──────────────┘
       ↓
┌──────────────┐
│   Summary    │
│              │
└──────────────┘
```

Read to Find Out

How did the emperor view himself?

Award Winning Selection

THE EMPEROR'S SILENT ARMY

TERRACOTTA WARRIORS *of* ANCIENT CHINA

BY JANE O'CONNOR

A Strange Discovery

Lintong County, People's Republic of China, March 1974

It's just an ordinary day in early spring, or so three farmers think as they trudge across a field in northern China. They are looking for a good place to dig a well. There has been a drought, and they must find water or risk losing their crops later in the year.

The farmers choose a spot near a grove of persimmon trees. Down they dig, five feet, ten feet. Still no water. They decide to keep on digging a little deeper. All of a sudden, one of the farmers feels his shovel strike against something hard. Is it a rock? It's difficult to see at the bottom of the dark hole, so the farmer kneels down for a closer look. No, it isn't a rock. It seems to be clay, and not raw clay but clay that has been baked and made into something. But what?

The terracotta army was discovered when well-diggers found the head of a "pottery man" like this one. No photographs were taken that day.

A buried army of terracotta soldiers was found in the countryside of northern China.

Now, more carefully, the men dig around the something. Perhaps it is a pot or a vase. However, what slowly reveals itself is the pottery head of a man who stares back at them, open-eyed and amazingly real looking. The farmers have never seen anything like it before. But they do remember stories that some of the old people in their village have told, stories of a "pottery man" found many years ago not far from where they are now. The villagers had been scared that the pottery man would bring bad luck so they broke it to bits, which were then reburied and forgotten.

The three well-diggers are not so **superstitious**. They report their discovery to a local official. Soon a group of archeologists arrives to search the area more closely. Maybe they will find pieces of a clay body to go with the clay head.

In fact, they find much more.

These soldiers' hands are clenched as if still holding their bronze weapons.

During the weeks and months that follow, the archeologists dig out more pottery men, which now are called by a more dignified term—terracotta figurines. The figurines are soldiers. That much is clear. But they come from a time long ago, when Chinese warriors wore knee-length robes, armor made from small iron "fish scales," and elaborate topknot hairdos. All of the soldiers are life-size or a little bigger and weigh as much as four hundred pounds. They stand at attention as if waiting for the command to charge into battle. The only thing missing is their weapons. And those are found too—hundreds of real bronze swords, daggers, and battle-axes as well as thousands of scattered arrowheads—all so perfectly made that, after cleaning, their ancient tips are still sharp enough to split a hair!

Summarize
If you had to summarize this paragraph, what three important details would you include?

Today, after years of work, terracotta soldiers are still being uncovered and restored. What the well-diggers stumbled upon, purely by accident, has turned out to be among the largest and most incredible archeological discoveries of modern times. Along with the Great Pyramids in Egypt, the buried army is now considered one of the true wonders of the ancient world. Spread out over several acres near the city of Xian, the soldiers number not in tens or hundreds but in the thousands! Probably 7,500 total. Until 1974, nobody knew that right below the people of northern China an enormous underground army has been standing guard, silently and watchfully, for more than 2,200 years. Who put them there?

One man.

Known as the fierce tiger of Qin, the divine Son of Heaven, he was the first emperor of China.

The Quest for Immortality

Before the time of Qin Shihuang (pronounced chin shir-hwong), who lived from 259 to 210 B.C., there was no China. Instead, there were seven separate kingdoms, each with its own language, currency, and ruler. For hundreds of years they had been fighting one another. The kingdom of Qin was the fiercest; soldiers received their pay only after they had presented their generals with the cut-off heads of enemy warriors. By 221 B.C. the ruler of the Qin kingdom had "eaten up his neighbors like a silkworm devouring a leaf," according to an ancient historian. The name China comes from Qin.

The map shows the Qin kingdom in brown and the Qin empire in stripes. The dot indicates where the terracotta army was found.

The king of Qin now ruled over an immense empire—around one million square miles that stretched north and west to the Gobi desert, south to present-day Vietnam, and east to the Yellow Sea. To the people of the time, this was the entire **civilized** world. Not for another hundred years would the Chinese know that empires existed beyond their boundaries. To the ruler of Qin, being called king was no longer grand enough. He wanted a title that no one else had ever had before. What he chose was Qin Shihuang. This means "first emperor, God in Heaven, and Almighty of the Universe" all rolled into one.

But no title, however superhuman it sounded, could protect him from what he feared most—dying. More than anything, the emperor wanted to live forever. According to legend, a magic elixir had granted eternal life to the people of the mythical Eastern Islands. Over the years, the emperor sent expeditions out to sea in search of the islands and the magic potion. But each time they came back empty-handed.

This painting from the seventeenth century shows the first emperor carried on a covered litter called a palanquin.

If he couldn't live forever, then Qin Shihuang was determined to live as long as possible. He ate powdered jade and drank mercury in the belief that they would **prolong** his life. In fact, these "medicines" were poison and may have caused the emperor to fall sick and die while on a tour of the easternmost outposts of his empire. He was forty-nine years old.

Summarize

Why is the information about Qin Shihuang important to the selection so far? Explain your answer.

325

For thousands of years, the Chinese have made silk fabric. This detail of a silk robe shows an embroidered dragon, the symbol of Chinese emperors.

If word of Qin Shihuang's death got out while he was away from the capital there might be a revolt. So his ministers kept the news a secret. With the emperor's body inside his chariot, the entire party traveled back to the capital city. Meals were brought into the emperor's chariot; daily reports on affairs of state were delivered as usual—all to keep up the appearance that the emperor was alive and well. However, it was summer, and a terrible smell began to come from the chariot. But the clever ministers found a way to account for the stench. A cart was loaded with smelly salted fish and made to **precede** the chariot, overpowering and masking any foul odors coming from the dead emperor. And so Qin Shihuang returned to the capital for burial.

The tomb of Qin Shihuang had been under construction for more than thirty years. It was begun when he was a young boy of thirteen and was still not finished when he died. Even incomplete, the emperor's tomb was enormous, larger than his largest palace. According to legend, it had a domed ceiling inlaid with clusters of pearls to represent the sun, moon, and stars. Below was a gigantic relief map of the world, made from bronze. Bronze hills and mountains rose up from the floor, with rivers of mercury flowing into a mercury sea. Along the banks of the rivers were models of the emperor's palaces and cities, all exact replicas of the real ones.

In ancient times, the Chinese believed that life after death was not so very different from life on earth. The soul of a dead person could continue to enjoy all the pleasures of everyday life. So people who were rich enough constructed elaborate underground tombs filled with silk robes, jewelry with precious stones, furniture, games, boats, chariots—everything the dead person could possibly need or want.

Qin Shihuang knew that grave robbers would try their best to loot the treasures in his tomb. So he had machines put inside the tomb that produced the rumble of thunder to scare off intruders, and mechanical crossbows at the entrance were set to fire arrows automatically should anyone dare trespass. The emperor also made certain that the workers who carried his coffin in to its final resting place never revealed its exact whereabouts. As the men worked their way back through the tunnels to the tomb's entrance, a stone door came crashing down, and they were left to die, sealed inside the tomb along with the body of the emperor.

Even all these measures, however, were not enough to satisfy the emperor. And so, less than a mile from the tomb, in underground **trenches**, the terracotta warriors were stationed. Just as flesh-and-blood troops had protected him during his lifetime, the terracotta troops were there to protect their ruler against any enemy for all eternity.

Beautiful silk robes, like this one from the nineteenth century, would be placed in the tomb of an important person to be worn in the afterlife.

Inside the Emperor's Tomb

What exactly is the terracotta army guarding so **steadfastly**? What, besides the body of the dead emperor, is inside the tomb? The answer is that nobody knows. And the government of China has no plans at present to **excavate** and find out.

In ancient China it was the custom to build a natural-looking hill on top of a person's tomb. The more important a person was, the bigger the hill. Thousands of years of harsh weather have worn down the emperor's mound; originally it was four hundred feet high, almost as high as the biggest of the three Great Pyramids in Egypt.

Like the ancient Egyptians, the ancient Chinese believed that the body of a dead person should be preserved as a "home" for the soul. However, the Chinese did not make a person's body into a mummy. They believed that jade had magic powers, among them the ability to keep a dead body from decaying. In Chinese tombs from the first century B.C., bodies of noblemen and princesses have been found wearing entire suits of jade. It is believed that Qin Shihuang is buried

The body of the emperor, which has never been uncovered, may wear a jade funeral suit like this one found in the tomb of a Chinese princess from the late second century.

in just such a suit, the thousands of small tiles all beautifully carved and sewn together with gold thread. And over this jade burial outfit, his body is supposedly covered in a blanket of pearls.

As for all the things placed with the emperor, certainly they must be grand beyond imagining—silk robes embroidered with dragons, gem-encrusted crowns and jewelry, musical instruments, hand-carved furniture, lamps, beautiful dishes, cooking pots, and golden utensils. Like the pharaohs of ancient Egypt, the first emperor would have made certain that he had everything he might possibly want in the afterlife. But unless his tomb is excavated, what these treasures look like will remain a mystery.

MEET THE AUTHOR

Jane O'Connor knows a lot about books. She's worked as an editor and a publisher, and has written more than thirty books. Sometimes she writes her books with her husband, her older son, or another author. Jane had lots of research to do for this book. She included many of the amazing details that she found in this story. She also had to help find just the right photographs to make the terracotta warriors come alive in our imaginations.

Author's Purpose

How can you tell Jane O'Connor probably admires archaeologists? How may that have affected her purpose for writing? How well did she achieve her purpose?

LOG ON Find out more about Jane O'Connor at **www.macmillanmh.com**

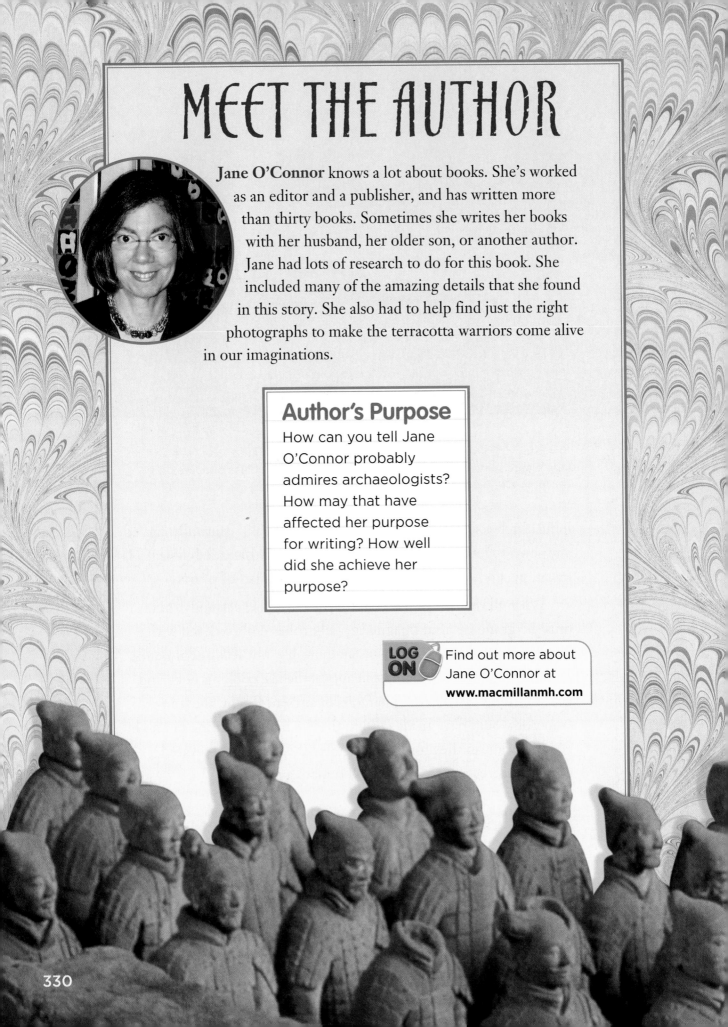

Comprehension Check

Summarize

STRATEGY SKILL

Use your Summary Chart to summarize *The Emperor's Silent Army*. What purpose did the silent army serve?

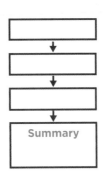

Summary

Think and Compare

STRATEGY SKILL

1. What details in the selection tell us about the person responsible for the building of the terracotta army? Use specific examples from the text. **Monitor Comprehension: Summarize**

2. Compare and contrast Qin Shihuang's tomb with what you know about the pyramids in Egypt. **Analyze**

3. The tomb of the emperor has not been fully explored. What would you say to the Chinese government to try to convince them to let archaeologists **excavate** the tomb further? **Synthesize**

4. The author tells us that the terracotta army is one of the most incredible archaeological discoveries of modern times. Why do you think this is true? **Evaluate**

5. Read "Bringing the Past to the Present" on pages 316-317. Think about what you have read in *The Emperor's Silent Army*. If the Chinese government were to approve further excavation of the emperor's tomb, what might they find? How might they find it? Use evidence from both texts to support your answer. **Reading/Writing Across Texts**

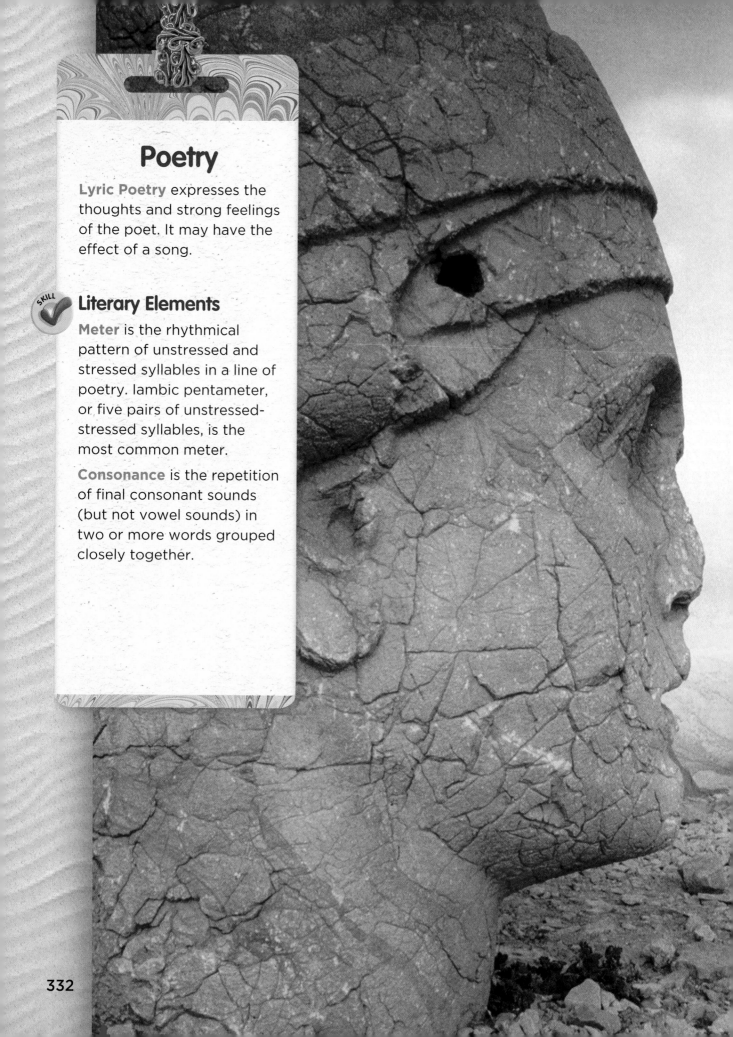

Poetry

Lyric Poetry expresses the thoughts and strong feelings of the poet. It may have the effect of a song.

Literary Elements

Meter is the rhythmical pattern of unstressed and stressed syllables in a line of poetry. Iambic pentameter, or five pairs of unstressed-stressed syllables, is the most common meter.

Consonance is the repetition of final consonant sounds (but not vowel sounds) in two or more words grouped closely together.

OZYMANDIAS

by Percy Bysshe Shelley

I met a traveler from an antique land
Who said: Two vast and trunkless legs of stone
Stand in the desert. . . Near them, on the sand,
Half sunk, a shattered visage lies, whose frown,
And wrinkled lip, and sneer of cold command,
Tell that its sculptor well those passions read
Which yet survive, stamped on these lifeless things,
The hand that mocked them, and the heart that fed:
And on the pedestal these words appear:
"My name is Ozymandias, king of kings:
Look on my works, ye Mighty, and despair!"
Nothing beside remains. Round the decay
Of that colossal wreck, boundless and bare
The lone and level sands stretch far away.

> The meter is iambic pentameter.

> The words "cold command" end in *d*, an example of consonance.

Connect and Compare

SKILL

1. What strong feelings can be found in the poem? How does the meter of the poem support the poem's meaning? **Meter**

2. Was King Ozymandias a just, kind ruler or a harsh tyrant? Use words and phrases from the poem to support your opinion. **Analyze**

3. Think about *The Emperor's Silent Army* and "Ozymandias." How are the emperor and King Ozymandias similar? **Reading/Writing Across Texts**

 LOG ON Find out more about poetry at **www.macmillanmh.com**

Write a Short Story

▼ Writer's Craft

Beginning, Middle, and End

Telling how things happen by using a conflict and resolution structure can help organize your writing in a clear beginning, middle, and end sequence.

I organized my story set in ancient Rome with a clear beginning and middle.

I offered a solution to clearly end my story.

 ## Octavia

by Helena C.

Marcus was late because his cat didn't wake him. Usually Octavia jumped on his chest and meowed. But today, thanks to Octavia's disappearing act, he would be late for school. Marcus couldn't find her anywhere.

He ran all the way. The streets of Rome were busy and Marcus had to dodge many people, carts of produce, and chariots driven by sleek horses.

The benches at school were hard, and the teacher was strict. The class was reading a book called <u>Roman Aqueduct</u>. Marcus wished he were out searching for Octavia. He was beginning to worry.

After school, he stopped at the public baths. The Romans went there to bathe and to see their friends. Marcus asked around, but no one had seen Octavia.

In the alley near his home Marcus passed a statue. Rome was full of incredible statues, but this one meowed. Sure enough, there was Octavia, and she wasn't alone. Lots of little Octavias were sleeping around her!

Marcus laughed. Now he would never be late again!

Your Turn

Write a short story that takes place in a historical setting. You might have to do some research to make your story ring true. Choose a setting that interests you. Your story should have a clear beginning, middle, and end. Use the Writer's Checklist to check your writing.

Greetings From THE COLOSSEUM

Writer's Checklist

 Ideas and Content: Is my story clear?

 Organization: Does my story have a clear beginning, middle, and end?

 Voice: Do the details tell how my main character feels?

 Word Choice: Did I choose strong descriptive words to tell what happened?

 Sentence Fluency: Did my sentences vary in length to help the flow of my story?

 Conventions: Did I capitalize and underline the title of a book correctly? Did I check my spelling?

SHOW TIME

Talk About It

What would you dramatize if you were putting on a class play? What type of music and dance would you include?

LOG ON Find out more about stage performances at **www.macmillanmh.com**

The Unusual Robot

by Wilson Jenkins

"Wow!" said Dominic as he finished reading the script for the school play. "We've got a winner."

Angela nodded. "Don't you love that detective robot?" she asked. "She really is **charismatic**. What a winning personality!"

"How about the line where she says a detective's job is **sleuthing**?" chimed in Bonnie.

"My favorite part is where she **mimics** the parrot. I mean a robot copying what a parrot says? It's too funny," said Carl.

The students chatted on about the **array** of different and colorful characters in the play. All the roles sounded good.

A Problem

Each year the students produce a play for the community. The money they raise helps pay for a sixth-grade trip to Washington, DC. It is an event of great pride and **significance** to the students.

"This play will be expensive to do," Ms. Tiroli warned the class. "We'll need special scenery, costumes, and even music. You'll have to figure out if you can do this play and have enough left for the trip."

The students began to list their expenses. Then they subtracted that amount from

what they would probably earn selling tickets to the play.

"It's not enough," said Carl. "Can we charge more for the tickets?"

Dominic said, "People won't come if we charge too much."

Ms. Tiroli suggested holding a meeting the next day.

Some Solutions

The students met and shared their ideas. One was to choose another play that didn't cost so much. "Oh!" said Angela **despondently**. "I'd be so sad if we didn't do *The Charismatic Robot*."

"I have an idea," piped up Paulo. "You know how some businesses in town are always **sponsoring** events for the high school sports teams? Maybe we can get them to sponsor our costumes."

"Great idea!" said Bonnie.

The students decided to talk to some business owners.

The Show Goes On

During the next few weeks, students were raising money, rehearsing the play, making posters, and selling tickets.

"We have enough to pay for all the materials," announced Paulo. "We'll list each sponsor in the program. None of them wants to be **anonymous**."

"Well, wait until they see the play," said Dominic. "They'll probably ask us to do one a month!"

"Actually," said Paulo, "they're all hoping to find a charismatic robot to work for them."

Reread for **Comprehension**

Monitor Comprehension

Draw Conclusions

A Conclusions Chart helps you to draw conclusions about information. When you draw a conclusion, look for facts or details about a character or event. Use these facts and logical reasoning to draw a conclusion.

Use the Conclusions Chart as you reread "The Unusual Robot."

Text Clues	Conclusion

339

Comprehension

Genre
A **Play** is a story that is intended to be performed and has features such as a prologue, stage directions, scene descriptions, and dialogue.

Monitor Comprehension
Draw Conclusions

As you read, use your Conclusions Chart.

Text Clues	Conclusion

Read to Find Out
Who is the Phantom Poet?

The Case of the Phantom Poet

Time: The present

Setting: A small suburban town in the U.S.A.

Prologue: A local newspaper, *The Town Caller*, is **sponsoring** a writing competition for sixth grade students. From a wide **array** of entries, a team of judges at the paper has narrowed the competition to two students: Delia Marcus and Latisha Walker. To decide the winning student, Mr. Tolliver, the school principal, has requested that both girls write a human interest story, featuring someone of special **significance** to the school. The race is on! It's Thursday and the deadline to submit the articles is Tuesday afternoon.

a play
by Karen English

illustrated by
Nicole Tadgell

Characters (in order of appearance):

Latisha Walker	A bright but shy young writer
Michael Johnson	Latisha's friend and star basketball player
Rhonda Watts	Latisha's friend since kindergarten
Carlos Hernandez	Michael's friend
Delia Marcus	Popular, overly confident winner of several writing competitions
Ms. Singh	School librarian
Miss Mackey	Woman who works in the cafeteria
Mr. Tolliver	School principal

SCENE 1

The school library; Latisha, Michael, Rhonda, and Carlos are huddled at a table, discussing the writing competition.

Michael: *(slowly, as if thinking aloud)* Someone of special significance to the school . . . someone dynamic, appealing, **charismatic**—*(pause)* Hey, why don't you just write about me! *(Everyone laughs, including Michael.)*

Latisha: Let's get serious. I'm facing major competition here. Delia Marcus wins just about every writing contest around.

Rhonda: There was the Robert Frost Poetry Contest last year and the haiku competition at the recreation center.

Carlos: And the short story competition that WBAE sponsored last month.

Draw Conclusions
Why is everyone concerned about competing against Delia?

Michael: *(shaking his head)* Hey, remember me? *(with pride)* Michael Johnson, Most Valuable Player at the school regionals this year! Slam dunk!

*(Everyone **mimics** cheering and applauding.)*

Latisha: *(holding a phony microphone up)* Michael, tell us how you got your start.

Michael: *(humble)* Well, I owe it all to Coach Greer. He's a great guy and a great role model. *(Everyone looks at one another, then, in unison . . .)*

All: Coach Greer!

Latisha: *(slowly)* Someone of significance to the school! *(puts arm around Michael's shoulder)* Michael, old friend, do you think you can get me an interview with Coach Greer?

(Enter Delia Marcus.)

Delia: *(smug)* Too late, Latisha. I just arranged an interview with him for tomorrow morning. Coach Julius Greer, college all-star and pride of our town, as my mom always says. She went to school with him! *(turns to leave)* Good try, Latisha, but life is like sports, you've got to be quick on your feet. *(walks away, leaving the other kids dumbfounded)*

Fade out.

The next day, back in the library; Latisha, Carlos, Rhonda, and Michael sit morosely, with their chins in their palms.

Latisha: Oh, well, back to square one.

(Carlos drums the table with a folded piece of paper.)

Rhonda: Stop that. I can't think.

(Carlos absentmindedly gives the table another tap and then opens the paper and reads to himself but audibly.)

Carlos: *(recites)* Do not despair of desserts not won; Soon you will find your place in the sun. *(sighs)* Courtesy, the Phantom Poet.

Latisha: *(absently)* What's that one about?

Carlos: This one? I didn't place in the last track meet and I was feeling kind of bad.

Michael: Are you going to turn it in to Ms. Singh? She's been collecting those couplets.

(All turn to look at the librarian writing at her desk. A large glass jar filled with folded paper sits on the desk.)

Rhonda: *(pause, as if thinking)* That's it! That's the subject of your human interest story—the Phantom Poet!

Latisha: Nobody knows who the Phantom Poet is.

Michael: We'll just have to find out. How long has this Phantom Poet been dropping those couplets all over the place? A year? A zillion of us have gotten them. Always when something disappointing has happened or when we need a boost.

Rhonda: Remember when the Student Council overlooked Mr. Sauer, the custodian, on Recognition Day? The whole Student Council got one. What'd it say?

Latisha: Um . . . *(recites)* Forgetting to include Mr. Sauer; Is like baking a cake without flour.

Carlos: I've got an idea. *(leaves the table, huddles with Ms. Singh, then returns with the jar)* Let's get to work! Latisha, you're going to write about the Phantom Poet.

(Light fades, then comes up on group sitting at the same table, this time covered with small squares of paper. Latisha and Michael are frowning at notes in their hands.)

Michael: I'm stumped. What do we have so far?

Carlos: The poet's got to be an adult. Check the style—no one our age writes this way.

Latisha: I think Carlos is right. They're too literary for a kid.

Michael: Mmm . . . literary . . . *(studies Ms. Singh, others follow his gaze)*

Draw Conclusions
Who does Michael think is the Phantom Poet?

Rhonda: You think Ms. Singh might be the Phantom Poet?

Latisha: There's only one way to find out. *(leaves the table to confer with Ms. Singh)*

Ms. Singh: How can I help you, Latisha?

Latisha: Um . . . Can I get a list of contemporary women journalists? I'm interested in reading about them.

Ms. Singh: No problem. *(consults her computer, writes something on a piece of paper, and hands it to Latisha)*

Latisha: *(returning to the table, waving paper)* I've got a writing sample. Now we can compare Ms. Singh's handwriting with the writing on the couplets.

(Heads bend over the writing sample.)

Michael: (**despondently**) It's not her. The poet's *e*'s have this little flourish. Not one of these *e*'s has that.

Latisha: *(disappointed)* Let's call it a day. Think about any adult who fits the profile of the poet. Tomorrow's Saturday. We can all meet at my house at 10:00 A.M. We've got to find the Phantom Poet!

Fade out.

SCENE 3

The next morning, Latisha's living room; Michael tosses a basketball. Kids are seated on the floor.

Michael: I hope you know I'm going to be late for basketball practice. Let's get started.

Carlos: *(clears throat)* You're going to thank me for this. I must admit my sleuthing has been pretty brilliant.

Michael: Speed it up, please.

Carlos: The poet's Mr. Tolliver.

All: Mr. Tolliver!

Carlos: Think about it. He's always giving us pep talks and little lessons at every opportunity.

Rhonda: But poems? How are we going to find out for sure? Latisha's deadline is Tuesday morning.

Carlos: Didn't I say I was brilliant? *(pulls paper from his pocket)* I suspected Mr. Tolliver on my way home, so I stopped by his office and asked him if he could write me an excuse for first period when I have to help put away sports equipment. Note the word *equipment*. Note it has two *e*'s.

Michael: Let's have it.

Carlos: Did I hear, "Thank you"?

Michael: *(snatching the note)* Thank you! *(He studies the note.)* Did you look at this, Einstein? The *e*'s are different.

Carlos: All right, they're different but check out the *a*'s. They look pretty similar.

(*Latisha also studies the note.*)

Latisha: No way, Carlos! Not at all!

Rhonda: (*continues studying the notes while the others argue*) Hold the phone! Check this out. Every single couplet has something to do with food or flowers. (*recites*) A time sweet as mangoes will resume; Take heart, a new day will chase your gloom. (*pause*) That was mine last winter—stuffed in my locker when my parents temporarily separated and I was all depressed.

Latisha: Who'd you confide in?

Rhonda: Only Miss Mackey in the caf . . . e . . . te . . . ri . . . a.

Carlos: Yeah, she's really great. And she always smells like . . . (*pause, as the kids look at one another*)

All: . . . flowers!

Latisha: (*thoughtfully*) Miss Mackey . . . Miss Mackey . . . Food, flowers . . . Looks like I have to go see Miss Mackey first thing Monday morning.

Fade out.

SCENE 4

Monday morning, the school cafeteria; Miss Mackey, in a hairnet and apron, with a pen and clipboard, is doing inventory. Latisha stands for a moment looking at her. She notes Miss Mackey's sweater with a flower in the lapel.

Latisha: It's you, isn't it?

Miss Mackey: Pardon me?

Latisha: You're the Phantom Poet. It all fits. *(points at the flower, waves her hand over the room)* Flowers . . . food . . . it's you.

Miss Mackey: *(sitting down, heavily)* Smart girl. Yes, it's me. I'm the poet. In fact, I've had a few of my poems published in *The Town Caller.*

Latisha: But without your name.

Miss Mackey: I never wanted a fuss. My reward comes from all of you. Giving you the right words when you need it.

Latisha: *(softly)* Miss Mackey, I want to write about you. I know it's for a selfish reason. Delia Marcus and I are finalists for the newspaper competition. We've got to write competing human interest stories to decide the winner. I want to be the winner, Miss Mackey, and your story will give me a good shot.

Miss Mackey: I can tell you my story, Latisha, but you can't give away my identity.

Latisha: I won't reveal your name.

Miss Mackey: Let's just say someone helped me with the right words when I needed it. I'm simply passing along the favor my way.

Latisha: Tell me more, Miss Mackey.

Both sit down to talk, quietly. Fade out.

SCENE 5

Mr. Tolliver's office; he's sitting behind his desk while Delia and Latisha stand holding their stories.

Mr. Tolliver: I look forward to your stories. And I'm curious about whom you chose to write about.

Delia: *(stepping forward, confidently)* I did my piece on Coach Greer, three time Most Valuable Player on his college basketball team, and the driving force behind our championship for the last two years.

Latisha: I chose the Phantom Poet.

Delia: *(shocked)* What?

Latisha: I found out who the poet is and interviewed *(pause)* the poet. The poet chooses to remain **anonymous** for personal reasons but I still got a great story. My article is about the rewards of writing words of inspiration to kids who need it.

Delia: How do we know you're not just making it up?

Mr. Tolliver: I'll know—since I, too, know the identity of the Phantom Poet. *(smiles at Latisha)* You'll have my decision by Friday. Good luck, girls.

Latisha: *(extending a hand to Delia; Delia takes it)* May the better story win.

Fade out.

353

Starring Karen and Nicole

Karen English has four children and has taught school for many years. She knows the joys and the problems of growing up. She used this reservoir of memory, and perhaps the psychology she studied in college, to write this play. It was clever the way she didn't quite tell us the ending. She knew it was a better story letting the reader guess who might win— Delia or Latisha. Whom do you want to win?

Nicole Tadgell was born in Highland Park, Michigan, and now makes her home in Spencer, Massachusetts, with her husband, Mark, and two border terriers. She has illustrated numerous books and is the winner of the Children's Africana Book Award for illustrating *Fatuma's New Cloth*.

LOG ON Find out more about Karen English and Nicole Tadgell at **www.macmillanmh.com**

Author's Purpose

A play is meant to be performed as entertainment. What text features tell you that this piece is a play and may be performed?

Comprehension Check

Summarize

Use your Conclusions Chart to help you summarize *The Case of the Phantom Poet*. What is the most important information in each scene?

Text Clues	Conclusion

Think and Compare

1. In what way was Miss Mackey someone who was "of special significance to the school"? Use information from the text to support your answer. **Monitor Comprehension: Draw Conclusions**

2. Miss Mackey mentions that someone once helped her with the right words. If that person were another character in the play, who do you think that person might be? **Evaluate**

3. The Phantom Poet chooses to remain **anonymous**. If you were the Phantom Poet, why would you choose to keep your identity a secret? **Synthesize**

4. Do you think small acts of kindness can make a difference in people's lives? Why or why not? **Evaluate**

5. Read "The Unusual Robot" on pages 338-339. How do the students in this story accomplish their goal? How are their methods similar to those of Latisha and her friends? **Reading/ Writing Across Texts**

Math

Genre

Informational Nonfiction can give instructions or directions with clear details.

Text Feature

Tables present information visually using rows (across) and columns (down).

Content Vocabulary

estimate
random sample
representative sample
biased sample

Students Who Would Attend _Annie_

Method of Selecting Sample	Percent
Frank asked 50 of his friends.	30%
Sue put the names of all sixth-grade students in a hat and selected 50 names from the hat.	80%
Ellen put the names of all the students in a hat and selected 50 names from the hat.	60%

This table shows the data from the surveys.

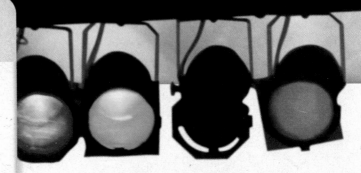

How to Conduct a Survey

Frank, Sue, and Ellen conducted surveys to **estimate** how many students in their school would attend a student production of _Annie_. What is the best prediction (or guess) for the percentage of students in the whole school that would attend _Annie_?

In a **random sample**, a group of subjects (a sample) is selected from a total group of people (a population). Each subject is chosen completely by chance and each member of the total group (the population) has an equal chance of being included in the sample. When you pick names out of a bag without looking, you are selecting a random sample of the names in the bag.

Ellen took a random sample of all the students in the school. Each student had an equal chance of being chosen. Frank and Sue did not take random samples.

In their samples, each student in the school did not have an equal chance of being selected.

A sample that gives you a good idea of what a total group (whole population) is like is called a **representative sample**.

A sample that does not represent the total group is called a **biased sample**. For example, Frank asked only his friends, and Sue asked only sixth-grade students.

Ellen's method is most likely to represent the total school. It is the best one to use for predicting (or guessing) the percentage of students in the school who would attend *Annie*. The best prediction is 60%.

Connect and Compare

1. Look at the table on page 356. What percentage of sixth-grade students would be likely to attend *Annie*? **Reading a Table**

2. Which method would you use to conduct a survey? Why? **Evaluate**

3. How should the students in *The Case of the Phantom Poet* plan and conduct a survey to find out who everyone thinks the mystery poet is? **Reading/Writing Across Texts**

Math Activity

Conduct a survey of your own. Include a random sample and a biased sample. Present your findings using a table.

 Find out more about surveys at **www.macmillanmh.com**

Writer's Craft

Tone

When you are writing a scene, you may set the tone you want by using sentence fragments because that is how people actually speak. Dialogue should always sound natural.

I used fragments and complete sentences to set the tone in my dialogue.

I tried to make the dialogue in the scene sound natural.

The Science Lesson

by Amelia L.

TIME: The present

SETTING: A sixth-grade classroom

Mr. Rosario: Please turn to page 303 in your books.

Nolan: (whispering to Tony) Where is it? Show it to me.

Tony: (pointing to his left hand) Here.

Mr. Rosario: Yesterday we read about amphibians. Who can name an amphibian? Kay?

Kay: A frog?

Mr. Rosario: Very good. Any other examples?

Jade: Toads are amphibians.

Mr. Rosario: That's right. (He turns to the board.)

Tony: No! Wait! (He dives under his desk.)

Mr. Rosario: (turning) Excuse me?

Nolan: I think he dropped something.

Mr. Rosario: Tony? What are you doing?

Tony: (going after something) Don't move, anyone!

Kay: (pointing) What's that moving like lightning?

Nolan: If only she knew.

Tony: (getting up with his hands cupped) Got it!

Mr. Rosario: Tony, what's going on?

Tony: (with hesitation) Oh, well . . . I have an amphibian. Would you like to see my frog?

Your Turn

Write a scene from a play. Try to make the dialogue sound natural, and set the tone by using both fragments and sentences. Your scene can be made-up or something that actually happened. Use the Writer's Checklist to check your writing.

Writer's Checklist

✓ **Ideas and Content:** Is it clear what is happening in my scene?

✓ **Organization:** Do the events and dialogue proceed naturally?

✓ **Voice:** Do the voices of my characters come through?

✓ **Word Choice:** Did I choose words that my characters would really use?

 ☑ **Sentence Fluency:** Did my use of fragments help establish the **tone** of my dialogue?

✓ **Conventions:** Did I punctuate my scene correctly? Did I check my spelling?

Test Strategy

Author and Me
The answer is not directly stated. Connect the clues to figure it out.

HOLLYWOOD HERE YOU COME

Step 1: Find a Director

There is an old saying that everybody has a story to tell.

The first movie cameras were invented way back before the turn of the twentieth century. They were bulky wood and metal contraptions; indeed, some were as big as pieces of furniture. A filmmaker had to crank the camera to turn the film, and the lighting had to be perfect.

Now because of amazing new technology, anyone can make movies! Digital video cameras, special computer software, and even camera phones are available to beginning filmmakers.

Alfred Hitchcock, legendary director of suspense movies, once said, "Drama is life with the dull bits cut out." Hitchcock certainly knew what he was talking about. He directed some of the cleverest and most exciting movies ever made, such as *The Lady Vanishes* and *The Man Who Knew Too Much*. Not all movies need to be complicated mysteries or action-packed adventures. There are many different kinds of movies. These categories are called genres. Some examples of movie genres are comedy, history, documentary, and, of course, drama. Often the most creative movies are those that break the mold and try something new.

Go On ▶

Step 2: Choose a Script

Movie critics say that good movies start with good scripts. Scripts, or screenplays, are the written version of the story. Dialogue, or what the characters in the movie say to each other, is the heart and soul of a movie script. Sounds, special effects, and music are also important.

Do you ever find yourself quoting classic movie lines to a friend? That all goes back to the work of a talented scriptwriter. Scripts are written in a unique way that makes them easy for actors to read and easy for the director to know what each scene should look like.

Step 3: Cast the Movie

The next step is to cast the movie. In Hollywood, there are people who spend all their time deciding which actors will be best for each part. The actors are important because they stay in the audience's memory long after the movie is over. Hold auditions to find the perfect person to play each character in the movie.

Step 4: Build the Set

Getting ready to shoot a movie is a lot of work. Many things need to be done before the cast and crew even arrive for the first day of filming. What shows up on screen depends on how well you plan the shoot. A shoot, when a director and actors get together to film the scenes of a movie, can be done in a studio or on location. A studio is a place that can be changed to fit whatever scene you are shooting. On location is when you film the scene in the place where it happens, or a place that looks like it.

For example, if the story takes place on the moon, you can shoot in a location that looks like the moon. You could even create your own moon set in the studio. The settings for the story are limited only by your imagination—and your ingenuity.

There are many kinds of movie directors. Some enjoy working closely with actors, and others enjoy letting the actors do their own thing. Regardless of directing style, it is the director's job to help the actors deliver the finest performances they can.

Step 5: Edit the Movie

In the can means a movie is done shooting. Still, there is more work to be done. Experts work many hours to put the different pieces of a movie together. Once the shoot is over, editors and mixers use computers to add sounds, music, and special effects. Then the film companies make posters, create commercials, and have press conferences to promote the movie.

Luckily, not every great movie needs special effects and press conferences. Many movies can be made with a crew of only a few people and a cast of just one person. That is the magic of the movies, especially today! Whichever genre you choose, filmmaking can be an art form.

Now set up the camera, point the lens, and get the actors in their places. Ready! Set! Action!

Go On ▶

Tip

Connect the clues or ideas from the selection to choose the best answer.

Directions: Answer the questions.

1. Based on the selection, which conclusion can you draw about making a movie?

A Choosing the actors is the most important part of making a movie.

B Every movie made today uses special effects.

C Good directors never tell the actors what to do.

D Preparing to shoot a movie and editing a movie require a lot of skill and planning.

2. What are some things that might stop a movie from being made on time?

A The script contains a lot of dialogue and the director wants to hear the actors read it aloud.

B The cast and crew want to work seven days a week.

C The film critics give the movie a bad review.

D The cast and crew must film outdoors, and the weather prevents them from working.

3. Which does not affect the cost of producing a movie?

A Digital cameras are very expensive.

B Shooting on location is very costly.

C The price of movie tickets has gone up.

D A lot of food is required to feed the cast and crew.

4. How has movie making become easier over time?

5. Do you think anyone can make a movie? Why or why not? Explain your response in two paragraphs, using examples from the selection in your answer.

Writing Prompt

What would it be like to be a movie director? Write a journal entry in which you describe one day on the set. Your entry should be at least three paragraphs.

UNCOMMON CHAMPIONS

Talk About It

All runners face challenges during races. How do you think the champion in this photo deals with challenges?

LOG ON Find out more about uncommon champions at **www.macmillanmh.com**

Vocabulary

typical	deteriorated
specialists	maturity
peripheral	summit
guidance	awesome

Context Clues

Synonyms are words with the same or nearly the same meanings. For example, *side* and *peripheral* are synonyms. When you come across an unfamiliar word, check to see if there is a synonym for it in the same paragraph.

Bethany Hamilton's COMEBACK

by Cesar Aparicio

Bethany Hamilton has never been a **typical** surfer like all the others. She surfs "goofy footed," with her right foot in front. Now, even more so, she goes against the norm. She surfs with one arm!

One day in late October, Bethany was surfing at Hawaii's Tunnel Beach. Around 7:30 A.M., a tiger shark attacked Bethany, biting off her left arm. Bethany was rushed to the hospital where **specialists** in limb loss worked on her injury.

Before her attack, Bethany was ranked second from her area in amateur surfing and was thought of as one of the best new women surfers. She hoped to become a professional surfer. To further her plans, Bethany was homeschooled, which gave her more time to surf.

Bethany didn't put her plans for the future to the side. She would not let the attack put her in a **peripheral** position. Instead, she moved back into the limelight when she returned to the water about four weeks after the attack. Three months later, she received a prosthetic arm and competed nationally.

She competed in the National Scholastic Surfing Association meet in Hawaii and took fifth place. In worldwide competitions, she shows her **maturity**, or development, as a person and as a surfer, refusing to let her work before the attack represent the **summit**, or peak, of her surfing career. She continues to progress with each contest. "I'm an athlete first, with a great second story," Bethany said to a reporter.

With the help and **guidance** of both her coach and her father, Bethany has been encouraged to keep up the sport and she continues to improve. Because she returned so quickly and works so hard, her surfing skills have not **deteriorated**.

Bethany has received an award as best comeback athlete, which is proof of her athletic ability and a testament to her personal strength. This young woman is an **awesome** example for athletes around the world. She is a picture of courage and grace in the face of tremendous challenges.

Reread for **Comprehension**

Evaluate

Author's Purpose
One way to evaluate a text is to examine the author's purpose. An author usually has one main purpose for writing. He or she might want to entertain, inform or persuade.

Use the Author's Purpose Chart as you reread "Bethany Hamilton's Comeback" to identify the author's purpose.

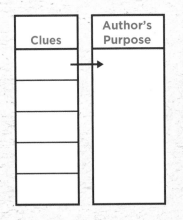

Comprehension

Genre

A **Biography** tells the story of a person's life written by another person.

Evaluate

Author's Purpose

As you read, use your Author's Purpose Chart.

Clues	Author's Purpose
→	

Read to Find Out

Why do you think the author wrote about Erik Weihenmayer?

Seeing Things His Own Way

by Marty Kaminsky

Erik Weihenmayer thrust his ice ax into the deep snow, hoping to grip a hold long enough to catch his breath. The howling winds, gusting up to 100 miles per hour, roared like a fleet of jet planes. To communicate with his climbing partners, Erik had to scream to be heard. It was only 3,000 more feet to the **summit**, but Erik's team was hopelessly trapped for five days in a blizzard on the high slopes of Mt. McKinley.

At 20,320 feet, Alaska's Mt. McKinley is the highest peak in North America. Freezing temperatures, sudden avalanches, and devastating storms make it one of the most difficult mountains in the world to climb. Nearly one hundred climbers have lost their lives there after falling into deep crevasses or being blown off the face by gale-force winds. For even the most experienced mountaineers and rugged explorers, climbing McKinley is the challenge of a lifetime.

Imagine climbing such a treacherous peak without being able to see a single step. That is the task that Erik Weihenmayer faced in June 1995. Erik is completely blind, having lost his vision at age thirteen due to a condition he was born with called retinoschisis. But blindness has never stopped him from living an exciting life and pursuing adventures most of us only dream about.

"I am not a daredevil," Erik explains. "I have a healthy fear and respect of the mountains, but I believe with proper training and skill a blind person can tackle some **awesome** challenges."

From a young age, life itself proved to be a challenge for Erik. When he was a three-month-old baby, Erik's eyes began to quiver and shake. His parents were alarmed and brought him to teams of **specialists** over a year and a half. The doctors diagnosed his problem as retinoschisis, a rare condition that causes pressure to build in the retina until it disintegrates, eventually leading to blindness. To view something directly in front of him Erik would have to look up, down, or sideways. He relied on his **peripheral** (side) vision to navigate his neighborhood and to do daily chores and tasks.

Erik at a base camp on Mt. McKinley

But Erik hated to be treated differently, so he learned to compensate for his poor vision. When he played basketball with friends, they helped him cover the court by playing zone defenses. They also learned to feed him the ball with a bounce pass. "Erik would hear a bounce pass," his father, Ed Weihenmayer, explains. "But lots of passes hit him in the face anyway. After most games Erik had a bloody nose and looked as if he was playing football, not basketball."

With the help of family and friends, Erik was encouraged to find creative ways to participate in everyday activities. When his brothers raced their mountain bikes over a ramp, Erik joined in, but sometimes he rode off the edge, picking up scraped knees for his efforts. Though he rarely complained or showed his frustration, Erik's family was aware of his struggles. His father solved the bike problem by painting the ramp bright orange. After two more months of bike stunts on the ramp, however, Erik's eyesight had **deteriorated** to the point that the ramp became an orange blur. He rode off his driveway one day and broke his arm.

Despite his failing vision Erik continued his attempts to blend in and be like everyone else. Frequently he walked into trees or doors, and he had constant bruises and black-and-blue shins. "I guess it was a lack of **maturity** on my part," Erik admits. "It was a sense of denial. I refused to learn to read Braille or to use a cane, even though I needed one for my own safety."

By the time he was thirteen, Erik's eyesight was completely gone. At first he tried to function without the use of canes or visual aids, but that proved dangerous. While visiting his grandparents, he stepped off a dock and fell eight feet into a boat. Though unharmed by the incident, it shook him up. Out of sheer desperation, Erik came to accept his blindness.

"I realized that if I got good at using the systems for the blind I would blend in better and be more like everyone else," he says. "If I didn't use my cane I would be stumbling about, and that would make me stand out more."

Erik and his dog, Wizard

Machu Picchu

At fifteen Erik joined his high school's wrestling team. Because the sport depends on physical contact, strength, and instinct, Erik found he could compete on even terms with his opponents. He did not win a match as a freshman, but by his senior year he was chosen team captain and sported a 30-3-3 record. He was selected to represent Connecticut in the National Freestyle Wrestling Championships and went on to wrestle at Boston College.

Just as Erik was beginning to accept his blindness and learning to function in a sightless world, tragedy struck hard. While he was away at summer wrestling camp, Erik's mother was killed in an automobile accident. The loss was devastating, but Erik's father exerted extra efforts to spend more time with his children. As a way to bring the family closer, Ed Weihenmayer brought his children together for adventurous treks around the world. Among many other journeys, they visited the Batura Glacier in Pakistan and the Inca ruins at Machu Picchu in Peru.

"Facing his mother's death and blindness so close together was difficult," Ed recalls. "But Erik never used them as an excuse for not measuring up and going for it." Rock-climbing trips to New Hampshire and other travels with his family whet Erik's appetite for adventure. He soon became a skillful rock climber, scuba diver, and sky diver.

After getting his master's degree from Lesley College in Massachusetts, Erik was hired to teach at an elementary school in Phoenix, Arizona. Managing a class of lively fifth graders was a challenge equal to any Erik had undertaken, but he loved his work and handled it well. "My dad worked on Wall Street for thirty years," he says. "He struggled to

Erik with students

find meaning in his work. I don't have that struggle as a teacher." The students in his classes quickly realize that Erik needs their help to make learning work for them. With his **guidance** they devise systems to communicate and get things done. Students pitch in taking turns writing on the board, hanging posters, and passing out papers. Although the class could take advantage of their sightless teacher, they rarely do. In fact, they fall over each other to be the first to fill his dog's water bowl.

As he settled into his teaching job, Erik and a buddy filled their weekends with climbing trips to the rock faces and mountains of Arizona. On the higher slopes Erik and his partners devised a climbing language that the lead climber would call out. If a teammate shouted, "Iceberg ahead," for example, Erik understood that a pointy rock sticking out of the ground was in his path. A cry of "ankle breaker" meant that little loose rocks lay ahead. By learning to follow in the footsteps of his partners and to rely on his other senses, Erik took on the tallest peaks in Africa and North and South America with his climbing friends.

Author's Purpose
What details does the author include to inform the reader about Erik's life as a teacher and a rock climber?

Erik rock climbing at the Phoenix, Arizona, Bouldering Competition

"Feeling the rock under my hand, feeling the wind and sensing I am hundreds of feet above tree line is an incredible experience," Erik says. "It's exciting to work on a team for a common goal." So great is his love of the mountains that Erik and his wife, Ellen, were wed at a rock altar 13,000 feet up the slopes of Mt. Kilimanjaro in Tanzania.

But pulling yourself up a sheer rock wall, balancing on an icy ridge, and handling sub-zero temperatures can prove frustrating for any mountaineer, particularly one who is blind. While climbing Mt. Rainier in 1985 Erik discovered he could not set up his tent in the freezing weather with his bulky gloves covering his hands. In **typical** fashion he refused to admit failure. "I was so embarrassed that I resolved never to let that happen again," he says. "When I returned to Phoenix I practiced setting up a tent in the one-hundred-degree heat with gloves on over and over. It is no longer a problem for me."

Careful planning and practice have always helped Erik work around the problems caused by his lack of vision. To prepare for the risky climb up Mt. McKinley, Erik's team practiced on Mt. Rainier in Washington and Long's Peak in Colorado. Back in Phoenix, Erik and a teammate strapped on fifty-pound packs and raced up and down the stairs of a forty-story skyscraper to build strength and endurance.

Before the McKinley trip Erik's climbing group, which called itself Team High Sights, secured the sponsorship of the American Foundation for the Blind. "I was hopeful that my climb would make a statement," Erik says.

Author's Purpose
Why does the author include the anecdotes about setting up the tent and running up the skyscraper's stairs?

Erik(right) in an igloo on Mt. McKinley at 17,000 feet.

Huddling in their ice-coated tents at 17,000 feet, Team High Sights was forced to wait out a five-day storm on Mt. McKinley. Their food supply was dwindling and all that could be seen of the summit was a plume of snow blowing hundreds of feet into the air. Unless the storm let up, all hope of reaching the summit would have to be abandoned. On the sixth day they heard on their weather radio the news they'd been waiting for: There would be a twelve-hour period of clear weather in which to reach the summit and return before the next storm system closed off the mountain.

Strapping on their ice shoes and insulated gear, the climbers tied themselves together with sturdy rope. Pushing through thigh-deep snow was exhausting work, but Team High Sights carefully moved up the mountain. For Erik, the climb to the summit seemed endless. At the top of a knife-edge ridge his ski pole slipped and all he could feel was air. "I was concentrating very hard with each step," he explains. "Finally I took a step and my friend Stacey said, 'Congratulations, you're on the top of North America.'"

With tears in their eyes, the climbers embraced and snapped photographs of each other. Erik held aloft a pair of banners—one designed by a girl at his school, and one for the American Foundation for the Blind. After fifteen minutes at the peak, the team headed down, safely making their way back to a lower camp.

The climb to the top of Mt. McKinley was a proud accomplishment for Erik, and one that he hopes provides inspiration for others. "Before McKinley I never thought I was extremely tough," Erik says. "I always felt I had the potential to do much more. I hope my climb proves that we can all push beyond what we think we can do."

Having climbed McKinley, the highest mountain in North America, Erik is well on the way to meeting one of his climbing goals. In the next few years he plans to summit the highest peak on each continent, including Mt. Everest in Asia. He has learned to step around every obstacle in his path, and though it will be a difficult task, Erik knows there is no reason a blind man cannot sit atop the tallest mountain in the world.

Erik reached his goal of climbing Mt. Everest in 2001.

On Top of the World with Marty Kaminsky

Marty Kaminsky is an elementary school teacher who loves to write. He started by writing for magazines, such as *Highlights* and *Sports Illustrated for Kids*. When he heard stories about athletes who are physically challenged, he was hooked. He had to write about them, he said, for his children, and for the children he has taught through the years. He says, "They are the reason I write anything at all."

Find out more about Marty Kaminsky at **www.macmillanmh.com**

Author's Purpose

This selection is a biography. Its main purpose is to give information about a person's life. Why might this piece also be persuasive?

Comprehension Check

Summarize

Summarize "Seeing Things His Own Way." Tell about the different situations that Erik Weihenmayer faced from childhood to adulthood.

Think and Compare

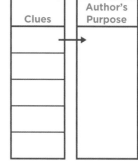

Clues	Author's Purpose

1. Why do you think the author included a section about Erik's childhood and his family? Use your Author's Purpose Chart to support your answer. **Evaluate: Author's Purpose**

2. Of all of Erik Weihenmayer's accomplishments, which do you find to be the most inspiring? Why? Support your answer. **Analyze**

3. Think about a time when you overcame a difficulty. What obstacles did you encounter? How did your experience contribute to your **maturity**? **Evaluate**

4. What, above all, is the message of "Seeing Things His Own Way?" Use references from the text to support your answer. **Synthesize**

5. Read "Bethany Hamilton's Comeback" on pages 366-367. If Bethany Hamilton were to meet Erik Weihenmayer, what do you think they might discuss with each other? **Reading/Writing Across Texts**

Amazing Artificial Limbs

by Jackie Glassman

Your day is full of activities you probably don't think much about, such as brushing your teeth, eating breakfast, walking to school, and riding your bike. Now imagine how you would accomplish these tasks if you were missing a limb, an arm or a leg.

Some people have lost limbs because of accidents or have had them **amputated** because of a disease. Other people are just born that way.

Throughout history, inventors have been developing **artificial** limbs, known as prostheses. A mechanically-operated arm was invented as early as the 1940s.

Today's modern medical **technology** has led to the development of new materials, advances in computers, and a greater understanding of the body. Many body parts can now be replaced with artificial ones that work almost as well as the originals. The science of designing electronic limbs is called **bionics**. New electronic limbs make it possible for people to control their artificial limbs in highly effective ways. These high-tech devices are improving the lives of many people.

Diamond Excell and Her Bionic Arms

Diamond Excell had to write, eat, and even brush her teeth with her feet because she was born without shoulders or arms. Then on her eleventh birthday, Diamond received a wonderful gift. She was fitted with myoelectric arms designed by inventor Ivan Yaeger.

How an Artificial Arm Works

SKILL

Reading a Diagram

This diagram shows an artificial arm. Inside are tiny electrical parts, motors, and batteries. Gears and motors inside allow the artificial arm to bend and work.

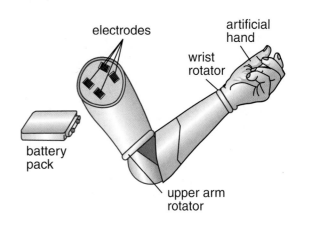

electrodes

artificial hand

wrist rotator

battery pack

upper arm rotator

The natural-looking limbs have tiny electrical parts and motors inside that made it possible for Diamond to hug her mother for the first time. By moving muscles in her back, Diamond creates electrical signals that control motors inside the prostheses. Each arm has motors that open and close the joints. The wrists and the elbows are designed so that when Diamond walks, her arms swing freely and naturally.

Until recently artificial legs were very low-tech. They were mainly controlled by the body's normal walking movements, which required a lot of energy. Today a myoelectric leg, like the myoelectric arm, is controlled by a person's muscles.

However, this is not as easy as it sounds. People with artificial limbs must go through lots of training to learn how to effectively control their replacement limbs. With the help of a myoelectric leg, many people can now participate in sports such as basketball and running.

With ongoing advances in science and technology, society can look forward to huge improvements in artificial limbs. For example, new materials allow prosthetic feet to press and spring much like real feet. One type of artificial foot transmits electronic information about pressure to the person using it. Feeling pressure helps people to balance because they can tell whether their weight is on the toes, heels, or sides of the feet.

Looking into the Future

In the very near future, scientists hope to create bionic limbs so that Diamond and others will have a first-rate sense of touch, making their artificial limbs that much closer to the real thing.

Connect and Compare

1. Look at the text and diagram on page 383. How do you think the wrist rotator works? **Reading a Diagram**

2. What improvements do you think can still be made to artificial limbs? **Evaluate**

3. How is Erik Weihenmayer's determination in "Seeing Things His Own Way" like Diamond's? **Reading/Writing Across Texts**

Science Activity

Research information about a high-tech innovation. Draw a diagram with accurate labels illustrating the innovation.

 Find out more about bionics at **www.macmillanmh.com**

Writer's Craft

A Strong Conclusion

State your main idea near the beginning. Follow with supporting details that relate to the main idea. End with a **strong conclusion** that connects to the introduction.

Interviewing a WINNER

The Reward of Helping Others

by LeShante B.

The first sentence states my main idea about my friend Jarvis.

My friend Jarvis may not have trophies or medals, but he feels like a winner when he's helping others.

LeShante: What is your proudest accomplishment?

Jarvis: Volunteering at the nursing home each week is my proudest accomplishment. I help people feel better.

LeShante: What do you do there?

Jarvis: I read to people and tell them about myself. They also tell me about themselves. We play games together.

LeShante: What do you enjoy doing most?

Jarvis: Once a month the volunteers help organize a special Bowling Night in the cafeteria. We form teams and even have prizes. Everyone has a great time. I also enjoy talking to older people because they have a lot of stories. You can learn a lot from them.

LeShante: Why would you encourage others to volunteer?

I included a strong conclusion about Jarvis.

Jarvis: It's a good way to serve the community, and you really gain from volunteering. I've made new friends and they're always happy to see me when I visit. I look forward to it each week.

Don't you agree with me that Jarvis is an outstanding winner?

Your Turn

Everyone is a winner in some way. Interview a classmate with three questions about his or her proudest accomplishment. Take notes and include his or her answers in your work. Be sure to provide supporting details for your main idea. Include a strong conclusion. Use the Writer's Checklist to check your work.

Writer's Checklist

☑ **Ideas and Content:** Did I ask questions about my subject's proudest accomplishment? Did I include a **strong conclusion**?

✓ **Organization:** Did I record details that supported my main idea?

✓ **Voice:** Did I include words and phrases that make the writing sound like me?

✓ **Word Choice:** Did I use descriptive words?

✓ **Sentence Fluency:** Did I vary the length of my sentences?

✓ **Conventions:** Did I make sure that all my pronouns agree with their antecedents? Did I check my spelling?

oceano

graphy

Vocabulary

edgy	formations
clockwise	intact
hovering	severed
interior	wreckage

Word Parts

A **Suffix** is added to the end of a word to change its meaning.

edge + y = on edge; nervous

Waves

by Alicia Reese

Part of Earth's beauty comes from its oceans. Oceanographers study the chemical makeup of the ocean as well as the currents in water, weather patterns, the geography of the ocean floor, and many other areas. Oceanographers' work is exciting, although sometimes it can be dangerous and cause them to become **edgy.** Using technology to do certain tasks helps. For example, robotic arms that rotate **clockwise** are sometimes used for the most dangerous tasks.

One basic part of oceanography is understanding waves and how they work. Sometimes ocean life can be seen in the wave. Creatures seem to be **hovering** within the **interior** of the wave, floating inside it as if they were weightless. Besides the beauty of waves, scientists are interested in their technical aspects. The diagram (right) shows how scientists examine waves.

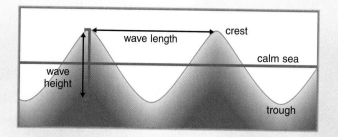

Waves are measured from the top (crest) to the bottom (trough). This allows scientists to find out the height of a wave. They also measure from crest to crest to determine the length of each wave.

Waves are classified by their height, length, and frequency. Some common kinds of waves are chop, swell, shallow, deep, and tsunami. Waves are created by specific conditions. The conditions that affect **formations** of waves include the ocean's temperature and depth, the wind's strength and speed, and the geological conditions of the area. Conditions must be favorable for certain kinds of waves to form, keep their shape, and remain **intact.**

A wave's height and length are directly related to its wind speed and duration, or how long it has been blowing. When it is really windy during a big storm, the waves grow in height and shrink in length.

During severe storms, huge and frequent waves might cut a sea vessel apart. Ships are at great risk of winding up as **severed** pieces after being hit by the force of a huge wave. By understanding the ocean, scientists can prevent this **wreckage** of ships by predicting when the water will be too dangerous for people and their ships.

The study of waves and the ocean also allows oceanographers to determine how certain beaches were formed. By studying the oceans a great deal can be learned about the surface we live on.

Reread for **Comprehension**

Evaluate

Fact and Opinion

In order to evaluate information in a text, it is important to know what is fact and what is opinion. A fact is something that can be proven true. An opinion is what someone thinks, feels, or believes. Nonfiction selections include facts, but may include some opinions, too.

Use your Fact and Opinion Chart as you reread "Waves."

Fact	Opinion

Comprehension

Genre

An **Autobiography** tells the story of a person's life written by that person.

Evaluate

Fact and Opinion

As you read, use your Fact and Opinion Chart.

Fact	Opinion

Read to Find Out

What is so fascinating about Robert D. Ballard's life?

The ocean liner R.M.S. *Titanic* was built in 1911 and deemed "virtually unsinkable." However, on its maiden voyage in 1912, the ship struck an iceberg in the North Atlantic and sank, killing 1,500 of the 2,200 passengers aboard. In 1985, Robert D. Ballard and his team discovered the remains of the *Titanic* on the ocean floor. A year later, the team returned to explore the ship in their submarine *Alvin*, with the help of *Jason Jr.*, or *JJ*, their robot.

EXPLORING THE
TITANIC

Our second view of the *Titanic* was breathtaking. As we glided soundlessly across the ocean bottom, the razor's edge of the bow loomed out of the darkness. The great ship towered above us. Suddenly it seemed to be coming right at us, about to run us over. My first reaction was that we had to get out of the way. But the *Titanic* wasn't going anywhere. As we gently brought our sub closer, we could see the bow more clearly. Both of her huge anchors were still in place. But the bow was buried more than sixty feet in mud, far too deep for anyone to pull her out of the ooze.

bow of the *Titanic*

It looked as though the metal hull was slowly melting away. What seemed like frozen rivers of rust covered the ship's side and spread out over the ocean bottom. It was almost as if the blood of the great ship lay in pools on the ocean floor.

As *Alvin* rose in slow motion up the ghostly side of the ship, I could see our lights reflecting off the still-unbroken glass of the *Titanic*'s portholes. They made me think of cats' eyes gleaming in the dark. In places the rust **formations** over the portholes looked like eyelashes with tears, as though the *Titanic* were crying. I could also see a lot of reddish-brown stalactites of rust over the wreck, like long icicles. I decided to call them "rusticles." This rust turned out to be very fragile. If touched by our sub, it disappeared like a cloud of smoke.

As we rose further and began to move across the mighty forward deck, I was amazed at the sheer size of everything: giant bollards and shiny bronze capstans that were used for winding ropes and cables; the huge links of the anchor chains. When you were there on the spot, the ship was truly titanic.

starboard railing

STRATEGY SKILL

Fact and Opinion
Is the first sentence on this page fact or opinion? Explain.

strained to get a good look at the deck's wood planking, just four feet below us. Then my heart dropped to my stomach. "It's gone!" I muttered. Most of the *Titanic*'s wooden deck had been eaten away. Millions of little wood-eating worms had done more damage than the iceberg and the salt water. I began to wonder whether the metal deck below the destroyed wood planking would support our weight when *Alvin* landed.

We would soon find out. Slowly we moved into position to make our first landing test on the forward deck just next to the fallen mast. As we made our approach, our hearts beat quickly. We knew there was a real risk of crashing through the deck. The sub settled down, making a muffled crunching noise. If the deck gave way, we'd be trapped in collapsing **wreckage**. But it held, and we settled firmly. That meant there was a good chance that the *Titanic*'s decks would support us at other landing sites.

We carefully lifted off and turned toward the stern. The dim outline of the ship's superstructure came into view: first B Deck, then A, finally the Boat Deck—the top deck where the bridge was located. It was here that the captain and his officers had guided the ship across the Atlantic. The wooden wheelhouse was gone, probably knocked away in the sinking. But the bronze telemotor control to which the ship's wheel had once been attached stood **intact**, polished to a shine by the current. We then safely tested this second landing site.

This scale drawing shows the enormous distance between Ballard's search ship *Knorr* and the *Titanic* wreck.

437 ft/133 m
This is the deepest a scuba diver has ever gone.

1,500 ft/465 m
Naval submarines dive no deeper than this. There is no light below this level.

3,028 ft/940 m
Pioneer underwater explorers William Beebe and Otis Barton reached this depth in a ball-shaped bathysphere in 1930.

1 mile/1,609 m
Many sea creatures here are transparent or can glow in the dark.

2 miles/3,218 m
The water temperature at this depth stays a few degrees above the freezing point.

12,460 ft/3,965 m
The water pressure where the Titanic lies is approximately 6,000 lbs. per square inch.

Great Pyramid of Cheops El Gizeh, Egypt

Eiffel Tower Paris, France

Empire State Building New York, U.S.A.

Sears Tower Chicago, U.S.A.

Ostankino Tower Moscow, Russia

CN Tower Toronto, Canada

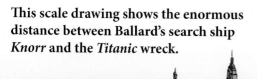

the submarine *Alvin*

I had an eerie feeling as we glided along exploring the wreck. As I peered through my porthole, I could easily imagine people walking along the deck and looking out the windows of the ship that I was looking into. Here I was at the bottom of the ocean looking at a kind of time capsule from history.

Suddenly, as we rose up the port side of the ship, the sub shuddered and made a clanging noise. A waterfall of rust covered our portholes. "We've hit something!" I exclaimed. "What is it?"

"I don't know," our pilot replied. "I'm backing off." Unseen overhangs are the nightmare of the deep-sub pilot. Carefully, the pilot backed away from the hull and brought us slowly upward. Then, directly in front of our forward porthole, a big lifeboat davit slid by. We had hit one of the metal arms that held the lifeboats as they were lowered. This davit was one of the two that had held boat No. 8, the boat Mrs. Straus had refused to enter that night. She was the wife of the owner of Macy's department store in New York. When she had been offered a chance to save herself in one of the lifeboats, she had turned to her husband and said, "We have been living together for many years. Where you go, I go." Calmly, the two of them had sat down on a pile of deck chairs to wait for the end.

steering motor on the bridge of the *Titanic*

Now, as we peered out our portholes, it seemed as if the Boat Deck were crowded with passengers. I could almost hear the cry, "Women and children first!"

We knew from the previous year's pictures that the stern had broken off the ship, so we continued back to search for the **severed** end of the intact bow section. Just beyond the gaping hole where the second funnel had been, the deck began to plunge down at a dangerous angle. The graceful lines of the ship disappeared in a twisted mess of torn steel plating, upturned potholes, and jumbled wreckage. We saw enough to know that the decks of the ship had collapsed in on one another like a giant accordion. With an unexpectedly strong current pushing us toward this twisted wreckage, we veered away and headed for the surface.

portside deck of the *Titanic*

The next day we landed on the deck next to the very edge of the Grand Staircase, which had once been covered by an elegant glass dome. The dome hadn't survived the plunge, but the staircase shaft had, and to me it still represented the fabulous luxury of the ship. *Alvin* now rested quietly on the top deck of the R.M.S. *Titanic* directly above the place where three elevators had carried first-class passengers who did not wish to use the splendid Grand Staircase.

We, however, would take the stairs with *JJ* the robot, our R2D2 of the deep. This would be the first deep-water test for our remote-controlled swimming eyeball, and we were very nervous about it. No one knew whether *JJ's* motors could stand up to the enormous ocean pressure of more than 6,000 pounds per square inch.

Using a control box with a joystick that operated like a video game, the operator cautiously steered *JJ* out of his garage attached to the front of *Alvin*. Slowly *JJ* went inching down into the yawning blackness of the Grand Staircase. More and more cable was let out as he dropped deeper and deeper.

We could see what *JJ* was seeing on our video in the sub. But at first *JJ* could see nothing. Then, as he dropped deeper, a room appeared off the portside foyer on A Deck. *JJ* swung around and our co-pilot saw something in the distance. "Look at that," he said softly. "Look at that chandelier."

the Grand Staircase in 1912

397

Now I could see it, too. "No, it can't be a chandelier," I said. "It couldn't possibly have survived."

I couldn't believe my eyes. The ship had fallen two and a half miles, hitting the bottom with the force of a train running into a mountain, and here was an almost perfectly preserved light fixture! *JJ* left the stairwell and started to enter the room, managing to get within a foot of the fixture. To our astonishment, we saw a feathery piece of coral sprouting from it. We could even see the sockets where the light bulbs had been fitted! "This is fantastic," I exulted.

Fact and Opinion
What facts and what opinions are stated in this second paragraph?

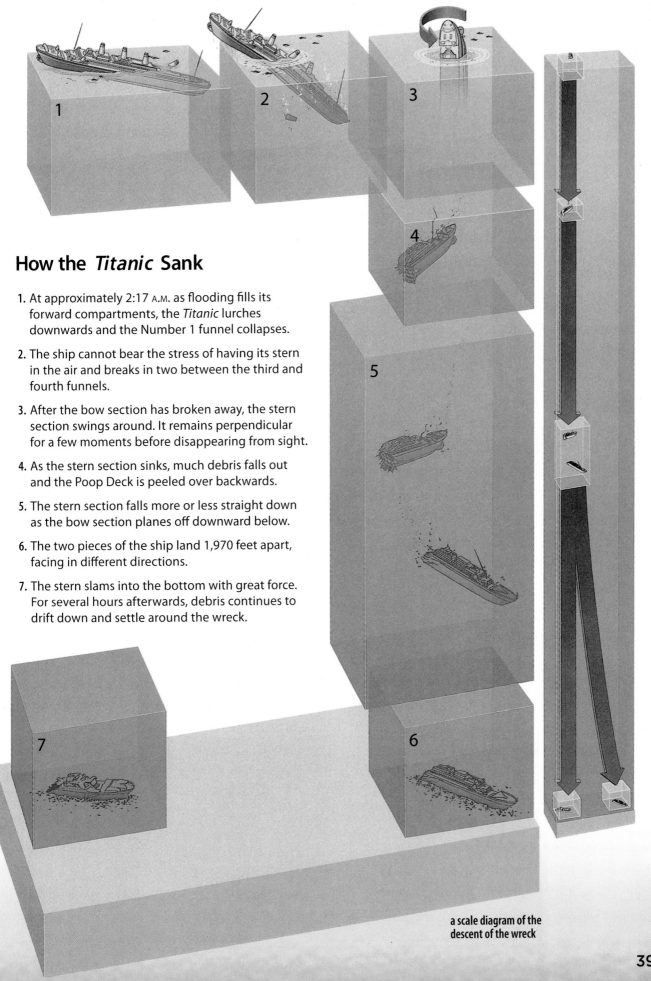

How the *Titanic* Sank

1. At approximately 2:17 A.M. as flooding fills its forward compartments, the *Titanic* lurches downwards and the Number 1 funnel collapses.

2. The ship cannot bear the stress of having its stern in the air and breaks in two between the third and fourth funnels.

3. After the bow section has broken away, the stern section swings around. It remains perpendicular for a few moments before disappearing from sight.

4. As the stern section sinks, much debris falls out and the Poop Deck is peeled over backwards.

5. The stern section falls more or less straight down as the bow section planes off downward below.

6. The two pieces of the ship land 1,970 feet apart, facing in different directions.

7. The stern slams into the bottom with great force. For several hours afterwards, debris continues to drift down and settle around the wreck.

a scale diagram of the descent of the wreck

"Bob, we're running short of time. We have to return to the surface." Our pilot's words cut like a knife through my excitement. Here we were deep inside the *Titanic*, actually going down the Grand Staircase, but we had used up all the time that we had to stay safely on the bottom. I knew our pilot was just following orders, but I still wanted to shout in protest.

Our little robot soldier emerged from the black hole and shone his lights toward us, bathing the **interior** of the sub in an unearthly glow. For a moment it felt as if an alien spaceship were **hovering** nearby. But that feeling quickly gave way to one of victory, thanks to our little friend. *JJ* had been a complete success.

On our next day's dive, we crossed over what had once been Captain Smith's cabin. Its outer wall now lay collapsed on the deck, as though a giant had brought his fist down on it. We passed within inches of one of the cabin's windows. Was this, I wondered, a window that Captain Smith had cranked open to let a little fresh air into his cabin before going to bed?

Suddenly a large piece of broken railing loomed out of the darkness. It seemed to be heading right for my viewport. I immediately warned the pilot who quickly turned *Alvin*'s stern around, rotating us free of the obstacle.

Now we began to drop onto the starboard Boat Deck. As we glided along, I felt as though I were visiting a ghost town where suddenly one day everyone had closed up shop and left.

An empty lifeboat davit stood nearby. Ahead I could see where the *Titanic*'s lifeboats had rested. It was on this very deck that the crowds of passengers had stood waiting to get into the boats.

the dining room in 1912; the dining room today

They had not known until the last moments that there were not enough lifeboats for everyone. It was also from this deck that you could have heard the *Titanic's* brave band playing cheerful music to boost the crowd's spirit as the slope of the deck grew steeper and steeper.

Jason Jr. now went for a stroll along the Boat Deck. As he slowly made his way along, he looked in the windows of several first-class cabins as well as into some passageways, including one that still bore the words, "First-Class Entrance." As *JJ* passed by the gymnasium windows, I could see bits and pieces of equipment amid the rubble, including some metal grillwork that had been part of the electric camel, an old-fashioned exercise machine. We could also see various wheel shapes and a control lever. Much of the gym's ceiling was covered with rust. This was where the gym instructor, dressed in white flannel trousers, had urged passengers to try the gym machines. And, on the last night, passengers had gathered here for warmth as the lifeboats were being lowered.

JJ examines a bollard on the Forecastle Deck

I could see *JJ* far off down the deck, turning this way and that to get a better view inside doorways and various windows. It was almost as though our little robot had a mind of his own.

But now we had to bring him home. We had been on the *Titanic* for hours. Once again it was time to head back to the surface.

The morning of July 18 was lovely and warm, but I felt **edgy** about the day's mission. We had decided to visit the *Titanic's* debris field. Along the 1,970 feet that separated the broken-off bow and stern pieces of the wreck, there was a large scattering of all kinds of objects from the ship. Everything from lumps of coal to wrought-iron deck benches had fallen to the bottom as she broke in two and sank. But I was anxious about what we might find down there among the rubble. I had often been asked about the possibility of finding human bodies. It was a chilling thought. We had not seen any signs of human remains so far, but I knew that if we were to find any, it would most likely be during this dive.

As the first fragments of wreckage began to appear on the bottom, I felt like we were entering a bombed-out museum. Thousands upon thousands of objects littered the rolling fields of ocean bottom, many of them perfectly preserved. The guts of the *Titanic* lay spilled out across the ocean floor. Cups and saucers, silver serving trays, pots and pans, wine bottles, boots, chamber pots, space heaters, bathtubs, suitcases, and more.

Then, without warning, I found myself looking into the ghostly eyes of a small, white smiling face. For a split second I thought it was a skull—and it really scared me. Then I realized I was looking at a doll's head, its hair and clothes gone.

My shock turned to sadness as I began to wonder who had owned this toy. Had the girl survived in one of the lifeboats? Or had she clutched the doll tightly as she sank in the icy waters?

We moved on through this amazing scenery. There were so many things scattered about that it became difficult to keep track of them. We came across one of the ship's boilers, and there on top of it sat an upright rusty metal cup like the ones the crew had used. It looked as though it had been placed there by a stoker moments before water had burst into the boiler room. It was astonishing to think that in fact this cup had just fluttered down that night to land right on top of a boiler.

one of the ship's safes

Then in the light of *Alvin*'s headlights, we spotted a safe ahead of us. I had heard about the story of fabulous treasure, including a leather-bound book covered with jewels, being locked in the ship's safes when she sank. Here was the chance of a lifetime, and I wanted to get a good look at it.

The safe sat there with its door face up. The handle looked as though it was made of gold, although I knew it had to be brass. Next to it, I could see a small circular gold dial, and above both a nice shiny gold crest.

402

Why not try to open it? I watched as *Alvin's* sample-gathering arm locked its metal fingers onto the handle. Its metal wrist began to rotate **clockwise**. To my surprise, the handle turned easily. Then it stopped. The door just wouldn't budge. It was rusted shut. I felt as if I'd been caught with my hand in the cookie jar. Oh, well, I thought, it was probably empty, anyway. In fact, when we later looked at the video footage we had taken, we could see that the bottom of the safe had rusted out. Any treasure should have been spread around nearby, but there was none to be seen. Fortunately, my promise to myself not to bring back anything from the *Titanic* was not put to the test.

robotic arm retrieves a leaded glass window

Two days passed before I went down to the *Titanic* again. After the rest, I was raring to go at it once more. This time we were going to explore the torn-off stern section that lay 1,970 feet away from the bow. It had been very badly damaged during the plunge to the bottom. Now it lay almost unrecognizable amidst badly twisted pieces of wreckage. We planned to land *Alvin* on the bottom directly behind the stern section and then send *JJ* in under the overhanging hull. Unless the *Titanic's* three huge propellers had fallen off when she sank, I figured they still ought to be there, along with her enormous 101-ton rudder.

We made a soft landing on the bottom and discovered that one of *JJ's* motors wouldn't work. Our dive looked like a washout. I sat glumly staring out of my viewport at the muddy bottom. Suddenly the mud started to move! Our pilot was slowly inching *Alvin* forward on its single ski right under the dangerous overhanging stern area. He was taking the sub itself to search for the huge propellers. Was he crazy? What if a piece of wreckage came crashing down? But our pilot was a professional, so I figured he must know exactly what he was doing.

In *Alvin* we explore under the overhanging deck of the *Titanic*'s severed stern section and photograph the buried rudder.

I could see an area ahead covered with rusticles that had fallen from the rim of the stern above. Until now we had had ocean above us. Crossing this point was like taking a dangerous dare. Once on the other side, there was no sure way of escaping if disaster struck. None of us spoke. The only sound in the sub was our breathing.

Slowly a massive black surface of steel plating seemed to inch down toward us overhead. The hull seemed to be coming at us from all sides. As we looked closely, we could see that like the bow, the stern section was buried deep in the mud—forty-five feet or so. Both the middle and the starboard propellers were under the mud. Only about sixteen feet of the massive rudder could be seen rising out of the ooze.

"Let's get out of here," I said. Ever so gently, *Alvin* retraced the path left by its ski. As we crossed over from the area covered with rusticles into the clear, we sighed with relief. We were out of danger. All of us were glad that this adventure was over.

Before we left the bottom this time, however, there was one mission that I wanted to complete. I wanted to place a memorial

plaque on the twisted and tangled wreckage of the stern, in memory of all those lost on the *Titanic*. Those who had died had gathered on the stern as the ship had tilted bow first. This had been their final haven. So we rose up the wall of steel to the top of the stern. With great care, *Alvin*'s mechanical arm plucked the plaque from where it had been strapped outside the sub, and gently

the plaque we placed on the stern in memory of those who died on the *Titanic*

released it. We watched as it sank quietly to the deck of the stern.

As we lifted off and began our climb to the surface, our camera kept the plaque in view as long as possible. As we rose, it grew smaller and smaller, until finally it was swallowed in the gloom.

MEET THE AUTHOR

A doll's head and a man's patent leather shoe are usually not objects of wonder. But they were truly haunting images to explorer and oceanographer **Dr. Robert D. Ballard**, because of where they were found—among the wreckage of the *Titanic*. Ballard saw those objects through the eyes of a small robot operated from a three-man submarine. Searching a 150-square-mile area of the ocean floor for the *Titanic* "makes

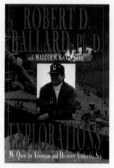

finding a needle in a haystack seem trivial," he says.

Ballard continues to be intrigued by technology and by what lies in the depths of the ocean.

Another book by Dr. Robert D. Ballard: *Explorations*

LOG ON Find out more about Dr. Robert D. Ballard at **www.macmillanmh.com**

Author's Purpose

Why might a reader think that Dr. Robert D. Ballard is fascinated by the *Titanic*? Identify text features and details from the selection that indicate the author's deep interest in the ship.

Comprehension Check

Summarize

Use your Fact and Opinion Chart to help you summarize *Exploring the* Titanic. Think about how the author's curiosity grew as he explored the *Titanic*.

Fact	Opinion

Think and Compare

1. Reread the first paragraph on page 394. What are the facts and what are the opinions? How do the facts help support the opinions? **Evaluate: Fact and Opinion**

2. According to the author, what are the advantages of using the *JJ* in the **interior** of the *Titanic*'s remains? **Evaluate**

3. If you wanted to be an oceanographer, what would you study in school? What special equipment would you have to learn to use? **Synthesize**

4. Do you think it was important to explore the remains of the *Titanic*? Why or why not? What can we learn from exploring ruins from the past? **Apply**

5. Read "Waves" on pages 390–391. Why would the information in "Waves" be important to the author of *Exploring the* Titanic? **Reading/Writing Across Texts**

A main character described in terms of hyperbole, or exaggeration, is an important feature of a tall tale.

Old Stormalong Finds a Man-Sized Ship

by Paul Robert Walker

Old Stormalong was the greatest sailor who ever sailed the seas. He stood four fathoms high, drank his soup from a Cape Cod dory, and ate a shark for dinner with ostrich eggs on the side. When he was finished, he stretched out on the deck and picked his teeth with an eighteen-foot oar.

Now, a fathom is the height of a good-sized man and a dory is a fair-sized rowboat. So Old Stormalong, well, he was a mighty big sailor. He had a hard time fitting on an ordinary ship, so he went from ship to ship, just trying to get comfortable. Finally he ended up as boatswain on the *Lady of the Sea*, the biggest ship in the Atlantic—at least that's what Stormy thought.

After a long voyage through the Caribbean, the *Lady* was heading for her home port of Boston. As she neared the Jersey coast, just off Barnegat Light, the weather turned bad, and the *Lady*—big as she was—tossed like a toy on the huge waves.

As Stormy peered through the growing tempest, he caught sight of something totally unexpected. A great new city was floating calm as could be on the stormy sea.

"It's unnatural!" he exclaimed. "How could the landlubbers build a city on the sea?" But as the *Lady* drew closer, he realized it wasn't a city at all. It was a ship! The biggest ship he'd ever seen—it made the *Lady of the Sea* look like a rowboat! Even from a distance he could read the name painted on the huge bow in letters twenty feet high: *Courser*.

Stormy leaned over the rail and gazed in admiration. "Now, that's a ship," he said with a sigh. "Aye, a man could stretch his legs on a ship like that."

Without bothering to take his gear from below, Stormy jumped over the side and swam toward the *Courser*. The seas were rough, but his powerful strokes brought him alongside the huge ship in a few minutes. He called for a rope and pulled himself aboard.

"And who might you be?" asked the captain.

"Alfred Bulltop Stormalong," Stormy replied. "At your service, sir."

"Well, sign the log," said the captain. "We can use a big man like you."

Stormy took a look around. The first thing he noticed was the horses—a whole stableful right on the deck!

"She's a horseboat, is she?" asked Stormy.

The captain laughed and patted Stormy on the back of the knee. "Horseboat, my eye!" he said. "Those are for the men on watch. The deck's so big, they have to ride around it."

This is a dialogue between Old Stormalong (Stormy) and the captain. Notice the quotation marks that surround each statement.

Stormy smiled and took a deep breath of the tangy salt air. "Aye," he said. "She's the ship for me."

And so she was. The *Courser* carried over six hundred men to keep her running trim. A man had to get out his compass to find his way from fore to aft. The sails were so big that they had to be made in the Sahara Desert—just to give the sailmakers room to spread them out. Bunkhouses and galleys were built up and down the masts, and the crow's nest was lost in the clouds. If a young man climbed the rigging, he was an old man by the time he came down.

Until Stormy came aboard, it took thirty-two men just to turn the wheel. But Old Stormalong could handle it steady by himself. Oh, he was a sight to see! A strong, handsome, four-fathom man in a peacoat as big as an ordinary sail. His black beard speckled with spray; his huge hands wrapped around the steering pegs; his dark eyes fixed on the horizon. Stormy was the only man aboard who could actually see where the ship was going.

The *Courser* could ride through an average storm as if she were floating on a millpond. In fact, during all the years that Old Stormalong handled the wheel, only two storms ever blew her off course.

The first was a September gale in the North Atlantic. The wind blew and blew—whipping the huge sails and spraying cold salt water across the decks until it was hard to tell whether a man was on the ship or in the sea. The fog was so thick that Stormy couldn't see the end of his beard. But he held the great wheel for two weeks straight—day and night—without eating or sleeping.

Finally, the winds died down and the fog lifted. When the sun rose over the cold blue water, the navigator discovered that they had been blown into the North Sea, and they were heading south—straight for disaster. You see, the *Courser* was much too big to turn around and a mite too big to pass through the English Channel.

Old Stormalong held the wheel steady while the officers rode around the deck shouting orders and watching the sides of the ship. As the *Courser* approached the narrowest point of the Channel—between Calais and the cliffs of Dover—the captain ordered the sails reefed and the men into the lifeboats.

"Hold fast!" shouted Stormy. "I think we can make it, sir."

"Are you sure?" asked the captain.

"It'll be close," said Stormy. "But if ye send all hands over and lay a coat of soap on the sides, we just might squeeze through. Better coat it extra heavy on the starboard— those Dover cliffs look mighty rough."

The captain ordered the crew to coat the sides as thick and slippery as they could. When the ship hit the bottleneck, she *just* squeezed through—it was so tight that the soap on the starboard side rubbed off against the cliffs. It's still there today, and that's why they're called the White Cliffs of Dover.

Connect and Compare

1. Find an example of hyperbole. How does hyperbole add humor to the story? **Hyperbole**

2. In what ways is Stormy a typical tall-tale hero? Find examples in the text to support your answer. **Analyze**

3. What details would you add to *Exploring the* Titanic to make it a tall tale? **Reading/Writing Across Texts**

411

Writer's Craft

Facts and Opinions

In an informative essay about science, history, or another serious subject, use precise details and descriptive language. Include only **facts** and avoid words that show emotion or **opinions**.

I wrote about observing clams at the beach. I used facts, not opinions, in my scientific observation.

My observation includes only precise, factual information.

Write a Scientific Observation

Quahogs

by Rose R.

My family took a trip to the beach this afternoon. I walked along the shore and saw hundreds of baby quahogs cover the sand between the high- and low-tide marks of the Atlantic Ocean. They had very hard shells with different colors. I walked closer and tapped them with my finger. I used my hand to measure their size, and they were no bigger than my fingernail. The end of the summer is the breeding season for these clams.

I watched the quahogs burrow themselves in the sand. They look for food under the surface. I could see these tiny clams use their "feet" to dig into the sand, disappearing from sight. It looked like they were wiggling down underground. Then before the next wave came in, they reappeared. The holes they made in the sand helped me recognize where they were.

Quahogs take in nutrients by sucking in water and filtering out the food. The filtered water then comes out the other side of the shell. My dad explained that when the quahogs get bigger, clammers will dig in the sand to find the ones ready to be eaten.

Your Turn

Write two or three paragraphs describing something you've observed in nature. Be sure to include precise details in your description. Do not include your own opinions. Use the Writer's Checklist to review your paragraphs.

Writer's Checklist

☑ **Ideas and Content:** Did I include important **facts** and observations? Did I avoid **opinions**?

✓ **Organization:** Did I organize my description in a logical way?

✓ **Voice:** Did I choose words that make the scientific observation sound formal and scientific?

✓ **Word Choice:** Did I use precise vocabulary? Did I avoid words that express opinions, such as *beautiful, amazing,* and *incredible*?

✓ **Sentence Fluency:** Did I use a variety of sentence beginnings?

✓ **Conventions:** Did I use subject and object pronouns properly? Did I check my spelling?

Talk About It

Helping others is often a choice rather than a requirement. What motivates people to help others?

LOG ON Find out more about ways to help others at **www.macmillanmh.com**

Helping Others

Vocabulary

- bewildering
- moderate
- hamper
- prohibit
- accessible

Claude Shirts combines facial expressions with signs to convey his message.

Talking With His Hands

"Go, greased lightning. Go. Go. Go. Go. Go. Go. Go."

Those lyrics are fun when you hear them with a rollicking beat in the musical *Grease!* But they would be **bewildering** if you couldn't hear the music. And even if you weren't confused, you would probably be just plain bored.

Being able to capture the spirit of that song and project it to the audience without sound was a challenge for Claude Shirts. He uses sign language to interpret plays for deaf audiences. "I try to tell the story that the music is telling," he says. Rather than repeating the sign for "go" over and over, he imitated the motions of driving. "I showed the character sitting in a car with his hair going straight back in the wind."

Shirts, 37, works with Hands On!, a group that interprets theater shows for deaf people. *Grease!* was tough enough to interpret. But that was a **moderate** challenge compared with interpreting the plays of Shakespeare. Shirts says Shakespeare's plays are really tricky because they are written in old-fashioned language. "At first, I had not a clue what the characters were saying," he admits. "I had to do so much preparation."

At Hands On! performances, Shirts positions himself so that he doesn't **hamper** deaf audience members' view of the on-stage action. If he does his job well, the crowd does not cheer and applaud. Instead, they reward Shirts with the unique applause given by deaf audiences: the sight of outstretched arms and waving palms moving in silent circles.

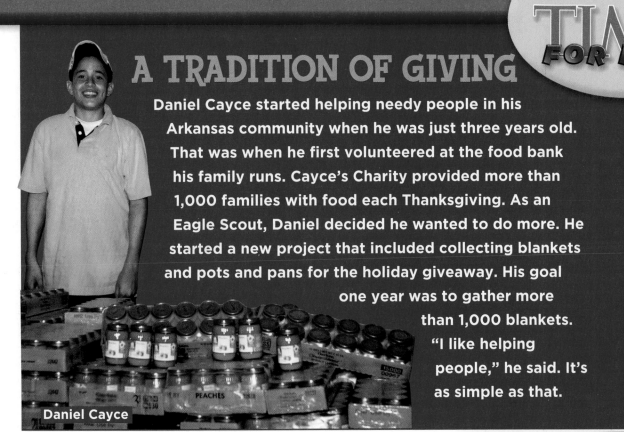

A TRADITION OF GIVING

Daniel Cayce started helping needy people in his Arkansas community when he was just three years old. That was when he first volunteered at the food bank his family runs. Cayce's Charity provided more than 1,000 families with food each Thanksgiving. As an Eagle Scout, Daniel decided he wanted to do more. He started a new project that included collecting blankets and pots and pans for the holiday giveaway. His goal one year was to gather more than 1,000 blankets. "I like helping people," he said. It's as simple as that.

Daniel Cayce

Able to Work

In 1990, a landmark law was passed in the United States. The Americans with Disabilities Act (ADA) gave an estimated 30 million Americans with disabilities "a fighting chance in the work force," according to former California Congressman Tony Coelho. Coelho himself was once denied the chance to have the career he wanted because he is epileptic.

The ADA was designed to **prohibit** discrimination in the workplace against those with disabilities. In large ways and small, the law has brought about changes for the disabled as well as for their employers. It requires businesses to make offices and other workplaces **accessible** to people with disabilities. And it's working. According to Coelho, "There is still job discrimination out there, but the tide is turning."

Ted Henter is blind. He runs a firm that makes software for others who are blind.

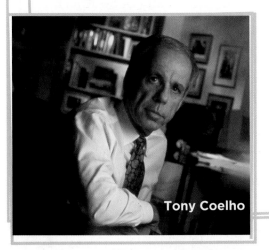

Tony Coelho

LOG ON Find out more about the Americans with Disabilities Act at **www.macmillanmh.com**

Comprehension

Genre
A **Nonfiction Article** in a newspaper or magazine presents facts and information.

Make Inferences and Analyze
Compare and Contrast
When you look for similarities, you compare things. When you look for differences, you contrast them.

Oseola McCarty (third from the right) and her family in 1922

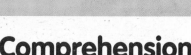

SAVING GRACE

How could a woman who spent her life doing laundry for others give $150,000 for university scholarships?

For most of her life, Oseola McCarty of Hattiesburg, Mississippi, did laundry for other people. It seems reasonable to assume that the modest income of a washerwoman would **prohibit** her from becoming a philanthropist. What people in Hattiesburg could not have guessed was that McCarty would wind up donating a small fortune to the local university. Large donations usually come from wealthy alumni. However, the University of Southern Mississippi announced that Oseola McCarty, then 87 years old, was giving the university $150,000 to finance scholarships for African American students. "I want them to have an education," said McCarty, who never married and had no children of her own. "I had to work hard all my life. They can have the chance that I didn't have."

HARD WORK

When McCarty was in the sixth grade, her aunt became unable to walk. McCarty left school to care for her. She also helped her mother and grandmother with their backyard laundry business. "Even when I was little," says McCarty, "I was always getting into the wash." By the time her aunt got back on her feet a year later, McCarty thought she was too far behind to return to school. "I was too big," she says. "So I kept on working."

McCarty's business was similar to running a Laundromat. However, unlike the owner of a Laundromat, she did not use washing machines and dryers. McCarty did all of the washing by hand. She had tried a washer and dryer, but found them inadequate. Instead, she boiled the clothes in a big black pot and hung them on the line to dry. Her place of business was the backyard of the wood-frame house she grew up in.

McCarty in 1997

"She had a bench in the backyard with three tubs on it," says Helen Tyre, 89, who hired McCarty back in 1943. "She and her mother and grandmother carried the water from a hydrant." Tyre remembers a time when McCarty charged just 50 cents a bundle (a week's worth of laundry for a family of four). Eventually her fee climbed to $10 a bundle, still a very **moderate** price.

SO OTHERS CAN LEARN

McCarty thought for years about the scholarship project. But it was only after arthritis forced her to stop taking in wash—at the age of 87—that she reached out to the university. Many people in McCarty's shoes would have kept the money. "Frankly, I didn't believe it at first," said Bill Pace, executive director of the University of Southern

President Bill Clinton awarded the Presidential Medal of Honor to McCarty in 1996.

Mississippi Foundation. The foundation manages gifts to the university. "I was amazed that someone who made their money that way could save that much and then would give it away."

The scholarship fund was established in 1995. The scholarships were not supposed to go into effect until after McCarty's death. But Pace and other university officials didn't want to **hamper** McCarty's chance to see at least one of her beneficiaries graduate. So less than a year after the gift was made they awarded the first Oseola McCarty Scholarship of $1,000 to Stephanie Bullock, 18.

Stephanie's mother taught school in Hattiesburg and her father supervised a water-treatment plant. Stephanie has a twin brother, Stephen, and the Bullocks were worried about paying college tuition for two kids at the same time. The help from the McCarty scholarship fund would make college **accessible** to both twins.

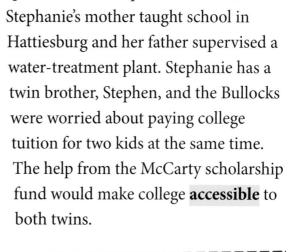

McCarty and Stephanie Bullock, the first student to receive the Oseola McCarty Scholarship

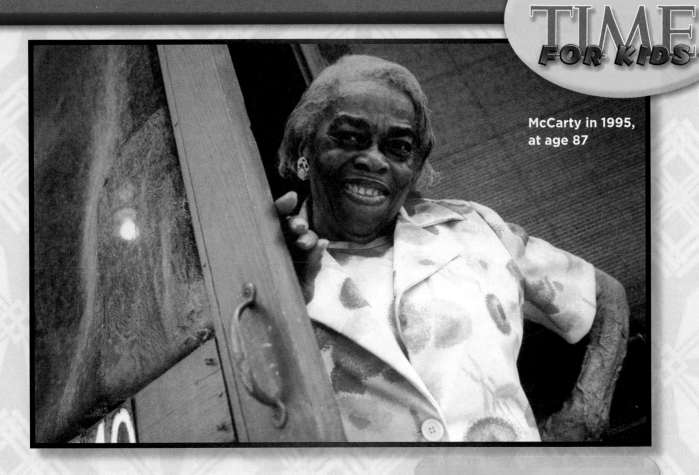

McCarty in 1995, at age 87

THE GIFT OF A LIFETIME

Word of McCarty's gift and her life story caused others to open their pocketbooks. Local businesspeople pledged to match McCarty's $150,000 contribution, and in addition, checks arrived at the university from all over. McCarty, meanwhile, found all the fuss a bit **bewildering**. She continued to project an air of genuine puzzlement by the question she heard over and over: Why didn't you spend the money on yourself? "I am spending it on myself," she answered with a smile.

Oseola McCarty died in 1999 at the age of 91.

Think and Compare

1. What did Oseola McCarty do for a living?

2. What benefit did Oseola McCarty receive from giving $150,000 to the University of Southern Mississippi?

3. If you had a large sum of money to use to help others, what would you do with it?

4. Compare and contrast the ways of helping others that are described in "Saving Grace" and the three stories on pages 416-417.

CYCLING

Talk About It

How would your life be different if you had to bicycle everywhere?

LOG ON Find out more about cycling at **www.macmillanmh.com**

Vocabulary

spectators

demonstration

prominent

luxury

prevail

maneuvered

collective

adept

Analogies

Analogies link pairs of words that relate in the same way.

Diners are *to eat* as *spectators* are to _____.

Answer: *watch*

Bike Ride, Anyone?

by Amy Leung

Some people might find it surprising that the present times are not considered the "Golden Age of Bicycling," since there are so many different bikes available. Believe it or not, this Golden Age occurred more than 100 years ago in the 1890s when horses were the main form of transport.

The first modern bicycle can be traced back to 1839 in Scotland. A variety of "bikes" followed. By the 1870s, James Starley of England was producing bikes. His bike, called the Ordinary, had a huge front and a small back wheel. Many **spectators** came to the 1876 U.S. Centennial Exhibition in Philadelphia to see a **demonstration** of how the Ordinary worked. Some models became more **prominent**, or well-known, than others. One bike designed in the United States was a real **luxury**. It cost more than some people made in a year!

In 1885 the Coventry Machinists Company in England produced a 50-pound machine called the Rover. It was built like the modern bicycle. By the 1890s the Ordinary and the Rover were

pitted against each other. Eventually, the Ordinary faded from production and the Rover would **prevail**. The Rover was simply faster and more easily **maneuvered**, or controlled, up and down hills and around corners.

Bicycling really became popular in the 1890s because it was nearly as fast as a horse and required less care and expense. People rode their bikes through the country and the city. Changes began to take place as bicycling increased in popularity.

As more people began biking, they formed the League of American Wheelmen. The league had one **collective** goal: All members wanted to improve bicycling conditions. The league worked to get roads paved for easier passage in all types of weather. It also published a bicycling magazine and established bicycle etiquette.

Women were good cyclists, just as **adept** at riding as men. Susan B. Anthony, the famous women's rights advocate, said that the bicycle had done wonders for women's freedom. Isn't it wonderful that a bike could improve women's rights?

In the 1970s the mountain bike made bicycling even more popular. Adults joined kids and teenagers on their bikes. Biking is a fun pastime and a fantastic alternative to driving.

Reread for **Comprehension**

 STRATEGY SKILL

Make Inferences and Analyze

Fact and Opinion
Making inferences and analyzing information can help you decide what is fact and opinion in a selection. A fact is a statement that can be proven true. An opinion is a statement of someone's feelings or beliefs. An opinion is not true or false.

Use the Fact and Opinion Chart as you reread "Bike Ride, Anyone?"

Fact	Opinion

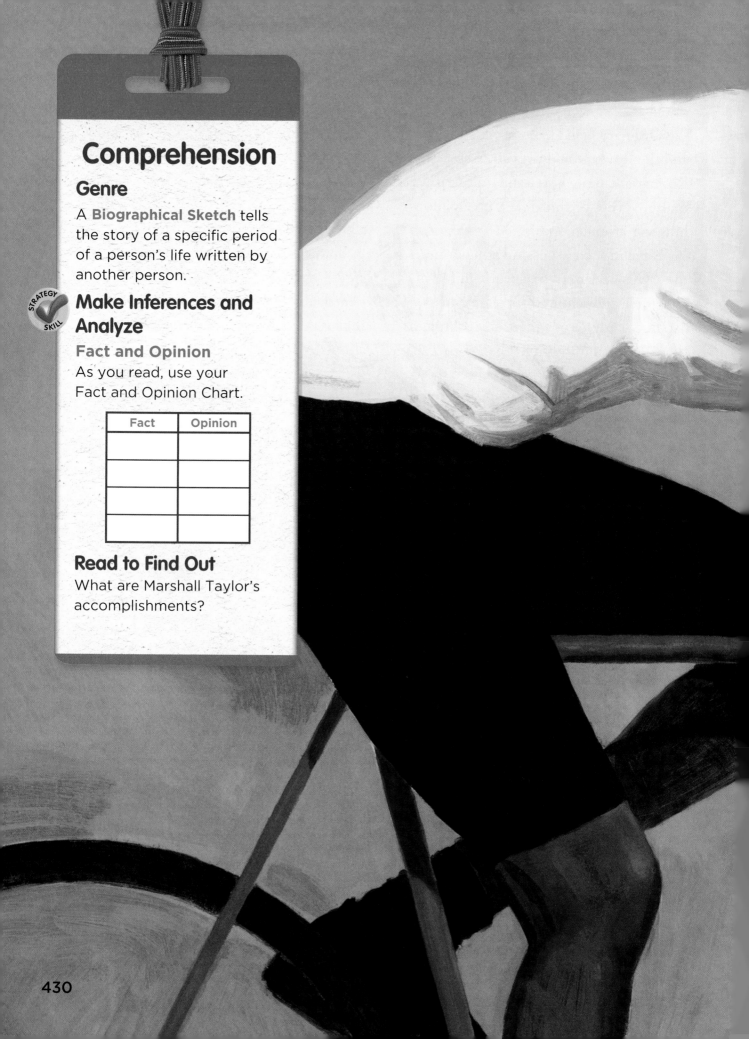

Comprehension

Genre

A **Biographical Sketch** tells the story of a specific period of a person's life written by another person.

Make Inferences and Analyze

Fact and Opinion

As you read, use your Fact and Opinion Chart.

Fact	Opinion

Read to Find Out

What are Marshall Taylor's accomplishments?

MAJOR TAYLOR
CHAMPION CYCLIST

Award Winning Illustrator

BY **Lesa Cline-Ransome**
ILLUSTRATED BY **James E. Ransome**

In Indianapolis, Indiana, there was a street lined with bicycle shops from one end to the other. Visitors would marvel at each window displayed with the most up-to-date models along that stretch of North Pennsylvania Avenue locals called Bicycle Row.

Right at the center sat the Hay and Willits Bicycle Shop: Thomas Hay, Bert Willits, proprietors.

It was this shop young Marshall Taylor visited when his own bicycle needed fixing. Marshall was thirteen years old, and waiting patiently was not one of the things he did best. So while he waited, he kept himself busy trying out new stunts. Then, the repairs made, he used one of his fancy mounts to climb quickly onto his bicycle. If he hurried, he could still finish his newspaper route before supper.

As Marshall left, Mr. Hay shouted, "Hey, son, that was some stunt work."

"Oh, those," said Marshall. "I have a lot more, wanna see?"

And without waiting for an answer, he began his **demonstration** with an acrobatic mount. Round and round the store he rode, first backward, then forward on the handlebars, each move more daring than the last. By the time he'd finished, everyone in the store was applauding for more.

"How'd you get so good?" Tom Hay asked the boy.

Marshall explained that he'd taught himself quite a collection of tricks riding on the long stretches of country road between his newspaper stops.

"Are you looking for work? For six dollars a week, all you need to do is sweep, straighten, and show off some of those stunts, and you've got yourself a job."

"Six dollars to clean and do tricks?" Marshall asked. Why, that paid a dollar more than his paper route.

"Okay, okay, we'll throw in a new bike, too," countered Bert Willits.

"I'll take it!" Marshall shouted.

How did a thirteen-year-old black teenager in 1891 come to be such a crackerjack cyclist—or even to own a bicycle? Mr. Hay and Mr. Willits wondered. And so Marshall told them of his father's job as a coachman to the **prominent** Southard family and how at the age of eight he'd been hired as the live-in companion of their only son. It was then that Marshall began his new life of **luxury**: private tutoring, fine clothing, a playroom stacked with toys.

But what Marshall loved most was the bicycle the Southards had given him. He'd never seen anything like its smooth curved lines of metal, so shiny and new and so utterly modern. He jumped on at once, knowing those wheels could carry him faster than his legs ever could.

And sure enough, in no time he became the top cyclist in the neighborhood. Amongst stately Victorian houses and tree-lined streets, in each and every race, Marshall breezed by the other boys, aware only of the wind against his face and the road he left behind.

For the days when Marshall was to perform, Mr. Hay outfitted him in a uniform with elaborate braidings and shimmery gold buttons.

Crowds gathered afternoons at 4:00 P.M. sharp to watch Marshall on the sidewalk outside the store. They were amazed by the young man in military uniform so **adept** on two wheels.

"He looks like a little major!" they would marvel.

Then they'd filter into the store to request private lessons and try out the bicycles that could make that little major do his tricks.

Hay and Willits Bicycle Shop had finally made a name for itself, and the owners had the kid everyone now called Major Taylor to thank for it.

The annual ten-mile road race, sponsored by Hay and Willits, was one of the biggest sporting events in Indianapolis. Each year an elaborate gold medal for the winner was displayed in their window, on view for all. Marshall liked to put down his cleaning rags and stop to admire it. He'd adjust it, polish it, and hold it up to the light to watch it sparkle. Once, he even tried it on, smiling at his own reflection in the window.

"Major Taylor, Champion Cyclist," he whispered to himself.

Early on the morning of the race, Marshall took his place among hundreds of **spectators**. He'd never seen a bicycle race up close and he didn't want to miss a single detail.

When Mr. Hay spotted Marshall, he waved to him. "Come on over here, young man; you must start in this race," he insisted.

"I don't think I can do it," Marshall protested.

"Why, it's no different than riding with your friends," he encouraged. "Look, just start up the road and come back when you're tired. The crowd will love it."

Bang! The starting pistol sounded, and Marshall was off, pedaling hard and fast, hoping only to keep pace with the others.

"Just till I get tired . . . just till I get tired . . . ," he kept repeating, his legs pumping as fast as his heart. Gradually the rhythmic creaks of the other bicycles faded and all he could hear was his own panting. Time fell away as he struggled to maintain speed, and the wind whipped his face. Out of nowhere Mr. Hay appeared, shouting and dangling the gold medal.

"You're a mile ahead! Keep going!"

Now he thought he could make out a swell of spectators gathered at the finish. Pushing, pushing with everything he had, his legs cramped with exhaustion, he burst through the winning tape . . . and then collapsed.

When he came to, sore, stiff, and exhausted, the crowd's cheers were ringing in his ears.

At thirteen years old, Marshall Taylor had won his first race.

Back at the shop, Marshall's dreams now stretched far beyond the walls of Hay and Willits. More than anything, he wanted to be a professional cyclist.

Fact and Opinion
Identify one fact and one opinion about Marshall Taylor.

437

One by one, he committed to memory the names of racers who'd visited the shop—Arthur Zimmerman, Willie Windle of Massachusetts, and Louis "Birdie" Munger, who had recently opened a racing workshop in town.

As Marshall grew to know Munger, he began spending more and more time at his shop. He'd follow him to the track, pleading, "Tell me about the race when . . . "

Birdie was tickled by Marshall. In fact, the boy reminded him of a younger version of himself. "You've got talent, but you've got to keep working," Birdie instructed after one of Marshall's many wins. Soon Marshall had been hired as his assistant, running errands and doing chores.

When Birdie decided to move to Worcester, Massachusetts, he invited Marshall along. After a fond farewell to his family, Marshall set off with Birdie to begin training. To anyone who'd listen, he would boast, "I am going to make Major Marshall Taylor the fastest bicycle rider in the world."

Marshall's talent grew as fast as his popularity. It wasn't long before racing fans—although they may not have known the name Marshall Taylor—knew there was a young Negro causing quite a stir.

But by the time Marshall turned professional at age eighteen, challenges off the track began to trail him like a shadow. All of the large purses won in races all over the country couldn't buy him a meal in a restaurant or a room in a hotel.

Cities like Louisville, St. Louis, and even Indianapolis wouldn't permit a black man on their tracks—their entry forms read, "For White Riders Only." Still that couldn't keep Marshall down. As the only Negro granted membership in the League of American Wheelmen, he was entitled to compete on any track he chose.

"You're never going to finish this race!" riders would holler above the noise of the crowd, or "This race is going to be your last," they'd taunt. Working as a group, they'd box him out. Racing next to him, they'd poke and jab him. They agreed that if they defeated him, the winner would split the prize money with the others. But usually there was no prize money to split: For every trick they tried, Taylor had his own.

439

Marshall's style had always been to stay behind the pack. "Save it for the finish," he would recite to himself. Wearing his lucky number 13 armband, he'd keep pace, then ride full speed in the final yards. But when the competition turned crueler, he had to adjust his style. As soon as he'd spot a clearing in the pack, he'd cut through and make his way to the front. And that's where he stayed, all the way across the finish line.

The "Black Whirlwind," as he was called by the press, had his own set of rules: "Ride clean and ride fair." Asked by reporters how he managed to keep calm despite attacks by other cyclists, Marshall answered, "I simply ride away."

Munger's prediction years earlier had come true. Major Marshall Taylor was now the fastest bicycle rider in the world. After he won the 1899 World Championship title, beating out the Butler brothers, offers to compete abroad flooded his home. Promises of money and racing against the world's best cyclists were too much to resist.

In 1900 friends and family said good-bye as Marshall boarded the *Kaiser Wilhelm der Grosse*, proud to be representing his country on his first European racing tour.

From the moment he arrived in France, fans swarmed around him, welcoming "le Nègre Volant," the Flying Negro. At every Parisian café, hotel, and track, they followed for a chance to shake his hand. The press reported his every move, and he was invited into the homes of aristocracy. Halfway around the world, Marshall Taylor was finally getting the recognition and respect he had worked for his whole life.

It was not on a starting line but rather at the Café Esperance that Marshall met the French champion, Edmond Jacquelin. "Welcome to Paris, Monsieur Taylor!" he greeted, smiling broadly. And with that, the two became instant friends.

Fact and Opinion
Can the statement " . . . the two became instant friends" be verified? Explain your answer.

440

Jacquelin, winner of the 1900 World Championship, French Championship, and Grand Prix of Paris—the Triple Crown of racing—was a sharp contrast to the 1899 World Champion. Everyone wondered who would **prevail** in the next race—the quiet, gentlemanly Taylor or the explosive, larger-than-life Jacquelin?

Long before Taylor and Jacquelin arrived at Le Parc des Princes velodrome for their race, crowds had gathered, straining for a glimpse of the two rivals. Shivering against the cold, Taylor stood at the starting line dressed in layers to protect himself from the biting wind. Was this the Flying Negro from America the fans had heard so much about?

Meanwhile Jacquelin strode onto the track.

"Vive Taylor! Vive Jacquelin!" shouted the crowd as more fans huddled beyond the gates.

The race was on.

When it was over, roars of applause rang out to the beat of the French national anthem.

"Edmond Jacquelin, the victor in two straight heats," came the announcement.

To schedule a rematch so close to the first race was unheard of, but the crowds demanded it.

"Who will be king?" asked *L'Auto Velo*. Would it be the 1899 or the 1900 World Champion, America or France, Taylor or Jacquelin?

As the men took their positions at the start of the first heat and strapped their feet to their pedals, the crowd held one **collective** breath.

Bang!

Jacquelin jumped comfortably into the lead. Marshall concentrated on erasing all thoughts of their first race from his mind. He leaned lower over his handlebars, and from high in the stands fans looked down on the shadow of a figure lying almost flat, inching closer and closer to his rival.

For one brief moment the two became one. Side-by-side and wheel-by-wheel they sped to the finish. It was only in the final lengths that one seemed to edge ahead.

In the blink of an eye, the heat was over. Taylor had come from behind to cross the finish line first. The crowd roared, yet the victor was still to be decided: The winner had to take the best of three heats.

In the second heat, again Marshall waited for just the right moment.

When he noticed a shift in Jacquelin's closely guarded position, he **maneuvered** his bike as adeptly as he had in front of Hay and Willits Bicycle Shop years ago. And once again all eyes were on little Major Taylor.

The wind, which Marshall had once so loved against his face, now pushed at his back, carrying him well ahead of his rival and first through the winning tape.

Two races and two straight heats brought American fans to their feet. While Jacquelin quietly rode off the track, Marshall tied the American flag to his waist. As he rode his victory lap, he heard the familiar tune of "The Star Spangled Banner," and all the world watched the colors red, white, and blue billow and fly in the wind.

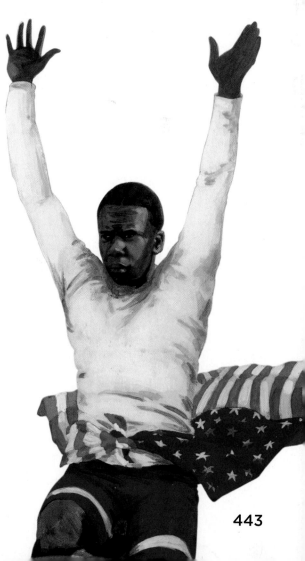

Take a Ride with Lesa Cline-Ransome and James E. Ransome

Lesa Cline-Ransome stood at the top of George Street, the hill in Worcester, Massachusetts, where Marshall Taylor trained. She visited the house he used to live in and read everything she could about his life. Her research helped this book feel real. Lesa wrote this book as a companion to *Satchel Paige*, her book about the renowned baseball player.

James E. Ransome started writing and illustrating books—about himself and his friends—in elementary school. He worked on this story with his wife, Lesa, and went with her to George Street. Seeing where Marshall Taylor trained, he says, "really brought him to life."

Another book by Lesa Cline-Ransome and James E. Ransome: *Satchel Paige*

 Find out more about Lesa Cline-Ransome and James E. Ransome at **www.macmillanmh.com**

Author's Purpose

The Ransomes wanted this biographical sketch to be both entertaining and informative. Give examples of how they achieved both purposes. How might the selection also be persuasive?

Comprehension Check

Summarize

Use your Fact and Opinion Chart to help you summarize *Major Taylor*. What are the facts of Marshall Taylor's life leading up to his victory in France?

Fact	Opinion

Think and Compare

1. Reread the first paragraph on page 441. What facts does the author include? What opinions does the author state? **Make Inferences and Analyze: Fact and Opinion**

2. Do you think the author approves or disapproves of how Marshall Taylor was treated during his bicycle races? Use specific references from the text to support your answer. **Analyze**

3. Marshall Taylor was called the "Black Whirlwind" and "le Nègre Volant." Think of your own nickname for Taylor based on his accomplishments using information from the text. **Synthesize**

4. Why do you think we should remember Marshall Taylor? What can we learn from his achievements? **Evaluate**

5. Pretend you are Marshall Taylor. Write a letter to the author of "Bike Ride, Anyone?" on pages 428–429 telling the author how learning to ride a bicycle changed your life. **Reading/Writing Across Texts**

445

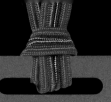

Poetry

Lyric Poems are short and songlike and express the feelings of the speaker.

Concrete Poems are shaped to look like the poem's subject matter.

Literary Elements

Assonance is the repetition of the same middle vowel sound in two or more closely grouped words.

Onomatopoeia is the use of words that sound like the action or thing they describe.

Bicycle Riding

by Sandra Liatsos

My feet rise
off the planet,
pedal wheels of steel
that sparkle as
they spin me through
the open space I feel
winging out
to galaxies
far beyond the sun,
where bicycles
are satellites,
their orbits never done.

The words *wheels* and *steel* repeat the middle vowel sound "ee" to create assonance.

The Sidewalk Racer or On the Skateboard

by *Lillian Morrison*

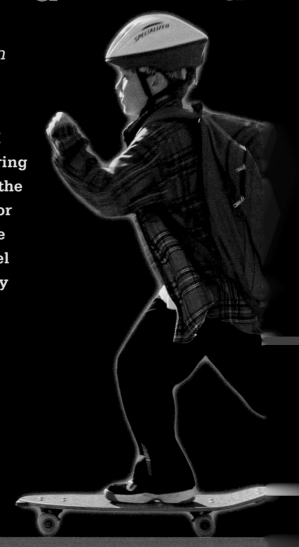

Skimming
an asphalt sea
I swerve, I curve, I
sway; I speed to whirring
sound an inch above the
ground; I'm the sailor
and the sail, I'm the
driver and the wheel
I'm the one and only
single engine
human auto
mobile.

Whirring **is like the sound it is describing. This is an example of onomatopoeia.**

Connect and Compare

1. How does the assonance in "Bicycle Riding" appeal to your senses? Which sense does it appeal to most? **Assonance**

2. Lyric poems are written to express strong feeling. How do the poets feel about bicycle riding and skateboarding? **Analyze**

3. Do you think Marshall Taylor would agree with the feelings expressed in "Bicycle Riding" and "The Sidewalk Racer"? Why or why not? **Reading/Writing Across Texts**

Write a News Article

The first sentence states the topic of the article.

I gave details about the Athens 2004 Olympic

U.S. Teen Takes Gold

by Josh A.

ATHENS 2004 — On August 19, Carly Patterson won the gold medal in the Olympic gymnastics all-around competition. This is the first time in 20 years that an American woman has won this prize. The last winner was Mary Lou Retton.

Patterson began the contest on the vault, scoring a 9.375. This low score motivated her to improve her performance. She raised her score on the next event by two-tenths of a point, earning her a 9.575 on the uneven bars.

Patterson knew that she must give a nearly perfect performance on her two final events, the balance beam and the floor exercise, and she did just that. She received a 9.725 on the balance beam. With this score, she took the lead over Svetlana Khorkina of Russia. She maintained the lead when she scored a 9.712 on her floor exercise to grab the gold.

The fifteen-year-old American was a proud winner. Svetlana Khorkina took the silver, and Nan Zhang of China took the bronze. Everyone in the final competition showed great talent.

Your Turn

Write a news article about a sports event.
It can be an event you watched in person or
on television. Make sure you state the topic
and most important facts in the first
sentence. Follow that with information
on when, where, why, and how.
Use the Writer's Checklist to
review your article.

Writer's Checklist

☑ **Ideas and Content:** Did I use a **topic sentence** at the beginning and include **details** that tell *when, where, why,* and *how*?

☑ **Organization:** Did I use time-order words to help organize my article?

☑ **Voice:** Did I choose words that express my interest in the topic?

☑ **Word Choice:** Did I use vivid words and precise verbs to capture readers' attention?

☑ **Sentence Fluency:** Did I write concise sentences that are clearly connected?

☑ **Conventions:** Did I use hyphens correctly? Did I check my spelling?

PIECES from the PAST

Talk About It

If you had to put together a museum exhibit of special items from your past, what would you include?

LOG ON Find out more about ceramics at
www.macmillanmh.com

Pottery dating from around sixth century B.C.

Minoan vase dating from around 1500 B.C.

A Change of Heart

by Matt Petrillo

Joe woke up in a bad mood. He didn't want to go to the museum with his school group today. The class had voted on their spring field trip, and Joe's suggestions did not win. He had wanted to do something outdoors, like visit a horse farm. He thought with **derision**, "What could I possibly find interesting about a museum dedicated to **ceramics**? Pottery is boring!"

But Joe had no choice. Most of the class had voted to go to the International Museum of Ceramics. With his brow **furrowed**, or wrinkled, Joe got ready for the trip. To try to cheer himself up, he noted, "It is raining today. We would have spent the whole outdoor trip standing under the **eaves** of the barn's roof trying to stay dry."

When the group reached the museum, they listened to the guide's introduction. Joe listened halfheartedly. "You might think that ceramics are just something your great aunt paints in a weekly class. Those are indeed ceramics, but the art form extends much further than that," the guide said. "As you tour the museum, you will learn about the importance of ceramics from ancient times. The pottery shards that have been found tell us a lot about the cultures they came from." Joe didn't know that ceramics was an ancient art. The guide was right. Joe did think of his great aunt and figurines when he thought of ceramics. Maybe this wouldn't be so bad after all.

Then the museum tour began. As they came upon the Native American pottery of the Southwest, the guide explained that the **arid**, or dry, climate helped the pottery dry faster. The guide showed a video of a woman **deftly** shaping a vase. Joe was fascinated by how skillful she was.

She looked as if she were born doing it; she looked so natural. Joe was amazed at the **symmetry** of the vases. It had to be difficult to get everything so balanced.

As the exhibits displayed works from more modern eras, the ceramics became fancier. Joe and his class saw sugar bowls, vases, statues, plates, and everything in between. He laughed at the odd shapes of Pablo Picasso's ceramic creations.

By the end of the day, Joe's mood had completely changed. He was glad he had come to the museum. He saw the **benefit** of learning about a variety of cultures through their ceramic works. He would definitely be happy to visit the museum again.

Cup, hands holding a fish (1953) by Pablo Picasso

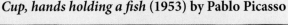

Reread for **Comprehension**

Evaluate

Author's Perspective

In order to evaluate the information in a text, it is important to understand the author's perspective. The attitude or opinions an author has toward the subject is his or her perspective.

An Author's Perspective Web can help you note clues about an author's perspective as you reread "A Change of Heart."

Author's Perspective

Comprehension

Genre

Historical Fiction may include fictional characters taking part in actual historical events from the past.

Evaluate

Author's Perspective

As you read, use your Author's Perspective Web.

Author's Perspective

Read to Find Out

How does the author make twelfth-century Korea come to life?

A Single Shard

by Linda Sue Park

illustrated by Julie Kim

Korea is an ancient country located on a peninsula on the eastern edge of Asia. In the 1100s, Korea was a kingdom of farmers and nobles. However, it also had potters, people who made beautiful vases and other objects from clay. The potters were considered to be artists. Tree-ear, the hero of this selection, has only one wish—to become a potter and make works of art from clay.

Tree-ear was so called after the mushroom that grew in wrinkled half-circles on dead or fallen tree trunks, emerging from the rotten wood without **benefit** of parent seed. A good name for an orphan, Crane-man said. If ever Tree-ear had had another name, he no longer remembered it, nor the family that might have named him so.

Tree-ear shared the space under the bridge with Crane-man—or rather, Crane-man shared it with him. After all, Crane-man had been there first, and would not be leaving anytime soon. The shriveled and twisted calf and foot he had been born with made sure of that.

Tree-ear knew the story of his friend's name. "When they saw my leg at birth, it was thought I would not survive," Crane-man had said. "Then, as I went through life on one leg, it was said that I was like a crane. But besides standing on one leg, cranes are also a symbol of long life." True enough, Crane-man added. He had outlived all his family and, unable to work, had been forced to sell his possessions one by one, including, at last, the roof over his head. Thus it was that he had come to live under the bridge.

Once, a year or so earlier, Tree-ear had asked him how long he had lived there. Crane-man shook his head; he no longer remembered. But then he brightened and hobbled over to one side of the bridge, beckoning Tree-ear to join him.

"I do not remember how long I have been here," he said, "but I know how long *you* have." And he pointed upward, to the underside of the bridge. "I wonder that I have not shown you this before."

On one of the slats was a series of deep scratches, as if made with a pointed stone. Tree-ear examined them, then shook his head at Crane-man. "So?"

"One mark for each spring since you came here," Crane-man explained. "I kept count of your years, for I thought the time would come when you would like to know how old you are."

Tree-ear looked again, this time with keen interest. There was a mark for each finger of both hands—ten marks in all.

Crane-man answered before Tree-ear asked. "No, you have more than ten years," he said. "When you first came and I began making those marks, you were in perhaps your second year—already on two legs and able to talk."

Tree-ear nodded. He knew the rest of the story already. Crane-man had learned but little from the man who had brought Tree-ear to the bridge. The man had been paid by a kindly monk in the city of Songdo to bring Tree-ear to the little seaside village of Ch'ulp'o. Tree-ear's parents had died of fever, and the monk knew of an uncle in Ch'ulp'o.

When the travelers arrived, the man discovered that the uncle no longer lived there, the house having been abandoned long before. He took Tree-ear to the temple on the mountainside, but the monks had been unable to take the boy in because fever raged there as well. The villagers told the man to take the child to the bridge, where Crane-man would care for him until the temple was free of sickness.

"And," Crane-man always said, "when a monk came to fetch you a few months later, you would not leave. You clung to my good leg like a monkey to a tree, not crying but not letting go, either! The monk went away. You stayed."

When Tree-ear was younger, he had asked for the story often, as if hearing it over and over again might reveal something more—what his father's trade had been, what his mother had looked like, where his uncle had gone— but there was never anything more. It no longer mattered. If there was more to having a home than Crane-man and the bridge, Tree-ear had neither knowledge nor need of it.

STRATEGY SKILL

Author's Perspective
What clues reveal how the author feels about Crane-man?

Breakfast that morning was a feast—a bit of the rice boiled to a gruel in a castoff earthenware pot, served up in a bowl carved from a gourd. And Crane-man produced yet another surprise to add to the meal: two chicken leg-bones. No flesh remained on the **arid** bones, but the two friends cracked them open and worried away every scrap of marrow from inside.

Afterward, Tree-ear washed in the river and fetched a gourd of water for Crane-man, who never went into the river if he could help it; he hated getting his feet wet. Then Tree-ear set about tidying up the area under the bridge. He took care to keep the place neat, for he disliked having to clear a space to sleep at the tired end of the day.

Housekeeping complete, Tree-ear left his companion and set off back up the road. This time he did not zigzag between rubbish heaps but strode purposefully toward a small house set apart from the others at a curve in the road.

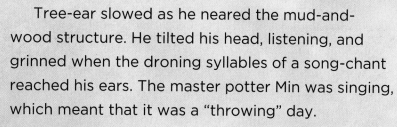

Tree-ear slowed as he neared the mud-and-wood structure. He tilted his head, listening, and grinned when the droning syllables of a song-chant reached his ears. The master potter Min was singing, which meant that it was a "throwing" day.

Min's house backed onto the beginnings of the foothills and their brushy growth, which gave way to pine-wooded mountains beyond. Tree-ear swung wide of the house. Under the deep **eaves** at the back, Min kept his potter's wheel. He was there now, his gray head bent over the wheel, chanting his wordless song.

Tree-ear made his way cautiously to his favorite spot, behind a paulownia tree whose low branches kept him hidden from view. He peeped through the leaves and caught his breath in delight. Min was just beginning a new pot.

Min threw a mass of clay the size of a cabbage onto the center of the wheel. He picked it up and threw it again, threw it several times. After one last throw he sat down and stared at the clay for a moment. Using his foot to spin the base of the wheel, he placed dampened hands on the sluggardly lump, and for the hundredth time Tree-ear watched the miracle.

In only a few moments the clay rose and fell, grew taller, then rounded down, until it curved into perfect **symmetry**. The spinning slowed. The chant, too, died out and became a mutter of words that Tree-ear could not hear.

Min sat up straight. He crossed his arms and leaned back a little, as if to see the vase from a distance. Turning the wheel slowly with his knee, he inspected the graceful shape for invisible faults. Then, "Pah!" He shook his head and in a single motion of disgust scooped up the clay and slapped it back onto the wheel, whereupon it collapsed into an oafish lump again, as if ashamed.

Tree-ear opened his mouth to let out his breath silently, only then realizing that he had been keeping it back. To his eyes the vase had been perfect, its width half its height, its curves like those of a flower petal. Why, he wondered, had Min found it unworthy? What had he seen that so displeased him?

Min never failed to reject his first attempt. Then he would repeat the whole process. This day Tree-ear was able to watch the clay rise and fall four times before Min was satisfied. Each of the four efforts had looked identical to Tree-ear, but something about the fourth pleased Min. He took a length of twine and slipped it **deftly** under the vase to release it from the wheel, then placed the vase carefully on a tray to dry.

As Tree-ear crept away, he counted the days on his fingers. He knew the potter's routine well; it would be many days before another throwing day.

The village of Ch'ulp'o faced the sea, its back to the mountains and the river edging it like a neat seam. Its potters produced the delicate celadon ware that had achieved fame not only in Korea but as far away as the court of the Chinese emperor.

Ch'ulp'o had become an important village for **ceramics** by virtue of both its location and its soil. On the shore of the Western Sea, it had access both to the easiest sea route northward and to plentiful trade with China. And the clay from the village pits contained exactly the right amount of iron to produce the exquisite gray-green color of celadon so prized by collectors.

Tree-ear knew every potter in the village, but until recently he had known them only for their rubbish heaps. It was hard for him to believe that he had never taken the time to watch them at work before. In recent years the pottery from the village kilns had gained great favor among those wealthy enough to buy pieces as gifts for both the royal court and the Buddhist temples, and the potters had achieved new levels of prosperity. The pickings from their rubbish heaps had become richer in consequence, and for the first time Tree-ear was able to forget about his stomach for a few hours each day.

During those hours it was Min he chose to watch most closely. The other potters kept their wheels in small windowless shacks. But in the warm months Min preferred to work beneath the eaves behind his house, open to the breeze and the view of the mountains.

Working without walls meant that Min possessed great skill and confidence to match it. Potters guarded their secrets jealously. A new shape for a teapot, a new inscribed design—these were things that the potters refused to reveal until a piece was ready to show to a buyer.

Min did not seem to care about such secrecy. It was as if he were saying, *Go ahead, watch me. No matter—you will not be able to imitate my skill.*

Author's Perspective
How do you think the author feels about the potters and their craft?

It was true, and it was also the main reason that Tree-ear loved watching Min. His work was the finest in the region, perhaps even in the whole country.

Tree-ear peered between the leaves of the paulownia tree, puzzled. Several days had passed since his last visit to Min's house, and he had calculated that it was time for another throwing day. But there was no sign of Min at his work, nor any wet clay on the wheel. The workshop area was tidy, with a few chickens in the yard the only signs of life.

Emboldened by the silence, Tree-ear emerged from his hiding place and approached the house. Against the wall was a set of shelves holding a few of Min's latest creations. They were at the stage the potters called "leather-hard"— dried by the air but not yet glazed or fired. Unglazed, the work was of little interest to thieves. The finished pieces were surely locked up somewhere in the house.

Tree-ear paused at the edge of the brush and listened hard one last time. A hen clucked proudly, and Tree-ear grinned—Min would have an egg for his supper. But there was still no sign of the potter, so Tree-ear tiptoed the last few steps to stand before the shelves.

For the first time he was seeing Min's work at close range. There was a duck that would have fit in the palm of his hand, with a tiny hole in its bill. Tree-ear had seen such a duck in use before. A painter had been sitting on the riverbank, working on a water scene. The painter had poured water from the duck's bill onto a stone a single drop at a time, mixing ink to exactly the correct consistency for his work.

Tree-ear stared at Min's duck. Though it was now a dull gray, so detailed were its features that he found himself half listening for the sound of a quack. Min had shaped and then carved the clay to form curve of wing and tilt of head. Even the little tail curled up with an impudence that made Tree-ear smile.

He tore his gaze away from the duck to examine the next piece, a tall jug with ribbed lines that imitated the shape of a melon. The lines were perfectly symmetrical, curving so gracefully from top to bottom that Tree-ear longed to run his finger along the smooth shallow grooves. The melon's stem and leaves were cleverly shaped to form the lid of the jug.

The last piece on the shelf was the least interesting—a rectangular lidded box as large as his two hands. It was completely undecorated. Disappointed in its plainness, Tree-ear was ready to turn away when a thought struck him. Outside, the box was plain, but perhaps inside . . .

Holding his breath, he reached out, gently lifted the lid, and looked inside. He grinned in double delight at his own correct guess and at Min's skill. The plain box held five smaller boxes— a small round one in the center and four curved boxes that fit around it perfectly. The small boxes appeared to completely fill the larger container, but Min had left exactly the right amount of space to allow any of them to be lifted out.

Tree-ear put the lid of the large box down on the shelf and picked up one of the curved containers. On the underside of its lid was a lip of clay that held the lid in place. Tree-ear's eyes flickered back and forth between the small pieces in his hand and the larger container, his brow **furrowed** in thought.

How did Min fit them together so perfectly? Perhaps he made the large box, then a second one to fit inside, and cut the smaller boxes from that? Or did he make an inside box first and fit the larger box around it? Maybe he began with the small central box, then the curved ones, then—

Someone shouted. The chickens squawked noisily and Tree-ear dropped what he was holding. He stood there, paralyzed for a moment.

It was the old potter. "Thief!" he screamed. "How dare you come here! How dare you touch my work!"

Tree-ear did the only thing he could think of. He dropped to his knees and cowered in a deep formal bow.

"Please! Please, honorable sir, I was not stealing your work—I came only to admire it."

The potter stood over the boy.

"Have you been here before, beggar-boy?"

Tree-ear's thoughts scrambled about as he tried to think what to answer. The truth seemed easiest.

"Yes, honorable sir. I come often to watch you work."

"Ah!"

Tree-ear was still doubled over in his bow, but he allowed himself a single sigh of relief.

"So is it you who breaks the twigs and bruises the leaves of the paulownia tree just beyond?"

Tree-ear nodded, feeling his face flush. He had thought he was covering his tracks well.

"Not to steal, you say? How do I know you do not watch just to see when I have made something of extra value?"

Now Tree-ear raised his head and looked at Min. He kept his voice respectful, but his words were proud.

"I would not steal. Stealing and begging make a man no better than a dog."

The potter stared at the boy for a long moment. At last, Min seemed to make up his mind about something, and when he spoke again, his voice had lost the sharpest edge of its anger.

"So you were not stealing. It is the same thing to me—with one part damaged, the rest is of no use." He gestured at the misshapen pottery box on the ground, badly dented from its fall. "Get on your way, then. I know better than to ask for payment for what you have ruined."

Tree-ear stood slowly, shame hot in his breast. It was true. He could never hope to pay Min for the damaged box.

Min picked it up and tossed it on the rubbish heap at the side of the yard. He continued to mutter crossly. "*Ai*, three days' work, and for what? For nothing. I am behind now. The order will be late . . . "

Tree-ear had taken a few dragging steps out of the yard. But on hearing the old potter's mutterings, he lifted his head and turned back toward him.

"Honorable potter? Sir? Could I not work for you, as payment? Perhaps my help could save you some time . . . "

Min shook his head impatiently. "What could you do, an untrained child? I have no time to teach you—you would be more trouble than help."

Tree-ear stepped forward eagerly. "You would not need to teach so much as you think, sir. I have been watching you for many months now. I know how you mix the clay, and turn the wheel—I have watched you make many things . . . "

The potter waved one hand to cut off the boy's words and spoke with **derision**. "Turn the wheel! Ha! He thinks he can sit and make a pot—just like that!"

Tree-ear crossed his arms stubbornly and did not look away. Min picked up the rest of the box set and tossed it too on the rubbish heap. He muttered under his breath, so Tree-ear could not hear the words.

Min straightened up and glanced around, first at his shelf, then at the wheel, and finally at Tree-ear.

"Yes, all right," he said, his voice still rough with annoyance. "Come tomorrow at daybreak, then. Three days it took me to make that box, so you will give me nine days' work in return. I cannot even begin to think how much greater the value of my work is than yours, but we will settle on this for a start."

Tree-ear bowed in agreement. He walked around the side of the house, then flew off down the road. He could hardly wait to tell Crane-man. For the first time in his life he would have real work to do.

Meet the Author and Illustrator

Linda Sue Park has been writing since she was four. When she was nine, she was paid a dollar by *Trailblazer Magazine* for a haiku she wrote. She never cashed the check. Today it is framed and hanging above her father's desk. Linda continued writing, but it wasn't until she had her second baby that she decided to write for children. For this story she reached deep into her Korean heritage. Linda now lives in upstate New York with her husband, their two children, and a dog named Fergus.

Other books by Linda Sue Park: *The Kite Fighters* and *Seesaw Girl*

Julie Kim, originally from Korea, now lives in Seattle, Washington, with her husband, Peter. She is a graduate of Rhode Island School of Design and has illustrated several magazines and books for children.

LOG ON Find out more about Linda Sue Park and Julie Kim at **www.macmillanmh.com**

Author's Purpose

This selection is historical fiction set in a specific time period. Do you think Linda Sue Park mainly wanted to inform readers about that time period or did she have another purpose? Explain.

Comprehension Check

Summarize

Summarize *A Single Shard*. What change takes place in Tree-ear's life by the end of the story? What leads up to this event?

Think and Compare

1. Use your Author's Perspective Web to think about how the writer paints a picture of life in twelfth-century Korea. Explain how the story would change if the author felt differently about the Korean potters. **Evaluate: Author's Perspective**

2. Compare and contrast the roles of Crane-man and Min, the potter in Tree-ear's life. How does each of them influence the boy? Use specific examples from the text. **Analyze**

3. Think about a person from whom you have learned a lot. What was his or her role in your life? How would you describe the **benefit** of his or her wisdom? **Synthesize**

4. Think about what you have read in *A Single Shard*. What qualities should a good teacher possess? **Evaluate**

5. Read "A Change of Heart" on pages 452-453. If Tree-ear were to talk to Joe about pottery, what do you think he might say? **Reading/Writing Across Texts**

Encyclopedias

Encyclopedia articles are arranged alphabetically. Article titles are in boldface type. Unless they are proper nouns, article titles may not be capitalized. Encyclopedia entries sometimes provide cross-references, often in capital letters.

apprentices in the past were young men who learned a trade or craft from an adult who was an expert in a chosen field. The young man's family would pay a set fee for him to live with the experienced worker, and in return, the adult would teach him all he knew about the field and give him room, **board**, clothing, and nurse him through any illnesses. The young man was usually required to stay for a fixed number of years. He was given hands-on training until he was ready to set himself up independently in the trade or craft, or to work for the master for wages. Apprentices have a long history, dating back to ancient Babylon, Egypt, Greece, and Rome. In Europe, they flourished until the 19th century. In **medieval** times, rules were established to **regulate** and supervise apprentices. The guidelines were meant to protect apprentices from abuse. Many apprenticeships faded from existence with the Industrial Revolution when machinery replaced various skilled laborers. However, some apprentice programs endure today, in trades such as plumbing and carpentry. See also TRADES.

Encyclopedias come in different formats, including sets of books, CD-ROMs, and online. Online encyclopedias have links to topics mentioned in the article. The links are often in a different color type.

Connect and Compare

1. What would you expect to find about apprentices in the cross-reference information under "trades"?
Reading an Encyclopedia Entry

2. How would a young person benefit from being an apprentice? How would an experienced worker benefit from having an apprentice? **Evaluate**

3. How did reading the entry about apprentices help you understand *A Single Shard*? **Reading /Writing Across Texts**

Social Studies Activity

Research a craft or job that still uses apprentices. Write a reference article about it.

 Find out more about apprentices at **www.macmillanmh.com**

Writer's Craft

Multiple Paragraphs

When writing **multiple paragraphs**, start each with a topic sentence. Use detail sentences to support the main idea. Transition words can help connect ideas between paragraphs. A strong conclusion sums up.

Write a Magazine Article

An Unusual Art

by Joyce S.

> I used transition words to connect ideas between paragraphs.

> I concluded by pointing out how extraordinary quilters are.

When you think of artwork, what do you picture? A painting? A sculpture? Few think of quilting, but quilting is a popular art form that has been around for hundreds of years.

In fact, handmade quilts show the quilter's skill and artistry. The stitching is very important and so is the pattern. There are traditional patterns for special events, such as marriage or the birth of a baby, and some quilts even tell stories. Since the 1700s, quilting has been a pastime mainly for women, which sets it apart from other art forms. The fact that quilts have an everyday use also sets them apart.

Quilting has played an important role around the globe. Victorian Crazy Quilts, Native American and African American quilts, and modern-day Amish quilts all come in a range of fabrics, styles, and prices. They show the extraordinary design talent of "ordinary" women.

Your Turn

Write a brief magazine article about the arts or a specific artist. For example, you might write about a local artist in your town or about a particular art form. Include interesting details about your topic. Add transition words to connect ideas between paragraphs. Use the Writer's Checklist to review your article.

Writer's Checklist

☑ **Ideas and Content:** Did I use enough details in each of my **multiple paragraphs** to keep readers interested?

✓ **Organization:** How is my article organized? Does the organization make sense?

✓ **Voice:** Did I use words and phrases that allow the article to reflect my personality?

✓ **Word Choice:** Did I use vocabulary appropriate for a magazine article? Did I include transition words?

✓ **Sentence Fluency:** Did I begin sentences in different ways? Did I use words properly?

✓ **Conventions:** Did I use words such as *there* and *their* correctly? Did I check my spelling?

Gwendolyn Brooks: A Voice

"Every day there's something exciting or disturbing to write about. With all that's going on, how could I stop?"

Gwendolyn Brooks never did stop. In her lifetime she witnessed some of the most pivotal events in modern American history and recorded them. Her poetry acted as a clear voice to help guide future generations through trouble and triumph.

The Voice of a Child

Born in 1917 in Topeka, Kansas, Gwendolyn moved with her family to Chicago later that year. She grew up watching her father work as a janitor, knowing that he had wanted to become a doctor but could not afford it. Early on, Gwendolyn knew that he was the kind of person she wanted to write about. She would write about the working man, the caring mother, the forgotten soldier, and the lonely child.

She began to write down her feelings and experiences. She wrote her first poem when she was only seven. When her parents saw how naturally she took to writing, they gave her a writing desk of her own. At the age of 13, Gwendolyn published a poem called "Eventide" in *American Childhood* magazine. Gwendolyn's voice

Go On ▶

continued to rush from her. By 16, she had collected a portfolio of work that included more than seventy-five published poems.

The Voice of a Teenager

"I felt that I had to write," Gwendolyn once said. "Even if I had never been published, I knew that I would go on writing, enjoying it and experiencing the challenge." Gwendolyn took a job at the *Chicago Defender*, a newspaper that focused on Chicago's African American community. Newspaper work taught Gwendolyn to view things from the outside, to observe and record the world in order to make sense of it. She saw life as a poem, a sad and wonderful song that took place every day for everyone. In particular, she felt the need to write about African Americans in Chicago, a world that was often overlooked.

Gwendolyn worked hard to learn everything she could about writing. She graduated with a degree in English and attended poetry workshops. Working with other talented young writers, she learned all of the techniques and tools of classic and modern poetry and began to shape her unique poetic voice.

The Voice of the Silent

Gwendolyn's first collection of poetry was published in 1945. It was called *A Street in Bronzeville*, which was a neighborhood in Chicago. It overflowed with life—real life that was rarely the subject of traditional poetry. Her subject was the African American community, but her voice appealed to everyone. She wrote about "life" as a universal truth, not as an experience to be divided into races, classes, or genders.

A Street in Bronzeville was a huge hit with both critics and audiences, but even Gwendolyn couldn't have predicted the success to come. Her next book, *Annie Allen* (1949), received even more attention. It was the story of an African American woman's journey from youth to adulthood. Critics loved it and readers applauded Gwendolyn's brave portrayal of an African American woman's experience in American society.

Annie Allen became the first book by an African American writer to win the prestigious Pulitzer Prize.

The Voice of Equality

All of those nights at her childhood writing desk had led Gwendolyn Brooks to America's top literary prize, yet she did not stop there. Her voice continued to speak to her.

Now famous and well-respected, Gwendolyn wrote what she felt needed to be written. She examined the changing experiences of African Americans all over the country. She wrote like a reporter, as an outsider looking in. That all changed in 1967, when Gwendolyn attended an African American writer's conference in Tennessee.

There she met young writers who had their own stories, poetry, and opinions. At that time civil rights was a key issue in American politics. Listening to all those writers, Gwendolyn felt a part of the struggle for freedom. The young thinkers and artists inspired her to rediscover her writing and herself.

A Voice for All Time

Gwendolyn Brooks spent her later years using poetry to advance the rights of African Americans in the United States. She knew that people were listening and she never let her voice grow quiet. Gwendolyn won many awards in her final years, but no award compared to her desire to spread the word of poetry to all. It was her gift. It was her voice.

On December 3, 2000, Gwendolyn Brooks died. Her voice fell silent, but her words live on.

Go On ▶

Directions: Answer the questions.

Tip

You have to think about the entire selection to choose the best answer.

1. **What does the author mean by saying Gwendolyn's voice rushed from her?**

   A She spoke quickly.
   B She wrote without thinking.
   C She produced many poems in a short time.
   D She rushed her ideas, and her poems were all very similar.

2. **Why did Gwendolyn want to write poetry?**

   A to get published
   B to explain her view of the world
   C that was all she was trained to do
   D it was the best way to make money quickly

3. **Why was *Annie Allen* an important book?**

   A It told about the difficulties of being an African American woman.
   B It shows that Gwendolyn could write about Asian women.
   C It brought Gwendolyn a large amount of prize money.
   D It changed people's opinions about poetry.

4. **How did Gwendolyn's poetry help African Americans?**

5. **Gwendolyn Brooks "never let her voice grow quiet." How does her voice speak in her writing? Write two paragraphs and use details from the selection to support your response.**

Writing Prompt

Gwendolyn Brooks is the Author of the Month. Write a news article about her life and the impact she has had on her audience. Your article should be at least three paragraphs long.

STOP 479

MENTORS

Talk About It

Think of a time when you helped a younger student. What did you learn from the experience?

LOG ON Find out more about mentoring at **www.macmillanmh.com**

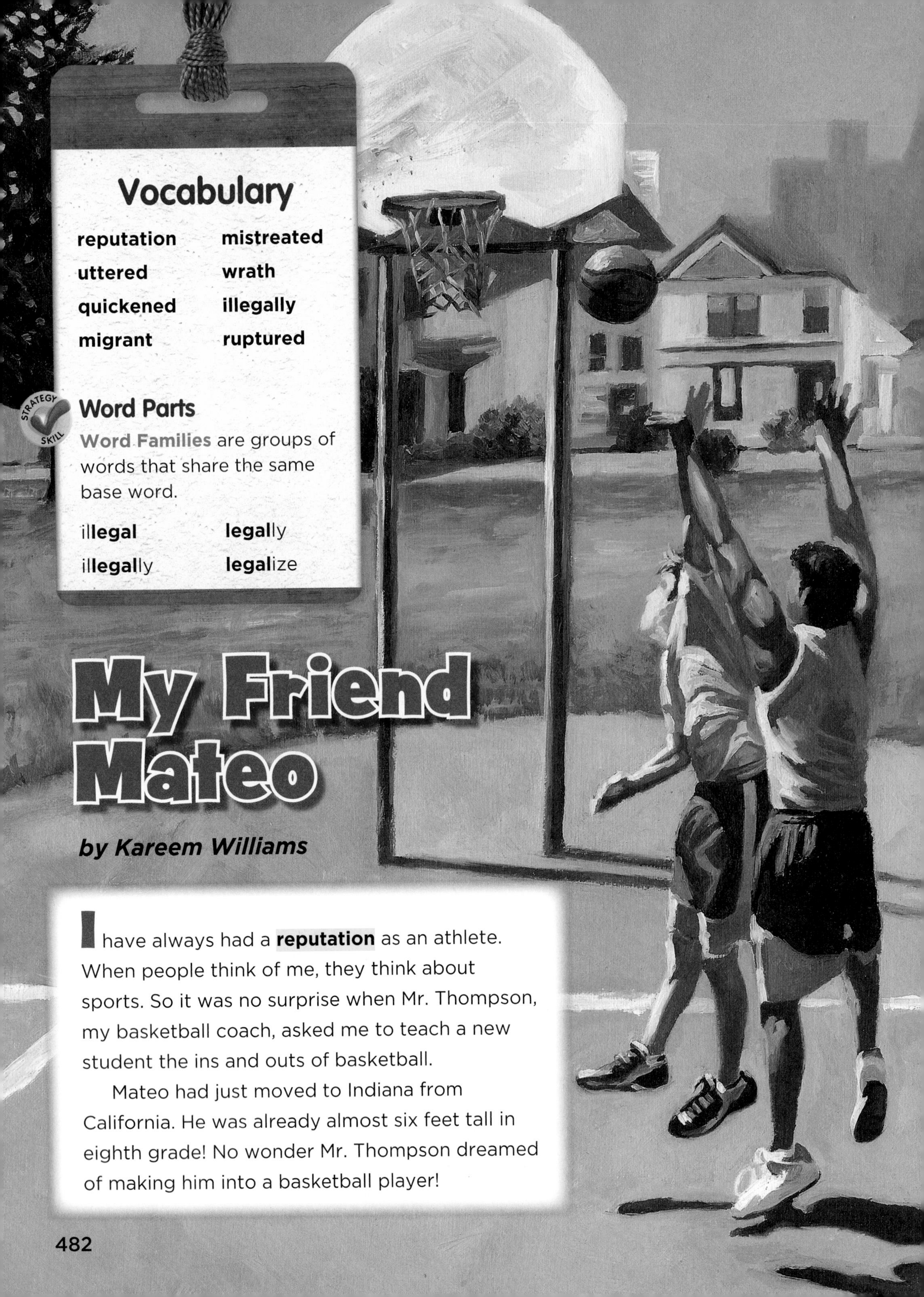

Vocabulary

reputation
uttered
quickened
migrant

mistreated
wrath
illegally
ruptured

Word Parts

STRATEGY SKILL

Word Families are groups of words that share the same base word.

il**legal**

il**legal**ly

legally

legalize

My Friend Mateo

by Kareem Williams

I have always had a **reputation** as an athlete. When people think of me, they think about sports. So it was no surprise when Mr. Thompson, my basketball coach, asked me to teach a new student the ins and outs of basketball.

Mateo had just moved to Indiana from California. He was already almost six feet tall in eighth grade! No wonder Mr. Thompson dreamed of making him into a basketball player!

Mateo was shy. The first time I met him at basketball practice he **uttered** the word "hello" to me, but he didn't move his eyes away from the floor. That shyness didn't last for long, however. Soon he had **quickened** his running and perfected his dribbling. Before long, I couldn't get him to stop talking!

The more I got to know Mateo, the more I liked him. He had lived a life that was different from mine, and I was very interested in the stories he told. He said that his parents were **migrant** farmworkers when they first moved to the United States. The family moved from town to town so his parents could find farmwork. He said that a few of the bosses were not kind to his parents and that some even **mistreated** them. Mateo said that sometimes his parents were treated unkindly when they made a mistake, but sometimes they suffered the boss's **wrath** just because the boss was in a bad mood. Often this anger would drive Mateo's family to move and find new work.

Mateo got to be pretty good at basketball. He was probably even better than I was! He could drive to the net without traveling **illegally**. But during our fourth game of the season, Mateo **ruptured** the tendon in his right knee. This means that the band of tissue holding his knee together had ripped or broken. All I know is that Mateo was done with basketball for a while. But I wasn't done with Mateo! We've been best friends ever since!

Reread for **Comprehension**

Evaluate

Author's Purpose
Understanding why an author wrote a selection will help you to better evaluate that piece. Authors write to inform, to persuade, or to entertain.

Use the Author's Purpose Chart to keep track of the clues that reveal the author's purpose as you reread "My Friend Mateo."

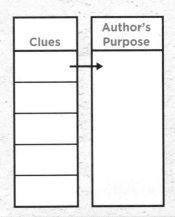

Clues	Author's Purpose

483

Comprehension

Genre

An **Autobiographical Story** tells of a specific period of a person's life written and often embellished by that person.

Evaluate

Author's Purpose

As you read, use your Author's Purpose Chart.

Clues	Author's Purpose

Read to Find Out

How does Francisco's drive help him succeed?

BREAKING THROUGH
by Francisco Jiménez

Francisco Jiménez has written several books about growing up in California after leaving Mexico. In this chapter, he writes about a special teacher and how she helped him to learn to enjoy reading, a discovery that changed his life.

At the end of my freshman year,

I received good grades in all subjects except English, even though I had worked the hardest in it. Writing was difficult for me. My freshman English teacher told me that my writing was weak. She suggested that I read more, that reading would improve my writing. "At least read the newspaper every day," she told me. "Read for enjoyment." I had little time to read. I read only for information for my classes, and I could barely keep up. Besides, we had no reading material at home and we didn't get the newspaper. I never got more free time to read all during high school, but I did learn to read for enjoyment. It happened in my sophomore year, in English class.

Miss Audrey Bell, my teacher, had a **reputation** for being hard. When she walked into the class the first day and wrote her name on the board, I heard moans from classmates sitting next to me. "I am sunk!" one of them said. "Hello, F," another **uttered**. Now I was even more worried.

Miss Bell had a round face, a small turned-up nose, full lips, and lively blue eyes, and she wore wire-rimmed glasses. Her smile never left her, even when she was upset. When she wrote on the board, her upper arm shook like jelly, just like Mamá's arms. The back of her hands were covered with small brown spots the size of raisins, and her shiny nails looked like the wings of red beetles. She teased students and often made comments that made the class laugh. I laughed too, even though sometimes I did not understand her jokes.

No one laughed at her homework assignments, though. Every week she gave us vocabulary and spelling lists and a poem to memorize. I wrote the poems on notecards and attached them to the broom handle or placed them in my shirt pocket and memorized them as I cleaned the offices after school. I did the same thing with spelling and vocabulary words. I had a harder time with reading and writing. I was a slow reader and often had to read each assignment twice. At times my mind wandered off as I worried about Papá.

A typical school and
classroom from the 1950s

When we discussed the readings in class, I was surprised to find out that I had not really understood what I read.

Writing was even more difficult for me. Miss Bell asked us to write short compositions analyzing short stories we read for class. I was happy whenever I understood the plot and summarized it, but this was not good enough. "Don't tell me the story," she would say, smiling. "I know it. I want you to analyze it." I thought I knew what she meant, so in my next composition I wrote about the lesson I learned from reading the story. I hoped this was what she wanted. The stories I had heard from Papá and Mamá, Tío Mauricio, and other **migrant** workers all had a lesson in them about right and wrong, like "La Llorona," "The Boy and His Grandfather," or "The Three Brothers."

When Miss Bell returned our compositions, I fixed my eyes on the stack of papers as she walked around the aisles passing them out, trying to spot mine. The one with the most writing in red was sure to be mine. My papers always came back looking as though she had poured red ink on them. My heart pounded faster with each step she took toward me. She grinned as she handed me my paper. I quickly grabbed it. It had fewer corrections than my previous papers, but the grade was only a disappointing C. I stuck it in my binder, and for the rest of the class I had a hard time concentrating. During study hall, I took out the paper. She had written "Good progress" at the bottom of it. I felt better. I then went over the corrections carefully to make sure I understood them. I did not want to make the same mistakes in my next writing assignment, which Miss Bell announced the following day.

Author's Purpose
Why does the author focus on his writing skills?

"Our next unit is on autobiography, the history of a person's life written or told by that person," she explained. "So for your next composition, I want you to write about a personal experience, something that happened to you." I liked the assignment, but it was harder than I expected. I thought of writing about being deported, but I did not want my teacher to know that my family had crossed the border **illegally** and that I was born in Mexico.

An idea finally came to me late that evening. As I was sitting at the kitchen table trying to figure out what to write, Trampita entered the room, pulling up his white shorts. "What are you doing up?" I asked.

Francisco, José Francisco (Trampita),
and Roberto, Tent City, Santa Maria, California

489

Papá, Trampita, and neighbor Don Pancho at Bonetti Ranch,
Santa Maria, California

"I am getting a glass of water," he responded, half asleep.
His small body cast a thin shadow on the wall. We called him
"Trampita," "little tramp," because Mamá had dressed him in
baby clothes we found in the city dump. As he passed me on
his way back to bed, I noticed his bulging navel, the size of
an egg, that had **ruptured** when he was a few months old.

We had been living in a farm labor camp in Santa Rosa.
It was winter. Papá and Mamá worked at an apple cannery at
night and left Roberto to take care of Trampita and me while
they were gone. One evening, before leaving for work, Mamá
prepared the milk bottle for Trampita and laid him on a wide

mattress that was on the dirt floor. After my parents left, Roberto and I sat on the mattress and told ghost stories until we got sleepy. We said our prayers and went to bed next to Trampita. We kept our clothes on because it was freezing cold. At dawn, we woke up, frightened by our parents' screams. "Where's Trampita?" Mamá cried out. "Where is he?" Papá shouted. They had terror in their eyes when they saw Trampita was gone.

"I don't know, Mamá," Roberto stuttered, shivering from the cold. Papá noticed an opening at the foot of the tent near the mattress. He rushed out. Seconds later he returned with Trampita in his arms. My baby brother was stiff and purple.

(left) José Francisco (Trampita) and Roberto, picking plums in Orosi, California. (right) José Francisco

I decided to write about that experience. I wrote three drafts, making sure I did not make any mistakes. I turned it in feeling confident. When I got my paper back, I was disappointed to see the red marks again. I had made a few errors. I felt worse when I read Miss Bell's note at the bottom of the paper, asking me to see her after class. *She must be pretty upset with the mistakes I made,* I thought. I half listened to what she said during the rest of class. When class was over, I waited until everyone had left the room before I approached her, folding the paper in half to hide the red marks.

"Is what you wrote a true story?" Miss Bell asked.

"Yes," I answered, feeling anxious.

"I thought so," she said, smiling. "It's a very moving story. Did your brother die?"

"Oh, no!" I exclaimed. "He almost did, but God saved him. He rolled off the mattress, landed outside the tent, and cried so much that he hurt his navel."

"His hernia must have really hurt," she said thoughtfully. "I am sorry." She looked away and cleared her throat. "Now, let's look at your paper." I handed it to her, lowering my head. "You're making a lot of progress," she said. "Your writing shows promise. If you're able to overcome the difficulties like the one you described in your paper and you continue working as hard as you have, you're going to succeed." She gave me back the paper and added, "Here, take it home, make the corrections, and turn it in to me tomorrow after class."

"I will. Thank you, Miss Bell." I floated out of the room, thinking about how lucky I was to be in her class. She reminded me of Mr. Lema, my sixth-grade teacher, who had helped me with English during the lunch hour.

That evening when I got home I worked on the paper. I looked at the mistakes I had made and corrected them, following Miss Bell's suggestions. As I retyped it on the kitchen table, Mamá came over and sat next to me. "It's late, Panchito," she said softly. "Time for bed."

An old typewriter
from the 1950s

"I am almost finished."

"What are you working on, *mijo?*"

"It's a paper I wrote for my English class on Trampita. My teacher liked it," I said proudly.

"On Trampita!" she exclaimed.

She got up and stood behind me. She placed her hands on my shoulders and asked me to read it. When I finished, I felt her tears on the back of my neck.

The next day after class I turned in my revised paper to Miss Bell. She glanced at it, placed it on a pile of papers on her desk, and picked up a book. "Have you read *The Grapes of **Wrath***?" she asked. "It's a wonderful novel by John Steinbeck."

"No," I said, wondering what the word *wrath* meant.

"I'd like for you to read it." She handed it to me. "I think you'll enjoy it. You can read it for your book report."

When am I going to find time to read such a thick book? I thought, running my fingers along its spine. I was planning to read a smaller book for my report. Miss Bell must have noticed the pain in my face because she added, "And you'll get extra credit because it's a long book." I felt better.

"Thanks!" I said. "It'll give me a chance to improve my grade." Her gentle smile reminded me of Mamá and the blessing she gave every morning when I left the house.

After my last class, I picked up the books and binders I needed from my locker and walked to the public library to study before going to work at five o'clock. I double-checked to make sure I had the novel with me. On the way, I kept thinking about how I was going to get through such a long book. I felt its weight on my shoulders and the back of my neck. I **quickened** my pace, passing students left and right. The honking of car horns from students cruising by sounded far away. I rushed into the library and went straight to my table in the left back corner, away from the main desk. I piled my books and binders on the table.

I took a deep breath, picked up the novel, and placed it in front of me. I grabbed my worn-out pocket dictionary from the stack and set it next to it. I muttered the title, *"The Grapes of Wrath."* The word *grapes* reminded me of working in the vineyards for Mr. Sullivan in Fresno. I looked up the word *wrath* and thought of the anger I felt when I lost my blue notepad, my *librito*, in a fire in Orosi. I began reading. It was difficult; I had to look up many words, but I kept on reading. I wanted to learn more about the Joad family, who had to leave their home in Oklahoma to look for work and a better life in California. I lost track of time. Before I knew it, five o'clock had passed. I was late for work.

When I got home that evening, I continued reading until one o'clock in the morning. That night I dreamed that my family was packing to move to Fresno to pick grapes. "We don't have to move anymore! I have to go to school!" I kept yelling, but Papá and Mamá could not hear me. I woke up exhausted.

Author's Purpose
What is the author's purpose in describing Francisco's fascination with the book?

Saturday night I skipped the school dance and stayed home to read more of the novel. I kept struggling with the reading, but I could not put it down. I finally understood what Miss Bell meant when she told me to read for enjoyment. I could relate to what I was reading. The Joad family was poor and traveled from place to place in an old jalopy, looking for work. They picked grapes and cotton and lived in labor camps similar to the ones we lived in, like Tent City in Santa Maria. Ma Joad

Francisco, freshman at Santa Maria High School

was like Mamá and Pa Joad was a lot like Papá. Even though they were not Mexican and spoke only English, they had many of the same experiences as my family. I felt for them. I got angry with the growers who **mistreated** them and was glad when Tom Joad protested and fought for their rights. He reminded me of my friend Don Gabriel, the *bracero* who stood up to Díaz, the labor contractor, who tried to force Don Gabriel to pull a plow like an ox.

After I finished reading the novel, I could not get it out of my mind. I thought about it for days, even after I had turned in the book report to Miss Bell. She must have liked what I wrote, because she gave me a good grade. My success made me happy, but, this time, the grade seemed less important than what I had learned from reading the book.

Meet the Author

Francisco Jiménez's family came to the United States from Mexico as migrant workers when he was four years old. Francisco worked in the fields, too. When he started school, he found it hard because he did not speak or understand English. He even failed first grade. But he soon realized that learning and knowledge were important. When he started writing, he wrote about how it felt to grow up in two cultures. Today he is a professor of modern languages at a university in California.

Francisco Jiménez

 LOG ON Find out more about Francisco Jiménez at **www.macmillanmh.com**

Author's Purpose

The author wants to persuade readers of the power of education, entertain readers with a story, and inform readers about migrant workers in the 1950s. Give an example from the story of each purpose.

 **Comprehension Check**

Summarize

Summarize what happens in *Breaking Through*. Miss Bell suggests that reading will help improve a person's writing skills. How does her suggestion shape the events in the story?

Think and Compare

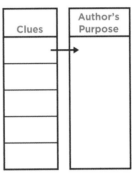

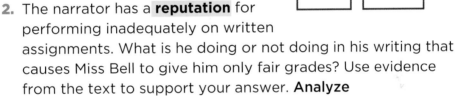

1. Why does the author choose to tell about his time in Miss Bell's class? Use the Author's Purpose Chart to help you support your answer. **Evaluate: Author's Purpose**

2. The narrator has a **reputation** for performing inadequately on written assignments. What is he doing or not doing in his writing that causes Miss Bell to give him only fair grades? Use evidence from the text to support your answer. **Analyze**

3. The teacher asks Francisco to read *The Grapes of Wrath* for his book report. What book has had the greatest impact on how you think and act? How did it change your ideas? **Apply**

4. How can writing change how people view themselves, other people, and the world? **Evaluate**

5. Read "My Friend Mateo" on pages 482–483. How are Mateo's family and the narrator's family in *Breaking Through* similar? **Reading/Writing Across Texts**

Genre

A **Letter to the Editor** is usually from a reader to a newspaper or magazine expressing an opinion.

Text Feature

Schedules are graphic aids that often show a timetable.

Content Vocabulary

persuade   exceptional

excel   commitment

Mentoring Matters

When members of a sixth-grade mentoring group realized they needed more mentors, they decided to invite other students. Mark, one of the mentors, offered to write a letter to **persuade** readers of the school newspaper to become mentors.

To the Editor:

I am writing on behalf of One-on-One, the sixth-grade mentoring group. Our group is two years old and our mission is to help students reach their goals through mentoring. You could consider this good classroom citizenship as it helps others in your school.

Our group consists of 14 students who **excel** in different subjects. Each member is assigned to a student who can use help in one of these subjects and has similar interests and schedules.

We hope the readers of this school newspaper will join our group. Many students would benefit from the **exceptional** skills of a mentor. Mentors can inspire other students who want to follow a similar path. This is my first year as a mentor, but I have already learned that everyone involved in mentoring gets something out of it. I was assigned to a mentor last year.

As it turns out, mentoring was one of the best things that happened to me. It helped me focus on certain math concepts that I just didn't get. I was able to turn the corner at an important point in my studies, going from nearly failing math, to not only passing, but to having math become one of my favorite subjects! It still amazes me that I completely changed from almost hating math to loving it! Would you believe I'm even thinking of studying math in college? Even if I don't, I have skills that I will use for the rest of my life.

My own experience convinced me to become a mentor this year and help other students like myself. Now that I am a mentor, I realize what a good feeling you get from helping someone else and knowing that you're making a difference in his or her life. In many cases, lasting friendships are made as well. My mentor and I hit it off right away, and we're still good friends today.

Becoming a mentor is a serious **commitment**. Mentors spend one hour every week with the student they are mentoring.

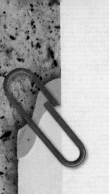

Considering your responsibilities, it may be difficult to add another commitment to your schedule. But I hope you will at least consider the possibility.

Please come to our next meeting on Wednesday at 1:00 P.M. (bring your lunch). You can meet the other mentors, learn more about what we do, and hear from a few students who will share their own personal stories.

Thank you for considering our invitation. We look forward to hearing from you.

Sincerely,

Mark Lopez

Time for Mentoring

Knowing your weekly schedule is just one of several factors you need to consider if you are thinking about becoming a mentor. By comparing your schedule with the schedule of the student you might be mentoring, you will be able to tell when you both are available. Meghann will have to compare her schedule with Christine's to see when it will be possible for them to meet.

Meghann's Schedule

	Monday	Tuesday	Wednesday	Thursday	Friday
8:15–8:30	Homeroom	Homeroom	Homeroom	Homeroom	Homeroom
8:30–10:00	Math	PE	Math	PE	Math/PE
10:00–11:30	Science	Spanish	Science	Spanish	Science/Spanish
11:30–1:00	Art/Chorus	Computer/Drama	Art/Chorus	Computer/Drama	Art/Chorus Computer/Drama
1:00–1:30	Lunch	Lunch	Lunch	Lunch	Lunch
1:30–3:00	Language Arts	Social Studies	Language Arts	Social Studies	Language Arts/Social Studies
3:00–5:00	Volleyball Practice		Volleyball Practice	Volleyball Practice	
5:00–7:00		Home Game			Away Game

Christine's Schedule					
	Monday	**Tuesday**	**Wednesday**	**Thursday**	**Friday**
8:15–8:30	Homeroom	Homeroom	Homeroom	Homeroom	Homeroom
8:30–10:00	Language Arts	PE	Language Arts	PE	Language Arts/ PE
10:00–11:30	Math	Spanish	Math	Spanish	Math/Spanish
11:30–1:00	Social Studies	Science	Social Studies	Science	Social Studies/ Science
1:00–1:30	Lunch	Lunch	Lunch	Lunch	Lunch
1:30–3:00	Art/Band	Computer/ Library	Art/Band	Computer/ Library	Art/Band/ Computer
3:00–5:00	Soccer Practice		Soccer Practice	Soccer Practice	
5:00–7:00					Soccer Game

Connect and Compare

1. Compare the two schedules. When can the girls meet? **Reading a Schedule**

2. How do you think Mark's experience last year will help him as a mentor this year? **Analyze**

3. Think about Mark and the student in *Breaking Through*. Explain why they both would be good mentors. **Reading/Writing Across Texts**

Social Studies Activity

Research mentoring programs in your area. Write a letter to your school newspaper about the value of mentors.

 Find out more about mentors at **www.macmillanmh.com**

Write a Speech

Meeting My Hero

by Bella L.

My purpose is to tell about the time I met my hero.

If you could meet anyone in the world, whom would you choose? Would you choose your hero? There was one special person I wanted to meet, and last year I did just that!

Sue Lopez is my hero. She is a dazzling basketball player who is going to try out for the WNBA team the Seattle Storm. In case you don't know, WNBA stands for Women's National Basketball Association, and Sue wants to be part of that league.

My cousin Sara lives in Seattle and plays basketball at school. In her spare time, Sue helped coach Sara's seventh-grade team last year. When I told my dad, he decided that we should visit Seattle during basketball season.

I used informal language in my speech.

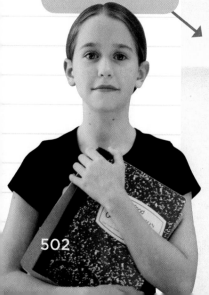

I went to Sara's practice with her, and she introduced me to Sue. Sue was glad I came to meet her. I told her how I wanted to grow up to be a basketball player just like her. Sue smiled and explained that she was once a young player like me who never imagined she would be trying out for a professional team. She said it took a lot of hard work, both in school and on the court, but she did it. Then she told me that I could do it, too!

Your Turn

Write a speech about someone you know or about someone you would like to know. Choose a formal or an informal tone, depending on your purpose, and make sure your voice is clear in your speech. Include adjectives that help describe the person. Use the Writer's Checklist to check your writing.

Writer's Checklist

 Ideas and Content: Is it clear whom I am describing and why I admire the person?

 Organization: Do I catch the listeners' attention in the beginning? Did I include details that will help my audience get to know the person?

Voice: Does my speech sound like me? Did I choose the appropriate **formal** or **informal language**?

 Word Choice: Do I use fresh and interesting language to describe the person?

 Sentence Fluency: Did I read my speech aloud to check the flow of language?

 Conventions: Did I proofread my speech, checking for proper spelling, grammar, and usage? Did I capitalize proper nouns and proper adjectives?

Talk About It

This mail carrier won't get stuck in traffic. What are some other problems he overcomes by using this vehicle?

LOG ON Find out more about smart thinking at **www.macmillanmh.com**

Smart Thinking

Vocabulary

participate	grimaced
ordeals	anticipated
nourishing	dejectedly
encounter	victorious

Word Parts

Many English words have **Latin Roots**. Prefixes and/or suffixes are added to the roots to form words.

The root *ject* means *throw*.

The prefix *de* means *down*.

Dejectedly means in a downcast manner.

Rites of Passage

by Luis Rivera

Carlos sat at his friend Aaron's house trying to prepare their oral report on "rites of passage." These are celebrations that mark a special moment in life, like growing up. All humans **participate** in rites of passage, but Carlos could not think of anything he would take part in.

In social studies they had read about Native Americans. Some of their young people went through **ordeals**, or challenges, which tested a young person's spirit and bravery.

Ana's quinceañera

Carlos learned that some of the tests required boys and girls to spend time alone in nature. They had to find **nourishing** food to stay healthy. They might have had to face a dangerous animal, which would have been a scary **encounter**. Carlos **grimaced** at the thought. Aaron noticed the look on his face.

"How is your research going?" Aaron asked.

"Well," Carlos said, "my sister, Ana, got to have a quinceañera. That means fifteenth year." Carlos thought of how Ana had **anticipated** the event all year, but he did not look forward to anything like that.

Aaron said, "Yeah, when I'm thirteen I get a bar mitzvah, which in the Jewish tradition means I'm a young man. My sister, Rachael, had her bat mitzvah, which means she's a young woman." Carlos sat **dejectedly** in his chair, almost giving up on the report, when an idea hit him.

"Wait a minute, Aaron! We have our report! You can talk about your family ceremonies and I can talk about Ana's!" They had solved their problem and felt **victorious**!

Aaron added, "You know what another rite of passage is, don't you, Carlos? A driver's license!"

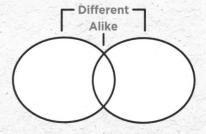

Rachael's bat mitzvah

Reread for **Comprehension**

Monitor Comprehension

Compare and Contrast

One way to monitor your understanding of a text is to compare and contrast characters or events. When you compare and contrast, you tell how things are alike and how they are different. You can use a Venn Diagram to compare and contrast things.

Use a Venn Diagram as you reread "Rites of Passage."

Different
Alike

Comprehension

Genre

Realistic Fiction tells an invented story that could have happened in real life.

Monitor Comprehension

Compare and Contrast
As you read, use your Venn Diagram.

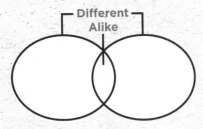

Read to Find Out

How are Grandfather's ideas different from Mary's?

Ta-Na-E-Ka

by
Mary Whitebird

illustrated by
Shonto Begay

Award
Winning
Illustrator

As my birthday drew closer, I had awful nightmares about it. I was reaching the age at which all Kaw Indians had to **participate** in Ta-Na-E-Ka. Well, not all Kaws. Many of the younger families on the reservation were beginning to give up the old customs. But my grandfather, Amos Deer Leg, was devoted to tradition. He still wore handmade beaded moccasins instead of shoes, and kept his iron-gray hair in tight braids. He could speak English, but he spoke it only with white men. With his family he used a Sioux dialect.

Grandfather was one of the last living Indians (he died in 1953 when he was 81) who actually fought against the U.S. Cavalry. Not only did he fight, he was wounded in a skirmish at Rose Creek—a famous **encounter** in which the celebrated Kaw chief Flat Nose lost his life. At the time, my grandfather was only eleven years old.

Eleven was a magic word among the Kaws. It was the time of Ta-Na-E-Ka, the "flowering of adulthood." It was the age, my grandfather informed us hundreds of times, "when a boy could prove himself to be a warrior and a girl took the steps to womanhood."

"I don't want to be a warrior," my cousin, Roger Deer Leg, confided to me. "I'm going to become an accountant."

"None of the other tribes make girls go through the endurance ritual," I complained to my mother.

"It won't be as bad as you think, Mary," my mother said, ignoring my protests. "Once you've gone through it, you'll certainly never forget it. You'll be proud."

I even complained to my teacher, Mrs. Richardson, feeling that, as a white woman, she would side with me.

She didn't. "All of us have rituals of one kind or another," Mrs. Richardson said. "And look at it this way: How many girls have the opportunity to compete on equal terms with boys? Don't look down on your heritage."

Heritage, indeed! I had no intention of living on a reservation for the rest of my life. I was a good student. I loved school. My fantasies were about knights in armor and fair ladies in flowing gowns, being saved from dragons. It never once occurred to me that being an Indian was exciting.

But I've always thought that the Kaw were the originators of the women's liberation movement. No other Indian tribe—and I've spent half a lifetime researching the subject—treated women more "equally" than the Kaw. Unlike most of the sub-tribes of the Sioux Nation, the Kaw allowed men and women to eat together. And hundreds of years before we were "acculturated," a Kaw woman had the right to refuse a prospective husband even if her father arranged the match.

The wisest women (generally wisdom was equated with age) often sat in tribal councils. Furthermore, most Kaw legends revolve around "Good Woman," a kind of super-squaw, a Joan of Arc of the high plains. Good Woman led Kaw warriors into battle after battle from which they always seemed to emerge **victorious**.

And girls as well as boys were required to undergo Ta-Na-E-Ka.

The actual ceremony varied from tribe to tribe, but since the Indians' life on the plains was dedicated to survival, Ta-Na-E-Ka was a test of survival.

"Endurance is the loftiest virtue of the Indian," my grandfather explained.

"To survive, we must endure. When I was a boy, Ta-Na-E-Ka was more than the mere symbol it is now. We were painted white with the juice of a sacred herb and sent naked into the wilderness without so much as a knife. We couldn't return until the white had worn off. It wouldn't wash off. It took almost eighteen days, and during that time we had to stay alive, trapping food, eating insects and roots and berries, and watching out for enemies. And we did have enemies—both the white soldiers and the Omaha warriors, who were always trying to capture Kaw boys and girls undergoing their endurance test. It was an exciting time."

Compare and Contrast
How is the grandfather's opinion of Ta-Na-E-Ka different from Mary's opinion?

"What happened if you couldn't make it?" Roger asked. He was born only three days after I was, and we were being trained for Ta-Na-E-Ka together. I was happy to know he was frightened, too.

"Many didn't return," Grandfather said. "Only the strongest and shrewdest. Mothers were not allowed to weep over those who didn't return. If a Kaw couldn't survive, he or she wasn't worth weeping over. It was our way."

"What a lot of hooey," Roger whispered. "I'd give anything to get out of it."

"I don't see how we have any choice," I replied.

Roger gave my arm a little squeeze. "Well, it's only five days."

Five days! Maybe it was better than being painted white and sent out naked for eighteen days. But not much better.

We were to be sent, barefoot and in bathing suits, into the woods.

Even our very traditional parents put their foot down when Grandfather suggested we go naked. For five days we'd have to live off the land, keeping warm as best we could, getting food where we could. It was May, but on the northernmost reaches of the Missouri River the days were still chilly and the nights were fiercely cold.

Grandfather was in charge of the month's training for Ta-Na-E-Ka. One day he caught a grasshopper and demonstrated how to pull its legs and wings off in one flick of the fingers and how to swallow it.

I felt sick, and Roger turned green. "It's a darn good thing it's 1947," I told Roger teasingly. "You'd make a terrible warrior." Roger just **grimaced**.

I knew one thing. This particular Kaw Indian girl wasn't going to swallow a grasshopper no matter how hungry she got. And then I had an idea. Why hadn't I thought of it before? It would have saved nights of bad dreams about squooshy grasshoppers.

I headed straight for my teacher's house. "Mrs. Richardson," I said, "would you lend me five dollars?"

"Five dollars!" she exclaimed. "What for?"

"You remember the ceremony I talked about?"

"Ta-Na-E-Ka. Of course. Your parents have written me and asked me to excuse you from school so you can participate in it."

"Well, I need some things for the ceremony," I replied, in a half-truth. "I don't want to ask my parents for the money."

"It's not a crime to borrow money, Mary. But how can you pay it back?"

"I'll babysit for you ten times."

"That's more than fair," she said, going to her purse and handing me a crisp, new, five-dollar bill. I'd never had that much money at once.

"I'm happy to know the money's going to be put to a good use," Mrs. Richardson said.

A few days later, the ritual began with a long speech from my grandfather about how we had reached the age of decision, how we now had to fend for ourselves and prove that we could survive the most horrendous of **ordeals**. All the friends and relatives who had gathered at our house for dinner made jokes about their own Ta-Na-E-Ka experiences. They all advised us to fill up now, since for the next five days we'd be gorging ourselves on crickets. Neither

Roger nor I was very hungry. "I'll probably laugh about this when I'm an accountant," Roger said, trembling.

"Are you trembling?" I asked.

"What do you think?"

"I'm happy to know boys tremble, too," I said.

At six the next morning, we kissed our parents and went off to the woods. "Which side do you want?" Roger asked. According to the rules, Roger and I would stake out "territories" in separate areas of the woods and we weren't to communicate during the entire ordeal.

"I'll go toward the river, if it's OK with you," I said.

"Sure," Roger answered. "What difference does it make?"

To me, it made a lot of difference. There was a marina a few miles up the river and there were boats moored there. At least, I hoped so. I figured that a boat was a better place to sleep than under a pile of leaves.

"Why do you keep holding your head?" Roger asked.

"Oh, nothing. Just nervous," I told him. Actually, I was afraid I'd lose the five-dollar bill, which I had tucked into my hair with a bobby pin. As we came to a fork in the trail, Roger shook my hand. "Good luck, Mary."

"N'ko-n'ta," I said. It was the Kaw word for *courage*.

The sun was shining and it was warm, but my bare feet began to hurt immediately. I spied one of the berry bushes Grandfather had told us about. "You're lucky," he had said. "The berries are ripe in the spring, and they are delicious and **nourishing**." They were orange and fat and I popped one into my mouth.

Argh! I spat it out. It was awful and bitter, and even grasshoppers were probably better tasting, although I never intended to find out.

I sat down to rest my feet. A rabbit hopped out from under the berry bush. He nuzzled the berry I'd spat out and ate it. He picked another one and ate that, too. He liked them. He looked at me, twitching his nose. I watched a red-headed woodpecker bore into an elm tree, and I caught a glimpse of a civet cat waddling through some twigs. All of a sudden I realized I was no longer frightened. Ta-Na-E-Ka might be more fun than I'd **anticipated**. I got up and headed toward the marina.

"Not one boat," I said to myself **dejectedly**. But the restaurant on the open shore, "Ernie's Riverside," was open. I walked in, feeling silly in my bathing suit. The man at the counter was big and tough-looking. He wore a sweatshirt with the words "Fort Sheridan, 1944," and he had only three fingers on one of his hands. He asked me what I wanted.

"A hamburger and a milk shake," I said, holding the five-dollar bill in my hand so he'd know I had money.

"That's a pretty heavy breakfast, honey," he murmured.

"That's what I always have for breakfast," I lied.

"Forty-five cents," he said, bringing me the food. (Back in 1947, hamburgers were twenty-five cents and milk shakes were twenty cents.)

"Delicious," I thought. "Better 'n grasshoppers—and Grandfather never once mentioned that I couldn't eat hamburgers."

While I was eating, I had a grand idea. Why not sleep in the restaurant? I went to the ladies' room and made sure the window was unlocked. Then I went back outside and played along the riverbank, watching the water birds and trying to identify each one. I planned to look for a beaver dam the next day.

The restaurant closed at sunset, and I watched the three-fingered man drive away. Then I climbed in the unlocked window. There was a night-light on, so I didn't turn on any lights. But there was a radio on the counter. I turned it on to a music program. It was warm in the restaurant, and I was hungry. I helped myself to a glass of milk and a piece of pie, intending to keep a list of what I'd eaten so I could leave money. I also planned to get up early, sneak out through the window, and head for the woods before the three-fingered man returned. I turned off the radio, wrapped myself in the man's apron, and in spite of the hardness of the floor, fell asleep.

"What the heck are you doing here, kid?"

It was the man's voice.

It was the morning. I'd overslept. I was scared.

"Hold it, kid. I just wanna know what you're doing here. You lost?

You must be from the reservation. Your folks must be worried sick about you. Do they have a phone?"

"Yes, yes," I answered. "But don't call them."

I was shivering. The man, who told me his name was Ernie, made me a cup of hot chocolate while I explained about Ta-Na-E-Ka.

"Darnedest thing I ever heard," he said, when I was through. "Lived next to the reservation all my life and this is the first I've heard of Ta-Na whatever-you-call-it." He looked at me, all goosebumps in my bathing suit. "Pretty silly thing to do to a kid," he muttered.

Compare and Contrast
How are Mary's experiences similar to and different from what she expected during Ta-Na-E-Ka?

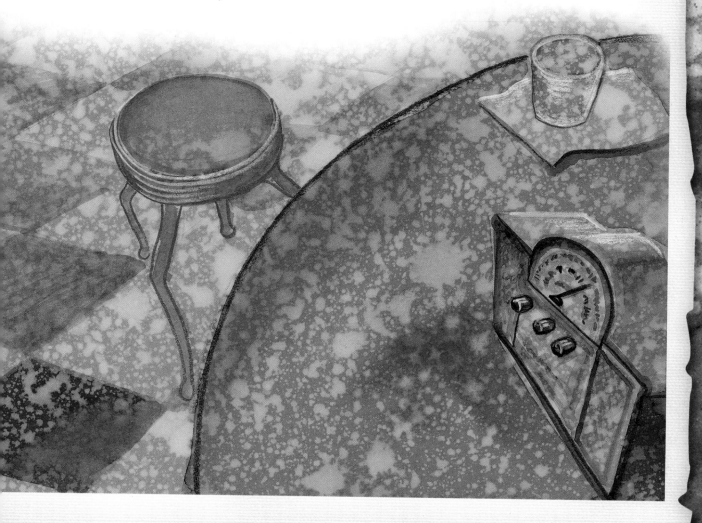

That was just what I'd been thinking for months, but when Ernie said it, I became angry. "No, it isn't silly. It's a custom of the Kaw. We've been doing this for hundreds of years. My mother and my grandfather and everybody in my family went through this ceremony. It's why the Kaw are great warriors."

"Okay, great warrior," Ernie chuckled, "suit yourself. And, if you want to stick around, it's okay with me." Ernie went to the broom closet and tossed me a bundle. "That's the lost-and-found closet," he said. "Stuff people left on boats. Maybe there's something to keep you warm."

The sweater fitted loosely, but it felt good. I felt good. And I'd found a new friend. Most important, I was surviving Ta-Na-E-Ka.

My grandfather had said the experience would be filled with adventure, and I was having my fill. And Grandfather had never said we couldn't accept hospitality.

I stayed at Ernie's Riverside for the entire period. In the mornings I went into the woods and watched the animals and picked flowers for each of the tables in Ernie's. I had never felt better. I was up early enough to watch the sun rise on the Missouri, and I went to bed after it set. I ate everything I wanted—insisting that Ernie take all my money for the food. "I'll keep this in trust for you, Mary," Ernie promised, "in case you are ever desperate for five dollars." (He did, too, but that's another story.)

I was sorry when the five days were over. I'd enjoyed every minute with Ernie. He taught me how to make western omelets and to make Chili Ernie Style (still one of my favorite dishes). And I told Ernie all about the legends of the Kaw. I hadn't realized I knew so much about my people.

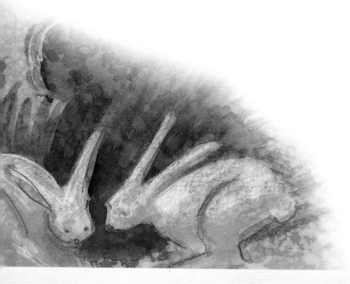

But Ta-Na-E-Ka was over, and as I approached my house, at about nine-thirty in the evening, I became nervous all over again. What if Grandfather asked me about the berries and the grasshoppers? And my feet were hardly cut. I hadn't lost a pound and my hair was combed.

"They'll be so happy to see me," I told myself hopefully, "that they won't ask too many questions."

I opened the door. My grandfather was in the front room. He was wearing the ceremonial beaded deerskin shirt which had belonged to his grandfather. "N'g'da'ma," he said. "Welcome back."

I embraced my parents warmly, letting go only when I saw my cousin Roger sprawled on the couch. His eyes were red and swollen. He'd lost weight. His feet were an unsightly mass of blood and blisters, and he was moaning: "I made it, see. I made it. I'm a warrior. A warrior."

My grandfather looked at me strangely. I was clean, obviously well-fed, and radiantly healthy. My parents got the message. My uncle and aunt gazed at me with hostility.

Finally my grandfather asked, "What did you eat to keep you so well?"

I sucked in my breath and blurted out the truth: "Hamburgers and milk shakes."

"Hamburgers!" my grandfather growled.

"Milk shakes!" Roger moaned.

"You didn't say we had to eat grasshoppers," I said sheepishly.

"Tell us about your Ta-Na-E-Ka," my grandfather commanded.

I told them everything, from borrowing the five dollars, to Ernie's kindness, to observing the beaver.

"That's not what I trained you for," my grandfather said sadly.

I stood up. "Grandfather, I learned that Ta-Na-E-Ka is important. I didn't think so during training. I was scared stiff of it. I handled it my way. And I learned I had nothing to be afraid of. There's no reason in 1947 to eat grasshoppers when you can eat a hamburger."

I was inwardly shocked at my own audacity. But I liked it. "Grandfather, I'll bet you never ate one of those rotten berries yourself."

Grandfather laughed! He laughed aloud! My mother and father and aunt and uncle were all dumbfounded. Grandfather never laughed. Never.

"Those berries—they are terrible," Grandfather admitted. "I could never swallow them. I found a dead deer on the first day of my Ta-Na-E-Ka—shot by a soldier, probably—and he kept my belly full for the entire period of the test!"

Grandfather stopped laughing. "We should send you out again," he said.

I looked at Roger. "You're pretty smart, Mary," Roger groaned. "I'd never have thought of what you did."

"Accountants just have to be good at arithmetic," I said comfortingly. "I'm terrible at arithmetic."

Roger tried to smile but couldn't. My grandfather called me to him. "You should have done what your cousin did. But I think you are more alert to what is happening to our people today than we are. I think you would have passed the test under any circumstances, in any time. Somehow, you know how to exist in a world that wasn't made for Indians. I don't think you're going to have any trouble surviving."

Grandfather wasn't entirely right. But I'll tell about that another time.

On a Journey with
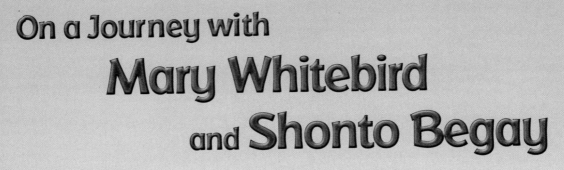
Mary Whitebird
and Shonto Begay

Mary Whitebird is a Native American. She first wrote this story for a young people's magazine. Although the story reflects the heritage of her culture, it is also about the challenges any young person might face in any culture. That makes it a classic coming-of-age story.

Shonto Begay was born on the Navajo Reservation in Arizona. His first canvas was the ground and his first brush a stick. He challenges all young people to find a space where they can think and dream. He calls this place a person's "story rock," where things are created from the heart and from the earth.

 LOG ON Find out more about Mary Whitebird and Shonto Begay at **www.macmillanmh.com**

Author's Purpose
Mary handled her challenge in her own way. How does the author feel about the way Mary survived Ta-Na-E-Ka? How can you tell?

Comprehension Check

Summarize

Use your Venn Diagram to help you summarize "Ta-Na-E-Ka." How does Mary's Ta-Na-E-Ka experience differ from her grandfather's?

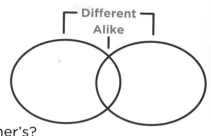

Different
Alike

Think and Compare

1. Compare and contrast Grandfather's generation of Kaw people with Mary's. How do you think the world of 1947 has affected the Kaw's traditions? **Monitor Comprehension: Compare and Contrast**

2. Mary completes the Kaw endurance test in an untraditional way. In your opinion, is Mary **victorious**? Why or why not? Use examples from the text to support your argument. **Evaluate**

3. Think of how you celebrate special occasions. What unique traditions do you have? How have those traditions changed over time? **Synthesize**

4. Mary's experience with Ta-Na-E-Ka represents a problem faced by many cultures: the desire to hold on to ancient traditions and the impulse to join with modern society. How is it possible to strike a balance between them? **Evaluate**

5. Read "Rites of Passage" on pages 506–507. Which experiences mentioned are the ones that Mary dreaded having to face? Which traditions are different from the Kaw tradition of Ta-Na-E-Ka? **Reading/Writing Across Texts**

Language Arts

Genre

A **Fable** is a brief story that teaches a moral, often through the actions of animals that act like people.

Literary Elements

A **Moral** is a lesson taught by a fable or story. It is usually stated outright at the end of the fable.

Personification is a literary device where human characteristics are given to animals or things.

A FABLE
by Aesop

retold by Jerry Pinkney

Introduction

The real Aesop was born a slave about the year 620 B.C. in the ancient republic of Greece, where he was later granted freedom as a reward for his learning and wit. Though he died about 565 B.C., for years his clever wisdom was passed down orally from generation to generation. Somewhere around 300 B.C., about 200 stories were gathered into a collection called *Assemblies of Aesopic Tales*. No one knows how many of the narratives attributed to Aesop were actually composed by him. Interestingly, motifs from many of them occur in the storytelling traditions of a variety of cultures—proof of the universality of the themes and lessons of these tales.

The Crow and the Pitcher

The crows speak. This is personification.

For weeks and weeks there had been no rain. The streams and pools had dried to dust, and all of the animals were thirsty. Two crows, flying together in search of water, spotted a pitcher that had been left on a garden wall. They flew to it and saw that it was half full of water. But neither one could reach far enough inside the pitcher's narrow neck to get a drink.

"There must be a way to get that water," said the first crow. "If we think it through, we'll find an answer."

The second crow tried to push the pitcher over, straining with all of his might. But it was too heavy to budge. "It's hopeless!" he croaked, and flew away to look for water elsewhere.

But the first crow stayed by the pitcher and thought, and after a time he had an idea. Picking up some small pebbles in his beak, he dropped them one by one into the pitcher until at last the water rose to the brim. Then the clever bird happily quenched his thirst.

Wisdom and patience succeed where force fails.

The moral of the fable.

Connect and Compare

1. Why does personification work especially well in fables? What would fables be like if they only featured humans? **Personification**

2. Why do you think an author who wanted to teach a lesson would choose to write a fable? **Analyze**

3. Compare "The Crow and the Pitcher" to "Ta-Na-E-Ka." How do the main characters in both stories use their brains to solve a problem in an unusual way? **Reading/Writing Across Texts**

 LOG ON Find out more about fables at **www.macmillanmh.com**

WRITE A Compare-and-Contrast ESSAY

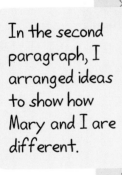
I Could Be a Character in a Book

by Lourdes M.

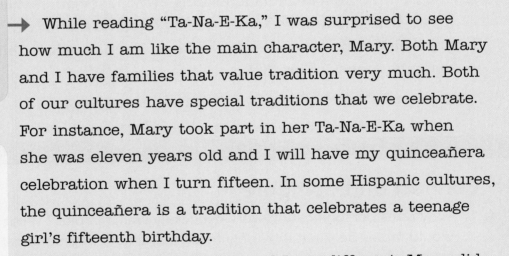

In the first paragraph, I talk about how Mary and I are alike.

→ While reading "Ta-Na-E-Ka," I was surprised to see how much I am like the main character, Mary. Both Mary and I have families that value tradition very much. Both of our cultures have special traditions that we celebrate. For instance, Mary took part in her Ta-Na-E-Ka when she was eleven years old and I will have my quinceañera celebration when I turn fifteen. In some Hispanic cultures, the quinceañera is a tradition that celebrates a teenage girl's fifteenth birthday.

In the second paragraph, I arranged ideas to show how Mary and I are different.

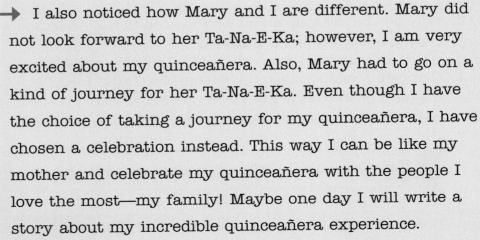

→ I also noticed how Mary and I are different. Mary did not look forward to her Ta-Na-E-Ka; however, I am very excited about my quinceañera. Also, Mary had to go on a kind of journey for her Ta-Na-E-Ka. Even though I have the choice of taking a journey for my quinceañera, I have chosen a celebration instead. This way I can be like my mother and celebrate my quinceañera with the people I love the most—my family! Maybe one day I will write a story about my incredible quinceañera experience.

Your Turn

Write a compare-and-contrast essay in which you compare yourself with a character from a story you have read. If you do not want to write about yourself, you may compare two characters, either from the same story or different stories. Be sure to arrange ideas in your essay carefully so that your comparisons are easy to follow and understand. Use the Writer's Checklist to check your writing.

Writer's Checklist

✓ **Ideas and Content:** Is it clear whom I am comparing? Did I point out similarities and differences?

✓ **Organization:** Did I **rearrange ideas** in my essay around the similarities and differences of my topic?

✓ **Voice:** Can you tell that I wrote this essay? Is my personality in my writing?

✓ **Word Choice:** Did I use fresh and snappy words to describe my subjects?

✓ **Sentence Fluency:** Did I use different kinds of sentences? Does my essay have natural rhythm?

✓ **Conventions:** Did I proofread my essay, checking for proper spelling, grammar, and usage? Did I use the articles *a* and *an* correctly?

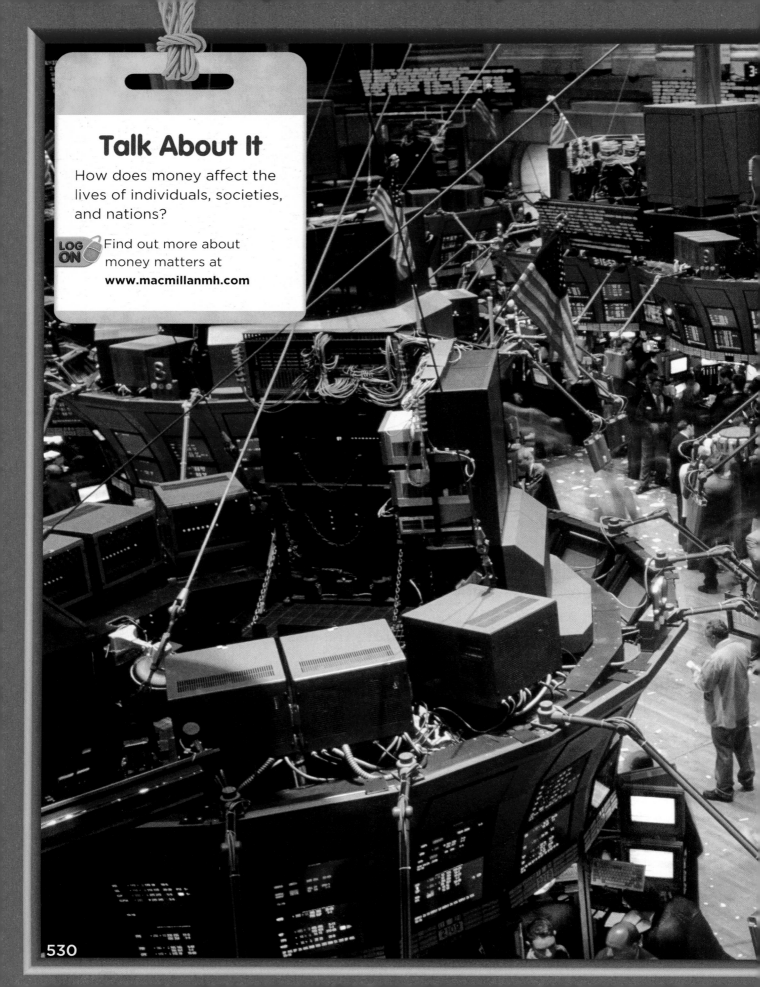

Talk About It

How does money affect the lives of individuals, societies, and nations?

LOG ON Find out more about money matters at **www.macmillanmh.com**

MONEY MATTERS

Vocabulary

economists

continuous

chronology

debut

periodic

MONEY TALK

Elections are often influenced by economic issues such as whether to cut or raise taxes. In a debate, here's how one student made the case for cutting taxes:

"If the President and Congress lower taxes, we will have more money to spend. More money would be available in the economy, because the money we spend would go to the businesses we buy from. This would have a good effect on the economy, because businesses would then have more money to expand. [Then they could] hire more people, who will work and pay taxes."

In order to truly evaluate this argument, it is important to understand how the economy works. But economists—scientists who study how money, goods, and services are used—sometimes seem to have their own language. Here are definitions of four words that are often used by economists and politicians.

ECONOMY: the system a country uses to manage money and resources

INFLATION: an increase in the availability of money and credit that is out of proportion to the goods and services available, causing a continuous, ongoing rise in prices and a decrease in the value of money

INTEREST: the fee paid to use borrowed money, such as the interest on a loan; or, the fee a financial institution pays to hold customers' money on deposit, such as the interest on a savings account

UNEMPLOYMENT RATE: the percentage of workers who don't have jobs and are actively looking for jobs

U.S. PAPER MONEY: WHO AND WHAT IS ON IT

Bill	Who's on the Front?	What's on the Back?
$1	George Washington	The front and back of the Great Seal of the U.S.
$2	Thomas Jefferson	The signing of the Declaration of Independence
$5	Abraham Lincoln	Lincoln Memorial
$10	Alexander Hamilton	U.S. Treasury Building
$20	Andrew Jackson	White House
$50	Ulysses S. Grant	U.S. Capitol
$100	Benjamin Franklin	Independence Hall in Philadelphia, Pennsylvania

DID YOU KNOW...?

- The **chronology** of currency in the American colonies dates back to 1690, when the Massachusetts Bay Colony issued the first paper money.

- The **debut** of paper money issued by the federal government occurred in 1862, during a coin shortage. The U.S. Treasury issued bills in denominations of $1, $5, $25, and 50 cents.

- While the government makes **periodic** use of larger bills, the $100 bill is the largest that is now in general circulation.

- Bills that get worn out from everyday use are taken out of circulation and replaced. A $1 bill usually lasts 18 months; $5 bill, two years; $10 bill, three years; $20 bill, four years; and $50 and $100 bills, nine years. In contrast, circulating coins last about 25 years.

OLD MONEY

BEFORE COINS, the ancient Greeks used iron nails as money, the ancient Britons used sword blades, and the ancient Chinese used swords and knives.

CHINESE COINS had holes in the center so they could be strung together like beads, which made carrying them easier.

EUROPEANS LEARNED about paper money from the Chinese.

SOME AMERICAN COLONISTS used wampum as money.

THE HERCULES COIN was introduced by Alexander the Great in 325 B.C.

COWRIE SHELLS have been used as money in many cultures.

LOG ON — Find out more about the history of money at www.macmillanmh.com

533

MANY COUNTRIES, ONE CURRENCY: EUROPE AND THE EURO

Comprehension

Genre

A **Nonfiction Article** in a newspaper or magazine presents facts and information.

Evaluate

Persuasion

Persuasion is a method used to convince others that they should act or think in a certain way.

HOW CAN MORE THAN A DOZEN COUNTRIES GIVE UP THEIR INDIVIDUAL CURRENCIES AND ADOPT A SINGLE FORM OF MONEY?

The euro symbol glows in front of the European Central Bank in Frankfurt, Germany, as fireworks welcome the new year and the new currency.

As spectacular New Year's Eve fireworks lit up the skies welcoming 2002, thousands of people across Europe lined up at ATMs to get crisp new bills. When the clock struck midnight, it didn't just usher in a new year—it marked the beginning of a new era. The 304 million residents of 12 European countries switched from their local coins and bills to a single currency: the euro.

THE EURO ROLLS OUT SMOOTHLY

The **chronology** of a common currency among members of the European Union dates back to at least 1992. The largest monetary changeover ever took years of **continuous** negotiations, planning, and preparation. Leaders of the countries making the switch believed the euro would strengthen ties among their nations and make trade, travel, and banking much easier. **Economists** believed the new European currency could become as important in the world as the mighty U.S. dollar.

535

THE EURO

FRONT: The European Central Bank's initials appear in five languages. A silvery foil hologram prevents counterfeiting. When the bill is tilted, the euro symbol and the value of the bill appear.

BOTH SIDES: Bridges and doorways represent co-operation among countries in Europe and with the rest of the world. The word "euro" appears in both Latin and Greek alphabets.

BACK: A map of Europe

Britain, Sweden, and Denmark, however, were stubbornly opposed to handing over control of their currency to the new European Central Bank. They refused to switch to euros. Greece wanted to join the euro movement but was rejected because its economy wasn't strong enough.

Banks worldwide started using euros years before the official changeover. At stores, prices were given in local currency and euros. In July 1999, mints began printing 15 billion bills and producing 56 billion coins. But it wasn't until January 1, 2002, that these bills and coins made their **debut**, and the euro became part of everyday life.

OUT WITH THE OLD

Many people were sad to say goodbye to some of the world's oldest and most charming currencies. "How ugly!" exclaimed Michela Moccia as she withdrew her first euros from a cash machine in Rome, Italy. "They look so cold, metallic, and boring."

The euros are very different from the old currencies, which included France's franc, Italy's lira, and Germany's mark. The colorful, old bills honored each country's unique history through art and mottoes. The euro notes show general styles of architecture from different periods in European history. Since euros were designed to be used in many countries, none of the images on the bills or coins could be associated with a specific place or historical figure.

Euro coins, however, allow for national expression. While they all look the same on the "tails" side, each country gets to pick its "heads." Italy's 1-euro coin features a famous sketch by Leonardo da Vinci. Austria's shows composer Mozart. Spain's depicts King Juan Carlos.

CHANGE IS GOOD

The changeover to euros caused a bit of confusion. There were **periodic** delays in cash transactions, with long lines at cash registers, tollbooths, and banks as people adjusted to the new currency. "It's slower because we have to concentrate more," said Isabell Schosstag, a cashier in Germany. In Italy, one woman reportedly tried to pay for a cup of coffee with the equivalent of $525 worth of euros!

Despite the small glitches, most Europeans have adapted well and accepted the new money. "It makes me feel like I am part of something bigger," said Alice Magnoni of Italy.

A currency dealer in Iraq exchanges a customer's 10-euro note for Iraqi dinar.

Think and Compare

1. Reread the last paragraph. How is this an example of persuasive technique?

2. Which three countries refused to adopt the euro?

3. In what ways do you think a change in the basic currency of your country would affect you?

4. How is the common theme of "money matters" treated in a different way in each of these selections?

In Frankfurt, Germany, workers hand out leaflets promoting a single currency for Europe.

CHANGE FOR A TWENTY

Goodbye, dull green and black. Hello, blue, peach, and yellow. In 2003, for the first time in 95 years, the United States changed the color of its paper money when it introduced the new twenty-dollar bill. To thwart counterfeiters, the new twenty has tiny number 20s and the phrase "Twenty USA" scattered in the background. The colorful new bill still features a portrait of Andrew Jackson, however.

The fifty-dollar bill was the next to have a makeover. Ulysses S. Grant is still on the new fifty, which was introduced in 2004. The bill features red and blue stars and stripes behind Grant's portrait.

On the fifty, a new security feature is thread embedded in the paper that glows under ultraviolet light. Treasury Secretary John Snow, speaking of the new design for the fifty, said, "We believe it will be extremely effective in discouraging counterfeiters." He continued, "It's also a lovely piece of currency . . . incorporating elements of other colors that are important to us in this country: red, white, and blue."

While the government changes the larger denominations every seven to ten years, the one-dollar bill stays the same. The reason is a simple one: Counterfeiters aren't very interested in making copies of it.

Go On ▶

Directions: Answer the questions.

1. The new twenty-dollar bill was changed by

   A   adding the portrait of U.S. Grant.

   B   using the portraits of different presidents.

   C   hiding numbers in the background.

   D   making it a larger size.

2. The new design of the twenty- and fifty-dollar bills is intended to

   A   encourage other countries to adopt the dollar.

   B   get people to save more.

   C   make them more difficult to counterfeit.

   D   make people think the bills are worth more.

3. The one-dollar bill is not being redesigned because

   A   there are too many of the old ones in circulation.

   B   it is usually not the target of counterfeiters.

   C   Treasury Secretary John Snow decided against it.

   D   it already has the same security features as the new bills.

4. Do you agree with the government decision not to change the one-dollar bill? Explain your answer.

5. If you could change the color of U.S. currency, what would you change it to, and why?

Tip

Form an opinion.

Write to a Prompt

Adopting the euro was a controversial move that faced resistance from some countries and their citizens. Great Britain, Sweden, and Denmark refused to go along with other members of the European Union. Write a persuasive essay from the perspective of a citizen of one of those countries, arguing either for or against adopting the euro.

I used examples to support my opinion.

Europe: We Are All in This Together

As a citizen of Sweden, I believe our government made a huge mistake when it decided not to adopt the euro. As a result of that decision, Sweden will not benefit from the obvious advantages a single currency brings to the countries of Europe.

The biggest benefit to having a single European currency is economic. With the euro, we would be able to trade with our European neighbors at better prices. We could enjoy more tourism, since it would be much easier for other Europeans to visit without changing their money. Finally, we would be able to share the cost savings of having our currency controlled by the European Central Bank rather than paying for a separate system.

Pride is not the issue here. If we could see beyond our nationalistic tendencies, we would see that adopting the euro is in our best interests.

Writing Prompt

There is a proposal being considered to establish a single currency for all of North America—Canada, the United States, and Mexico. Write a persuasive essay expressing your point of view on this topic, either in favor of or against the proposal.

Writer's Checklist

- ☑ Ask yourself, who is my audience?
- ☑ Think about your purpose for writing.
- ☑ Choose the correct form for your writing.
- ☑ Form an opinion about the topic.
- ☑ Use reasons to support your opinion.
- ☑ Be sure your ideas are logical and organized.
- ☑ Use your best spelling, grammar, and punctuation.

Collections

Talk About It

What do the boys in this photo collect? If you could collect anything in the world, what would it be? Why?

LOG ON Find out more about collections at **www.macmillanmh.com**

543

GRANDPA and ME

by Susan Reilly

For six weeks in the summer of 1986, I went to live with my grandfather. When my mom first told me about the plans, without thinking, I **instinctively** groaned. Somewhere inside me a voice told me that I would be miserable. This meant no afternoon baseball games with my neighborhood friends. Plus, I just knew my popularity would **decrease**, or lessen, if I wasn't around all summer.

The first week with Grandpa was fine. We went out to dinner and watched TV together. One day, Grandpa was sitting at the table reading the newspaper. I sat on the couch and flipped through my baseball card collection. I had all my cards in a binder with plastic sleeve protectors. "Wish I had a Hank Aaron card," I muttered to myself.

When Grandpa heard me, he **swiveled** around on his chair so fast that the wheels almost flew off! He said, "I didn't know you liked baseball, Susan."

I explained that it was my favorite sport and that I usually play it all summer with my friends. Grandpa stood up **shakily**, balancing himself with his hand on the wall, and walked to the door. "Let's go," he said, smiling. "I want to show you something."

We drove for quite a while, and when Grandpa finally stopped the car, we were in front of some **dilapidated** old houses. They were abandoned and falling apart. A sign on each house said "Land will be sold to highest bidder. City Hall **auction**. Call for details." I started to say something, but I noticed that Grandpa had a faraway look in his eyes. "I haven't been here for **decades**," he whispered, "probably twenty or thirty years."

We walked onto one of the old porches. Grandpa pointed down the street and said, "That's the field where I used to play baseball every summer." Then I realized where we were: This was the house Grandpa grew up in! We peeked inside a window to see a big mess. The ceiling was falling down so that you could see the wooden **rafters**, or beams, hidden behind it. No one had lived here for a long time.

On the ride home, Grandpa was very quiet. I thought about how he must miss his old home and the friends he grew up with. Then I realized that six weeks away from home was not too bad, especially with Grandpa around.

Reread for **Comprehension**

Evaluate

Make Judgments

Good readers usually make judgments while they are reading. Evaluating the actions of the characters helps readers make judgments about the characters.

You can use a Judgment Chart to help you evaluate the characters in a story. Use the chart as you reread "Grandpa and Me."

Action	Judgment

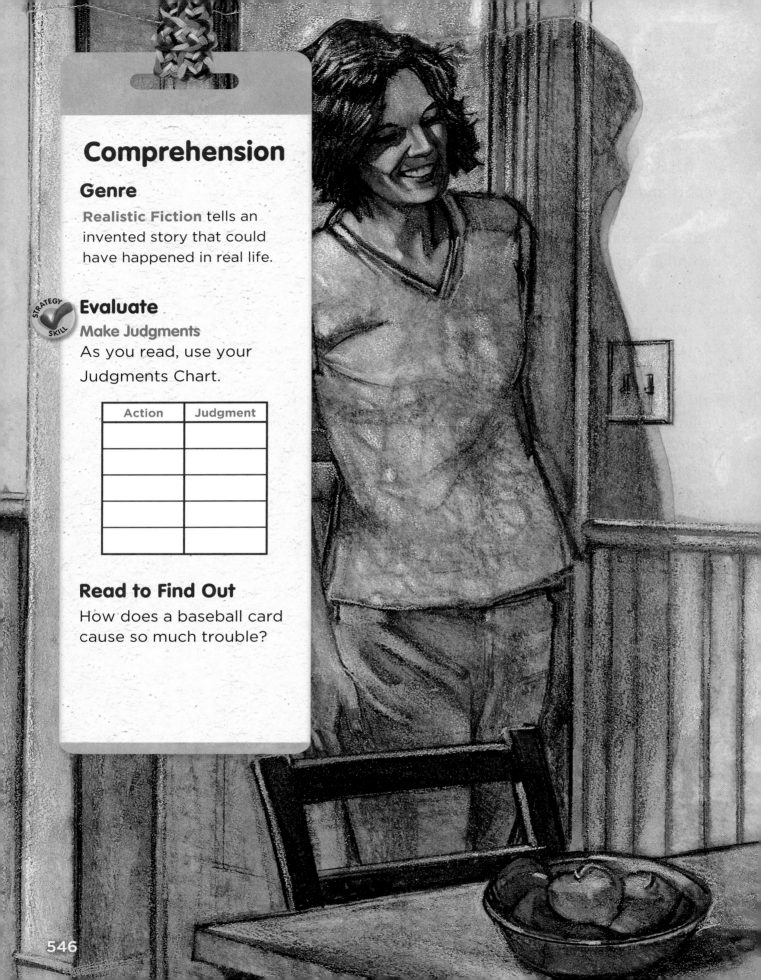

Comprehension

Genre

Realistic Fiction tells an invented story that could have happened in real life.

Evaluate

Make Judgments
As you read, use your Judgments Chart.

Action	Judgment

Read to Find Out

How does a baseball card cause so much trouble?

546

I may not have been a great hitter, but I knew more about cards than any kid around. I put together a complete set of guys who played shortstop. That was always my position.

Mom says buying baseball cards is like throwing money into a garbage can. But I figure a kid should be allowed to have one harmless vice.

And besides, my baseball cards actually *saved* us money. When I got holes in my sneakers, I would slip a card inside so I didn't need to buy a new pair right away. I always used lousy cards, of course. I wouldn't think of stepping on a card that was worth anything.

"I got you some work today, Joe," Mom said as we chowed down on leftovers.

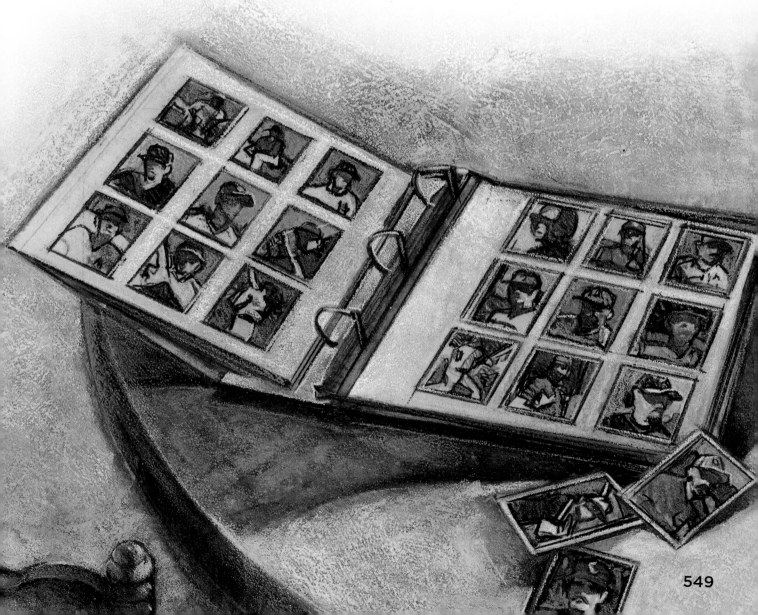

550

"Oh, yeah? What?"

"Miss Young needs her attic cleaned out. She'll pay you five dollars. I told her you'd take it."

"Oh, *man!*"

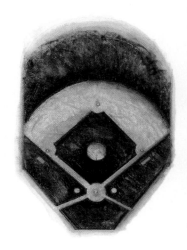

Amanda Young is this really old lady who lives next door. I know she's way over one hundred, because my mom showed me an article from the paper that talked about Louisville's Century Club. She's pretty peppy for an old lady. Her skin is really wrinkly, though.

Miss Young never had any kids, and she was never married. I don't even think she has any relatives who are still alive. She's been living by herself in that **dilapidated** old house for as long as anybody can remember. She never comes outside. Her groceries are brought in.

My mom stops over to Miss Young's now and then to see if she's okay. I guess that's how I got this job.

It's not like I don't appreciate the work or anything. It's just that Amanda Young is kinda weird. I've run a few errands for her, and she starts talking to me about nothing and she goes on and on. I can't understand what she's saying half the time. I nod my head yes to be polite.

Sometimes, I must admit, I pretend my mom is calling so I can go home. Miss Young doesn't hear very well, so she can't tell I'm lying.

I've never seen Miss Young smile. She seems really sad, as if somebody did something terrible to her a long time ago and she never got over it.

I've heard kids say that Amanda Young is a witch. Kids always make up stories like that. I think she's just a lonely old lady. I feel a little sorry for her.

Cleaning out Miss Young's attic isn't my idea of a fun afternoon, but five bucks is five bucks. There is a new set of baseball cards coming out next month, and I can use the money to buy a few packs.

Make Judgments
Was it appropriate for Joey's mother to accept a job offer without talking to Joey about it first? Explain.

I'm sure I would have felt differently about the job if I'd known what Miss Young had up in her attic.

We only had a half day of school the next day, so I thought it would be a good time to go over to Amanda Young's house. The shutters were hanging off the windows at an angle, and the place hadn't had a coat of paint in **decades**. You could tell home maintenance was not very important to the old lady.

Miss Young was in worse financial shape than we were. My mom said she could barely live off her Social Security checks.

After I rang the doorbell, I didn't hear a sound inside for a minute or two. I was afraid that maybe Miss Young was hurt or something, but then I heard her shuffling feet coming toward the door. She was really small, so when she opened the door a crack I could barely see her.

"Come in," she creaked. "Why Joseph Stoshack, you're getting to be *so* big!"

Inside, the house was like one of those historical houses some famous guy lived in and has been preserved just the way he left it when he died. It was filled with antiques, though I don't know if stuff is still called antique if somebody never stopped using it. The walls were covered with hats and dried flowers.

"Pirates, eh?" she said, peering at my baseball cap. "Are you a Pittsburgh rooter?"

"No, I just like this baseball cap, Miss Young."

"I used to root for the Pirates when I was a girl," she said. "Well, one Pirate anyway." She stopped for a moment and let out a sigh before changing the subject. "We didn't have television back then, or even radio. But we used to *pore* over the newspaper. Did you know that the manager of the Pirates invented those flip-up sunglasses outfielders wear?"

"Really?"

Miss Young had never brought up baseball the other times we'd spoken. For the first time, she had my interest.

"That's right," she continued. "His name was Fred Clarke. He's a Hall of Famer, you know."

I had heard of Clarke, but I didn't know too much
about him.

"And the baseball bat was invented right here in
Louisville, Joseph. There was this fella named Pete
Browning. He broke his bat one day, and a little boy took
him home and carved Pete a new one on his daddy's lathe.
His dad was a woodworker you see, who made wooden
butter churns. Do you know what a butter churn is, Joseph?
Oh, of course not. You're too young. Well, anyway, Pete took
his new bat and got three hits the next day. Naturally, his
teammates *all* wanted new bats. The woodworker stopped
making butter churns and went into the bat business. And
that's how the Louisville Slugger was born. Of course, that
was before my time."

I couldn't imagine *anything* being before her time.

"I want to show you something, Joseph."

She put on a pair of old-lady glasses and opened a
drawer in the bureau in her front hallway. After sifting
through the junk in there for a minute, she pulled out a
photo and held it under a lamp. It was an old-time baseball
player. The image was fuzzy, but I could make out the word
"Louisville" across the chest of his uniform.

The photo looked like it had originally been larger, but it was ripped in half. There was a white border at the top, bottom, and left side, but the right side had no border and the edge was jagged.

The picture had been taken in a garden. The ballplayer was facing the camera and his left arm was extending out to the jagged edge, like he was holding hands with someone. It was impossible to tell who the other person was, because that half had been ripped off.

I looked up and saw there were tears in Miss Young's eyes.

"I was supposed to hold onto this half of the picture until we saw each other again," she said softly. "I waited and waited. But he never came back."

She handed me the picture abruptly. "Throw it away with the rest of the junk upstairs. It's worthless."

I'm a collector. I never throw *anything* away. Who knows? A ripped picture of an old-time ballplayer might be

worth something to somebody. It certainly meant something to Miss Young a long time ago. As I stuffed the picture in my backpack, I wondered why it had made her so upset.

Miss Young led me upstairs and told me she wanted me to take everything out of the attic and put it on the street for the garbage men to take away. I figured she knew she wasn't going to live forever, and she wanted to clean up her affairs while she was still around.

As soon as I stepped up into the attic, I knew it had been a mistake to take the job. It was dark, filthy, and it looked like a junkyard. This was no five-dollar job, I thought to myself.

But a deal is a deal. I started picking through the trash and hauling it out to the street. The whole time I was thinking I should have gotten a paper route or some other real job.

Being a collector and all, I couldn't resist peeking into a few of Miss Young's old boxes to see what kind of stuff she had decided to hang on to all these years. But it was exactly what she said it was—worthless junk. Broken candlesticks. Old clothes. A set of encyclopedias. I chucked it all out.

After a couple of hours I had cleared the entire attic except for a few boxes. I was dog tired, and I picked up the next box without holding it from the bottom. The box had deteriorated with age, and the bottom ripped open in my arms. The contents spilled all over the floor. I was angry at myself for not being more careful.

I decided to take a short break before cleaning up the mess, so I lay down on the dusty wooden slats and stared at the **rafters.** In a few minutes I felt rested and rolled over on my side to look at the junk strewn across the floor.

It was papers, mostly. Nothing too interesting. Bank statements and tax returns from a long time ago. I started picking them up and putting them into a pile. When I picked up the stack, a single piece of cardboard fell out and fluttered to the floor.

It didn't register at first. But when I picked up the card, I felt a strange tingling sensation.

I turned over the card and looked at the other side. I couldn't believe my eyes.

It was a picture of a man's face. I gasped. **Instinctively**, I looked around to see if anybody was watching. Of course nobody was there.

The man in the picture was a young man, with short brown hair parted in the middle. He had a solemn expression on his face, with his head **swiveled** slightly so he was looking off to the left. His shirt collar was navy blue, and the shirt was muddy gray. It had four white buttons.

On the right side of his chest were the letters "PITTS" and on the left were the letters "BURG." There was no H.

The background of the card was burnt-orange. There was a thin white border on all four sides. Across the bottom border, centered in the middle, were these magic words . . .

WAGNER, PITTSBURG

My breath came in short bursts. I suddenly felt warm. My heart was racing. My *brain* was racing. The tingling sensation was all over me, and stronger than I had ever experienced it.

No doubt about it. I had just stumbled upon a T-206 Honus Wagner card—*the most valuable baseball card in the world.*

Every serious collector knows the legend behind the Wagner card. These early baseball cards were printed by tobacco companies and were included with their products. All the players agreed to be on the cards except for Honus Wagner, the star shortstop of the Pittsburgh Pirates.

Wagner was against cigarette smoking, and he didn't want his name or picture used to sell tobacco. He forced the American Tobacco Company to withdraw his card—but they had already started printing them. A small number of the cards reached the public before the card was discontinued.

That's why the Honus Wagner card is so valuable. Only about forty of them are known to exist in the whole world, most of them in bad condition.

I just found No. 41, and it was *mint.* Nobody had *touched* it in over eighty years.

I knew the piece of cardboard in my hand was worth thousands of dollars, but I didn't know exactly how *many* thousands. I remembered that a few years ago some famous athlete had bought one at an **auction**, but I couldn't recall who he was or how much he paid for it. It was a huge amount of money, that was for sure.

All my problems, I suddenly realized, were solved. Or so I thought.

I slipped the card in my backpack, being careful not to bend any of the corners or damage it in any way. A tiny nick in a card this rare might **decrease** its value by thousands of dollars.

Quickly, I gathered up the rest of the junk in the attic and hauled it out to the curb.

I had almost forgotten about Miss Young, but she called me over just as I was about to run home.

"Aren't you forgetting something, Joseph?"

She held out a five-dollar bill and **shakily** placed it in my palm. She grabbed my other hand and looked me in the eye.

"Thank you for helping out an old lady," she said seriously. "And because you did such a fine job, I want you to have *ten* dollars. I bet that's a lot of money to a boy your age."

Ten bucks? In my head I was thinking that I had a fortune in my backpack.

"Yeah, I could use ten dollars," I sputtered. "Thanks Miss Young."

"Buy something nice for yourself," she called out as I dashed away. "Money won't do *me* any good."

"I will," I called out as I left. "Believe me, I *will*."

Mom wouldn't be home from work for an hour or so. I grabbed my bike, hopped on, and started pedaling east on Chestnut Street past Sheppard Park and Founders Square.

As I cruised down the streets I was filled with an overwhelming feeling of joy. Happiness washed over my body. Nobody could touch me. Nobody could hurt me. Nobody could tell me what to do. It was a feeling I had never experienced before.

I didn't know if I should tell the whole world about my good fortune, or if maybe I shouldn't tell *anybody* in the world.

As I whizzed down the street, I felt like everyone was looking at me. I felt like everyone must somehow know what had happened to me. They knew what I had in my backpack. It was as if the news had instantly been picked up and broadcast around the globe.

Those feelings lasted about a minute, when a different feeling came over me. A bad feeling. The baseball card wasn't mine to take, really. It was Miss Young's card. If anybody deserved to get rich from it, it was *her*. She had been nice enough to pay me *double* for cleaning out her attic, and I had stolen her fortune.

Almost as quickly, my brain came up with reasons I shouldn't feel badly. Miss Young herself said that money wouldn't do her any good, so why *shouldn't* I keep the card? After all, *she* told me to throw the stuff away. If I hadn't found the card, *she* wouldn't have found it. It would have ended up buried in a landfill someplace, worth nothing to anyone.

Finder's keepers, right?

And besides, I thought, Miss Young isn't going to live much longer.

I felt bad, again, thinking that last thought.

I was feeling very mixed up. Deep inside I knew the right thing would be to give Miss Young back her baseball card.

But that didn't necessarily mean I was going to *do* the right thing.

Make Judgments
Was Joey's action appropriate, or should he return the baseball card to Miss Young? Explain.

At Bat with DAN GUTMAN

DAN GUTMAN has a section on his Web site called "Read My Rejection Letters." *Honus and Me* was rejected seven times before a publisher accepted the manuscript. Dan said that during the three years he tried to get "Honus" published, he learned that persistence pays off! In the end, *Honus and Me* was nominated for 11 state book awards and won a California Young Reader's Award.

 LOG ON Find out more about Dan Gutman at **www.macmillanmh.com**

Author's Purpose
Dan Gutman worked very hard to get *Honus and Me* published. What do you think was his main purpose for writing? Explain.

Comprehension Check

Summarize

Use your Judgments Chart to help you summarize *Honus and Me*. Consider how money has an impact on the events of the story.

Action	Judgment

Think and Compare

1. If Joey offered to split what the baseball card was worth with Miss Young, would this be an appropriate solution to his problem? Use facts from the text to support your answer. **Evaluate: Make Judgments**

2. Why do you think Joey is so excited to find the baseball card? How can it change his life? **Analyze**

3. This selection ends before we know what Joey decides to do about the baseball card. How would you end the story? Why? **Synthesize**

4. Joey could use the wealth from the Wagner card to help his family. Is it all right to take unfair advantage of a situation, as long as you help someone in the end? Explain. **Evaluate**

5. Read "Grandpa and Me" on pages 544–545. How do Susan and Joey in *Honus and Me* make false judgments about the elder characters in the stories? **Reading/Writing Across Texts**

Math

Genre

A **Nonfiction Article** gives information and facts about a topic.

Text Feature

Photographs and Captions give more detail to an article and make it more interesting.

Content Vocabulary

lures
antique
memorabilia

Cool Collections

The Smithsonian Center for Education and Museum Studies has a Web site devoted completely to collecting. "Smithsonian Kids Collecting" features amazing collections belonging to real kids. Here are two of their stories.

bass lure

Will Yeingst

I have a collection of fishing objects. I began collecting about a year ago when I was looking through my grandfather's old salt-water tackle box. There were lots of **lures**, weights, and plugs. After that I started looking through **antique** price guides and became very interested in all types of lures, nets, and fishing **memorabilia**. Some of my collection comes from objects that belonged to both my grandfathers.

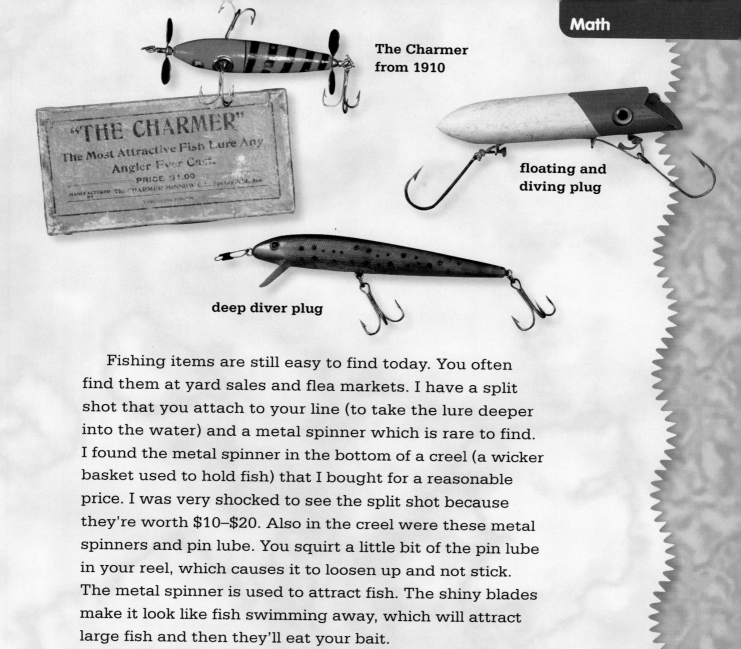

The Charmer
from 1910

"THE CHARMER"
The Most Attractive Fish Lure Any
Angler Ever Cast.
PRICE $1.00
MANUFACTURED The CHARMER MINNOW CO., Spring Md, Ind.
BY

floating and
diving plug

deep diver plug

Fishing items are still easy to find today. You often find them at yard sales and flea markets. I have a split shot that you attach to your line (to take the lure deeper into the water) and a metal spinner which is rare to find. I found the metal spinner in the bottom of a creel (a wicker basket used to hold fish) that I bought for a reasonable price. I was very shocked to see the split shot because they're worth $10–$20. Also in the creel were these metal spinners and pin lube. You squirt a little bit of the pin lube in your reel, which causes it to loosen up and not stick. The metal spinner is used to attract fish. The shiny blades make it look like fish swimming away, which will attract large fish and then they'll eat your bait.

My grandfather's fishing license was from 1947. You often see them at flea markets ranging from $10–$30. My favorite lure is a rubber frog made in 1900 by Pfleuger. I found my Civil War era fish hooks in a Civil War shop.

I have a lot of antique fishing poles in my collection like the bamboo rod owned by an "early Yeingst" who would fly fish for trout with it. I have a lure called the punkinseed that is manufactured by Heddon. I bought 13 lures for $50 and soon I found out that the punkinseed lure alone is worth $50. I got a good deal on it!

jig lures

silver coin
of a Gupta
horseman
(below)

elephant and
rhinoceros coins,
4th–5th century
(left)

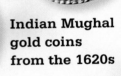

Indian Mughal
gold coins
from the 1620s

Gayatri Mani

I collect international stamps, coins, pens and pencils, erasers, comic books, birds' eggs, rocks, Indian clothing and jewelry. But I'm just going to talk about my money, stamps, and Indian book collection.

I've been collecting coins since I was about six years old. It started when we were taking my first trip back to India and I got a coin from Bahrain in a gift shop. I got a lot of my B.C. coins from my great uncle. I also have some from 974 A.D. and some pre-British coins, which are from the 1500s or 1600s, before the British took over India.

Whenever I got a new coin, my mom would make me study the capital of that country. I have coins from countries from every continent except for Antarctica.

My stamps are from all over the world too. I started collecting stamps because my aunt is from Indonesia and my grandparents live in India and my uncle lives in Germany. They used to write letters to me, so I would cut the stamps off the corners of the envelopes.

Indonesia
stamps (left)

Indian
stamps
(left and
below)

German
stamp
(right)

564

I also collect Indian comic books, which have stories about Indian mythology, which is a lot like Greek mythology. A lot of Indian comics are also like *Aesop's Fables*. They're called *Jataka Tales* and the *Panchatantra*. They have animal stories with morals at the end.

two popular retellings of Indian tales

Connect and Compare

1. Based on the photographs and captions, which of these collections would you like to read more about? Why? **Photographs and Captions**

2. What kinds of things would you like to collect? Why? **Evaluate**

3. Do you think the collections in "Cool Collections" and Joe's baseball card collection in *Honus and Me* are equally interesting? Explain. **Reading/Writing Across Texts**

Math Activity

Research what resources you would need to start a collection. Then write a budget and calculate how much money you will need for starting a collection.

 Find out more about collections at **www.macmillanmh.com**

Writer's Craft

Figurative Language

When you use **figurative language**, your readers get a clear picture of what you are describing. For example, personification is a comparison in which human qualities are given to objects or animals.

My favorite baseball sits on a throne as if it were a king.

The baseball is portrayed as encouraging me to succeed.

My Championship Baseball

by Troy B.

I have a baseball
that sits on a throne
above what my mother calls
the most cluttered desk in Kentucky.

I have a baseball
that has thirteen signatures
in smeared blue ink
of my teammates, my friends.

I have a baseball
that is made of cork and cowhide,
with grass stains and summertime dirt
stuck between the stitches of crimson string.

I have a baseball
that whispers to me, every time I feel down,
"You can do it!"
and reminds me that I did it before.

Your Turn

Write a poem that describes an object that is important to you. Your poem can rhyme or it can be unrhymed, like Troy's poem. Choose colorful figurative language to describe your object. It might help to imagine that you are creating a photograph of the object with your words. Use the Writer's Checklist to check your writing.

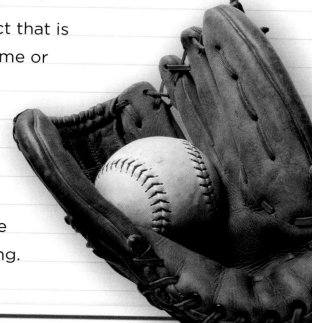

Writer's Checklist

☑ **Ideas and Content:** Is it clear what object I am describing? Did I include **figurative language** to create a vivid picture?

✓ **Organization:** Do the details I chose fit into the poem like pieces of a puzzle?

✓ **Voice:** Do I capture the way I feel about this object? Does the poem sound like only I sound?

✓ **Word Choice:** Did I include lively and vivid adjectives?

✓ **Sentence Fluency:** Does my poem have natural rhythm? Do the words flow smoothly?

✓ **Conventions:** Did I use the words *more* or *most* properly in my poem? Did I check my spelling?

TAKING A STAND

Talk About It

These people took a stand for equality in 1963. What is something in your life that you would take a stand on?

Find out more about taking a stand at
www.macmillanmh.com

569

Rosa Parks and the Institute

by Alana Phillips

What do you think of when you hear the name Rosa Parks? Do you think of the word *freedom*? Do you see a public bus in your mind's eye? Rosa Parks is known for her **defiance** when she was faced with unfair treatment. In other words, Rosa Parks refused to follow the rules when she knew in her heart that those rules were wrong. She wanted to help make the unjust treatment **evident**, or easy to see. This is why people admire

Rosa Parks. To some, her actions have **resonated** like an echo that says, "Fight for your beliefs. Fight for your beliefs. Fight for your beliefs."

Throughout her life, Rosa Parks was **persistent** in fighting for her beliefs. For example, she never stopped trying to help Americans. This is why she started the Rosa and Raymond Parks Institute for Self-Development.

In 1987, Rosa Parks and her friend Elaine Easton Steele started the institute together. Rosa Parks wished her husband could have been included, but he passed away in 1977. Rosa Parks remembered her husband's strong **convictions**. One of his strongest beliefs was in civil rights for all. Raymond Parks, like his wife, believed that no person should suffer **oppression**, or cruel treatment, just because of the color of his or her skin. Rosa Parks honored her husband's memory by including his name in the institute's title.

The institute offers many programs for today's youth. One of the main programs is called Pathways to Freedom. Children in the program can trace the path of the Underground Railroad. They learn about history and about the civil rights movement of the 1950s and 1960s.

The success of this program helped the institute gain **momentum**. With this strength and force, new programs have moved forward. One of its most popular programs has youngsters teaching senior citizens how to use computers! Like the **remedies** that doctors offer the sick, the institute offers a cure for those who suffer from loneliness. The Rosa and Raymond Parks Institute offers people a place to connect to the past, to the future, and to each other.

Reread for **Comprehension**

Monitor Comprehension

Summarize

When you summarize, you retell the most important parts of a selection. This helps you to monitor your understanding of the story. A Summary Chart will help you take notes on the selection. You can use these notes to write a summary. Use the Summary Chart as you reread "Rosa Parks and the Institute."

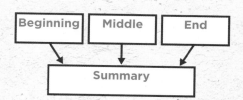

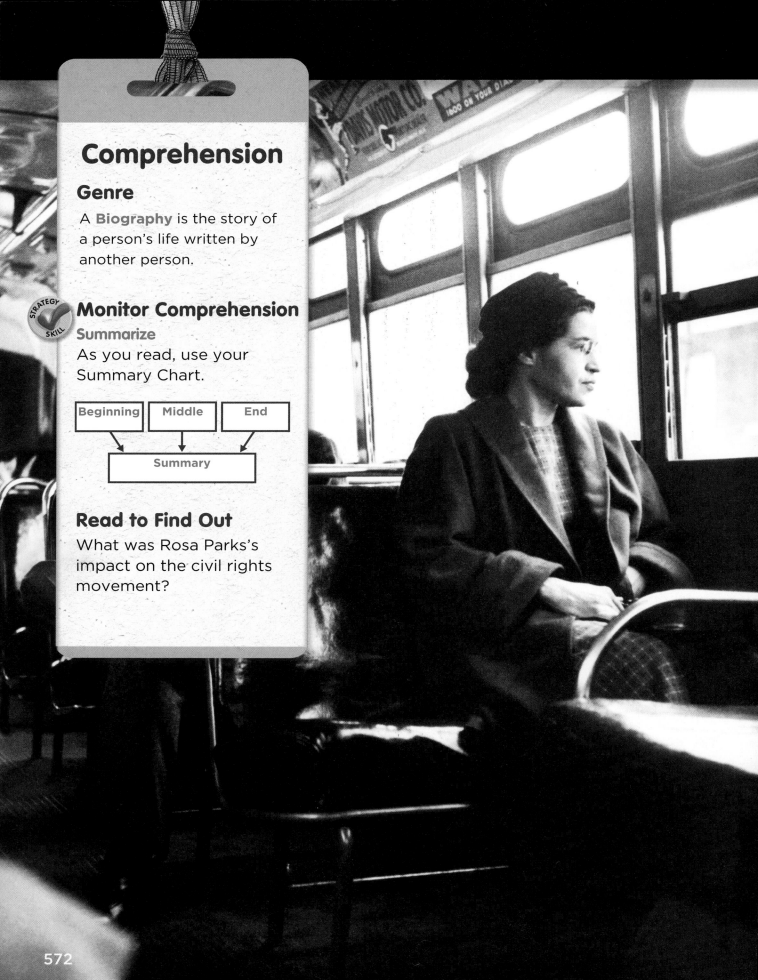

Comprehension

Genre

A **Biography** is the story of a person's life written by another person.

Monitor Comprehension

Summarize

As you read, use your Summary Chart.

Beginning	Middle	End
↓	↓	↓

Summary

Read to Find Out

What was Rosa Parks's impact on the civil rights movement?

572

from

Let It Shine

by Andrea Davis Pinkney

Rosa Parks

Leona and James McCauley with their daughter Rosa Louise

Rosa McCauley was named after her maternal grandmother, Rose Edwards. The name fit her perfectly. She was a beautiful, delicate child, who was always blossoming with enthusiasm. Rosa's father, James McCauley, worked as a carpenter. He traveled through the South building homes. Rosa saw very little of her father while she was growing up. His work kept him away from his family for long periods of time.

Rosa's mother, Leona, was a schoolteacher who settled with her children in Pine Level, Alabama, the place where she was raised. Rosa and her baby brother, Sylvester, lived on an eighteen-acre farm with their mother and their grandparents, Grandma Rose and Grandpa Sylvester.

Because there were so few black schools in the immediate community, Leona often traveled to other towns to find teaching assignments. She also earned money by styling hair for the women in Pine Level and by mending clothes for neighbors and friends.

Although Rosa missed having her father nearby, she loved living with her grandparents. Grandpa Sylvester was an outspoken man, who was solid in his **convictions**. He believed that no human being had just cause to mistreat another, and that if somebody did you wrong, you should not stand for it.

From a very young age, Rosa learned about racial hatred. Both her grandparents had been slaves. They told her many stories about the wicked treatment black people had endured at the hands of white slave masters. But even though slavery had ended by the time Rosa was born, she still experienced the **oppression** of racism firsthand. This bigotry was **evident** mostly in laws that demanded separate schools, drinking fountains, restaurants, and public bathrooms for black people and white people.

When Rosa was six, she began to attend Pine Level's only black school, a shabby one-room schoolhouse where students from first through sixth grades crammed together on benches. There were no desks, no windows, a handful of tattered books, and one teacher for fifty kids. During the winter, the sixth-grade boys had to build a fire in a woodstove to keep the classroom warm.

The school for white students was a place black children could only dream about. It was made of bricks. It had a playground. There were books galore. There were plenty of teachers. And there was lots of heat. It wasn't fair that the amenities that made the white schools so fine were purchased with public tax money that came from the pockets of both Pine Level's white *and* black residents.

Leona saved every penny she could, and when Rosa was eleven years old, her mother sent her to the Montgomery

Early twentieth century African American classroom

Industrial School for Black Girls, a private school in Montgomery, Alabama. During the school year, Rosa lived with her aunt Fannie. At her new school Rosa learned everything, from how to read world maps to how to mix **remedies** for sick and ailing souls. She even took cooking lessons.

But a private education couldn't shield Rosa from the public humiliation of racism that was common in the South in the 1920s. Rosa often rode streetcar trolleys to school—segregated streetcars in which she, along with every other black rider, was forced to sit in the back.

When Rosa was sixteen, her grandma Rose died. Soon after that Rosa's mother got sick. Rosa quit school and returned to Pine Level so that she could work to help support her family. She spent the final years of her childhood running the Edwards's farm and earning money cooking and sewing, two skills she had perfected at the Montgomery Industrial School.

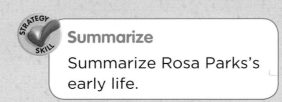

Summarize

Summarize Rosa Parks's early life.

In 1931 a neighbor introduced Rosa to Raymond Parks. Raymond was as dandy as they come. He was smart, smooth talking, forthright, and **persistent**. And he drove a red car that had a rumble seat in the back. Raymond was a barber who worked in downtown Montgomery. He took a quick liking to Rosa. But she was not immediately impressed with him. He came to Rosa's house several times to ask Rosa's mother if he could take Rosa for a drive in his car. It was clear to Leona that Raymond Parks was intelligent and sincere. She agreed to let him spend time with her daughter, but it was Rosa who kept turning down Raymond's offers.

Finally, when Rosa said yes to a short ride with Raymond, she saw that he was more than just a pretty boy with a flashy car. Like Rosa's grandfather, Raymond was a man of conviction. He was well-spoken and cared deeply about the plight of black people in the South. And he was an active member of the National Association for the Advancement of Colored People (NAACP).

NAACP branch office, Detroit, Michigan, 1940's

The more Raymond told Rosa about his commitment to helping black people, the more Rosa's awareness grew. Her love for Raymond grew, too. In December 1932 Rosa McCauley and Raymond Parks were married, in Pine Level at the home of Rosa's mother. Rosa was nineteen years old.

Alabama State Teachers College

Raymond knew that Rosa had been forced to quit high school to take care of her family. It troubled him that his wife had to give up something she enjoyed so much. Soon after Rosa and Raymond married, Raymond encouraged Rosa to complete her education. Rosa was happy to return to school. She graduated from Alabama State Teachers College in 1933, with a high school diploma.

Rosa found work as a helper at Saint Margaret's Hospital in Montgomery. At night she worked as a seamstress at home, mending and tailoring clothes. Rosa was grateful for her job, but going to work drove home the sad reality of segregation. When Rosa took the city bus to work, she had to go through the same degrading ritual day after day. She would step on the bus at the front and buy a ticket from the driver. Then she'd have to leave the bus, walk around to the back, and enter the bus again through the rear door. All black passengers had to sit in the back. Only white people were allowed to ride at the front of the bus. This was the law. If you were black and the back of the bus was too crowded, tough. You had to wait for the next bus, go through the same drill, and pray you would get to work on time.

Rosa was growing tired of this daily disgrace. Sometimes she would get onto the bus at the front and pay her fare, like always. Then before the driver had a chance to take full notice of her, Rosa would breeze through the front section of the bus to find her seat in the back.

577

Several drivers came to associate Rosa with her **defiance**. Once, in 1943, a driver kicked Rosa off his bus because she refused to enter the bus through the back door. He told Rosa that if she thought she was too high-and-mighty to follow the rules, she should find another bus to ride. But there *was* no other bus for her to ride. And there were no drivers bold enough to turn their backs on the ugly ways of discrimination.

As the wife of a civil rights activist (and the granddaughter of a civil rights believer), Rosa had learned three important things about changing the unjust treatment black people had suffered: Change takes time. Change takes strength. Change takes the help of others. Rosa Parks had all three.

She knew that one of the best ways to put these advantages to work would be to join the NAACP. But becoming an NAACP member wasn't as simple as it seemed. Rosa's husband didn't think it was a good idea. The NAACP existed under the constant threat of white vigilantes who looked for violent ways to sabotage group meetings. Sometimes NAACP meetings had to be held during late-night hours, in dark, secret places where Klansmen and the police couldn't find the group.

Raymond supported his wife's wish to stop segregation, but at the same time, he feared for her safety. And there were very few women enrolled as NAACP members. If Rosa were to join, she would be shrouded by the influence of men. Rosa respected her husband's concerns. But in 1943 when she spotted a picture in the *Alabama Tribune* of Johnnie Carr, a friend of hers from the Montgomery Industrial School, who was acting as a temporary secretary for the local NAACP Montgomery branch, Rosa knew she had to join. Soon after Rosa saw the newspaper article, she attended the annual NAACP Montgomery meeting. This was the meeting to elect new officers. There were sixteen people at the meeting—fifteen men and Rosa Parks.

African American citizens sitting in the rear of the bus during the time of segregation laws

When it came time to elect a permanent volunteer secretary, everybody looked to Rosa. They all figured secretarial work was women's work and she was the natural choice. Rosa accepted the job gladly. What better way to serve the cause than to document its progress?

Rosa wasted no time. She put her pen to paper right then and there, and recorded the remaining minutes of the meeting. From that day on for the next twelve years, Rosa took her position as the NAACP Montgomery chapter secretary very seriously. And when he saw the commitment that Rosa brought to her volunteer work, so did her husband.

Rosa organized branch meetings, kept the books, wrote and mailed letters and press releases, and at every turn, drummed up new members. When the office phone rang, Rosa answered it. When someone had a question about the workings of the branch, Rosa answered that, too.

Montgomery NAACP meeting, 1950s. Rosa is at the right and Mr. E. D. Nixon is the first in the middle row.

As branch secretary, Rosa worked closely with E. D. Nixon, the chapter president. Under E. D.'s direction, she recorded all of the cases of discrimination and violence against black people in the state of Alabama. The cases seemed never ending. There were hundreds of them.

Documenting these cases showed Rosa that racism in Alabama was big. It was powerful. It gathered **momentum** with each mile it covered. It would take the force of one woman's iron will to stop it in its tracks.

Turns out, Rosa Parks was that woman.

December 1, 1955, started out like any other Thursday for Rosa. She went to her job at the Montgomery Fair department store, where she then worked as a seamstress. When the workday ended, Rosa gathered her purse and coat and walked to the Court Square bus stop. She waited patiently for the Cleveland Avenue bus—the bus she'd taken to and from work many times. When she stepped onto the bus and paid her dime to ride, she immediately spotted an empty seat on the aisle, one row behind the whites-only section of the bus. It was rush hour. Any seat on any bus at this time of day was a blessing. Rosa sat back and gave a quiet sigh of relief.

When the bus stopped to pick up passengers at the Empire Theater stop, six white people got on. They each paid the ten-cent fare, just as Rosa had done. All but one of them easily found seats at the front of the bus. The sixth passenger, a man, didn't mind standing. He curled his fingers around a holding pole and waited for the bus to pull away.

But according to the bus segregation laws for the state of Alabama, black people were required to give up a bus seat if a white person was left standing. And each bus driver in the state was allowed to lay down the letter of the law on his bus.

As it turned out, Rosa was sitting on the bus that was driven by the same driver who, twelve years before, had kicked Rosa off his bus because she would not enter through the back door. The driver remembered Rosa. And Rosa sure remembered him. He glared at Rosa through his rearview mirror. He ordered her up and out of her seat. But she wouldn't move. Instead, she answered him with a question. Why, she asked, should she have to endure his bossing her around?

Well, the driver didn't take kindly to Rosa challenging him. Next thing Rosa knew, he was standing over her, insisting that she give up her seat to the white man who needed a seat. Rosa clenched her purse, which rested in her lap. When the driver asked Rosa to move a second time, Rosa put it to him plainly and firmly: No.

He told Rosa he would call the police if she didn't move. Rosa didn't flinch. Maybe she was thinking about her grandpa Sylvester's solid belief in not allowing mistreatment from others. Or maybe she was just fed up with giving in to segregation's iron fist.

Even the threat of police couldn't rouse Rosa. Once again her answer to the bus driver was simple: Do it. And he did— lickety-split. The police came right away. They arrested Rosa and took her to the city jail. Rosa called her husband and told him the whole story. News of Rosa's arrest had already begun to spread through Montgomery's black community. Several friends of Rosa's and Raymond's had seen Rosa get arrested. E. D. Nixon from the NAACP was one of the first to hear about Rosa. He immediately collected enough bail money to release Rosa from jail. He told Rosa and Raymond that though the incident was an unfortunate one, it had the power to pound out segregation. If Rosa was willing—and brave enough—to bring a case against Alabama's segregation laws, she could help end segregation in the state.

Rosa didn't have to think long about E. D. Nixon's proposal. Just a short time earlier, Rosa had been staring segregation in the face and saying *no*. Now she was looking the law in the eyes, and without blinking, she said *yes*. She agreed to attack the system that kept her and every black person in the United States of America from being treated equally. Years later, in reflecting on the events that led to her decision, Rosa said, "People always say that I [didn't give] up my seat because I was tired, but that isn't true. I was not tired physically . . . The only tired I was, was tired of giving in."

On December 5, 1955, Rosa and her attorney, Fred Gray, appeared before Judge John B. Scott in the city court of Montgomery, Alabama. Rosa was found guilty of breaking the Alabama State segregated bus law. She was fined ten dollars. Although Rosa was convicted, her act had ignited the Montgomery bus boycott, a civil rights movement that would change the face of segregation forever.

Summarize

Summarize how Rosa Parks decided to help end segregation in her state.

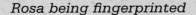
Rosa being fingerprinted

Rev. Martin Luther King Jr. outlining boycott strategies to his organizers, including Rosa Parks.

The Reverend Martin Luther King Jr. helped the boycott get off to a strong start. On the evening of December 5, 1955, he addressed nearly one thousand people at the Holt Street Baptist Church in Montgomery. He said, "We're going to work with grim and firm determination to gain justice on the buses in this city. And . . . we are not wrong in what we are doing. If we are wrong, the Constitution of the United States is wrong . . . If we are wrong, justice is a lie. And we are determined here in Montgomery to work and fight until justice runs down like water and righteousness like a mighty stream . . ."

Martin Luther King's words **resonated** like thunder on a dark night. The kind of thunder that stirs you from the inside out. As a protest to the treatment they and Rosa had received, every black resident of Montgomery stopped riding the city's buses. They walked to where they wanted to go. They walked miles and miles—to work, to church, to the bank, to the grocery store. They organized car pools. And by denying money to the city bus system, they showed white people that black men and women were valuable paying customers. No matter how tired of walking they may have been—some had to wake up long before dawn to get to work on time—they refused to give up.

583

*African Americans car pool, during bus boycott, deserted bus
in background*

Rosa lost her job as a result of her arrest and the
boycott. To earn money, she tailored clothes in her home.
She spent the rest of her time helping the boycott stay
organized. The boycott rolled on for more than a year.
Finally, on December 20, 1956, the Supreme Court ruled
that in the state of Alabama segregated buses were illegal.
Black people went back to riding buses the very next day,
and you can best believe that on buses in Montgomery—and
throughout the state—black people sat in the front, enjoying
their view of justice.

The Montgomery bus boycott was an important triumph
for African Americans. It was the beginning of the end of *all*
segregation. But it was a victory that came at a cost to Rosa.
Soon after the boycott ended, Rosa received angry threats
from white people who were in favor of segregation. A few
months later Rosa and Raymond Parks, and Rosa's mother,
Leona, moved to Detroit, Michigan, where Rosa's brother
had settled.

Living in the North enabled Rosa to continue her civil rights interests peacefully. In 1965 she began working in the office of John Conyers, a young black congressman. As she had done at the NAACP, Rosa kept the congressman's office running smoothly. She also helped him find housing for the city's homeless.

Whenever Rosa saw an opportunity to serve fellow African Americans, she took it. In 1987 she founded the Rosa and Raymond Parks Institute for Self-Development, a means for teaching young people about civil rights.

Over time Rosa has gained many impressive titles. She has been called the Mother of the Civil Rights Movement and the Patron Saint of the Civil Rights Movement. She even has two streets named after her, one in Detroit, the other in Montgomery. Montgomery's Cleveland Avenue, where Rosa caught the bus on that landmark day in 1955, was later renamed Rosa Parks Boulevard.

No single pronouncement can ever fully capture the impact that Rosa Parks has had on the condition of civil rights in America—and beyond.

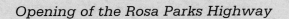

Opening of the Rosa Parks Highway

Rosa Parks in 1999

Meet the Author
Andrea Davis Pinkney

Andrea Davis Pinkney writes every day. Some of her best story ideas come to her when she is riding on the subway in New York City, where she lives with her husband, artist Brian Pinkney, and their children. Andrea grew up surrounded by civil rights activists. Maybe that is why all her books are about people who did extraordinary things to help change the world.

Another book by Andrea Davis Pinkney: *Silent Thunder*

 Find out more about Andrea Davis Pinkney at **www.macmillanmh.com**

Author's Purpose
How can you tell that the author considers Rosa Parks an American hero? What details in *Let It Shine* show that Andrea Davis Pinkney admires Rosa Parks?

Comprehension Check

Summarize

Use your Summary Chart to help you summarize *Let It Shine*. Why is Rosa Parks known as "the Mother of the Civil Rights Movement"?

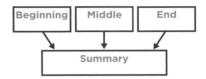

Think and Compare

1. How did the events and people in Rosa Parks's early life shape her work in the civil rights movement? **Monitor Comprehension: Summarize**

2. How would you describe Rosa Parks's personality? Pick an event described in *Let It Shine* to illustrate her character. Use specific evidence from the text. **Evaluate**

3. Think about a time when someone you know stood up for his or her **convictions**. What happened? What were the potential consequences? **Synthesize**

4. Think about the bus driver, the man to whom Rosa was supposed to give her seat, and the police officer who arrested her. Why would some people support such an unjust law? **Evaluate**

5. Read "Rosa Parks and the Institute" on pages 570–571. How do the activities at the Institute reflect the goals of Rosa Parks in *Let It Shine?* **Reading/Writing Across Texts**

Caged Bird

by Maya Angelou

Poetry

Lyric Poems convey the strong feelings of the poet and may sound like songs.

Literary Elements

Words **Rhyme** when their endings sound the same or nearly the same. Rhymes mostly occur at the end of lines of poetry.

A **Simile** is a comparison between two unlike things using *like* or *as*.

Repetition involves repeating a word or phrase for rhythmic effect and emphasis.

The free bird leaps
on the back of the wind
and floats downstream
till the current ends
and dips his wings
in the orange sun rays
and dares to claim the sky.

But a bird that stalks
down his narrow cage
can seldom see through
his bars of rage
his wings are clipped and
his feet are tied
so he opens his throat to sing.

The caged bird sings
with a fearful trill
of things unknown
but longed for still
and his tune is heard
on the distant hill
for the caged bird
sings of freedom.

"Trill," "still," "hill" all rhyme, as do "heard" and "bird."

I Dream a World

by Langston Hughes

I dream a world where man
No other will scorn,
Where love will bless the earth
And peace its paths adorn.
I dream a world where all
Will know sweet freedom's way,
Where greed no longer saps the soul
Nor avarice blights our day.
A world I dream where black or white,
Whatever race you be,
Will share the bounties of the earth
And every man is free,
Where wretchedness will hang its head
And joy, like a pearl,
Attend the needs of all mankind—
Of such I dream, my world!

The title is repeated throughout the poem to emphasize the importance of this idea.

Here joy is compared to a pearl to form a simile.

Connect and Compare

1. Langston Hughes repeats the phrase "I dream a world" throughout the poem. How does this repetition give the last line of the poem greater emphasis? **Repetition**

2. How does the poet of "Caged Bird" use the image of birds to express her feelings about humans? **Analyze**

3. How do you think Rosa Parks would have felt about these poems? Would she have agreed or disagreed with the poets' ideas? **Reading/Writing Across Texts**

 Find out more about poetry at **www.macmillanmh.com**

Write an Eyewitness Account

The Birth of a Twister

by Tyrone W.

When I stepped out of my house that afternoon, I knew that something was very different. It was 3:30 P.M. and I noticed that no birds were chirping. Usually, you can hear dozens of birds singing and see them in the trees.

The next thing I noticed was that there was no breeze. The leaves in the trees seemed to be standing still. If you had been there, you would have thought it was weird, too!

I walked to the end of my street and then I saw it. There was a gigantic cloud looming in the far-off sky. Thick and dark, its shape reminded me of a bull charging a red flag. It was the worst thing I had ever seen. I stood still and watched the giant cloud come closer. Suddenly, a strange line became visible near its front. When the line came close to touching the ground, I realized that it was a tornado! I had just watched a tornado being born! I ran home as fast as I could, told my parents, and hurried to the basement.

Fortunately, the tornado had touched down for only a few minutes in some fields on the outskirts of town. Those just happened to be the same few minutes that I was watching it!

I established an ominous mood.

I used words such as weird.

Your Turn

Write an eyewitness account of an important event. This event can be something that happened in your life or it can be an event from history. If you write about a historical event, remember to write as if you were there watching it happen. Be sure to use a strong, original voice, and try to speak directly to the audience when it is appropriate. Use the Writer's Checklist to check your writing.

Writer's Checklist

☑ **Ideas and Content:** Did I retell my experience clearly? Did I include strong descriptions?

☑ **Organization:** Did I organize my paper in a logical way? Did I share events in the correct order?

☑ **Voice:** Did I share my experience in a way that only I could?

☑ **Word Choice:** Did I use precise words to reinforce **mood**?

☑ **Sentence Fluency:** Did I use different kinds of sentences to add interest to my writing?

☑ **Conventions:** Did I edit and proofread my essay?

After Apple Picking

by Robert Frost

My long two-pointed ladder's sticking through a tree

Toward heaven still,

And there's a barrel that I didn't fill

Beside it, and there may be two or three

Apples I didn't pick upon some bough. 5

But I am done with apple-picking now.

Essence of winter sleep is on the night,

The scent of apples: I am drowsing off.

I cannot rub the strangeness from my sight

I got from looking through a pane of glass 10

I skimmed this morning from the drinking trough

And held against the world of hoary grass.

It melted, and I let it fall and break.

Go On ▶

But I was well

Upon my way to sleep before it fell,   15

And I could tell

What form my dreaming was about to take.

Magnified apples appear and disappear,

Stem end and blossom end,

And every fleck of russet showing clear.   20

My instep arch not only keeps the ache,

It keeps the pressure of a ladder-round.

I feel the ladder sway as the boughs bend.

And I keep hearing from the cellar bin

The rumbling sound   25

Of load on load of apples coming in.

For I have had too much

Of apple-picking: I am overtired

Of the great harvest I myself desired.

There were ten thousand thousand fruit to touch,   30

Cherish in hand, lift down, and not let fall.

For all

That struck the earth,

No matter if not bruised or spiked with stubble,

Went surely to the cider-apple heap   35

As of no worth.

One can see what will trouble

This sleep of mine, whatever sleep it is.

Were he not gone,

The woodchuck could say whether it's like his   40

Long sleep, as I describe its coming on,

Or just some human sleep.

A Bump on the Head

Probably the most famous apple in history belonged to English physicist Sir Isaac Newton. His apple became the symbol for one of history's greatest scientific discoveries: the force of gravity.

However, some historians question whether or not the apple even existed. When examining history, people try to separate the fact from the fiction. And in Newton's case, his scientific work was the fact, and the story about the apple was all fiction.

Isaac Newton was born in 1642 in England. As a young man, he left home to study science at Cambridge University. One day while resting under an apple tree, an apple fell from a branch above and hit him right on the head. He looked at the apple and began to think. He thought about why the apple fell, applying some of the scientific knowledge from school.

Newton realized that forces inside Earth were always pulling objects toward its center. That's why the apple fell down and did not stay floating high up in the tree. When a person jumps, he or she does not go flying, soaring into space like a lost balloon. Gravity pulls everything toward the ground.

What's the problem with this famous and inspiring apple story? Most historians and scholars don't believe the bump on the head ever happened.

Then why did he tell this story? Today the general belief is that Newton invented that apple to make his work with gravity more memorable. Ask some people and they won't even remember why the apple fell on Sir Isaac Newton's head. Not everyone remembers the work Newton did to change the world. Much of the time, people remember the apple more than they remember him.

Would Newton live on in the minds of people without his famous story? Would we remember him at all without that apple?

What if it had been a peach?

Go On ▶

Directions: Answer the questions.

Tip

You have to think about the entire selection to choose the best answer.

1. **Why would a scientist invent a story like Newton's falling apple?**

   A   to get people's interest
   B   to explain why apples grow on trees
   C   to help the cause of medicine
   D   to make the audience laugh

2. **Why is history filled with both fact and fiction?**

   A   to confuse people
   B   to make major events and abstract ideas more understandable
   C   so we can make up characters
   D   so we can decide for ourselves what is true

3. **In the poem, the poet is trying to show that**

   A   an apple a day keeps the doctor away.
   B   picking apples is good exercise.
   C   nature's seasons are like the stages in a person's life.
   D   picking apples is like picking oranges.

4. **Explain how the speaker in the poem "After Apple Picking" has a different experience with apples from the one Newton does.**

5. **Explain why Robert Frost's poem "After Apple Picking" is a metaphor for life. Write at least one paragraph. Include examples from the poem in your answer.**

Writing Prompt

Think of a time when an ordinary experience caused you to learn something new. Write a speech about the experience and reflect on what you learned from it. Your speech should be at least three paragraphs long.

STOP 595

Great Designs Last Forever

Talk About It

Flight is intriguing. If you were to design a flying machine, what would it look like?

LOG ON Find out more about great designs at **www.macmillanmh.com**

Artists
of the Past

by Lisa Darwood

Suppose that you could travel back in time to the period of the **Renaissance**. This was an exciting age when there was a rebirth of interest in learning and the arts. It began in Italy in the 1300s and spread throughout Europe.

You arrive in Florence, a beautiful city in Italy. This is the city of the Medici family. The Medici are wealthy bankers and merchants who have **commissioned**, or sponsored, artists to create many paintings, statues, and buildings for the city. They have also supported poets and writers.

One of the people you meet is Michelangelo Buonarroti. Like fellow artist Leonardo da Vinci, he is a genius of many talents. Known for his beautiful paintings in the Sistine Chapel in Rome, he is also a great sculptor and is making sketches for a statue. Most artists of this period are concerned that parts of statues be in **proportion**. They want their work to show how one part of the body relates to other parts. Michelangelo's sketches show more than the figure's proportions, though. They show the power and spirit of the figure. Once Michelangelo is happy with his drawings, he will make a model of his statue. The model is a **miniature** version of the statue, which will be huge.

Michelangelo's *David*

Vocabulary

Renaissance
commissioned
proportion
miniature
philosopher
elaborate
envisioned
recommend

Word Parts

Many English words have **Greek Roots**.

phil = love
soph = wise

Philosopher originally meant one who loves wisdom.

Another artist you meet is Leonardo da Vinci, also a leader of the Renaissance. One of his most famous paintings is the *Mona Lisa*. But Leonardo is more than a painter; he is a **philosopher** who studies the nature of the universe. He wants to know how everything works. He draws **elaborate** and detailed scientific pictures of plants, animals, humans, and the many inventions he has **envisioned** in his mind. Leonardo fills more than 4,000 pages in his notebooks with drawings. He shows you drawings of flying machines and undersea boats. How amazing for the fifteenth century!

A third artist of the Renaissance is Raphael. He is younger than Leonardo and Michelangelo and has studied their work. Some of the people you meet think his paintings are more delicate in color and have softer lines. Raphael shows you a work called *The School of Athens*.

Detail of Plato and Aristotle from *The School of Athens* by Raphael

It pictures an imaginary group of great thinkers. You are interested to see that included in the painting are Michelangelo, Leonardo, and Raphael.

When you return to the twenty-first century, you can't wait to tell your friends about these artists of the past. You **recommend**, or suggest, that they too pay a visit to the Renaissance Era.

Reread for **Comprehension**

Generate Questions

Make Generalizations

It is important to generate or ask questions as you read. How accurate is the information? As you read a selection, look for facts. Compare what you read to other information that you know. Then make a generalization about the information.

Use a Generalizations Chart as you reread "Artists of the Past."

Important Information	Generalization

Comprehension

Genre

Nonfiction gives an account of actual people, situations, or events.

Generate Questions

Make Generalizations

As you read, use your Generalizations Chart.

Important Information	Generalization

Read to Find Out

What makes Leonardo's designs so timeless?

by **Jean Fritz**
illustrated by **Hudson Talbott**

LEONARDO'S HORSE

Award Winning Book

Anyone who watched the young Leonardo wander the countryside around his home in Vinci might have guessed that he would be an artist. He stopped to examine everything. He looked at the landscape as if he were memorizing it. So it was no surprise when his father took him as a young teenager to Florence to study art.

People noticed that Leonardo was different.

He dressed differently. While other young men wore long togas, Leonardo wore short, rose-colored velvet togas.

He wrote differently. Backwards. From the right side of the paper to the left. A person would have to use a mirror to read his writing.

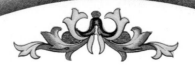

And he wouldn't eat meat. He liked animals too much to
eat anything that had once been alive. Nor could he stand the sight
of caged birds. If he saw a man selling birds, he would buy them all.
Then he would open the cages and watch the birds fly away. What
a flurry they made! How did they do it? All his life Leonardo tried
to discover their secret of flying so he could make a flying machine
for himself.

For a man who liked to ask questions, Leonardo da Vinci
was born at the right time—April 15, 1452. Everybody was asking
questions then. The age was called the **Renaissance**, a time of
rebirth when people who had forgotten how to be curious became
curious again. They were exploring new countries, discovering,
inventing, looking at old things in new ways. What was the point,
Leonardo asked, in copying what had already been done? He had to
bring his own experience into whatever he painted. You wouldn't
catch him putting a halo around the head of a saint. How could he?
He had never seen a halo.

Leonardo da Vinci turned out to be a famous artist; still, he
was not just an artist. He could never be just one thing. He was an
engineer, an architect, a musician, a **philosopher**, an astronomer.
Once he fashioned a special kind of flute made of silver in the shape
of a horse's head. The ruler of Florence, Lorenzo de' Medici, asked
him to deliver it as a gift to the duke of Milan. This was lucky for
Leonardo. He had heard that the duke of Milan wanted to honor
his father with a bronze horse in front of his palace. And Leonardo
wanted to be the one to make it.

This would be his mark on history. Hundreds of years later
people would point to the horse. "Leonardo made that," they
would say.

Make Generalizations
Is the statement "Everybody was
asking questions then" a valid
generalization? Explain your answer.

602

Parachute

Catapult

So he wrote to the duke, listing all the things that he could do. He could make cannon, lightweight bridges, and covered chariots that couldn't be broken or harmed. On and on he went, but he saved the most important point for the last. He could make a bronze horse. In the end, he didn't send the letter. He simply left for Milan. Never mind that he was in the midst of painting a large religious picture in Florence. Let someone else finish it. He had planned the picture and that was the important part.

Leonardo was thirty years old now, handsome with curly blond hair. The duke gave him the job of working on the horse, but at the same time he was expected to take charge of entertainment in the palace. He had a beautiful singing voice, he could play musical instruments, he could juggle and ask riddles, and he was also asked to stage **elaborate** plays for special occasions. Whenever he had a chance, he went back to the horse.

He visited the stables, studying how a horse was put together.

He needed to understand everything about his subject. He measured and drew pictures until he knew where all the bones and muscles of a horse were. But you couldn't show all the muscles on a statue, he said, or the horse would look like a bag of turnips. You should show only those muscles the horse was using or getting ready to use.

He visited statues of horses. Many were shown in an amble— left front leg moving at the same time as the left back leg. This was not easy for a horse; he had to be taught to do it. Leonardo saw one horse, however, that he described as free—left front leg and right back leg moving together, in a trot. Moreover, both ears were pointed forward. (Some horses pointed one ear back to hear the rider's orders.)

Leonardo was ready to begin.

But the duke wasn't quite ready. He wanted a much bigger horse than the one he had originally planned. One three times larger than life. Could Leonardo manage anything that large? the duke wondered. He wrote to Lorenzo, asking him to **recommend** someone who could do the job.

Lorenzo replied: Leonardo da Vinci was the only one.

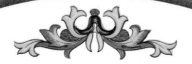

On April 23, 1490, Leonardo wrote in his notebook: "I resumed work on the horse." The hardest part would be the casting. He collected 58,000 pounds of metal—tin and copper—which would be heated until it was fluid. This would be turned into bronze and used to cast the horse. But should he pour the bronze all at once? No one had tried a single pouring of anything this large.

In November 1493, he had completed the clay model—twenty-four feet high. It was shown off at one of the duke's special occasions, and it was a sensation.

But Leonardo seemed to be in no hurry to start casting. Perhaps he wasn't sure how he'd do it. Besides, he was planning a new project. He had been **commissioned** to cover the wall of a convent with a picture of Jesus and his disciples at the Last Supper. Since he wanted to present the disciples realistically, each with his own personality, Leonardo walked the streets of Milan, looking for the right faces. He had trouble with Judas. He could never find anyone in Milan who looked evil enough. So he left Judas for someone else to do.

Later, in 1498, there were rumors that the French were preparing to invade Milan, and the duke wanted to be ready. And there was all the metal that Leonardo had collected. Just what the duke needed. So he sent it off to be made into cannon. Well, this is war, Leonardo reasoned. What else could they do?

When the French came in 1499, Leonardo and the duke fled. But the horse couldn't leave. There he was when the French arrived. The archers laughed. Never would they find as perfect a target, they said. Pulling back the strings on their bows, they let their arrows fly. Ping! Ping! Ping! The horse sagged. Ping!

Then it rained. And the horse became smaller and smaller. At last it was nothing but a pile of mud stuck with arrows.

Make Generalizations
The author states that many statues showed horses in an amble. Is this a valid generalization? Explain.

Leonardo went back to inventing and painting, but he never forgot his horse.

He still wanted to invent a flying machine. But he still couldn't do it.

His greatest disappointment, however, was his horse.

As Leonardo became older, his hair turned white and grew down to his shoulders. His beard reached to his waist.

And he became depressed. What had he achieved? he asked himself. He complained to his notebook: "Tell me," he asked, "if anything has been achieved by me. Tell me. Tell me." It was especially hard when his rival, Michelangelo, taunted him.

"You," Michelangelo said, "who made a model of a horse you could never cast in bronze and which you gave up, to your shame."

In his notebook Leonardo mourned, "I have wasted my hours."

On May 2, 1519, Leonardo da Vinci died. It was said that even on his deathbed, Leonardo wept for his horse.

Leonardo has been remembered for hundreds of years, especially for his paintings *Mona Lisa* and *The Last Supper*. But not for his horse. That story was almost forgotten until 1977, when it was told in a magazine. And the right man read it. His name was Charles Dent. And Charlie loved art—reading about it, making it, looking at it, collecting it. Leonardo would have liked Charlie. They were both dreamers with big dreams. Yet Leonardo may have been envious. Charlie did what Leonardo had always longed to do. He flew, soaring through the sky like a bird freed from its cage. Charlie was an airline pilot, and whenever he traveled, he looked for art to take home.

The more Charlie read about Leonardo and his horse, the more he cared about Leonardo. When he read that Leonardo died still grieving for his horse, Charlie couldn't stand it. Right then he had the biggest dream of his life.

"Let's give Leonardo his horse," he said. It would be a gift from the American people to the people of Italy.

But could he really give Leonardo his horse? Could anyone? Charlie went to see famous scholars who had specialized in the study of Leonardo. When he came home, Charlie was smiling; he could go ahead.

But where would he build his horse? He needed a special
building, he decided—a round building shaped like a dome, tall
enough for a horse. On top there would be windows to let in
the light.

Charlie didn't know a thing about domes, but luckily he found
a man who did. When at last the Dome was finished, Charlie hung
the pictures he had collected on the walls and arranged other art
objects around the room.

All that was needed was the horse.

Every day Charlie could see the horse more clearly. Wherever
he went, he carried a small piece of wax or a piece of clay and made
miniature models of the horse. But he needed to be around real
horses. He borrowed two champion Morgan horses and studied
them for months, running his hands over their bodies so he could
feel where the muscles and bones were. He measured every inch of
the horses just as Leonardo would have done.

Then, in 1988, he began the eight-foot model of the horse.
Over the wooden skeleton, he applied one thousand pounds of clay.
To hold the horse steady, a post ran through the belly of the horse

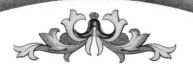

to the ground. To fill the belly, the horse was stuffed with slats of wood and Styrofoam. So now the Dome had a clay horse—his left foreleg raised and bent, his right rear leg off the ground. Free. The muscles in his hindquarters were tense, his ears pointed forward, his nostrils were beginning to flare.

By 1993 the eight-foot plaster model of the clay horse was completed and ready to be cast into a twenty-four-foot bronze horse.

For that it would have to be sent to a foundry where it could be enlarged; a twenty-four-foot clay model sculpted; then the twenty-four-foot bronze horse cast.

In 1994, however, the people at the Dome were less concerned about the horse than they were worried about Charlie. He became sick and no one knew what was the matter. Then he was told that he had Lou Gehrig's disease and it could not be cured. He would not be alive when the horse arrived in Milan. All Charlie said was what he always said: He had never been interested in taking credit for the horse; the gift of the horse was a gesture of friendship from the American people to the Italian people, a salute across the centuries to Leonardo.

On December 13, Charlie's family and friends gathered around his bedside and promised him that the horse would be finished.

On Christmas morning 1994, Charlie died.

On August 1, 1995, the horse was ready to go to the foundry. He was hoisted into a van, tied, padded, and driven off for his great adventure.

At the Tallix Foundry in Beacon, New York, his transformation began. He was enlarged and cut up into sixty separate pieces. They were laid against the wall of the foundry while the Dome people gathered to watch the pieces being put together. It was certainly a huge horse, but was it as grand as Charlie had **envisioned**?

The Dome friends walked quietly around the horse. They seemed uneasy.

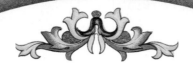

The horse wasn't right.

Art experts were called in. They shook their heads.

No, the horse wasn't right.

He looked awkward. Out of **proportion**. One of his rear legs appeared to be short. His eyes were not exactly parallel. He needed help.

Fortunately, a talented sculptor from New York City, Nina Akamu, agreed to try to fix him. But when she went to work on the twenty-four-foot horse, she found that the cementlike plaster that covered him resisted change. No matter how hard she tried, she couldn't fix him.

Everyone recognized that there was only one thing to do, but it took a while for anyone to say it out loud. Yet it had to be said. Nina would have to start from scratch and make another horse. For some, the idea of doing away with Charlie's horse was almost more than they could bear, yet they all knew that Charlie would want his horse to be as perfect as possible.

The horse would always be Charlie's dream, but as soon as Nina went to work, he had to become her horse, too. She had studied in Italy for eleven years. Her favorite Renaissance artist was Verrochio, Leonardo's teacher. It was lucky that she was there to carry on with Charlie's dream.

First Nina made an eight-foot clay horse. From it a second eight-foot horse was made of plaster. Using the plaster model as a guide, a twenty-four-foot horse was made in clay.

Everyone went to work to get the horse exactly right. Finally he was ready to be cast in bronze.

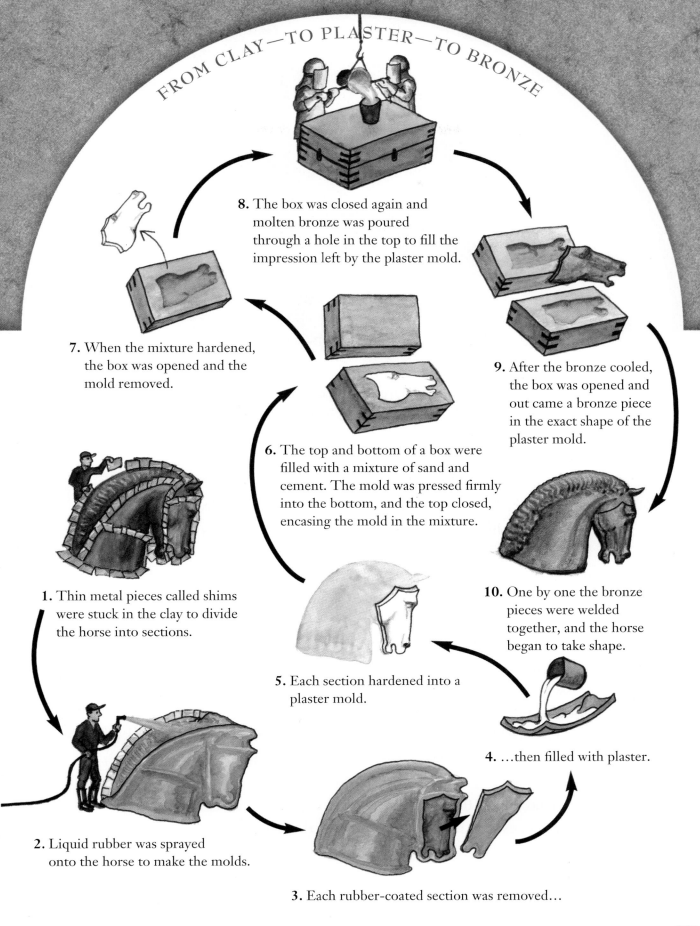

FROM CLAY—TO PLASTER—TO BRONZE

8. The box was closed again and molten bronze was poured through a hole in the top to fill the impression left by the plaster mold.

7. When the mixture hardened, the box was opened and the mold removed.

9. After the bronze cooled, the box was opened and out came a bronze piece in the exact shape of the plaster mold.

6. The top and bottom of a box were filled with a mixture of sand and cement. The mold was pressed firmly into the bottom, and the top closed, encasing the mold in the mixture.

1. Thin metal pieces called shims were stuck in the clay to divide the horse into sections.

5. Each section hardened into a plaster mold.

10. One by one the bronze pieces were welded together, and the horse began to take shape.

4. …then filled with plaster.

2. Liquid rubber was sprayed onto the horse to make the molds.

3. Each rubber-coated section was removed…

611

But how could such a large bronze sculpture stand on two legs? First they built a steel skeleton inside the body of the horse to support the sides, and then they inserted steel tubes in the two legs. The tubes were bolted to steel anchor plates below the hooves and embedded in concrete.

Finally, the horse was complete. Everyone stood back and looked up at him. They agreed that he was ready for his new home.

If Leonardo had finished his horse, he would only have had to move it from the vineyard where he worked to the front of the duke's palace. Charlie's horse had to cross the ocean to Italy. But he was too big.

So he was cut up into separate pieces, crated, and flown to Milan, where the Tallix people and the Dome people waited to reassemble him. Workers would crawl through a trapdoor in the horse's belly to fasten the pieces together.

He would stand on a pedestal in a small park in front of Milan's famous racetrack, within whinnying distance of the racing stable.

On June 27, 1999, the horse took off.

September 10, 1999, was the date set for the unveiling of the statue, exactly five hundred years to the day since the French invaded Milan and destroyed Leonardo's horse.

An enormous cloth was spread over the horse so he couldn't be seen. Two huge clusters of blue and white balloons were attached to either end of the cloth. On the pupil of one eye of the horse, Nina had written in tiny letters *Leonardo da Vinci*. On the other eye she had written *Charles Dent*. She had put her own name in the curly mane of the horse.

As a large crowd of Italians and Americans took their seats, the horse stayed in hiding. Speeches were made. The Italian national anthem was sung. Then the American national anthem.

Finally, the strings anchoring the balloons were cut and the cloth rose into the sky.

Ahhhhhhh!

At last Leonardo's horse was home.

Share a Historical Perspective with
Jean Fritz and Hudson Talbott

Jean Fritz lived in China until she was 13. "Having to wait to get to America," she says, "I needed to make up for lost time." That's one of the reasons she writes stories about America's history. When she gets letters from children saying she added the "fun" to history, she says she didn't add anything. There was as much fun in the past as there is today. One of the most exciting writing adventures she had was going to Italy for the celebration of the bronze horse in this story.

Another book by Jean Fritz: *Can't You Make Them Behave, King George?*

Hudson Talbott's

books have taken him to Africa, England, Ireland, and to the heart of the Amazon rainforest — by dugout canoe! What he loves the most about traveling is sharing his experiences with others.

 LOG ON Find out more about Jean Fritz and Hudson Talbott at **www.macmillanmh.com**

Author's Purpose
What details in the selection suggest that Jean Fritz admires the artists of the Italian Renaissance, particularly Leonardo da Vinci? Explain.

Comprehension Check

Summarize

Summarize the story of *Leonardo's Horse*. Remember to include the most important details and retell them in your own words.

Think and Compare

1. What generalizations can you make about the method used to make the horse— from clay to plaster to bronze? Use your Generalizations Chart. **Generate Questions: Make Generalizations**

Important Information	Generalization

2. Do you think Charles Dent and Nina Akamu created the horse that Leonardo had **envisioned**? Use examples from the text. **Analyze**

3. How does the author describe a Renaissance person? Think about the talents and skills you possess today. What more do you think you would need to learn to be called a Renaissance person? **Synthesize**

4. The building of Leonardo's horse was meant to be a gift of friendship from the American people to the Italian people. Can great works of art bring cultures closer together? How? **Evaluate**

5. Read "Artists of the Past" on pages 598–599. What characteristics do Michelangelo, Leonardo da Vinci, and Nina Akamu have in common? **Reading/Writing Across Texts**

Leonardo da Vinci

by Diane Stanley

As an inventor, Leonardo is probably most famous for having tried to build a flying machine. He was convinced that "the bird is an instrument functioning according to mathematical laws, and man has the power to reproduce an instrument like this with all its movements." So he analyzed the flight patterns of birds and bats, studied the **anatomy** of their wings, and observed air currents.

Leonardo da Vinci wrote, "I believe that if this screw device is well manufactured, that is, if it is made of linen cloth, the pores of which have been closed with starch, and if the device is promptly reversed, the screw will engage its gear when in the air and it will rise up on high."

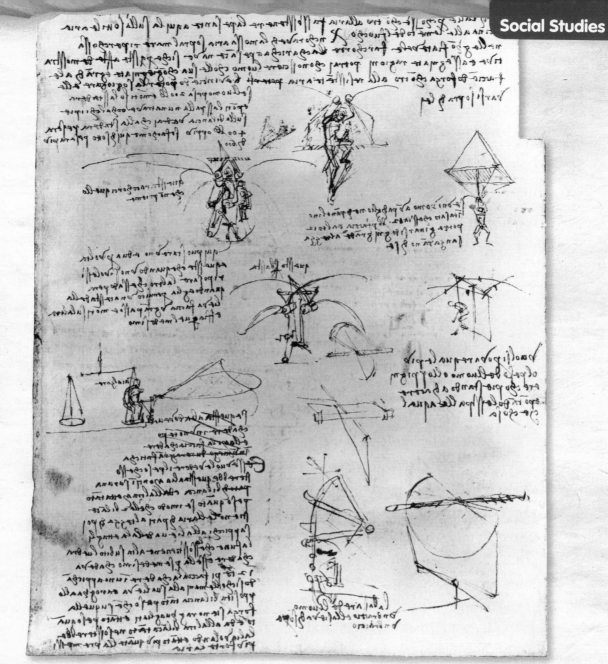

Drawings of *Parachute Experiments and Flying Machines* by Leonardo da Vinci

He sketched a variety of designs and finally, after years of preparation, built a model in a secret upstairs room at his workshop. On January 2, 1496, he wrote in his notebook, "Tomorrow morning, I shall make the strap and the attempt." Either he lost his nerve or it didn't work. At any rate, we have no record of it. But the next time he wrote of trying to fly, he was more cautious. "You will experiment with this machine over a lake," he wrote to himself, "and you will wear attached to your belt a long wineskin . . . so that if you fall in, you will not be drowned."

Model of airscrew built after sketch by Leonardo da Vinci

In 1503 he felt certain of success. Twice he wrote about it in his notebook, speculating grandly that the flight would dumbfound the universe and bring him eternal glory. Yet after years of work and study, Leonardo failed. We don't know any of the details, but much later the son of one of Leonardo's friends wrote these words about the attempt: "Vinci tried in vain."

At least he finally understood the problem. Birds are designed to fly—half the weight of their bodies is in the muscles of flight. Humans, on the other hand, with less than a quarter of their body weight in the arm and chest muscles, would never have the strength to fly like birds.

In his notes, Leonardo remarked that with this linen parachute, if it is held open, a person can jump without risk.

As a casual afterthought he designed a parachute as well as an airscrew, based on a toy, which some call the first helicopter. He also sketched the pattern of a leaf drifting to earth and under it showed a man on a winglike **glider**. If he had only worked along these lines instead of trying to imitate the flapping motion of birds, he might have been the first man to fly.

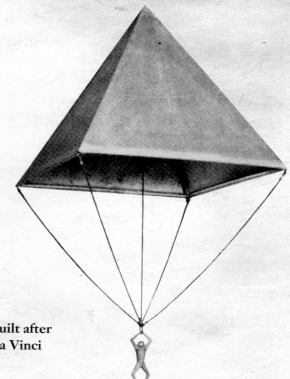

Model of parachute built after sketch by Leonardo da Vinci

Connect and Compare

1. How does the reader learn more about Leonardo da Vinci from his notebook entries and drawings? **Primary Source**

2. How does reading Leonardo da Vinci's own words help you understand his ideas and feelings? **Apply**

3. The notebook entries and *Leonardo's Horse* introduce you to Leonardo da Vinci. Which piece helped you get to "know" him better? Why? **Reading/Writing Across Texts**

Social Studies Activity

Research other great minds from the Italian Renaissance. Select one and write a summary of this person's greatest innovation. Did this person keep a journal?

Find out more about early flying machines at **www.macmillanmh.com**

Write About
How to Make Something

How to Make a Wax-Press Leaf Collage

by Dorothy B.

You can bring the outdoors indoors with a leaf collage. It is easy to make one, with a little adult supervision.

Begin by collecting leaves, a large piece of cardboard, two pieces of wax paper, glitter, and a dry rag. You'll also need an iron to press the leaves between the wax paper.

First, cover your work area with the cardboard. Make sure you cover it well. Plug in the iron and set it on its end on a safe surface nearby. Then, on top of the cardboard, arrange the leaves on one piece of wax paper. Sprinkle on some glitter. When you are satisfied with your arrangement, cover it with the other piece of wax paper to make a "sandwich."

Next, cover the wax paper sandwich with the dry rag. Iron slowly over the rag. This will melt the wax paper and trap the leaves and glitter in place.

Finally, after you have ironed the wax paper well, gently remove the rag. Remember to unplug the iron! Transfer the collage to a flat surface while it cools. You can add trim around the wax paper to make a border if you like.

I used the time-order words *first*, *then*, *next*, and *finally*.

I used the position word *top*.

620

Your Turn

Think of something that you know how to make. Then write the steps for how to make it. Be sure to give the steps in order and to use signal words such as *first, next*, and *then* to help your reader follow your directions. Use the Writer's Checklist to check your writing.

Writer's Checklist

✓ **Ideas and Content:** Did I pick a project that I can explain clearly? Are my directions concise?

✓ **Organization:** Did I give the steps in the correct order? Did I give enough details to help the reader understand what to do?

✓ **Voice:** Can the reader tell that I am talking right to them?

✓ **Word Choice:** Did I use **time-order words** and position words?

✓ **Sentence Fluency:** Do the beginnings of my sentences vary and show how my ideas connect?

✓ **Conventions:** Did I use correct spelling and punctuation? Did I use *good* and *well* correctly in my sentences?

Talk About It

If you could travel to any time period in history, which one would it be? Explain your answer.

LOG ON Find out more about time travel at **www.macmillanmh.com**

TIME TRAVEL

Sci-Fi Prep

by Gary Hillerman

Marge slumped into the apartment.

"Hi. What's the matter?" Her mother could always tell when Marge was upset.

"We have to read a science fiction story for homework tonight," Marge said **glumly**. "Why can't we read a sports story or a story about something that really happened?"

"Well," said her mother, "lots of people think science fiction is interesting. Did you know many ideas that appeared in this type of literature have actually come true at a later time?"

"Like what?" asked Marge. She was **tinkering** with the headset to her cell phone, adjusting the knobs.

"Robots, for example," said her mother. "When science fiction writers such as Isaac Asimov first wrote about robots, they really were imaginary. Today robots exist and are used in lots of ways."

"That's right," said Marge's brother, William, as he entered the kitchen. "In the 1940s, Asimov and another writer set up three rules to control the way robots act in science fiction. The first rule says that robots may not injure a person or allow a person to be harmed if robots can help."

"That's very **honorable**," sniffed Marge. "I'll keep that good behavior in mind if I meet a robot."

She didn't wait to hear what the other rules were. She went to her room and began her homework.

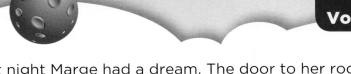

That night Marge had a dream. The door to her room opened and in came a robot. Despite her words to William, she was trembling.

"Good evening, Marjorie," said the robot, speaking very **formally,** not using her nickname. "I have come to escort you on a special journey."

"Where?" whispered Marge.

"Our **destination** is a lost world," answered the robot. "I left my home and **immigrated** here many years ago. Now it is time for me to return. . . and you must come with me."

"Why?" Marge's voice was **unsteady** and she stammered. Her fingers began to **fidget** with the cover on the bed, picking at loose threads. Too bad she hadn't stayed to hear the other rules for controlling robots.

"Ah, good question," said the robot. "Tomorrow you will be assigned to write a science fiction story for homework. It's time you learned more about the subject. Come!"

Slowly, Marge got out of bed and followed the robot into the world of science fiction.

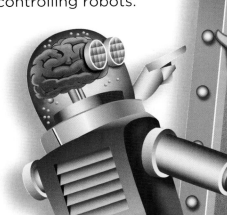

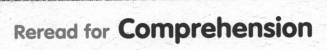

Reread for **Comprehension**

Generate Questions

Sequence

Generating, or asking, questions as you read can help you to summarize a story. As you read, ask yourself what the most important events are. Then list in order what happened first, next, and last.

Use a Sequence Chart as you reread "Sci-Fi Prep."

Event
↓
↓
↓

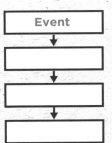

Comprehension

Genre

Science Fiction is a story that tells of fictional events, usually set in the future, and is based on science or technology.

Generate Questions

Sequence

As you read, use your Sequence Chart.

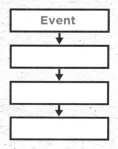

Event

Read to Find Out

How does the use of a time machine in the story affect the sequence of events?

LAFFF

by Lensey Namioka
illustrated by Raúl Colón

Award Winning
Author
and
Illustrator

In movies, geniuses have frizzy white hair, right? They wear thick glasses and have names like Dr. Zweistein.

Peter Lu didn't have frizzy white hair. He had straight hair, as black as licorice. He didn't wear thick glasses, either, since his vision was normal.

Peter's family, like ours, had **immigrated** from China, but they had settled here first. When we moved into a house just two doors down from the Lus, they gave us some good advice on how to get along in America.

I went to the same school as Peter, and we walked to the school bus together every morning. Like many Chinese parents, mine made sure that I worked very hard in school.

In spite of all I could do, my grades were nothing compared to Peter's. He was at the top in all his classes. We walked to the school bus without talking because I was a little scared of him. Besides, he was always deep in thought.

Peter didn't have any friends. Most of the kids thought he was a nerd because they saw his head always buried in books. I didn't think he even tried to join the rest of us or cared what the others thought of him.

Then on Halloween he surprised us all. As I went down the block trick-or-treating, dressed as a zucchini in my green sweats, I heard a strange, deep voice behind me say, "How do you do."

I yelped and turned around. Peter was wearing a long, black Chinese gown with slits in the sides. On his head he had a little round cap, and down each side of his mouth drooped a thin, long mustache.

"I am Dr. Lu Manchu, the mad scientist," he announced, putting his hands in his sleeves and bowing.

He smiled when he saw me staring at his costume. It was a scary smile, somehow.

Some of the other kids came up, and when they saw Peter, they were impressed. "Hey, neat!" said one boy.

I hadn't expected Peter to put on a costume and go trick-or-treating like a normal kid. So maybe he did want to join the others after all—at least some of the time. After that night he wasn't a nerd anymore. He was Dr. Lu Manchu. Even some of the teachers began to call him that.

When we became too old for trick-or-treating, Peter was still Dr. Lu Manchu. The rumor was that he was working on a fantastic machine in his parents' garage. But nobody had any idea what it was.

One evening, as I was coming home from a baby-sitting job, I cut across the Lus' backyard. Passing their garage, I saw through a little window that the light was on. My curiosity got the better of me, and I peeked in.

Sequence

What events happened to change the narrator's opinion of Peter?

628

I saw a booth that looked like a shower stall. A stool stood in the middle of the stall, and hanging over the stool was something that looked like a great big shower head.

Suddenly a deep voice behind me said, "Good evening, Angela." Peter bowed and smiled his scary smile. He didn't have his costume on and he didn't have the long, droopy mustache. But he was Dr. Lu Manchu.

"What are you doing?" I squeaked.

Still in his strange, deep voice, Peter said, "What are *you* doing? After all, this is my garage."

"I was just cutting across your yard to get home. Your parents never complained before."

"I thought you were spying on me," said Peter. "I thought you wanted to know about my machine." He hissed when he said the word *machine*.

Honestly, he was beginning to frighten me. "What machine?" I demanded. "You mean this shower-stall thing?"

He drew himself up and narrowed his eyes, making them into thin slits. "This is my time machine!"

I goggled at him. "You mean . . . you mean . . . this machine can send you forward and backward in time?"

"Well, actually, I can only send things forward in time," admitted Peter, speaking in his normal voice again. "That's why I'm calling the machine LAFFF. It stands for Lu's Artifact For Fast Forward."

Of course Peter always won first prize at the annual statewide science fair. But that's a long way from making a time machine. Minus his mustache and long Chinese gown, he was just Peter Lu.

"I don't believe it!" I said. "I bet LAFFF is only good for a laugh."

"Okay, Angela. I'll show you!" hissed Peter.

He sat down on the stool and twisted a dial. I heard some *bleeps, cheeps,* and *gurgles.* Peter disappeared.

He must have done it with mirrors. I looked around the garage. I peeked under the tool bench. There was no sign of him.

"Okay, I give up," I told him. "It's a good trick, Peter. You can come out now."

Bleep, cheep, and *gurgle* went the machine, and there was Peter, sitting on the stool. He held a rose in his hand. "What do you think of that?"

I blinked. "So you produced a flower. Maybe you had it under the stool."

"Roses bloom in June, right?" he demanded.

That was true. And this was December.

"I sent myself forward in time to June when the flowers were blooming," said Peter. "And I picked the rose from our yard. Convinced, Angela?"

It was too hard to swallow. "You said you couldn't send things back in time," I objected. "So how did you bring the rose back?"

But even as I spoke I saw that his hands were empty. The rose was gone.

"That's one of the problems with the machine," said Peter. "When I send myself forward, I can't seem to stay there for long. I snap back to my own time after only a minute. Anything I bring with me snaps back to its own time, too. So my rose has gone back to this June."

I was finally convinced, and I began to see possibilities. "Wow, just think: If I don't want to do the dishes, I can send myself forward to the time when the dishes are already done."

"That won't do you much good," said Peter. "You'd soon pop back to the time when the dishes were still dirty."

Too bad. "There must be something your machine is good for," I said. Then I had another idea. "Hey, you can bring me back a piece of fudge from the future, and I can eat it twice: once now, and again in the future."

"Yes, but the fudge wouldn't stay in your stomach," said Peter. "It would go back to the future."

"That's even better!" I said. "I can enjoy eating the fudge over and over again without getting fat!"

It was late, and I had to go home before my parents started to worry. Before I left, Peter said, "Look, Angela, there's still a lot of work to do on LAFFF. Please don't tell anybody about the machine until I've got it right."

A few days later I asked him how he was doing.

"I can stay in the future time a bit longer now," he said. "Once I got it up to four minutes."

"Is that enough time to bring me back some fudge from the future?" I asked.

"We don't keep many sweets around the house," he said. "But I'll see what I can do."

A few minutes later, he came back with a spring roll for me. "My mother was frying these in the kitchen, and I snatched one while she wasn't looking."

I bit into the hot, crunchy spring roll, but before I finished chewing, it disappeared. The taste of soy sauce, green onions, and bean sprouts stayed a little longer in my mouth, though.

It was fun to play around with LAFFF, but it wasn't really useful. I didn't know what a great help it would turn out to be.

Every year our school held a writing contest, and the winning story for each grade got printed in our school magazine. I wanted desperately to win. I worked awfully hard in school, but my parents still thought I could do better.

Winning the writing contest would show my parents that I was really good in something. I love writing stories, and I have lots of ideas. But when I actually write them down, my stories never turn out as good as I thought. I just can't seem to find the right words, because English isn't my first language.

I got an **honorable** mention last year, but it wasn't the same as winning and showing my parents my name, Angela Tang, printed in the school magazine.

The deadline for the contest was getting close, and I had a pile of stories written, but none of them looked like a winner.

Then, the day before the deadline, *boing,* a brilliant idea hit me.

I thought of Peter and his LAFFF machine.

I rushed over to the Lus' garage and, just as I had hoped, Peter was there, **tinkering** with his machine.

"I've got this great idea for winning the story contest," I told him breathlessly. "You see, to be certain of winning, I have to write the story that would be the winner."

"That's obvious," Peter said dryly. "In fact, you're going around in a circle."

"Wait, listen!" I said. "I want to use LAFFF and go forward to the time when the next issue of the school magazine is out. Then I can read the winning story."

After a moment Peter nodded. "I see. You plan to write down the winning story after you've read it and then send it in to the contest."

I nodded eagerly. "The story would *have* to win, because it's the winner!"

Peter began to look interested. "I've got LAFFF to the point where I can stay in the future for seven minutes now. Will that be long enough for you?"

"I'll just have to work quickly," I said.

Peter smiled. It wasn't his scary Lu Manchu smile, but a nice smile. He was getting as excited as I was. "Okay, Angela. Let's go for it."

He led me to the stool. "What's your **destination**?" he asked. "I mean, *when's* your destination?"

Suddenly I was nervous. I told myself that Peter had made many time trips, and he looked perfectly healthy.

Why not? What have I got to lose—except time?

I took a deep breath. "I want to go forward three weeks in time." By then I'd have a copy of the new school magazine in my room.

"Ready, Angela?" asked Peter.

"As ready as I'll ever be," I whispered.

Bleep, cheep, and *gurgle.* Suddenly Peter disappeared.

What went wrong? Did Peter get sent by mistake, instead of me?

Then I realized what had happened. Three weeks later in time Peter might be somewhere else. No wonder I couldn't see him.

There was no time to be lost. Rushing out of Peter's garage, I ran over to our house and entered through the back door.

Mother was in the kitchen. When she saw me, she stared. "Angela! I thought you were upstairs taking a shower!"

Sequence
Why is Angela's mother confused by her presence?

"Sorry!" I panted. "No time to talk!"

I dashed up to my room. Then I suddenly had a strange idea. What if I met *myself* in my room? Argh! It was a spooky thought.

There was nobody in my room. Where was I? I mean, where was the I of three weeks later?

Wait. Mother had just said she thought I was taking a shower. Down the hall, I could hear the water running in the bathroom. Okay. That meant I wouldn't run into me for a while.

I went to the shelf above my desk and frantically pawed through the junk piled there. I found it! I found the latest issue of the school magazine, the one with the winning stories printed in it.

How much time had passed? Better hurry.

The shower had stopped running. This meant the other me was out of the bathroom. Have to get out of here!

Too late. Just as I started down the stairs, I heard Mother talking again. "Angela! A minute ago you were all dressed! Now you're in your robe again and your hair's all wet! I don't understand."

I shivered. It was scary, listening to Mother talking to myself downstairs. I heard my other self answering something, then the sound of her—my—steps coming up the stairs. In a panic, I dodged into the spare room and closed the door.

I heard the steps—my steps—go past and into my room.

The minute I heard the door of my room close, I rushed out and down the stairs.

Mother was standing at the foot of the stairs. When she saw me, her mouth dropped. "But . . . but . . . just a minute ago you were in your robe and your hair was all wet!"

"See you later, Mother," I panted. And I ran.

Behind me I heard Mother muttering, "I'm going mad!"

I didn't stop and try to explain. I might go mad, too.

It would be great if I could just keep the magazine with me. But, like the spring roll, it would get carried back to its own time after a few minutes. So the next best thing was to read the magazine as fast as I could.

It was hard to run and flip through the magazine at the same time. But I made it back to Peter's garage and plopped down on the stool.

At last I found the story: the story that had won the contest in our grade. I started to read.

Suddenly I heard *bleep, cheep,* and *gurgle,* and Peter loomed up in front of me. I was back in my original time again.

But I still had the magazine! Now I had to read the story before the magazine popped back to the future. It was hard to concentrate with Peter jumping up and down impatiently, so different from his usual calm, collected self.

I read a few paragraphs, and I was beginning to see how the story would shape up. But before I got any further, the magazine disappeared from my hand.

So I didn't finish reading the story. I didn't reach the end, where the name of the winning writer was printed.

That night I stayed up very late to write down what I remembered of the story. It had a neat plot, and I could see why it was the winner.

I hadn't read the entire story, so I had to make up the ending myself. But that was okay, since I knew how it should come out.

The winners of the writing contest would be announced at the school assembly on Friday. After we had filed into the assembly hall and sat down, the principal gave a speech. I tried not to **fidget** while he explained about the contest.

Suddenly I was struck by a dreadful thought. Somebody in my class had written the winning story, the one I had copied. Wouldn't that person be declared the winner, instead of me?

The principal started announcing the winners. I chewed my knuckles in an agony of suspense, as I waited to see who would be announced as the winner in my class. Slowly, the principal began with the lowest grade. Each winner walked in slow motion to the stage, while the principal slowly explained why the story was good.

At last, at last, he came to our grade. "The winner is . . ." He stopped, slowly got out his handkerchief, and slowly blew his nose. Then he cleared his throat. "The winning story is 'Around and Around,' by Angela Tang."

I sat like a stone, unable to move. Peter nudged me. "Go on, Angela! They're waiting for you."

I got up and walked up to the stage in a daze. The principal's voice seemed to be coming from far, far away as he told the audience that I had written a science fiction story about time travel.

The winners each got a notebook bound in imitation leather for writing more stories. Inside the cover of the notebook was a ballpoint pen. But the best prize was having my story in the school magazine with my name printed at the end.

Then why didn't I feel good about winning?

After assembly, the kids in our class crowded around to congratulate me. Peter **formally** shook my hand. "Good work, Angela," he said, and winked at me.

That didn't make me feel any better. I hadn't won the contest fairly. Instead of writing the story myself, I had copied it from the school magazine.

That meant someone in our class—one of the kids here—had actually written the story. Who was it?

My heart was knocking against my ribs as I stood there and waited for someone to complain that I had stolen his story.

Nobody did.

As we were riding the school bus home, Peter looked at me. "You don't seem very happy about winning the contest, Angela."

"No, I'm not," I mumbled. "I feel just awful."

"Tell you what," suggested Peter. "Come over to my house and we'll discuss it."

"What is there to discuss?" I asked **glumly**. "I won the contest because I cheated."

"Come on over, anyway. My mother bought a fresh package of humbow in Chinatown."

I couldn't turn down that invitation. Humbow, a roll stuffed with barbecued pork, is my favorite snack.

Peter's mother came into the kitchen while we were munching, and he told her about the contest.

Mrs. Lu looked pleased. "I'm very glad, Angela. You have a terrific imagination, and you deserve to win."

"I like Angela's stories," said Peter. "They're original."

It was the first compliment he had ever paid me, and I felt my face turning red.

After Mrs. Lu left us, Peter and I each had another humbow. But I was still miserable. "I wish I had never started this. I feel like such a jerk."

Peter looked at me, and I swear he was enjoying himself. "If you stole another student's story, why didn't that person complain?"

"I don't know!" I wailed.

"Think!" said Peter. "You're smart, Angela. Come on, figure it out."

Me, smart? I was so overcome to hear myself called smart by a genius like Peter that I just stared at him.

He had to repeat himself. "Figure it out, Angela!"

I tried to concentrate. Why was Peter looking so amused?

The light finally dawned. "Got it," I said slowly. "*I'm* the one who wrote the story."

"The winning story is your own, Angela, because that's the one that won."

My head began to go around and around. "But where did the original idea for the story come from?"

"What made the plot so good?" asked Peter. His voice sounded **unsteady**.

"Well, in my story, my character used a time machine to go forward in time . . ."

"Okay, whose idea was it to use a time machine?"

"It was mine," I said slowly. I remembered the moment when the idea had hit me with a *boing*.

"So you s-stole f-from yourself!" sputtered Peter. He started to roar with laughter. I had never seen him break down like that. At this rate, he might wind up being human.

When he could talk again, he asked me to read my story to him.

I began. "'In movies, geniuses have frizzy white hair, right? They wear thick glasses and have names like Dr. Zweistein. . . .'"

Fast Forward with Lensey Namioka and Raúl Colón

Lensey Namioka was born in China. She is the only person in the world named Lensey because her father made it up just for her! She started learning to read Chinese at age two. In college Lensey studied mathematics but decided she liked being a writer better. Since then she has written more than 20 books.

Another book by Lensey Namioka: *Half and Half*

Raúl Colón is an artist who has done work for the *New York Times* and *Time* magazine. He has also created theater posters and artwork for the advertising industry. But he is best known for the picture books he has illustrated. And now he has written one too: *Orson Blasts Off!*

 Find out more about Lensey Namioka and Raúl Colón at **www.macmillanmh.com**

Author's Purpose
What makes science fiction different from other types of fiction? Do science fiction writers usually write for a different purpose than other fiction writers? Explain.

Comprehension Check

Summarize

Use your Sequence Chart to help you summarize "LAFFF." Think about how the events of the story lead back to the beginning.

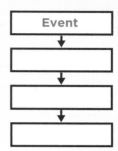

Event
↓
↓
↓

Think and Compare

1. How does Angela's opinion of Peter Lu change throughout the course of the story? What events are responsible for this change? **Generate Questions: Sequence**

2. What events in the story would change if Angela had met herself in the future? **Analyze**

3. Suppose that, after scientists spend years **tinkering**, time travel becomes possible. To what time period would you like to travel? What are the potential drawbacks of time travel? **Synthesize**

4. What if Angela did steal another student's story? Do you think Angela and Peter were right or wrong to use the time machine to steal the winning story? Support your answer. **Evaluate**

5. Read "Sci-Fi Prep" on pages 624–625. How might Peter Lu's time machine help Marge write a science-fiction story? **Reading/Writing Across Texts**

Time Travel

Science

Genre

An **Internet Article** is a form of nonfiction that gives verifiable information and facts about a topic.

Text Features

A **Hyperlink** is an electronic connection within the text that provides direct access to more information. A **Keyword** is a specific word typed into the search box that helps you find information on the Internet.

Content Vocabulary

universally   aeronautics
fleeting

There are many different sources of information on the Internet. There are search engines, encyclopedias, newspapers, and other online reference sources. However, it is crucial to evaluate the sources you choose.

Evaluate your source. Decide if the online source of information is both reliable and appropriate. Historical records, encyclopedias, magazine articles, and newspaper articles usually contain reliable information.

Decide if you should check more than one source. Determine if you need to check more than one site to confirm your findings.

Use menus, toolbars, and links. Web sites are constructed to offer lots of choices while you are reading an article. Menus can help you decide what you want to read next. If you want to look for another topic, conduct a search simply by typing a key word in the search box and clicking "Go" or "Search." The computer will find it for you. Toolbars and links give you related information.

Choose your hyperlink. Click on one or more of the available hyperlinks within the text to get direct access to other information you need.

Science Online
Offering great articles on science topics

Search Time Travel **Go**

You Are a Time Traveler
by Louis Kamsky

Time travel has long fascinated people. Traveling to the past or future would allow you to live in exciting periods of history or to get a glimpse of what the world would be like in the future. You might even travel to the near future and see yourself as a grandparent! Think about it. If you were allowed to go back to the past, whom would you want to meet? Michelangelo? King Henry VIII? Eleanor Roosevelt? What historical event would you like to witness? The French Revolution? The Allied invasion of Normandy? You might set your sights more modestly with a visit to yourself as a baby.

Since these ideas are so **universally** tempting, it is natural that time travel would interest so many writers, filmmakers, and scientists. But you might be surprised to realize that in the smallest sense of the term, we are all time travelers. Even as you sit here reading this article, time is racing forward. The future becomes the past as soon as it happens. Think about it: the present is so **fleeting**! Everything you do quickly becomes part of the past, and so it is that we move through time. The famous scientist, Albert Einstein, assigned a mathematical formula to this idea, which is called the Theory of Relativity.

Black hole at the center of a galaxy

Albert Einstein

| Jules Verne | Time Machines in Movies | Time Machines in Fiction | Albert Einstein | Black Holes |

Back

Forward

Home

Reload

Images

Open

Print

Find

Stop

Science Online

Jules Verne

LINKS

Jules Verne (1828-1905)

Jules Verne was a French novelist and a pioneer writer of science fiction. After he tried to run away to become a sailor at age 11, he promised his family he would only travel in his imagination. He fulfilled this promise, writing at least 50 tales of extraordinary voyages.

Verne was very interested in geography and new discoveries in **aeronautics** and travel. His first famous work, *Five Weeks in a Balloon* (1863), gained him fame and wealth. Most of his books are adventure stories based on wide research. He is best known for his classic works of science fiction such as *From the Earth to the Moon* (1865) and 20,000 Leagues Under the Sea (1870), which show extraordinary cleverness in predicting submarines and space travel. In general, Verne influenced literature by giving credibility to scientific efforts.

Science Fiction Writers ▶

19th Century Science Predictions ▶

Search [ ] **Go**

Black Holes

When stars that are more than four times the mass of the sun reach the end of their life and have used all their fuel, they collapse under the pressure of their own weight. The center of this collapse becomes a black hole. Black holes have such a strong force that even light cannot escape from them. They suck everything in and are shaped like an ice cream cone, whose point is called a *singularity*.

Black Hole

Connect and Compare

1. In what ways would hyperlinks in this article be useful? **Using Hyperlinks**

2. Why might an online science article be a reliable source? **Analyze**

3. What facts discussed in "You Are a Time Traveler" complement the ideas in *LAFFF?* How does *LAFFF* qualify as science fiction? Explain. **Reading/Writing Across Texts**

 Science Activity

Research the concept of time travel on the Internet. Then write your own evaluation of time travel.

 Find out more about science fiction at **www.macmillanmh.com**

Write an EXPLANATORY ESSAY

The Water Glass Problem

by Ruben J.

Sometimes small problems can be really annoying. Insects are a good example.

Last summer we spent two weeks in my uncle's cabin on a lake. The swimming, boating, and fishing were great, but the bugs bugged me. Every night I put a glass of water by my bed in case I got thirsty. The problem was that insects kept getting into the glass. Yuck!

After a few nights I decided to solve my problem. First, I looked for holes in the window screens and put patches on them, but some insects got in anyway. Next, I thought about keeping a spoon next to my glass so I could scoop out the bugs. Somehow that was the least appealing solution. I thought harder. Then I put a small plate over the top of the glass. That night I knocked over the plate and it broke. As I wiped up the pieces with a tissue, the solution was suddenly clear. I would place a tissue over the glass top—no bugs, no breakage, no mess.

Finally, this solution worked perfectly, and it was so simple. I'm a genius!

I tried to write paragraphs that flow smoothly.

I used transitions between my paragraphs.

Your Turn

Think about a problem you have solved. It can be a big problem or a small one like the one that Ruben described. Write an explanatory essay telling how you solved your problem. Be sure that your main idea is clear and that you use transitions between paragraphs. Use the Writer's Checklist to check your writing.

Writer's Checklist

 Ideas and Content: Does the beginning of my essay grab the reader's attention? Do I state my problem clearly?

 Organization: Does my essay have **transitions** between paragraphs?

 Voice: Are my feelings about my problem and solution clear?

Word Choice: Do I use strong verbs and fresh adjectives to explain my problem and solution?

 Sentence Fluency: Do my sentences have variety? Do my sentences flow when I read my paper aloud?

 Conventions: Are my spelling and punctuation correct? Do I use comparative forms of adverbs correctly?

Talk About It

Why do you think it has always been important for people to figure out ways to communicate with each other?

Find out more about communication at
www.macmillanmh.com

KEEPING *in* TOUCH

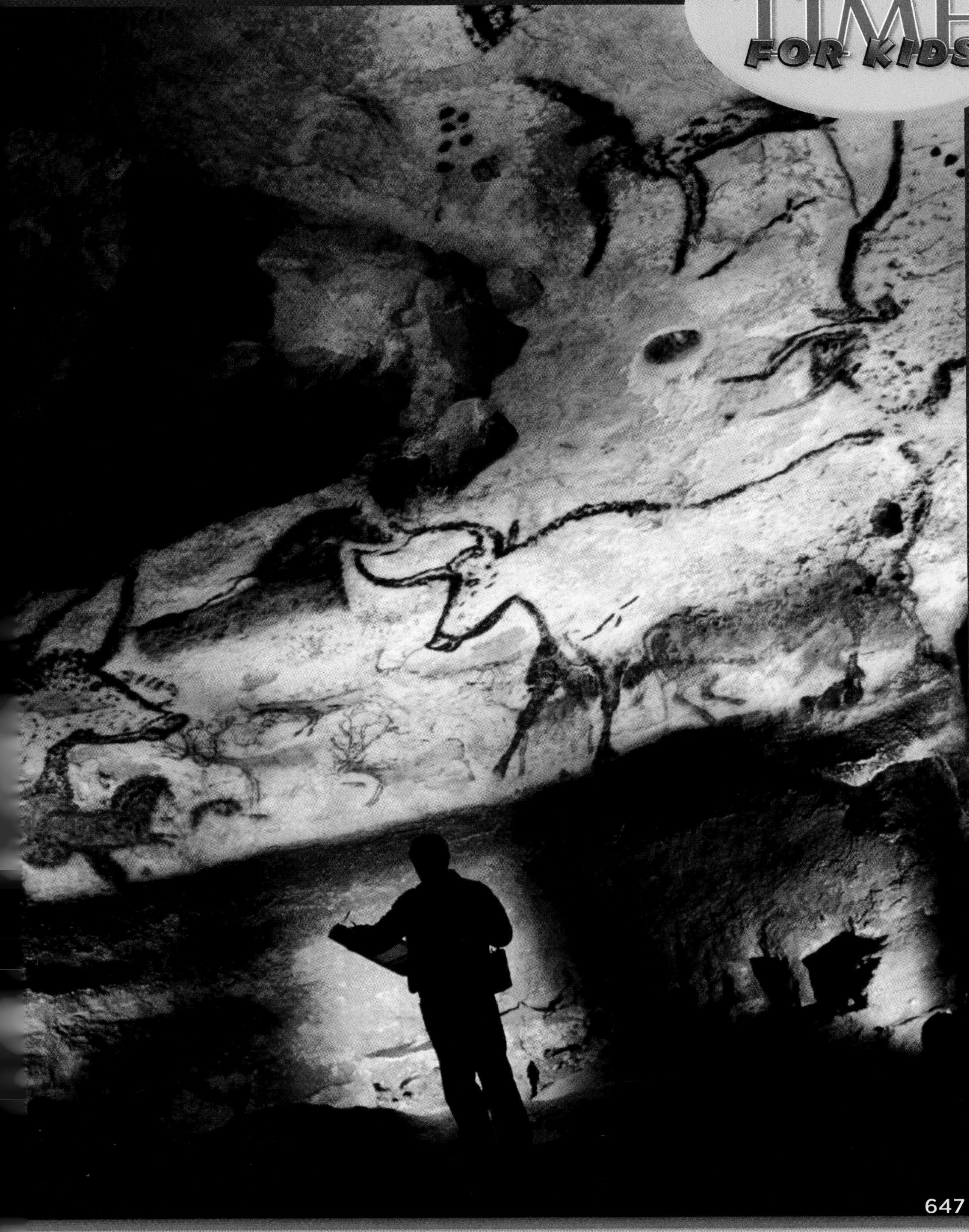

TIME FOR KIDS®

Vocabulary

anthropologists

presumably

immense

portable

nuisance

This 2,600-year-old stone cylinder was found in La Venta, Mexico.

AMERICA'S OLDEST WRITTEN WORDS

Scientists made a discovery in southern Mexico. The group's project leader, Mary E. D. Pohl, made the announcement: a 2,600-year-old stone cylinder, carved with symbols that seem to represent words, had been found. Pohl believes the cylinder shows the earliest known system of writing in the Americas. Although some experts doubt this claim, Pohl's report could change history as we know it!

Pohl and her team made the discovery near the city of La Venta. The Olmec lived there from 1300 B.C. to 400 B.C. The Olmec are best known for creating large stone sculptures. They also built massive pyramids and cities and created a formal government long before the Maya.

Anthropologists are scientists who study human beings and their cultures. Before this discovery, they believed that ancient civilizations in what is now Mexico didn't have a writing system until about 300 B.C. That's when the Olmec's neighbors, the Zapotec, began writing. Pohl's findings suggest that the Olmec wrote 300 years earlier.

Olmec traditions were later adopted by other cultures and, **presumably**, they adopted Olmec writing, too. "It makes sense that they would be the first to use a system of writing," says Pohl, who will look for more proof.

UNITED STATES OF AMERICA

MEXICO

Gulf of Mexico

La Venta

PACIFIC OCEAN

Mexico City

Oaxaca

0   500 Miles

SAY IT IN QUECHUA

Quechua (KETCH•wah) is the ancient language of the Inca—the native people of Peru, in South America. About 5 million people in Peru still speak it. You may already know a little Quechua. *Cocoa, lima* (bean), *condor,* and *llama* are Quechua words. Try saying these words and phrases. (See if you can say, "Hello, friend.")

Napaykullayki

ENGLISH	QUECHUA	HOW YOU SAY IT
Hello	Napaykullayki	(nah•pie•coo•YAH•key)
Friend	Kuchuqmasi	(coo•chew•MAH•see)
Father	Tayta	(TIE•ta)
Mother	Mama	(MAH•mah)
Please	Allichu	(ah•YEE•chew)
Yes	Ari	(ah•REE)
No	Mana	(MAH•nah)
My name is _____.	Noqa kani _____.	(Nee•OH•ha CHA•nee _____)

 Find out more about the Inca at **www.macmillanmh.com**

Communication Time

In the past two hundred years, we have made immense strides in the ways we communicate with each other.

- **1829** Braille, which allows blind people to read, is created.
- **1837** Invention of the telegraph.
- **1876** Invention of the telephone.
- **1893** Thomas Edison opens the first motion-picture studio.
- **1906** The first radio program is broadcast.
- **1928** Television is invented.
- **1972** Electronic mail (later called e-mail) is introduced.

- **1973** First call on a **portable** cell phone is made.
- **1989** The first provider of dial-up Internet access for consumers debuts.
- **2003** Spam, unsolicited e-mail, becomes a server-clogging **nuisance**—and accounts for about half of all e-mails.

An early TV and its inventor, August Karolus, in 1928

649

THESE WALLS CAN TALK

How did the earliest human beings express themselves through art?

If you're looking for archaeological finds that really rock, you can travel to Europe, Africa, and Australia to find some of the earliest examples of the human creative spirit.

EXPLORING EUROPE'S CAVES

In 1994, three people exploring a cliff in southeastern France felt a breeze wafting from a pile of rock and debris. "That was a sign that there was a cave beneath it," recalls Jean-Marie Chauvet. With his companions, Chauvet cleared away an opening, then wriggled through a tunnel into a complex of large caves.

Then, in the pale glow of their headlamps, the explorers noticed two red lines on a cavern wall. Chauvet recognized the markings as "characteristic of the Stone Age." They had discovered an **immense** archaeological trove and, **presumably**, a clear window on prehistoric life.

Six days later they returned with **portable** lighting and plastic sheets that they spread about to avoid disturbing artifacts on the cavern floors. Probing deeper into the cavern system, they began coming upon exquisite, intricately detailed wall paintings and engravings of animals, as well as numerous images

A colleague of Jean-Marie Chauvet inspects the Stone Age cave paintings found in France.

of human hands, some in red, others in black pigment. "I thought I was dreaming," says Chauvet.

The art was in pristine condition, apparently undisturbed for up to 20,000 years. The walls show images of lions, bison, deer, bears, horses, and some 50 woolly rhinos.

For now, tourists are not allowed in this amazing cave. The French Culture Ministry has put the Chauvet cave off-limits to all but a handful of **anthropologists** and other experts. The French learned a lesson from a cave at Altamira in Spain, another site where amazing rock art has been discovered. Early unrestricted access to this Spanish

cave obliterated archaeological clues and led to the rapid deterioration of artwork. At another well-known site of cave art in France—the Lascaux caves—the caves have also been sealed. Visitors tour a carefully created replica instead.

SAVING THE ROCK ART OF AFRICA

Equally beautiful works can be found in great abundance on rock shelters, walls, and overhangs throughout the African continent. Unfortunately, these ancient masterpieces are deteriorating at an alarming rate, and they may disappear entirely unless something is done to save them.

In an effort to record Africa's vanishing trove of rock art, David Coulson, a Nairobi-based photographer, and Alexander Campbell, former director of Botswana's National Museum and Art Gallery, began crisscrossing the continent. They visited known sites and stumbled across new ones, photographing as much of the art as they could. Campbell is convinced that if examples of Africa's rock art were counted, they would total many hundreds of thousands of individual images.

Everywhere Coulson and Campbell went, they found images dulled by sunlight, wind, and water, and damaged by chemical seepage from mining operations, tourism, and outright vandalism. An unthinking tourist, unaware of the art's significance and value, can be much more than just a **nuisance**. Amateur photographers have been known to throw water and cola drinks on the art to enhance its contrast and make the colors more vivid.

HOW OLD IS THE ROCK ART OF AUSTRALIA?

The Australian continent abounds in Aboriginal rock art, both paintings and engravings. Much of it lies in a 1,500-mile-long, boomerang-shaped area along the country's north coast.

Archaeologist Darrell Lewis of the Australian National University estimates that there are at least 10,000 rock-art sites on the Arnhem Land plateau alone, in the Northern Territory. "Each of these sites," he says, "can have several hundred paintings." But unlike early inhabitants of Europe, who often decorated caves over a short period and then abandoned them, the Australian Aborigines would return

Ancient carvings show a herd of giraffes on a stone outside a cave in Niger.

Scientists date these ancient drawings by Australian Aborigines to 23,000 B.C.

over and over to the same sites. This is a practice that still goes on today. Unraveling the history of a single site can thus be extremely complicated.

How old is Australia's art? It is clear that artists were at work in Australia at roughly the same time as their European cousins. Anthropologist Alan Thorne of the Australian National University claims that a small piece of red ochre (a kind of clay), dated to 50,000 years ago, was worn down on one side—like a piece of chalk—by humans. "Whether it was ground to paint a shelter or a person or part of a wall, I don't think anyone would disagree that it is evidence of art," says Thorne.

These ancient masterpieces found around the world offer windows into the rich lives of our prehistoric ancestors. But if nothing is done to save and preserve the rock art, some of these windows could close forever.

Think and Compare

1. What problem is discussed in this selection, and what solutions are described?

2. What difference between European and Australian cave art is described?

3. If you were given the task of preserving for the future a single work of art from the present, what would it be? Explain your choice.

4. Summarize the common thread in all the selections you've read in this section.

Test Strategy
Think and Search
Read on to find the answer. Look for information in more than one place.

LeRoy Sealy helps his niece Patricia learn Choctaw.

Languages at Risk

When you hear the words *endangered* or *extinct,* you may think of rhinos, tigers, and other wildlife. But languages can also become endangered or extinct. Linguists, people who study languages, say about half of the world's 6,500 languages are in trouble. Some have fewer than five living speakers, and nearly 3,000 may disappear in the next 100 years.

Concerned linguists are working to save endangered languages. They are publishing books and making recordings of languages that are at risk.

The most common reason for a language to become endangered is that a small group of people speaking one language comes into contact with a larger community speaking another language. Over time, the smaller group begins speaking the dominant language. Technology and travel have also contributed to the problem by helping the rapid spread of common languages such as English and Spanish.

Says one linguist, "Every language has its way of expressing ideas about the world. When a language dies, we lose that insight."

Go On ▶

Directions: Answer the questions.

1. What problem is described in this selection?

    A   Certain languages are being banned in some places.

    B   Because of technology and travel, the world needs a single, common language.

    C   Thousands of the world's languages are in trouble and may become extinct.

    D   People who speak one language have trouble learning to speak a new language.

2. Concerned linguists are working on this problem by

    A   teaching common languages such as Spanish and English in schools.

    B   publishing books and recordings to preserve languages that could disappear.

    C   introducing new languages in communities where only one language is spoken.

    D   simplifying the spelling of words in endangered languages.

3. A linguist is a person who

    A   teaches foreign languages to high school students.

    B   studies and preserves languages.

    C   publishes books about technology and travel.

    D   works with endangered animals.

4. Explain the most common cause of a language becoming endangered or extinct.

5. Do you believe that it is important to preserve every language currently being spoken in the world? Explain your ideas. Use details from the article in your response.

> **Tip**
>
> Look for information in more than one place.

Write to a Prompt

A wall-size mural in the entrance to your school was created 75 years ago by the school's first graduating class. The paint is peeling. Preserving it will cost a lot of money. Most students think it is ugly and should be painted over. However, some think it should be preserved. Write a persuasive editorial for the school paper giving your view.

Save the Mural!

I've never paid much attention to it myself, but maybe that's because it is so faded. Still, I believe strongly that we should save the Garden Valley School mural.

Styles of art and tastes change all the time. But we don't go around burning paintings from the past because they are old and no one paints like that anymore. Think about what we'd lose if that happened.

That mural was there when our grandparents were born. The first students who ever walked through these halls made it. They were expressing their pride in their school. They were thinking about the students who would follow them; they were thinking about us.

The mural is part of school. It's part of us. If we don't save it, we'll be saying we don't care about the past, and we don't care about the future, either.

I kept my audience in mind as I chose ideas to emphasize.

Writing Prompt

When construction begins on a new community fitness center, a network of caves is discovered. The cave walls are painted with what appear to be ancient images and symbols. The local university wants to stop the construction and preserve the caves for their historical and cultural value. The developer wants to continue. Write a persuasive editorial for your local paper giving your opinion.

Writer's Checklist

- ☑ Ask yourself, who is my audience?
- ☑ Think about your purpose for writing.
- ☑ Choose the correct form for your writing.
- ☑ Form an opinion about the topic.
- ☑ Use reasons to support your opinion.
- ☑ Be sure your ideas are logical and organized.
- ☑ Use your best spelling, grammar, and punctuation.

Print, Past and Present

Talk About It

Through the centuries humans have invented many ways to write. Which do you think is more important to the history of the world—the invention of the printing press or the computer? Why?

LOG ON Find out more about printing at **www.macmillanmh.com**

Comprehension

Genre

Informational Nonfiction gives a detailed account of real situations and people using verifiable facts.

Generate Questions

Description

As you read, use your Description Web.

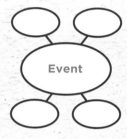

Read to Find Out

How did the printing press revolutionize the world?

Breaking into Print

Before and After the Invention of the Printing Press

by Stephen Krensky
illustrated by Bonnie Christensen

Award Winning Selection

Of all the inventions; of all discoveries in science and art; of all the great results in the wonderful progress of mechanical energy and skill; the printer is the only product of civilization necessary to the existence of free man.

Charles Dickens

In a long room with seven tables and seven windows, a French monk sat hunched over a parchment page. He dipped a goose quill in some ink and began to write. The quill made a scratching sound, like a cat clawing at a closed door.

Parchment was made from a specially prepared animal skin, usually from sheep or goats. The best parchment, called vellum, was made from calfskin.

Monks worked only in natural light. The risk of fire from candles posed too great a danger to their precious **manuscripts.**

If a monastery library had 100 books, it was considered a lot. The books were so valuable, they were chained to their shelves.

The monk worked six hours almost every day for many months. He hoped to finish before the first snow fell.

The monk was making a book.

STRATEGY SKILL

Description
Describe how books were first made.

Charlemagne founded many schools that taught arithmetic, basic grammar, and the Bible.

In classrooms, only teachers had books. The students memorized information or took notes on wax slates.

*Under Charlemagne's rule (800– 814 A.D.) Latin was firmly **established** as the language of the court and education.*

Charlemagne's scribes also pioneered leaving spaces between words and starting phrases with capital letters.

The monastery was a small part of a great empire, an empire with far more soldiers than books. Its emperor, Charlemagne, both read and spoke Latin, but he could write little more than his name.

His **scribes**, however, created a new script that made writing easier to understand.

In the Middle Ages, people believed in superstitions and magic to explain things such as thunderstorms and diseases.

Rome had a population of about 500,000 in 300 A.D. After the fall of its empire, no European city had more than 20,000 people for hundreds of years.

In England, William the Conqueror ordered a record made of the land and its owners so he could tax them accurately. This Domesday Book was finished in 1086.

Across the countryside, reading and writing counted for little. Few roads were free of robbers or wolves. In the villages, warring peasants lived and died without ever seeing a book.

In time, the villages knew longer periods of peace. The peasants began to eat better and made goods to trade on market day. Successful merchants learned to read and write so that they could keep records of their business. Sometimes their children were taught as well.

Book-making shops were centered in Paris. There, one person wrote the text, another added fancy letters in red ink, and a third painted colored borders and decorations. Two others checked the text for mistakes, and another team bound the pages together.

Books were still very expensive. One fine book was traded for 200 sheep, 5 measures of wheat, and 5 measures of barley.

Paper was invented in 105 A.D., when Ts'ai Lun reported its development to the Chinese emperor. It was made from the pulp of mulberry, bamboo, and other fibers. The paper in Europe was made from rags. It was introduced in Spain around 1150.

Block printing was first developed in Asia in the eighth century. No press was used for the printing process. After the blocks were etched and inked, paper was rubbed on them to make a print.

More books were now needed, more than the monks could manage alone. In the new book-making **guilds**, many hands worked together.

Many such books were made with a new material called paper. It was much cheaper than parchment and especially useful for wood or metal block printing.

The world's oldest known printed book, a Buddhist scripture called The Diamond Sutra, *was printed from wooden blocks in 868.*

Korean experiments with movable type began in the 1200s.

The writing of Dante's Divine Comedy *in Italian (1321) and Chaucer's* The Canterbury Tales *in English (1387) marked the rise of national languages over Latin.*

In faraway China, printers had been using paper for centuries. And around 1050, the Chinese printer Pi Sheng had invented movable type using baked clay tablets. Yet few Chinese printers were excited about the invention. Their alphabet has thousands of characters. Only in a dream could printers create so much type. And even if they managed this feat, organizing the type would turn the dream into a nightmare.

The Koreans made further progress. They were actually printing books with movable type around 1400. But their written language is as complicated as Chinese, which discouraged them from making too much of the process.

Eyeglasses were invented around 1290 and were common by 1400. This invention enabled many more people to read by the time Gutenberg was born.

It was very expensive for Gutenberg to conduct his experiments. He was always borrowing money for supplies and to give himself more time to work.

In the German town of Mainz, one young man knew nothing of Chinese or Korean printing methods. But he was interested in the idea and process of printing. His name was Johannes Gensfleisch, but he followed the old custom of taking his mother's name: Gutenberg.

As a young goldsmith and gem cutter, Gutenberg had learned how to cut steel punches and cast metal in molds. He knew which metals were hard and which were soft, which melted easily and which could take great heat without melting. Over the next few years, Gutenberg tinkered with the printing process.

After much experimenting, Gutenberg cast his metal type from an **alloy** made of 80% lead, 15% antimony, and 5% tin.

Gutenberg cast 290 different letters, numbers, punctuation marks, and other symbols in preparation to printing his first book.

Although he had a simpler alphabet than the Chinese or Koreans, he still faced many **obstacles**. There was no room for sloppy or careless design. Printed letters had to fit as closely together as handwritten ones. Printed words had to fall in a straight line. Printed lines had to leave even spaces above and below.

Gutenberg also had to find the proper metal to cast letters and the right ink to use. If the metal was too hard, it would break too easily. If the metal was too soft, it would lose its shape too quickly. As for the ink, it could not be too thick or too thin or likely to fade over time.

Description
Identify the obstacles Gutenberg faced with the printing process.

Gutenberg's ink was made from boiled linseed oil colored with a kind of soot called lampblack.

Gutenberg's platen, a metal plate that flattened the paper onto the metal type, was raised and lowered by a large screw and lever.

Screw-style presses were used to press olives and grapes and for printing designs on cloth. They were also used for squeezing water out of damp sheets of paper.

Gutenberg began working on the Bible project in 1452. It took more than three years to complete.

Gutenberg was very practical. He did not believe in reinventing things that already worked fine. So he adapted a winepress for printing. He made it taller, so that the work could be done at waist height, and he created a rolling tray for sliding the paper in and out.

Gutenberg spent almost twenty years building and tinkering. He invented adjustable molds to make letters in different widths. He found the right alloy for casting his letters.

The Gutenberg Bible, published in 1456, was printed in a run of 200 copies. Though it was started with two presses, six presses were eventually used together. As many as 50 copies were printed on vellum, requiring up to 5,000 animal skins.

Shortly before Gutenberg's Bible was completed, he lost his business when he was unable to repay a loan. Although he eventually published again, he was never free of debt. He died **penniless** in 1468.

Lower costs played a great part in the success of printing. By 1463, ten printed Bibles sold for the price of one manuscript copy.

In 1462, when Mainz became the site of political battles, the printers packed up their presses and spread out across Europe.

He built the upper and lower type cases for storing capital and small letters. He even created the long, grooved composing stick for quickly assembling lines of print.

Gutenberg's great project was a two-column Bible.

It reflected everything he knew of the art of printing.

Soon, other printers were building on Gutenberg's work. They added more than one ink to a page. They added illustrations to the text.

Englishman William Caxton was unusual among printers because his main interest was actually creating and translating books, not just running a successful business. In 1475, he produced the first printed book in English, Recuyell of the Historyes of Troye.

By the year 1500, there were more than 1,000 printers in Europe, and they had printed millions of books.

Despite the success of printed books, some wealthy people looked down on them as plain and coarse.

They began printing more than religious works and public notices. They began printing philosophy and poetry and stories of the imagination.

In almost no time at all, printing grew beyond the reach of one man or firm. New printers were setting up shop as fast as they could learn the craft. A generation earlier, printers had produced a single book in a few months. Now they were printing thousands of books a year.

New schools sprang up to teach people how to read. And since books were no longer rare or costly, students as well as teachers could own them. This freed the students from memorizing so much and gave them more time to think.

There were geography books for Christopher Columbus and science books for Nicolaus Copernicus. And there were art and science and engineering and many other books for Leonardo da Vinci, who studied almost everything.

Reading and writing were no longer just for studious monks or highborn lords and ladies. Books were no longer chained up in private libraries or boldly sold for a king's ransom.

The printing press took learning and knowledge from just a **privileged** few and shared them with everyone else. And that change, more than any other act, set the stage for the modern world to come.

Although many schools were for rich students, some poor students were educated for free.

When Columbus planned his trip to Asia, he studied many printed books and maps.

In 1543, when Copernicus first showed the solar system with the sun in the middle, a lot of people didn't believe him. They thought the earth was the center of everything.

When da Vinci wasn't painting, he drew up plans for inventions, including a flying machine that resembled a helicopter.

The History

3500–2500 B.C.	Pictographic writing, in which simple pictures represent objects and actions, develops in the Middle East.
circa 3100 B.C.	Egyptians begin hieroglyphic writing, which they continue to use for more than 3,000 years.
circa 2360 B.C.	Babylonians create cuneiform symbols, which they write on clay tablets.
circa 2000 B.C.	Sheets of papyrus are developed from the Egyptian papyrus plant. Writing is done with a brushlike reed. The sheets are then rolled into scrolls.
300 B.C.	Mesoamericans create scrolls on bark paper.
200s B.C.	Parchment, a writing surface made from animal skin, comes into use. The split pen is developed as a writing instrument.
105 A.D.	Paper is invented in China by Ts'ai Lun.
200s	Romans replace the long scroll format with the codex, in which the scrolls have been cut into pages, creating the first books.
circa 400	The Chinese start writing with ink.
700s	The Chinese start printing with woodblocks.
800s	Carolingian scribes begin leaving spaces between words to make reading easier.
868	The earliest certain date of the printing of an entire book, *The Diamond Sutra*, in China by Wang Chich.
1150	The invention of paper first reaches Europe, in Spain.
1200s	The Koreans begin experimenting with movable type.
1300s	Book-making guilds thrive.
1390	The first European paper mill is established in what will later become Germany.
circa 1398	Johannes Gensfleisch, or Gutenberg, is born at Mainz.

# of Printing

Gutenberg's 42-line Bible is finished.	**1456**
The first printed book in English, *Recuyell of the Historyes of Troye*, is produced by William Caxton with Colard Mansion.	**1475**
More than 1,000 printers are active in Europe.	**1500**
The Italian printer Aldus Manutius creates a standard for mixing typefaces and for including illustrations on the printed page.	**early 1500s**
The first book is printed in the Americas, in Mexico City.	**1539**
The first Bible is printed in the American colonies by Samuel Green.	**1663**
English typefounders William Caslon and John Baskerville develop new standard type fonts.	**1700s**
A machine for casting fonts is introduced in England.	**1822**
The monotype machine is patented. It combines a typewriter-like keyboard with a type casting unit to create individual letters at the stroke of a finger.	**1868**
The Linotype machine begins setting complete lines of "hot" type automatically in single pieces of cast lead.	**1886**
More efficient printing presses are developed, including self-inking capabilities and some motorization.	**late 1800s**
Phototypesetting is introduced. "Cold" type replaces "hot" type in many situations as columns of type are reproduced on photosensitive paper instead of being cast in lead.	**1950s**
Computerized typesetting is created at video screens, storing text and illustrations on a computer disk.	**1980s to present**

Breaking into Print
with Stephen Krensky and Bonnie Christensen

Stephen Krensky used to make up stories in bed at night, before he fell asleep. He would imagine a character and then tell himself a story about that character. With 72 books published, Stephen is still imagining characters, plots, and scenes, and is always researching interesting things. Writing is hard and fun, he says, but it's the best job he can think of having.

Another book by Stephen Krensky: *The Printer's Apprentice*

Bonnie Christensen still remembers her third and fourth grade art teacher who helped her see the world in a different way. "She gave me the key to a world that traveled with me wherever I moved," says Bonnie. And Bonnie did move a lot. She went to nine schools in twelve years! Today she lives in Vermont with her daughter and two cats.

 Find out more about Stephen Krensky and Bonnie Christensen at **www.macmillanmh.com**

Author's Purpose
Why did the author use two different columns of text on most pages? Was this format effective? Explain.

Comprehension Check

Summarize

Use your Description Web to help you summarize *Breaking into Print*. Think about how the printing press enabled so many changes to take place in the lives of ordinary people.

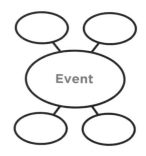

Event

Think and Compare

1. Use the descriptive details on pages 672–673 to describe what Gutenberg accomplished in almost twenty years of building and tinkering. **Generate Questions: Description**

2. What **obstacles** did the printing press overcome, either directly or indirectly? Use specific examples from the information in the side text to support your answer. **Evaluate**

3. Think about an invention that makes your life easier. What do you think life was like before the invention came into use? **Evaluate**

4. Like the printing press, the computer has changed how we share and shape information. How is such easy access to information both good and bad for people today? **Analyze**

5. Read "A Writing Story" on pages 660–661. How do the authors of "A Writing Story" and *Breaking into Print* present their information in the same way? How do they present the information in different styles? **Reading/Writing Across Texts**

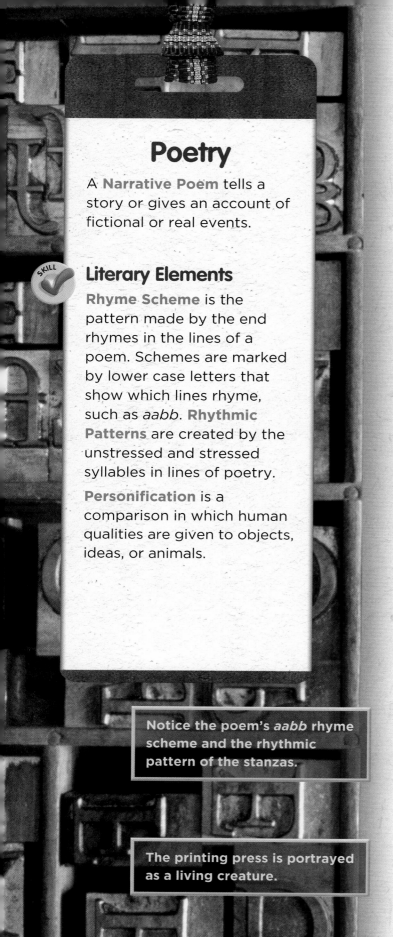

Poetry

A **Narrative Poem** tells a story or gives an account of fictional or real events.

Literary Elements

Rhyme Scheme is the pattern made by the end rhymes in the lines of a poem. Schemes are marked by lower case letters that show which lines rhyme, such as *aabb*. **Rhythmic Patterns** are created by the unstressed and stressed syllables in lines of poetry.

Personification is a comparison in which human qualities are given to objects, ideas, or animals.

> Notice the poem's *aabb* rhyme scheme and the rhythmic pattern of the stanzas.

> The printing press is portrayed as a living creature.

Future Bookmaker

by Constance Andrea Keremes

When I was but a lad of ten,
I joined the world of working men.
Apprentice was the name I took,
I learned to print all kind of book.

The print shop had an air of gloom,
And sunlight seemed to shun the room.
My master was a man I feared,
He raged at me and pulled his beard.

The printing press groaned fearfully,
As though it might devour me.
And yet I grew to love that place,
My heart would sing, my pulse would race.

Each time I worked with type and ink,
I always trembled just to think,
That all those many rows of words,
Would soon fly up and out like birds.

Those books were tutors glad to share,
Their words with people everywhere.
So many books for eager hands,
The rich and poor throughout the land.

And now my youth has passed away,
Beside the hearth I spend my day.
I like to sit and contemplate,
The many books I helped create.

Each book a lifelong friend to be,
To everyone—but most to me.

Connect and Compare

1. How does personification help dramatize the narrator's tale?
   Personification

2. What makes this a narrative poem? Cite examples from the text.
   Analyze

3. Consider "Future Bookmaker" and *Breaking into Print*. How do they
   work together to help you understand the role of the printing press
   through the years. **Reading/Writing Across Texts**

 Find out more about narrative poetry at **www.macmillanmh.com**

681

Write About a Process

Fast Food

by Emily R.

When it comes to getting food as fast as possible, the chameleon is the champion. That's because a chameleon can catch an insect in less than a quarter of a second! That is even faster than a frog. How does a chameleon, a type of lizard, do this?

It has a long, sticky tongue that is more than one and a half times the length of its body. When an insect is nearby, a chameleon quickly sticks out its tongue toward it. The way the tongue works is similar to a telescope that is being extended. A set of nine tubelike sleeves in the chameleon's tongue slide along one another to make the tongue longer. Zip! The outstretched tongue snatches the insect. Zip! The tongue slides back and the chameleon has a tasty meal of insect.

Scientists believe the chameleon's tongue is the fastest in the animal kingdom. Somehow, I don't think these animals go hungry for too long.

I defined the chameleon as a type of lizard.

I explained how the tongue extends.

Your Turn

Think about a process you can explain. It can be about something that interests you in nature or something that people have made. Choose a topic that you know a lot about or can research easily. Write an explanation of how the process works. Choose words and phrases that will help clarify your meaning. Use the Writer's Checklist to check your writing.

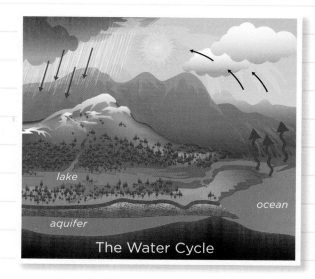

lake

ocean

aquifer

The Water Cycle

Writer's Checklist

✓ **Ideas and Content:** Did I choose a process that I know a lot about? Did I explain the process clearly?

✓ **Organization:** Did I explain the steps of the process in order? Did I use enough details?

✓ **Voice:** Does my language convey why I think this process is interesting?

✓ **Word Choice:** Did I vary **word choice** to make my explanations clear?

✓ **Sentence Fluency:** Did I vary the lengths of my sentences?

✓ **Conventions:** Are my spelling and punctuation correct? Did I use commas after introductory phrases?

VOLCANOES
PAST AND PRESENT

Talk About It

What words can you think of to describe what is taking place in this photo?

LOG ON Find out more about volcanoes at **www.macmillanmh.com**

685

Vocabulary

ambitious	revived
drowsy	dwelling
lounge	pondering
agonized	vapors

Dictionary

Many words have more than one meaning. Dictionaries define **Multiple-meaning Words**.

For example:

¹ *lounge (verb)* = to pass time lazily

² *lounge (noun)* = a room for lounging or being at ease

³ *lounge (noun)* = a couch or sofa

Voice from Vesuvius

by Isabel Kamsly

Tammi and Brian are in southern Italy with their parents. Their mother is an archaeologist, and their father heads a computer graphics company. Both are working at the excavations of Herculaneum on the Bay of Naples. It is an impressive, **ambitious** project.

The hot sun was making Tammi and Brian tired and **drowsy**. They had spent the morning watching a computer-generated exhibit of Herculaneum in A.D. 79 that their dad made. Now they decided to **lounge** on the ground at the archaeological site itself.

"Just think," said Brian, "about sixty-five feet of matter from Mt. Vesuvius fell on this city. That's much more than covered Pompeii."

(left) Vestibule of a Thermae at Herculaneum

"Mom says that when it cooled, the volcanic ash covered the city like cement," added Tammi. "That's why things have been so well-preserved all these years."

"It was horrifying," said an **agonized** voice that sounded as if it were in pain.

Startled, the children turned to see who was speaking. No one was there. Suddenly, they were **revived** and wide awake. Was the voice coming from the ancient home in front of them?

"Some said the gods were punishing us," the voice said. "Is that what it was?"

Tammi peered into the **dwelling**, but the house was empty. Still she felt she should answer.

"I know people believed that," she said, "but it was really the volcano erupting. You know, Mt. Vesuvius."

"But why?" asked the voice.

"There's a scientific explanation," said Brian. "Earth is covered with large plates. They are always moving. When one plate pushes under another, it melts and becomes liquid rock called *magma*. This super hot rock creates gas and steam. Then it can burst through Earth's surface as a volcano. Mt. Vesuvius has erupted more than seventy times since Herculaneum and Pompeii were covered in A.D. 79."

For a minute there was silence. Brian's scientific explanation required some **pondering**, or thinking about.

"There was so much ash, rock, and fumes. The **vapors** killed people as they ran for the sea," said the voice sadly.

"Er . . . you speak as if you were there," said Tammi.

"Yes, I was there . . . it was my fate." The voice trailed off, "I will always be there . . ."

The children looked at one another. "It must be the sun," gasped Tammi. "Let's go find Mom and Dad."

Reread for **Comprehension**

Summarize

Theme

When you summarize what you read, it is helpful to identify the theme, or subject, of the story. Ask yourself how all the parts of the story relate to the theme.

A Theme Chart can help you summarize a story. Use the chart to identify the theme as you reread "Voice from Vesuvius."

Setting
What the Characters Want
Plot Problem
Outcome
Theme

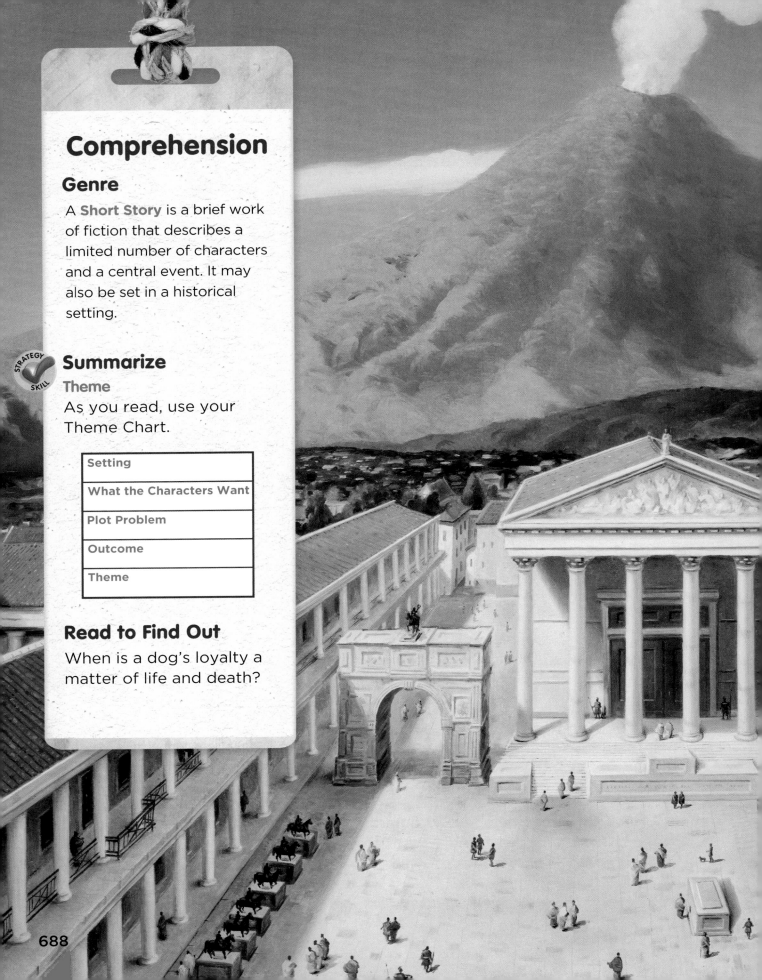

Comprehension

Genre

A **Short Story** is a brief work of fiction that describes a limited number of characters and a central event. It may also be set in a historical setting.

Summarize

Theme

As you read, use your Theme Chart.

Setting
What the Characters Want
Plot Problem
Outcome
Theme

Read to Find Out

When is a dog's loyalty a matter of life and death?

The Dog of
POMPEII

BY LOUIS UNTERMEYER
ILLUSTRATED BY MICHAEL JAROSZKO

Award
Winning
Author

Tito and his dog Bimbo lived (if you could call it living) under the wall where it joined the inner gate. They really didn't live there; they just slept there. They lived anywhere. Pompeii was one of the liveliest of the old Latin towns, but although Tito was never an unhappy boy, he was not exactly a merry one. The streets were always lively with shining chariots and bright red trappings; the open-air theaters rocked with laughing crowds; sham-battles and athletic sports were free for the asking in the great stadium. Once a year the Caesar visited the pleasure-city and the fire-works lasted for days; the sacrifices in the Forum were better than a show. But Tito saw none of these things. He was blind—had been blind from birth. He was known to every one in the poorer quarters. But no one could say how old he was, no one remembered his parents, no one could tell where he came from. Bimbo was another mystery. As long as people could remember seeing Tito—about twelve or thirteen years—they had seen Bimbo. Bimbo had never left his side. He was not only dog, but nurse, pillow, playmate, mother and father to Tito.

Did I say Bimbo never left his master? (Perhaps I had better say comrade, for if any one was the master, it was Bimbo.) I was wrong. Bimbo did trust Tito alone exactly three times a day. It was a fixed routine, a custom understood between boy and dog since the beginning of their friendship, and the way it worked was this: Early in the morning, shortly after dawn, while Tito was still dreaming, Bimbo would disappear. When Tito awoke, Bimbo would be sitting quietly at his side, his ears cocked, his stump of a tail tapping the ground, and a fresh-baked bread—more like a large round roll—at his feet. Tito would stretch himself; Bimbo would yawn; then they would breakfast. At noon, no matter where they happened to be, Bimbo would put his paw on Tito's knee and the two of them would return to the inner gate. Tito would curl up in the corner (almost like a dog) and go to sleep, while Bimbo, looking quite important (almost like a boy) would disappear again. In half an hour he'd be back with their lunch.

Sometimes it would be a piece of fruit or a scrap of meat, often it was nothing but a dry crust. But sometimes there would be one of those flat rich cakes, sprinkled with raisins and sugar, that Tito liked so much. At supper-time the same thing happened, although there was a little less of everything, for things were hard to snatch in the evening with the streets full of people. Besides, Bimbo didn't approve of too much food before going to sleep. A heavy supper made boys too restless and dogs too stodgy—and it was the business of a dog to sleep lightly with one ear open and muscles ready for action.

But, whether there was much or little, hot or cold, fresh or dry, food was always there. Tito never asked where it came from and Bimbo never told him. There was plenty of rain-water in the hollows of soft stones; the old egg-woman at the corner sometimes gave him a cupful of strong goat's milk; in the grape-season the fat wine-maker let him have drippings of the mild juice. So there was no danger of going hungry or thirsty. There was plenty of everything in Pompeii—if you knew where to find it—and if you had a dog like Bimbo.

Breadseller in Public Square, from House of the Baker, Pompeiian fresco

Theme
What message about friendship does the author want readers to understand?

Musicians. Street scene. Mosaic from Cicero's Villa, Pompeii.

As I said before, Tito was not the merriest boy in Pompeii. He could not romp with the other youngsters and play Hare-and-Hounds and I-spy and Follow-your-Master and Ball-against-the-Building and Jack-stones and Kings-and-Robbers with them. But that did not make him sorry for himself. If he could not see the sights that delighted the lads of Pompeii he could hear and smell things they never noticed. He could really see more with his ears and nose than they could with their eyes. When he and Bimbo went out walking he knew just where they were going and exactly what was happening.

"Ah," he'd sniff and say, as they passed a handsome villa, "Glaucus Pansa is giving a grand dinner tonight. They're going to have three kinds of bread, and roast pigling, and stuffed goose, and a great stew—I think bear-stew—and a fig-pie." And Bimbo would note that this would be a good place to visit tomorrow.

Or, "H'm," Tito would murmur, half through his lips, half through his nostrils. "The wife of Marcus Lucretius is expecting her mother. She's shaking out every piece of goods in the house; she's going to use the best clothes—the ones she's been keeping in pine-needles and camphor—and there's an extra girl in the kitchen. Come, Bimbo, let's get out of the dust!"

Or, as they passed a small but elegant **dwelling** opposite the public-baths, "Too bad! The tragic poet is ill again. It must be a bad fever this time, for they're trying smoke-fumes instead of medicine. Whew! I'm glad I'm not a tragic poet!"

Or, as they neared the Forum, "Mm-m! What good things they have in the Macellum today!" (It really was a sort of butcher-grocer-market-place, but Tito didn't know any better. He called it the Macellum.) "Dates from Africa, and salt oysters from sea-caves, and cuttlefish, and new honey, and sweet onions, and—ugh!—water-buffalo steaks. Come, let's see what's what in the Forum." And Bimbo, just as curious as his comrade, hurried on. Being a dog, he trusted his ears and nose (like Tito) more than his eyes. And so the two of them entered the center of Pompeii.

The Forum was the part of the town to which everybody came at least once during each day. It was the Central Square and everything happened here. There were no private houses; all was public—the chief temples, the gold and red bazaars, the silk shops, the town hall, the booths belonging to the weavers and jewel merchants, the wealthy woolen market, the shrine of the household gods. Everything glittered here. The buildings looked as if they were new—which, in a sense, they were. The earthquake of twelve years ago had brought down all the old structures and, since the citizens of Pompeii were **ambitious** to rival Naples and even Rome, they had seized the opportunity to rebuild the whole town. And they had done it all within a dozen years. There was scarcely a building that was older than Tito.

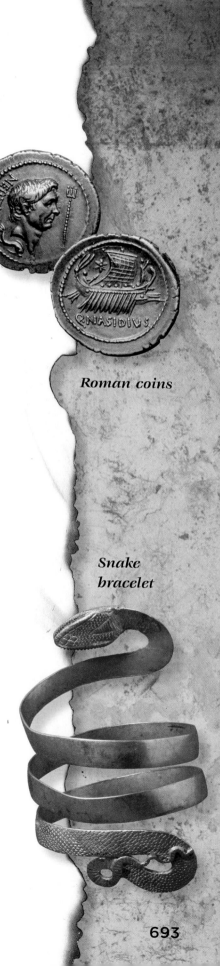

Roman coins

Snake bracelet

Tito had heard a great deal about the earthquake though, being about a year old at the time, he could scarcely remember it. This particular quake had been a light one— as earthquakes go. The weaker houses had been shaken down, parts of the out-worn wall had been wrecked; but there was little loss of life, and the brilliant new Pompeii had taken the place of the old. No one knew what caused these earthquakes. Records showed they had happened in the neighborhood since the beginning of time. Sailors said that it was to teach the lazy city-folk a lesson and make them appreciate those who risked the dangers of the sea to bring them luxuries and protect their town from invaders. The priests said that the gods took this way of showing their anger to those who refused to worship properly and who failed to bring enough sacrifices to the altars and (though they didn't say it in so many words) presents to the priests. The tradesmen said that the foreign merchants had corrupted the ground and it was no longer safe to traffic in imported goods that came from strange places and carried a curse with them. Every one had a different explanation—and every one's explanation was louder and sillier than his neighbor's.

They were talking about it this afternoon as Tito and Bimbo came out of the side-street into the public square. The Forum was the favorite promenade for rich and poor. What with the priests arguing with the politicians, servants doing the day's shopping, tradesmen crying their wares, women displaying the latest fashions from Greece and Egypt, children playing hide-and-seek among the marble columns, knots of soldiers, sailors, peasants from the provinces—to say nothing of those who merely came to **lounge** and look on— the square was crowded to its last inch. His ears even more than his nose guided Tito to the place where the talk was loudest. It was in front of the Shrine of the Household Gods that, naturally enough, the householders were arguing.

Roman statue found in Pompeii

"I tell you," rumbled a voice which Tito recognized as bathmaster Rufus's, "there won't be another earthquake in my lifetime or yours. There may be a tremble or two, but earthquakes, like lightnings, never strike twice in the same place."

"Do they not?" asked a thin voice Tito had never heard. It had a high, sharp ring to it and Tito knew it as the accent of a stranger. "How about the two towns of Sicily that have been ruined three times within fifteen years by the eruptions of Mount Etna? And were they not warned? And does that column of smoke above Vesuvius mean nothing?"

"That?" Tito could hear the grunt with which one question answered another. "That's always there. We use it for our weather-guide. When the smoke stands up straight we know we'll have fair weather; when it flattens out it's sure to be foggy; when it drifts to the east—"

"Yes, yes," cut in the edged voice. "I've heard about your mountain barometer. But the column of smoke seems hundreds of feet higher than usual and it's thickening and spreading like a shadowy tree. They say in Naples—"

"Oh, Naples!" Tito knew this voice by the little squeak that went with it. It was Attilio, the cameo-cutter. "*They* talk while we suffer. Little help we got from them last time. Naples commits the crimes and Pompeii pays the price. It's become a proverb with us. Let them mind their own business."

Cameo

"Yes," grumbled Rufus, "and others, too."

"Very well, my confident friends," responded the thin voice which now sounded curiously flat. "We also have a proverb—and it is this: Those who will not listen to men must be taught by the gods. I say no more. But I leave a last warning. Remember the holy ones. Look to your temples. And when the smoke-tree above Vesuvius grows to the shape of an umbrella-pine, look to your lives."

Tito could hear the air whistle as the speaker drew his toga about him and the quick shuffle of feet told him the stranger had gone.

"Now what," said the cameo-cutter, "did he mean by that?"

"I wonder," grunted Rufus, "I wonder."

Theater mask mosaic

Tito wondered, too. And Bimbo, his head at a thoughtful angle, looked as if he had been doing a heavy piece of **pondering**. By nightfall the argument had been forgotten. If the smoke had increased no one saw it in the dark. Besides, it was Caesar's birthday and the town was in holiday mood. Tito and Bimbo were among the merry-makers, dodging the charioteers who shouted at them. A dozen times they almost upset baskets of sweets and jars of Vesuvian wine, said to be as fiery as the streams inside the volcano, and a dozen times they were cursed and cuffed. But Tito never missed his footing. He was thankful for his keen ears and quick instinct—most thankful of all for Bimbo.

They visited the uncovered theater and, though Tito could not see the faces of the actors, he could follow the play better than most of the audience, for their attention wandered—they were distracted by the scenery, the costumes, the by-play, even by themselves—while Tito's whole attention was centered in what he heard. Then to the city-walls, where the people of Pompeii watched a mock naval-battle in which the city was attacked by the sea and saved after thousands of flaming arrows had been exchanged and countless colored torches had been burned. Though the thrill of flaring ships and lighted skies was lost to Tito, the

Roman ships fresco from Pompeii

shouts and cheers excited him as much as any and he cried out with the loudest of them.

The next morning there were *two* of the beloved raisin and sugar cakes for his breakfast. Bimbo was unusually active and thumped his bit of a tail until Tito was afraid he would wear it out. The boy could not imagine whether Bimbo was urging him to some sort of game or was trying to tell something. After a while, he ceased to notice Bimbo. He felt **drowsy**. Last night's late hours had tired him. Besides, there was a heavy mist in the air—no, a thick fog rather than a mist—a fog that got into his throat and scraped it and made him cough. He walked as far as the marine gate to get a breath of the sea. But the blanket of haze had spread all over the bay and even the salt air seemed smoky.

He went to bed before dusk and slept. But he did not sleep well. He had too many dreams—dreams of ships lurching in the Forum, of losing his way in a screaming crowd, of armies marching across his chest, of being pulled over every rough pavement of Pompeii.

He woke early. Or, rather, he was pulled awake. Bimbo was doing the pulling. The dog had dragged Tito to his feet and was urging the boy along. Somewhere. Where, Tito did not know. His feet stumbled uncertainly; he was still half asleep. For a while he noticed nothing except the fact that it was hard to breathe. The air was hot. And heavy. So heavy that he could taste it. The air, it seemed, had turned to powder, a warm powder that stung his nostrils and burned his sightless eyes.

Then he began to hear sounds. Peculiar sounds. Like animals under the earth. Hissings and groanings and muffled cries that a dying creature might make dislodging the stones of his underground cave. There was no doubt of it now. The noises came from underneath. He not only heard them—he could feel them. The earth twitched; the twitching changed to an uneven shrugging of the soil. Then, as Bimbo half-pulled, half-coaxed him across, the ground jerked away from his feet and he was thrown against a stone-fountain.

Theater mask mosaic

The water—hot water—splashing in his face **revived** him. He got to his feet, Bimbo steadying him, helping him on again. The noises grew louder; they came closer. The cries were even more animal-like than before, but now they came from human throats. A few people, quicker of foot and more hurried by fear, began to rush by. A family or two—then a section—then, it seemed, an army broken out of bounds. Tito, bewildered though he was, could recognize Rufus as he bellowed past him, like a water-buffalo gone mad. Time was lost in a nightmare.

It was then the crashing began. First a sharp crackling, like a monstrous snapping of twigs; then a roar like the fall of a whole forest of trees; then an explosion that tore earth and sky. The heavens, though Tito could not see them, were shot through with continual flickerings of fire. Lightnings above were answered by thunders beneath. A house fell. Then another. By a miracle the two companions had escaped the dangerous side-streets and were in a more open space. It was the Forum. They rested here a while—how long he did not know.

Tito had no idea of the time of day. He could *feel* it was black—an unnatural blackness. Something inside—perhaps the lack of breakfast and lunch—told him it was past noon. But it didn't matter. Nothing seemed to matter. He was getting drowsy, too drowsy to walk. But walk he must. He knew it. And Bimbo knew it; the sharp tugs told him so. Nor was it a moment too soon. The sacred ground of the Forum was safe no longer. It was beginning to rock, then to pitch, then to split. As they stumbled out of the square, the earth wriggled like a caught snake and all the columns of the temple of Jupiter came down. It was the end of the world—or so it seemed.

To walk was not enough now. They must run. Tito was too frightened to know what to do or where to go. He had lost all sense of direction. He started to go back to the inner gate; but Bimbo, straining his back to the last inch, almost pulled his clothes from him. What did the creature want? Had the dog gone mad?

Theme

How do Bimbo's actions reinforce the theme of the story?

Submarine fauna, mosaic, 1st century from Pompeii

Then, suddenly, he understood. Bimbo was telling him the way out—urging him there. The sea gate of course. The sea gate—and then the sea. Far from falling buildings, heaving ground. He turned, Bimbo guiding him across open pits and dangerous pools of bubbling mud, away from buildings that had caught fire and were dropping their burning beams. Tito could no longer tell whether the noises were made by the shrieking sky or the **agonized** people. He and Bimbo ran on—the only silent beings in a howling world.

New dangers threatened. All Pompeii seemed to be thronging toward the marine gate and, squeezing among the crowds, there was the chance of being trampled to death. But the chance had to be taken. It was growing harder and harder to breathe. What air there was choked him. It was all dust now—dust and pebbles, pebbles as large as beans. They fell on his head, his hands—pumice-stones from the black heart of Vesuvius. The mountain was turning itself inside out. Tito remembered a phrase that the stranger had said in the Forum two days ago: "Those who will not listen to men must be taught by the gods." The people of Pompeii had refused to heed the warnings; they were being taught now—if it was not too late.

Suddenly it seemed too late for Tito. The red hot ashes blistered his skin, the stinging **vapors** tore his throat. He could not go on. He staggered toward a small tree at the side of the road and fell. In a moment Bimbo was beside him. He coaxed. But there was no answer. He licked Tito's hands, his feet, his face. The boy did not stir. Then Bimbo did the last thing he could—the last thing he wanted to do. He bit his comrade, bit him deep in the arm. With a cry of pain, Tito jumped to his feet, Bimbo after him. Tito was in despair, but Bimbo was determined. He drove the boy on, snapping at his heels, worrying his way through the crowd; barking, baring his teeth, heedless of kicks or falling stones. Sick with hunger, half-dead with fear and sulphur-fumes, Tito pounded on, pursued by Bimbo. How long he never knew. At last he staggered through the marine gate and felt soft sand under him. Then Tito fainted. . . .

Some one was dashing sea-water over him. Some one was carrying him toward a boat.

"Bimbo," he called. And then louder, "Bimbo!" But Bimbo had disappeared.

Voices jarred against each other. "Hurry—hurry!" "To the boats!" "Can't you see the child's frightened and starving!" "He keeps calling for some one!" "Poor boy, he's out of his mind." "Here, child—take this!"

They tucked him in among them. The oar-locks creaked; the oars splashed; the boat rode over toppling waves. Tito was safe. But he wept continually.

"Bimbo!" he wailed. "Bimbo! Bimbo!"

He could not be comforted.

Eighteen hundred years passed. Scientists were restoring the ancient city; excavators were working their way through the stones and trash that had buried the entire town. Much had already been brought to light—statues, bronze instruments, bright mosaics, household articles; even delicate paintings had been preserved by the fall of ashes that had taken over two thousand lives. Columns were dug up and the Forum was beginning to emerge.

It was at a place where the ruins lay deepest that the Director paused.

"Come here," he called to his assistant. "I think we've discovered the remains of a building in good shape. Here are four huge millstones that were most likely turned by slaves or mules—and here is a whole wall standing with shelves inside it. Why! It must have been a bakery. And here's a curious thing. What do you think I found under this heap where the ashes were thickest? The skeleton of a dog!"

"Amazing!" gasped his assistant. "You'd think a dog would have had sense enough to run away at the time. And what is that flat thing he's holding between his teeth? It can't be a stone."

"No. It must have come from this bakery. You know it looks to me like some sort of cake hardened with the years. And, bless me, if those little black pebbles aren't raisins. A raisin-cake almost two thousand years old! I wonder what made him want it at such a moment?"

"I wonder," murmured the assistant.

MEET THE AUTHOR

LOUIS UNTERMEYER was a poet, an author, and a humorist. He was born in 1885 and lived to the age of 92. During his life, he took a trip to Italy, where he said these stories were waiting for him. When he saw the plaster cast of the dog in Pompeii, who had died almost 2,000 years before, he knew he must tell a story about it.

LOG ON Find out more about Louis Untermeyer at **www.macmillanmh.com**

Author's Purpose

Louis Untermeyer wrote this story to entertain readers, but he also informs them about a spectacular historical setting. Describe the setting and its importance.

Comprehension Check

Summarize

Use your Theme Chart to help you summarize "*The Dog of Pompeii.*" What is the major event of the story? How does this event affect the main characters?

Setting
What the Characters Want
Plot Problem
Outcome
Theme

Think and Compare

1. The author uses much of the story to describe the wealth and beauty of Pompeii. The story ends with scientists amazed at finding an ordinary dog with a raisin cake. How do these two different story elements relate to the theme? **Summarize: Theme**

2. In the afterword, the author of this selection muses that Tito becomes a famous friend to and healer of animals. How is this idea an extension of the story's theme? **Synthesize**

3. Bimbo seems to be Tito's only comrade and ends up saving the boy from Vesuvius's suffocating **vapors**. What qualities do you think pets should possess? **Evaluate**

4. Tito uses Bimbo to see for him. How do animals today make life easier for the physically challenged? **Analyze**

5. Read "Voice from Vesuvius" on pages 686–687. How would the information presented in the story have helped Tito? **Reading/Writing Across Texts**

Science

Genre

An **Informational Essay** is a nonfiction piece about a particular topic and can tell a story about a real-life experience.

Text Features

Graphic Aids, such as maps, photographs, captions, and subheadings, help you more fully understand the information in an article.

Content Vocabulary

lava
billow
fire-resistant

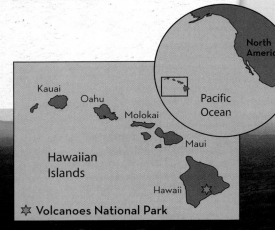

Kauai
Oahu
Molokai
Maui
Hawaiian Islands
Hawaii
North America
Pacific Ocean
☆ **Volcanoes National Park**

VOLCANO!

by Forrest Gale, as told to Lora Gale
photos by G. Brad Lewis

How would you like to live on an island way out in the middle of the Pacific Ocean? I do and it's really incredible. There are coral reefs and rainforests and, best of all, an erupting volcano!

My dad's a park ranger at Hawaii Volcanoes National Park, on the "big island" of Hawaii. (See map.) A volcano named Kilauea (kill-uh-WAY-uh) has been erupting here for more than 20 years. Watching it erupt is really exciting. So when the volcano is putting on a show, my friend Heather and I grab our gear and hit the trail!

GO TO THE FLOW

Usually we go on a **lava** hike late in the day. That's because it's easier to see the glow of the lava as the sky starts to darken, especially from far away. By now we know the safety rules by heart: Hike with an adult, stay on the trails, wear sturdy shoes, carry a flashlight (so we can find our way home after dark), and *never* touch hot lava.

We rush to a volcano-viewing area that's been set up by the park rangers. Then we sit and watch for hours. We see fiery colors, from yellow to orange to cherry-red. The lava crackles and pops and forms weird, wrinkly shapes.

Getting close to an erupting volcano is like having front-row seats at the best fireworks show ever!

You can see a vent, or opening, in the side of Kilauea. That's where blobs of hot lava blast out from inside Earth. Golden rivers of lava then race down the side of the volcano and toward the coast.

When the hot lava reaches the cool ocean, huge clouds of steam **billow** hundreds of feet into the sky. And as the lava cools and hardens, it adds more solid rock to the edge of our ever-growing island.

VOLCANO-WATCHERS

When we aren't looking for lava, Heather and I go to the Volcano School of Arts and Sciences. Kids at our school get to help scientists working at Hawaii Volcanoes National Park and the Hawaiian Volcano Observatory.

One of the scientists is Christina Heliker. Once a week, she suits up for an important—and dangerous—job. Her work clothes are sturdy boots, a **fire-resistant** suit and hood, a gas mask, and two pairs of heavy gloves. One of her tools is the heavy head of a sledgehammer tied to a long steel cable. The challenge is to use it to snag a sample of super-hot lava.

Christina has to get as close as she safely can to Kilauea's vent. Then she lowers the hammer head into the flowing lava until a glob sticks to it. "You can't imagine the heat," she says. "The hammer and cable glow red."

Christina and the other scientists are trying to learn all they can about lava and volcanoes. That will help them find better ways to predict when dangerous volcanoes might erupt. And knowing that will allow people who live near those volcanoes more time to get safely away.

Above: **Christina Heliker, a scientist, goes "fishing" for lava samples. Special clothes protect her from the heat.**

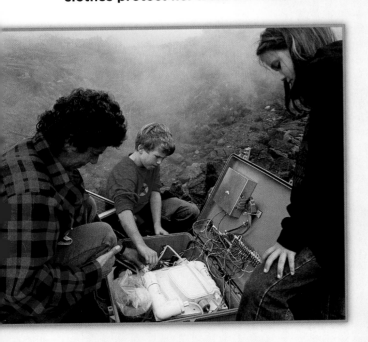

Left: **We're helping scientist Tamar Elias. She's collecting samples of gas from steam that's spewing from the volcano. (You can see clouds of steam in the background.) By learning more about the gas, she can learn more about how volcanoes erupt.**

A LIVING EARTH

It's great to know and help these scientists. Their research not only helps people—it also helps us learn how Earth works. And one thing's for sure: Here in Hawaii, we never forget that Earth is *alive!*

So, why not come visit us sometime? You won't want to miss Kilauea, one of the world's greatest and longest-running lava shows.

Connect and Compare

1. How do the map, photographs, and captions help you understand the information more thoroughly? **Graphic Aids**

2. If you visited Kilauea or another volcano, what would you do to stay safe? **Evaluate**

3. If the people of Pompeii had the same knowledge and tools to understand what causes volcanoes to erupt as modern-day scientists do, how might events have turned out differently in "The Dog of Pompeii"? Explain. **Reading/Writing Across Texts**

 Science Activity

Research volcanoes. Create a fact card for a volcano that interests you.

 Find out more about volcanoes at **www.macmillanmh.com**

Writer's Craft

Precise Words

Think about your audience, the people who will be reading your writing. Use **precise words** to convey your meaning. Make sure your words are appropriate for those readers.

Write an Explanation for Two Audiences

I used words that third-graders would understand.

Hello, Surtsey

(for a third-grade class)
by Tomás M.

Surtsey is an island near Iceland. This island is the newest one on Earth. It was formed in 1963 when a volcano erupted. The volcano sent up lava for two years, covering about one and a half square miles, until it finally stopped. The lava had made a new island. The island was named Surtsey for the Viking fire god called Surtur.

I used harder words for the high school students.

The Story of Surtsey

(for a high school class)

Below the island of Surtsey lies the Mid-Atlantic ridge. Here, two of Earth's plates–the North American and the Eurasian–touch. However, these plates are slowly pulling apart as magma oozes up between them to form volcanoes along the ridge. Such undersea volcanoes are called rift volcanoes.

It was a rift volcano that erupted and formed Surtsey in 1963. Red-hot lava poured from the new volcano, building up gradually over two years, to form the island.

Your Turn

Think of a short explanation of a natural phenomenon, such as a tornado or how a canyon is formed, that you can write for two different audiences. As you write, think about your audience and choose the best words for that audience. Vary your sentences by combining sentences using adjectives, adverbs, and prepositional phrases. Use the Writer's Checklist to check your writing.

Writer's Checklist

 Ideas and Content: Are my explanations clear for both audiences? Did I include all the important information?

 Organization: Do my explanations have a main idea and supporting details?

 Voice: Am I successful in communicating my interest in this topic?

 Word Choice: Did I use **precise words** that are appropriate for each audience?

 Sentence Fluency: Did I vary my sentence lengths? Did I combine sentences using adjectives, adverbs, and prepositional phrases?

Conventions: Did I use correct spelling and punctuation?

Test Strategy

On My Own
The answers for questions 4 and 5 are not in the selection. Form an opinion about what you read.

Portable Music:
Taking It with You

Turn It Down

In July of 1979, life for the music lover was about to change. Family sing-alongs would be no more. Never again would people have to hum their favorite song while waiting at the doctor's office. And all the kids who had ever heard "Turn that music down!" were about to get what they always wanted. They were going to be able to turn it up loud, really loud.

The portable tape player arrived on the music scene and changed the world. Music, and how people listened to it, was never the same.

The Music in Your Head

Before the birth of the portable tape player, people were stuck having to listen to whatever was playing. Everyone knows that feeling, the frustration of being trapped in a long line as the worst song you've ever heard blasts from a speaker in the ceiling. Most of us also know the feeling of being trapped when buckled into a friend's car but not allowed to touch the radio. Before it was portable, music was something that groups of people shared.

Go On ▶

Whole rooms were forced to listen to the same music. The radio or tape player was too big to carry from room to room.

As early as 1954, the American public got its first taste of radio freedom. The first transistor radio went on sale and allowed the buyer to take his or her music anywhere. That is, if the radio signal went uninterrupted. It was a start. There was even an earpiece for private listening. People got their first taste of listening to music on their own terms and they liked it. Change was a good thing!

An Amazing Accident

The event that changed portable music took place in 1979. The invention of the portable tape player became the foundation for the shift in how people listened.

There is a legend about how the first portable tape player was built. The story suggests that it was more the result of an accident than smart business sense. The president of a Japanese electronics company asked his designers to make him a small tape player to take with him on an airplane. He wanted to listen to a tape of classical music during the long flight overseas to America. It was a new, but simple, request. The designers at the company took one of their older devices, a tape player and recorder, and removed the record feature. They also took off the speaker. In its place they gave the player a plug for earphones. Sound simple? It was—so simple that it was strange no one had ever thought of it before.

However, things didn't quite work out as planned. Once the president of the company arrived in the United States, he called his designers. It turned out that the batteries in the tape player had died and the tape they had given him was blank. Not the best beginning for what would become one of the world's most popular inventions.

As soon as the rest of the company heard about this new product, they were already planning its release to the public. They perfected it and made sure the batteries were fresh and the tapes weren't blank. Within months of its release, the portable tape player became a cultural phenomenon. Music had been set free.

Answer Questions

Going Digital

The freedom of music depends on how it is played. If all music is put on analog tapes, then more tape players are needed. The same is true with vinyl records, eight-track tapes, and compact discs—they all depend on the machines that play them. Therefore, when the popularity of computers began to make the world a digital planet, portable music had to catch up.

In the 1980s and 1990s, compact discs proved that digital music was superior to old-fashioned tape recordings. Musicians and designers realized how good music sounded digitally and how easy it was to store. The clutter of old tapes could be eliminated because slimmer, better sounding CDs were taking over. What did you do with a box full of old tapes? Sell them at a garage sale or use them to prop up a couch with three legs? People didn't need them any more. Along with CDs themselves, portable CD players became the portable toys of choice.

MP3 computer files are the newest trend in music. They are individual songs or recordings that have been created for storage on a computer. These files can be played on special players called DAPs, or digital audio players. Now even the days of CDs seem numbered. In the old days, the size of a tape or CD actually mattered. Only a certain amount of information could fit onto a tape or CD, which limited how much music you could take along with you. MP3 files make it possible to have more music in less space because they exist only inside the memory of a computer chip. Computer chips are becoming smaller while the amount of memory is getting bigger. The choice of what to listen to has become almost endless.

What happens now? One small portable music player can hold thousands of MP3 songs in a machine the size of a credit card. Music freedom has exploded in a way that no one had ever dreamed possible. It's only a matter of time until a DAP is in the pocket of every music lover.

Go On ▶

Directions: Answer the questions.

1. **Which BEST describes the theme of this selection?**

   A   Change is a good thing in portable music.
   B   Music never changes.
   C   Portable tape players are outdated.
   D   Everyone should have an MP3 player.

2. **The invention of the portable tape player**

   A   was the well-thought-out idea of an engineer.
   B   made television popular.
   C   took over ten years.
   D   became the foundation in the shift in how people listened to music.

3. **What is the advantage of digital music?**

   A   It is louder.
   B   The earphone is built in.
   C   It has improved sound.
   D   It uses tape players.

4. **Now that we can take our music with us, we can play it anywhere at any time. Is this always a good thing? Explain your answer.**

5. **"Music is the universal language." What do you think this means? Explain your answer.**

Tip

Form an opinion.

Writing Prompt

Think about something you use to play or record music. Write directions explaining how to use the device. Write the steps in a clear order.

Glossary
What Is a Glossary?

A glossary can help you find the **meanings** of words in this book that you may not know. The words in the glossary are listed in **alphabetical order**. **Guide words** at the top of each page tell you the first and last words on the page.

Each word is divided into syllables. The way to pronounce the word is given next. You can understand the pronunciation respelling by using the **pronunciation key**. A shorter key appears at the bottom of every other page. When a word has more than one syllable, a dark accent mark (ˊ) shows which syllable is stressed. In some words, a light accent mark (ˋ) shows which syllable has a less heavy stress. Sometimes an entry includes a second meaning for the word.

Guide Words

First word on the page   Last word on the page

Sample Entry

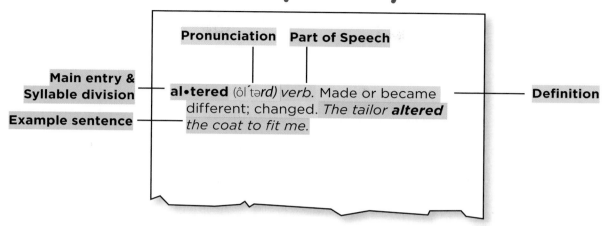

Pronunciation   Part of Speech

Main entry &
Syllable division

Definition

Example sentence

al•tered (ôl´tərd) *verb.* Made or became different; changed. *The tailor **altered** the coat to fit me.*

Pronunciation Key

Phonetic Spelling	Examples	Phonetic Spelling	Examples
a	at, bad, plaid, laugh	d	dear, soda, bad
ā	ape, pain, day, break	f	five, defend, leaf, off, cough, elephant
ä	father, calm		
âr	care, pair, bear, their, where	g	game, ago, fog, egg
e	end, pet, said, heaven, friend	h	hat, ahead
ē	equal, me, feet, team, piece, key	hw	white, whether, which
i	it, big, give, hymn	j	joke, enjoy, gem, page, edge
ī	ice, fine, lie, my	k	kite, bakery, seek, tack, cat
îr	ear, deer, here, pierce	l	lid, sailor, feel, ball, allow
o	odd, hot, watch	m	man, family, dream
ō	old, oat, toe, low	n	not, final, pan, knife, gnaw
ô	coffee, all, taught, law, fought	ng	long, singer
ôr	order, fork, horse, story, pour	p	pail, repair, soap, happy
oi	oil, toy	r	ride, parent, wear, more, marry
ou	out, now, bough	s	sit, aside, pets, cent, pass
u	up, mud, love, double	sh	shoe, washer, fish, mission, nation
ū	use, mule, cue, feud, few	t	tag, pretend, fat, dressed
ü	rule, true, food, fruit	th	thin, panther, both
u̇	put, wood, should, look	t͟h	these, mother, smooth
ûr	burn, hurry, term, bird, word, courage	v	very, favor, wave
		w	wet, weather, reward
ə	about, taken, pencil, lemon, circus	y	yes, onion
b	bat, above, job	z	zoo, lazy, jazz, rose, dogs, houses
ch	chin, such, match	zh	vision, treasure, seizure

Aa

a•brupt•ly (ə brupt′lē) *adverb.* Happening in a quick way or without warning. *Ben **abruptly** dropped the hot potato onto the floor.*

ab•sorb (ab sôrb′, ab zôrb′) *verb.* To soak up or take in. *Use a towel to **absorb** the spilled water.*

ac•ces•si•ble (ak ses′ə bəl) *adjective.* Able to be reached, entered, or approached. *Ramps make buildings **accessible** to those who cannot climb stairs.*

a•dept (ə dept′) *adjective.* Highly skilled, expert. *Bonnie is **adept** on the balance beam in gymnastics.*

ad•min•is•ter (ad min′ə stər) *verb.* To give or provide something. *The nurse will **administer** first aid.*

ad•verse (ad vûrs′, ad′vûrs) *adjective.* Not helpful to what is wanted; not favorable. *The football game was played under **adverse** conditions because of the heavy rain.*

aer•o•nau•tics (âr′ə nô′tiks) *noun.* The science or art of flight. *The pilots studied **aeronautics**.*

ag•o•nized (ag′ə nīzd′) *verb.* Experienced great discomfort, pain, or stress. *The owner **agonized** over money problems after he closed the store for the day.*

al•loy (al′oi) *noun.* A metal formed by fusing two or more metals, or a metal and another substance. *Brass is an **alloy** of copper and zinc.*

al•tered (ôl′tərd) *verb.* Made or became different; changed. *The tailor **altered** the coat to fit me.*

am•bi•tious (am bish′əs) *adjective.* Eager to succeed. *The **ambitious** assistant would work all weekend in hopes of becoming a manager someday.*

am•pu•tat•ed (am′pyə tā′tid) *verb.* Having had any limb or digit cut off by surgery. *After her arm was crushed in the car accident, it was **amputated**.*

an•a•lyz•ing (an′ə lī′zing) *verb.* Examining carefully and in detail in order to understand something. *By **analyzing** the soil sample, the scientist learned that the land was safe for a playground.*

a•nat•o•my (ə nat′ə mē) *noun.* The branch of science dealing with the structure of animals or plants and the relationships of their parts. *The teacher held classes in **anatomy**.*

a•non•y•mous (ə non′ə məs) *adjective.* Of unknown origin or authorship; without any name given. *All the donations were **anonymous**, so the hospital did not know whom to thank for all the money.*

Word History

Anonymous comes from the Greek word *anōnymos. Onyma* means "name," and the *a-* placed at the beginning means "without."

an•thro•pol•o•gists (an′thrə pol′ə gists) *noun, plural.* Students or experts in the science that deals with physical, cultural, and social development of humans. *Several **anthropologists** showed up at the construction site after the workers found the artifacts.*

an•tic•i•pat•ed (an tis′ə pā′tid) *verb.* Expected or looked forward to. *All day we **anticipated** getting our test scores from our teacher.*

an·tique (an tēk´) *adjective.* Of, belonging to, or in the style of long ago; dating from an early time period. *My grandmother had an antique dining room table that was worth a lot of money.*

anx·i·e·ty (ang zī´i tē) *noun.* A feeling of fearful uneasiness or worry about what may happen. *The family felt anxiety when no one could find the lost dog.*

ap·pa·rat·us (ap´ə rat´əs, ap´ə rā´təs) *noun.* A device or mechanism used for a particular purpose. *One of the apparatus in the gym required repairing.*

aq·ue·ducts (ak´wə dukts´) *noun, plural.* Large pipes or other channels that carry water over a long distance. *Aqueducts were built for easier access to the water supply through the village.*

ar·id (ar´id) *adjective.* Dry; lifeless. *After the long drought, the ground was arid.*

ar·ray (ə rā´) *noun.* A large collection or display. *The shop window offered a wide array of objects for the home.*

ar·ti·fi·cial (är´tə fish´əl) *adjective.* Produced by humans; made in imitation or as a substitute. *The artificial knee my uncle received worked as well as his natural one.*

as·pir·ing (ə spīr´ing) *verb.* Wanting or trying very hard to achieve some goal. *John is aspiring after fame and fortune.*

auc·tion (ôk´shən) *noun.* A public sale at which property or possessions are sold to the highest bidder. *My brother bid twenty dollars for some lamps at an auction.*

awe·some (ô´səm) *adjective.* Inspiring great wonder combined with fear or respect. *The Grand Canyon is an awesome sight.*

ax·is (ak´sis) *noun.* A real or imaginary straight line through the center of an object, around which the object turns. *Earth rotates on its axis once every twenty-four hours.*

Bb

ben·e·fit (ben´ə fit) *noun.* Something that helps or betters a person or thing. *We all knew the benefit of eating fresh green vegetables.*

be·wil·der·ing (bi wil´də ring) *verb.* Confusing or puzzling. *This math problem is bewildering to me.*

bi·ased sam·ple (bī´əst sam´pəl) *noun.* A group of subjects in a survey that does not represent the total group. *In order for Kim to get the results she wanted in her survey, she polled a biased sample.*

bil·low (bil´ō) *verb.* To rise in waves. *Watch the curtains billow in the breeze.*

bi·on·ics (bī on´iks) *noun.* The study of the parts of the bodies of humans and other animals in order to devise improvements in various machines, especially computers and artificial limbs. *Since I am so interested in sports and computers, I decided to study bionics at college.*

at; āpe; fär; câre; end; mē; it; īce; pîerce; hot; ōld; sông; fôrk; oil; out; up; ūse; rüle; pull; tûrn; chin; sing; shop; thin; this; hw in white; zh in treasure.

The symbol ə stands for the unstressed vowel sound in about, taken, pencil, lemon, and circus.

board (bôrd) *noun.* Meals provided regularly for pay or in exchange for services. *The student received room and **board** for a reasonable fee.*

bol•ster (bōl´stər) *verb.* To support or strengthen. *The sight of land can **bolster** a sailor's low spirits after many days at sea.*

broad•cast (brôd´kast´) *noun.* Information or entertainment that is sent out by radio or television. *We all listened to Rita's **broadcast** of the news and the weather.*

Cc

ca•lam•i•ties (kə lam´i tēz) *noun, plural.* Disasters causing great destruction and loss. *The relief agency helped people through many kinds of **calamities**.*

cal•cu•la•tions (kal´kyə lā´shənz) *noun, plural.* The products or results of a mathematical process. *By performing careful **calculations**, the astronomer was able to locate a new star.*

can•vass (kan´vəs) *verb.* To examine or discuss carefully or thoroughly. *I had to **canvass** my class to find out who the most popular person was.*

cas•cade (kas kād´) *noun.* A waterfall or series of small waterfalls; anything resembling this. *The clothes fell out of the suitcase in a **cascade** down the staircase.*

ce•ram•ics (sə ram´iks) *noun.* The art or technique of making objects by shaping clay and then baking it at a high temperature. *Connie displayed beautiful **ceramics** throughout her home.*

Word History

The word **ceramics** comes from the Greek *keramikos*, which stems from *keramos* meaning "potter's clay" or "pottery."

cha•me•leon (kə mēl´yən) *noun.* Any of various small, slow-moving lizards that can change the color of their skin to match their surroundings. Also used in reference to a person who is very changeable. *Since he tended to look different every time we saw him, we called him a **chameleon.***

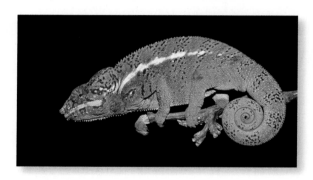

char•is•mat•ic (kar´iz mat´ik) *adjective.* Having the rare personal quality of attracting the loyalty and devotion of a large following of people. *People are drawn to **charismatic** politicians.*

chro•nol•o•gy (krə nol´ə jē) *noun.* The arrangement of events in the order in which they happened. *In class the teacher showed us the **chronology** of events that led to the War of Independence.*

civ•i•lized (siv´ə līzd´) *adjective.* No longer savage or primitive; educated. *He was a very **civilized** young man and had excellent manners.*

clock•wise (klok´wīz´) *adverb.* Going in the direction that the hands of a clock move. *The popular new dance involved spinning around* **clockwise** *several times.*

co•in•ci•den•ces (kō in´si dən ses) *noun, plural.* Remarkable occurrences of events or circumstances at the same time and apparently by chance. *A series of* **coincidences** *led me to meet my group of friends in the museum.*

col•lec•tive (kə lek´tiv) *adjective.* Of, relating to, or done by a group of persons or things; united. *The book was written by a* **collective** *effort; all the writers added something.*

com•mis•sioned (kə mish´ənd) *verb.* Being assigned to create a work of art. *My art teacher was* **commissioned** *to paint a huge mural at the new hotel.*

com•mit•ment (kə mit´mənt) *noun.* The act of devoting oneself; an obligation. *Since joining the drama club was a huge time* **commitment**, *I had to think twice before signing up.*

con•cen•trat•ed (kon´sən trā´tid) *verb.* Close together in one place. *The population of our country is* **concentrated** *in the cities.*

con•quis•ta•do•res (kon kēs´tə dôr´ēz) *noun, plural.* The Spanish conquerors in Mexico and Peru during the sixteenth century. *In history class we are learning about Hernando Cortés and the* **conquistadores** *who conquered the Aztec Empire.*

con•scious (kon´shəs) *adjective.* **1.** Knowing or realizing; aware. *Linda was* **conscious** *of her own tendency to exaggerate.* **2.** Awake. *Despite the blow to his head, Al remained* **conscious**.

con•serve (kən sûrv´) *verb.* To preserve. **Conserve** *your strength.*

con•tin•u•ous (kən tin´ū əs) *adjective.* Unbroken or without a break. *The* **continuous** *screaming of the baby ruined our lunch at the restaurant.*

con•vic•tions (kən vik´shənz) *noun, plural.* Firm beliefs or opinions. *Many people voted for the politician because of his deep* **convictions**.

Dd

da•ta (dā´tə, dat´ə) *noun, plural.* Information from which conclusions can be drawn; facts and figures. *The* **data** *from the reports must be accurate.*

de•but (dā bū´, dā´bū) *noun.* A first public appearance. *It was difficult to get tickets to the* **debut** *of the movie because of the great advance reviews it received.*

dec•ades (dek´ādz) *noun, plural.* Periods of ten years. *At my grandmother's party, she told stories that spanned the eight* **decades** *of her life.*

Word History

The word **decade** comes from the Greek word, *deka*, which means "ten."

de•crease (di krēs´) *verb.* To lessen or reduce. *Our class made a list of ways to* **decrease** *pollution in our state.*

de•fi•ance (di fī´əns) *noun.* Bold or open resistance to authority or opposition. *The general was getting very angry at the strong* **defiance** *of the small number of enemy troops.*

at; **ā**pe; **fä**r; **câ**re; **e**nd; **mē**; **i**t; **ī**ce; **pî**erce; **ho**t; **ō**ld; **sô**ng; **fô**rk; **oi**l; **ou**t; **u**p; **ū**se; **rū**le; **pu**ll; **tû**rn; **ch**in; si**ng**; **sh**op; **th**in; **th**is; **hw** in **wh**ite; **zh** in trea**s**ure.

The symbol **ə** stands for the unstressed vowel sound in **a**bout, tak**e**n, penc**i**l, lem**o**n, and circ**u**s.

deft•ly (deft´lē) *adverb.* In a skillful or nimble way. *The dancer* **deftly** *performed her moves across the stage.*

de•hy•drat•ed (dē hī´drā tid) *adjective.* To have had water or moisture removed. *The marathon runner was* **dehydrated** *after the race because she sweated so much.*

de•ject•ed•ly (di jek´tid lē) *adverb.* Showing disheartened, downcast, or low spirits. *I* **dejectedly** *kicked the ball against the wall after we lost the soccer game.*

dem•on•stra•tion (dem´ən strā´shən) *noun.* Something that proves clearly; an explaining or showing by the use of visible examples. *It's a thrill when scientists prove a new theory in a* **demonstration.**

de•ri•sion (di rizh´ən) *noun.* Scornful contempt; ridicule; mockery. *The bully treated all the class with* **derision.**

de•scend•ing (di sen´ding) *verb.* Moving or coming from a higher place to a lower one. *They were* **descending** *the mountain on skis.*

de•spon•dent•ly (di spon´dənt lē) *adverb.* In a way that shows having lost heart; in a depressed or dejected way. *As the team lost more points, they walked* **despondently** *along the sidelines.*

des•ti•na•tion (des´tə nā´shən) *noun.* A place to which a person or thing is going. *The train conductor asked us what our* **destination** *was when we boarded the train.*

de•te•ri•o•rat•ed (di tîr´ē ə rā´tid) *verb.* Lessened in character, quality, condition, or value; worsened. *The newspaper* **deteriorated** *rapidly in the rain.*

dev•as•tat•ing (dev´ə stā´ting) *adjective.* Wreaking or capable of wreaking complete destruction; ruinously destructive. *The hurricane proved to be* **devastating;** *it completely destroyed 1000 houses.*

di•lap•i•dat•ed (di lap´i dā´tid) *adjective.* Fallen into ruin or decay. *Everyone on our street decided to help paint the* **dilapidated** *old house on the corner.*

drow•sy (drou´zē) *adjective.* Feeling sleepy. *The guard was* **drowsy** *after working extra shifts every day of the week.*

dwell•ing (dwel´ing) *noun.* A place where a person lives. *While walking along the beach, the children found an old* **dwelling** *made of wood and canvas.*

Ee

eaves (ēvz) *noun, plural.* The overhanging edge or edges of a sloping roof. *The new window was placed upstairs under the* **eaves.**

e•con•o•mists (i kon´ə mists) *noun, plural.* Students of or experts in economics or money matters. *Many* **economists** *predicted that sales during the holiday season would be low.*

edg•y (ej´ē) *adjective.* Very nervous or impatient. *Sam felt* **edgy** *when he was called down to the principal's office.*

e•lab•o•rate (*adjective,* i lab´ər it; *verb,* i lab´ə rāt´) *adjective.* Worked out with great care and great detail. *The committee spent one year planning the* **elaborate** *ceremony.* —*verb.* To give additional or fuller treatment to something spoken or written. *I was too tired to* **elaborate** *on the events of the trip, so I just gave a basic account of it.*

em•barked (em bärkt´) *verb.* To begin or set out, as on an adventure. *The vacationers* **embarked** *on a two-week cruise in the Caribbean.*

em•bar•rass•ment (em bar´əs mənt) *noun.* The act or state of feeling uncomfortable or ashamed. *Aunt Tillie's crass behavior at the dinner party was an* **embarrassment** *to the whole family.*

em•bed•ded (em be´did) *verb.* To set in surrounding matter; to place or plant firmly. *The seeds were deeply* **embedded** *in the soil.*

em•ploy•ee (em ploi´ē) *noun.* A person who works for a person or business for pay. *A good* **employee** *is one who always does his or her best on the job.*

en•coun•ter (en koun´tər) *noun.* Any kind of meeting between friends, enemies, or colleagues. *My grandfather told me about the violent* **encounter** *when he was wounded in the war.*

en•gulf (en gulf´) *verb.* To swallow up or completely surround. *The flames may* **engulf** *the whole hillside unless we put the fire out soon.*

en•thralled (en thrôld´) *verb.* Held spellbound; charmed. *The crowd was* **enthralled** *by the magician and his bag of magic tricks.*

en•vi•sioned (en vizh´ənd) *verb.* Formed a picture in the mind. *The principal* **envisioned** *a big, new gym for his school.*

ep•i•dem•ic (ep´i dem´ik) *noun.* **1.** The rapid spread of a disease among people at the same time. *The elementary school experienced an* **epidemic** *of chicken pox last winter.* **2.** The rapid spread or sudden, widespread appearance of anything. *An* **epidemic** *of burglaries hit our town.*

e•qua•tor (i kwā´tər) *noun.* An imaginary line around Earth halfway between the North and South poles. *The United States and Canada are north of the* **equator**.

e•rode (i rōd´) *verb.* To wear or wash away slowly. *Ocean waves will* **erode** *the shore.*

es•cort (es´kôrt) *noun.* A person or persons who go along with another as a courtesy or for protection. *Cinderella's stepsisters wanted the prince to be their* **escort** *to the ball.*

es•tab•lished (e stab´lisht) *verb.* Set up permanently. *The restaurant where we ate lunch was* **established** *in 1897!*

es•ti•mate (*verb*, es´tə māt´; *noun*, es´tə mit) *verb.* To come to a conclusion by reasoning or an educated guess. *We* **estimate** *that the trip will take an hour, but it might take longer if there is heavy traffic.* —*noun.* An approximate judgment or calculation. *The painters gave me an* **estimate** *of what the job would cost.*

e•vac•u•ate (i vak´ū āt´) *verb.* To leave or cause to leave. *Firefighters must* **evacuate** *the people from the burning building.*

ev•i•dent (ev´i dənt) *adjective.* Easily seen or understood. *It was* **evident** *to everyone that the thief had stolen the money.*

---

at; āpe; fär; câre; end; mē; it; īce; pîerce; hot; ōld; sông; fôrk; oil; out; up; ūse; rüle; pull; tûrn; chin; sing; shop; thin; **th**is; hw in white; zh in treasure.

The symbol ə stands for the unstressed vowel sound in about, taken, pencil, lemon, and circus.

ex•ca•vate (eks´kə vāt´) *verb.* To uncover by digging. *The miners work to* **excavate** *coal.*

ex•cel (ek sel´) *verb.* To do very well; to succeed. *The teacher told us that it takes a lot of studying to* **excel** *in our classes.*

ex•cep•tion•al (ek sep´shə nəl) *adjective.* Unusual or out of the ordinary. *I liked the* **exceptional** *architecture of the building.*

ex•trav•a•gant (ek strav´ə gənt) *adjective.* Lavish or wasteful in the spending of money. *Mary made many* **extravagant** *purchases that she really could not afford.*

Ff

fam•ine (fam´in) *noun.* A great lack of food in an area or country. *The* **famine** *affected nearly all the people in the village.*

feat (fēt) *noun.* An act or deed that shows great courage, strength, or skill. *Climbing that mountain was quite a* **feat***.*

fidg•et (fij´it) *verb.* To be nervous or make restless movements. *The girl tried not to* **fidget** *in the long line.*

fire-re•sist•ant (fīr ri zis´tənt) *adjective.* Being constructed specifically against getting set on fire at a certain temperature and certain amount of time. *The* **fire-resistant** *outfit worked well.*

fleet•ing (flē´ting) *adjective.* Passing very quickly. *We only had a* **fleeting** *look at the famous actress as she hurried into the theater.*

flour•ish (flûr´ish) *verb.* To grow or develop strongly or prosperously; thrive. *In order for a child to grow and* **flourish***, he or she must eat nutritious food and get lots of rest and exercise.*

fore•man (fôr´mən) *noun.* A worker who supervises a group of workers, as in a factory or on a farm. *The* **foreman** *was in charge of seeing that the cars came off the assembly line on time.*

fore•told (fôr tōld´) *verb.* Told of ahead of time. *The game played out just as my coach* **foretold***: we won the championship!*

for•mal•ly (fôr´mə lē) *adverb.* Acting with stiff, proper, or polite behavior. *The governor* **formally** *welcomed the guests to the party.*

for•ma•tions (fôr mā´shəns) *noun, plural.* Something that is formed. *The tourists took a boat to see the strange rock* **formations** *in the lake.*

ful•fill (fùl fil´) *verb.* To carry out or bring to completion; cause to happen. *Miguel was able to* **fulfill** *his promise as a musician by mastering the piano.*

fur•rowed (fûr´ōd) *adjective.* Having deep wrinkles. *Whenever I asked for money, my dad's brow looked* **furrowed***.*

Word History

The word **furrow** comes from the Old English *furh* which is "a channel made by a plow."

Gg

gen•er•ate (jen´ə rāt´) *verb.* To bring about or produce. *That machine will* **generate** *electricity.*

gen•er•os•i•ty (jen′ə ros′i tē) *noun.* Willingness to give or share freely. *We thanked the community for its **generosity** and helpfulness during the crisis.*

glee•ful•ly (glē′fə lē) *adverb.* In a joyous or merry way. *The children **gleefully** ran toward the ice-cream truck.*

glid•er (glī′dər) *noun.* An aircraft that flies without a motor and rides on currents of air. *We entered a contest to see who could build a model **glider** that could fly the farthest.*

gloat•ed (glō′tid) *verb.* Thought about with satisfaction or, sometimes, mean-spirited pleasure. *The town **gloated** over its team's victory in the state tournament.*

glum•ly (glum′lē) *adverb.* To act in a sad or depressed manner. *Vincent **glumly** walked home after he got his bad report card.*

gri•maced (grim′əst) *verb.* To twist the face to show disgust, pain, or displeasure. *The carpenter **grimaced** when he stepped on a nail.*

grit•ted (gri′tid) *verb.* Ground or held tightly clamped together, as with the teeth. *The weightlifter **gritted** her teeth as she lifted 300 pounds.*

grouch•y (grou′chē) *adjective.* In a bad mood; irritable; sulky. *Working with **grouchy** people is no fun at all.*

guid•ance (gī′dəns) *noun.* The act or process of guiding; giving direction or leading. *Before embarking on a law career, Maria sought **guidance** from lawyers she had met.*

guilds (gildz) *noun, plural.* In the Middle Ages, a group of merchants or artisans in one trade or craft, organized to maintain standards of work and to protect the interests of members. *Representatives from all the **guilds** went to a meeting to discuss work conditions.*

Hh

ham•per[1] (ham′pər) *verb.* To interfere or slow the action or progress of something. *The rain did not **hamper** people from enjoying themselves at the outdoor concert.*

ham•per[2] (ham′pər) *noun.* A large basket or container, usually with a cover. *After getting caught in the rain, I threw my wet clothes in the laundry **hamper**.*

hob•bled (hob′əld) *verb.* Moved or walked awkwardly with a limp. *After he sprained his ankle, Brad **hobbled** around for three weeks.*

hon•or•a•ble (on′ər ə bəl) *adjective.* Characterized by or having a sense of what is right or moral. *The young girl was considered very **honorable** when she returned the wallet she found.*

hov•er•ing (huv′ə ring) *verb.* Remaining in the same spot for a period of time. *The bees were **hovering** above the chocolate cake at our picnic.*

---

at; āpe; fär; câre; end; mē; it; īce; pîerce; hot; ōld; sông; fôrk; oil; out; up; ūse; rüle; pull; tûrn; chin; sing; shop; thin; this; hw in white; zh in treasure.

The symbol ə stands for the unstressed vowel sound in about, taken, pencil, lemon, and circus.

Ii

il·le·gal·ly (i lē′gə lē) *adverb.* Acting in an unlawful manner. *The police officer wrote tickets for all the cars that were parked* **illegally***.*

im·mense (i mens′) *adjective.* Very large or huge. *The crowd at the outdoor concert left an* **immense** *amount of garbage on the ground.*

im·mi·grat·ed (im′i grā′tid) *verb.* Entered a country or region in which one was not born in order to make a permanent home there. *Saskia's parents* **immigrated** *here from Russia about fifteen years ago.*

in·no·va·tions (in′ə vā′shənz) *noun, plural.* Things or ideas that are of value and newly introduced. *The development of the first antibiotic was one of the great* **innovations** *in medicine.*

in·scribed (in skrībd′) *verb.* Written, carved, engraved, or marked on something. *The stone walls were* **inscribed** *with the names of people who had given money to the museum.*

in·stinc·tive·ly (in stingk′tiv lē) *adverb.* Of or relating to a natural tendency. *Birds* **instinctively** *feed their young in the nest.*

in·tact (in takt′) *adjective.* Not damaged and in one whole piece. *The flower vase was still* **intact** *after it was found in the bottom of the box.*

in·ter·cept (in′tər sept′) *verb.* To stop on the way; to stop the course or progress of. *The defensive back managed to* **intercept** *the quarterback's pass.*

Word History

Intercept comes from the Latin, *interceptus*, which is the past participle of *intercipere*, meaning "interrupt" or "to catch between."

in·te·ri·or (in tîr′ē ər) *noun.* The inside of something. *The* **interior** *of the building was very cool compared to the heat outside.*

in·ter·pret·er (in tûr′pri tər) *noun.* One who helps to make something clear or understandable. *The* **interpreter** *at the United Nations translated English into Swahili.*

in·ter·sec·tion (in′tər sek′shən, in′tər sek′shən) *noun.* A place of intersecting, especially where two or more roads or streets meet or cross. *We stopped our car at the* **intersection** *of 70th Street and Second Avenue.*

Ll

la·ment·ed (lə men′təd) *verb.* Expressed sorrow, grief, or regret. *We all* **lamented** *the loss of the best player on the team to a knee injury.*

la·va (lä′və, lav′ə) *noun.* Very hot, melted rock that comes out of an erupting volcano. *The* **lava** *destroyed everything in its path as it flowed out of the volcano.*

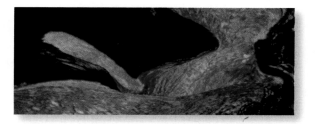

leg•a•cy (legʹə sē) *noun.* Something handed down by custom or tradition. *The mansion was passed down to my uncle by a **legacy** specifying that he never modernize it.*

lim•ou•sine (limʹə zēnʹ) *noun.* A large sedan, often with a glass partition between the front and back seats, often driven by a chauffeur. *When the **limousine** pulled up, a crowd gathered to see the movie star.*

lounge (lounj) *verb.* To lean, sit, or lie lazily. *During the summer, I love to **lounge** around the pool and read magazines.* —*noun.* **1.** A place for sitting, waiting, or relaxing within a public setting. *In the Victorian era, there was a ladies' and a gentlemen's **lounge** at the railway station.* **2.** A couch or sofa. *I sat on a comfortable **lounge**.*

lures (lu̇rz) *noun, plural.* Artificial bait used in fishing. *The **lures** were in the tackle box.*

lux•u•ry (lukʹshə rē, lugʹzhə rē) *noun.* Something that adds to a person's comfort or pleasure but is not really necessary. *A yacht is a **luxury** that most of us cannot afford.*

Mm

maize (māz) *noun.* A grain that grows on the ears of a tall plant. ***Maize** is usually called corn.*

Word History

Maize comes from the Spanish word *maíz* which means "Indian corn" and originates from the native South American Taino tribe's word *mahiz*.

ma•neu•vered (mə nüʹvərd) *verb.* Used skillful or clever moves or plans. *Jackson **maneuvered** the large boat skillfully past the smaller ones.*

man•u•scripts (manʹyə skriptsʹ) *noun, plural.* The handwritten versions of books, articles, or other works, especially ones from before the invention of printing presses. *The editor spent the weekend reading the **manuscripts** available in the museum's library.*

mar•veled (märʹvəld) *verb.* To become filled with wonder or astonishment. *The class **marveled** at Henry's ability to answer math problems so quickly and accurately.*

ma•tu•ri•ty (mə chu̇rʹi tē) *noun.* The state or quality of reaching full physical and mental development, or full growth. *The crops are ready to be harvested when they have reached **maturity**.*

me•di•e•val (mēʹdē ēʹvəl, mid ēʹvəl) *adjective.* Belonging to or happening in the Middle Ages, the period of European history from about the fifth century to the middle of the fifteenth century. *James came to class in a **medieval** costume to present his report on tenth-century Europe.*

---

at; āpe; fär; câre; end; mē; it; īce; pîerce; hot; ōld; sông; fôrk; oil; out; up; ūse; rüle; pu̇ll; tûrn; chin; sing; shop; thin; this; hw in white; zh in treasure.

The symbol ə stands for the unstressed vowel sound in about, taken, pencil, lemon, and circus.

mem•o•ra•bil•i•a (mem´ər ə bil´ē ə) *noun, plural.* Things that are worth being collected or recorded. *At the flea market there was a lot of* **memorabilia**.

mi•grant (mī´grənt) *adjective.* Moving from one region to another in search of work. *The* **migrant** *worker returned every April.*

mim•ics (mim´iks) *verb.* To imitate the speech, manners, or gestures of; to copy closely or reproduce. *The way Lucy* **mimics** *Harpo Marx is a classic bit of comedy.*

min•i•a•ture (min´ē ə chər) *adjective.* Greatly reduced in size or very small. *On their vacation, my parents bought me a* **miniature** *model of the Eiffel Tower.*

mis•treat•ed (mis trē´tid) *verb.* To be treated badly. *The veterinarian said the dog we found had been* **mistreated** *by its owner.*

mit•i•gate (mit´i gāt´) *verb.* To make milder or less severe or painful. *The nurse tried to* **mitigate** *the suffering of the patient.*

mod•er•ate (*adjective,* mod´ər it; *verb,* mod´ə rāt) *adjective.* Not extreme; balanced. *We have had* **moderate** *temperatures this winter.* —*verb.* To preside over or at. *My class wanted me to* **moderate** *the middle school debate, but I was too shy.*

mo•men•tum (mō men´təm) *noun.* The force or speed resulting from motion. *I was gaining* **momentum** *as I rode down the hill.*

muf•flers (muf´lərz) *noun, plural.* Scarves of wool or other material worn around the neck for warmth. *The children were dressed in hats, coats, and* **mufflers** *so they could play in the snow.*

myth•o•log•i•cal (mith´ə loj´i kəl) *adjective.* Of, relating to, or found in mythology. *The* **mythological** *character of Zeus was the ruler of all the gods on Mount Olympus.*

Nn

non•re•new•a•ble (non´ri nü´ə bəl, non´ri nū´ə bəl) *adjective.* Easily used up or exhausted. *Coal and petroleum are* **nonrenewable** *natural resources.*

nour•ish•ing (nûr´ə shing) *adjective.* Promoting health and growth. *So that I could grow up to be healthy and strong, my mother made me eat many* **nourishing** *foods.*

nui•sance (nü´səns, nū´səns) *noun.* A person, thing, or action that annoys or offends. *The bees were a huge* **nuisance** *during the picnic.*

Oo

ob•sta•cles (ob´stə kəlz) *noun, plural.* Persons or things that get in the way of or block progress. *After the big storm, there were many* **obstacles** *in the road that blocked traffic.*

op•pres•sion (ə presh´ən) *noun.* The act of controlling or governing by cruel and unfair use of force. *The citizens protested against the* **oppression** *of their strict leader.*

or•deals (ôr dēlz´) *noun, plural.* Very difficult tests or painful experiences. *Auditioning for the two ballet companies made for exhausting* **ordeals***.*

or•i•gin (ôr´i jin, or´i jin) *noun.* **1.** The source from which something begins. *What is the* **origin** *of that folk song?* **2.** Parentage; ancestry. *Settlers of European* **origin** *arrived in Plymouth, Massachusetts, in 1620.*

out·skirts (outʹskûrtsʹ) *noun, plural.* The regions or sections surrounding or at the edge of an area, as in a city. *On the* **outskirts** *of the town we discovered beautiful woodland.*

Pp

par·tic·i·pate (pär tisʹə pātʹ) *verb.* To take part in an activity with others. *My teacher asked me to* **participate** *in the class discussion about NATO.*

pa·thet·ic (pə thetʹik) *adjective.* Bringing about pity, sadness, or sympathy. *The lost puppy looked so* **pathetic**, *we brought him home.*

ped·es·tri·ans (pə desʹtrē ənz) *noun, plural.* Persons who travel on foot; walkers. *At busy intersections,* **pedestrians** *must cross only when the light stops traffic.*

Word History

The word **pedestrians** stems from the Latin word *pedester* that originally comes from the Latin *pes,* meaning "foot."

pen·nant (penʹənt) *noun.* A long, often triangular flag, used especially for school or team identification. *Each fan carried a* **pennant** *saying, "Go Panthers!"*

pen·ni·less (penʹē lis) *adjective.* Very poor or having no money. *The man was* **penniless** *after the fire destroyed his business.*

pe·ri·od·ic (pîrʹē odʹik) *adjective.* Happening at regular times. *There was a rainbow in the sky between the* **periodic** *showers.*

pe·riph·er·al (pə rifʹər əl) *adjective.* Relating to, located at, or forming the outermost part or edge. *Even though Ivan was facing the window, he saw in his* **peripheral** *vision that Karen had come in the door.*

per·sist·ent (pər sisʹtənt) *adjective.* Continuing firmly and steadily in spite of opposition or difficulty. *The* **persistent** *fan finally got his favorite actor's autograph after trying for two months.*

per·suade (pər swādʹ) *verb.* To cause someone to believe or do something by pleading or arguing. *The manager tried to* **persuade** *her employees to work extra hours during the holidays.*

phase (fāz) *noun.* A stage of development of a person or thing. *On the third* **phase** *of the journey, we traveled by sea.*

phi·los·o·pher (fə losʹə fər) *noun.* An expert in or student of the purpose of humanity, the universe, and life itself. *Many people showed up to listen to the* **philosopher** *speak on the human condition.*

at; āpe; fär; câre; end; mē; it; īce; pîerce; hot; ōld; sông; fôrk; oil; out; up; ūse; rüle; pùll; tûrn; chin; sing; shop; thin; **th**is; hw in white; zh in treasure.

The symbol ə stands for the unstressed vowel sound in about, taken, pencil, lemon, and circus.

plight (plīt) *noun.* A bad situation or condition. *The drought created a terrible* **plight** *for farmers.*

pon•der•ing (pon´də ring) *noun.* The act of thinking something through. *Before deciding which summer camp to attend, Lisa spent a week of* **pondering***.*

pores (pôrz) *noun, plural.* Very small openings. *The* **pores** *in the fabric occur naturally.*

port•a•ble (pôr´tə bəl) *adjective.* Able to be moved easily or carried by hand. *The manager brought a* **portable** *television to the store so he could watch the baseball game while he worked.*

post•marked (pōst´märkt´) *verb.* Stamped with an official mark to cancel the postage stamp, showing the date and place of mailing. *The tax return must be* **postmarked** *no later than midnight on April 15.*

pre•car•i•ous (pri kâr´ē əs) *adjective.* Dependent on chance or circumstance; dangerous. *The climber was in a* **precarious** *position on the cliff.*

pre•cede (pri sēd´) *verb.* To go or come before or ahead of. *The bridesmaids* **precede** *the bride down the aisle.*

pref•er•enc•es (pref´ər əns əz) *noun, plural.* That which is preferred, liked better. *My* **preferences** *didn't seem to count when my family opted to go to the seashore rather than the mountains.*

pre•sum•a•bly (pri zü´mə blē) *adverb.* Likely, probably, or taken for granted. *Many students* **presumably** *stayed home when they saw all the snow this morning.*

pre•vail (pri vāl´) *verb.* **1.** To be greater in power or influence; triumph or succeed. *We must try to* **prevail** *over everyday obstacles.* **2.** To be widespread; persist. *Colds still* **prevail** *in our school during the winter.*

priv•i•leged (priv´ə lijd) *adjective.* A special person, group, or class enjoying or possessing special rights, advantages, or benefits. *Several of Maria's* **privileged** *classmates were invited to a special dinner by the mayor.*

pro•ce•dure (prə sē´jər) *noun.* A particular course of action, especially one that follows a definite series of steps. *The children followed the correct* **procedure** *during the fire drill.*

pro•hib•it (prō hib´it) *verb.* To forbid or prevent. *We need to* **prohibit** *smoking on the bus.*

pro•long (prə lông´) *verb.* To make longer, especially in time. *The host was happy to* **prolong** *the dinner, since the guests were having such a good time.*

prom•e•nade (prom´ə nād´, prom´ ə näd´) *noun.* A leisurely walk, especially one taken in a public place for pleasure or display. *The ladies made their evening* **promenade** *to show off their finery.*

prom•i•nent (prom´ə nənt) *adjective.* Well-known or important; very noticeable. *Mr. Rodriguez and Mr. Johnson are* **prominent** *community leaders.*

pro•pelled (prə peld´) *verb.* Caused to move forward or onward; kept in motion. *The engine blast* **propelled** *the rocket into space.*

pro•por•tion (prə pôr´shən) *noun.* The relation of one thing to another with respect to size, number, degree or amount. *The number of seats in the gym was not in* **proportion** *to the number of students who arrived.*

pros•pered (pros´pərd) *verb.* Having had success, wealth, or good fortune. *The owners of the business finally **prospered** after years of hard work.*

Qq

quar•an•tine (kwôr´ən tēn´, kwor´ən tēn´) *noun.* The isolation of persons, animals, ships, or goods exposed to infectious disease, to prevent the spread of the disease. *The doctors placed the family under **quarantine** when influenza broke out.*

quick•ened (kwik´ənd) *verb.* To move more rapidly. *Sally **quickened** her pace so she wouldn't miss her bus.*

qui•pu (kē´pü) *noun.* A device consisting of a cord with knotted strings of various colors attached, used by the ancient Peruvians for recording events, keeping accounts, etc. *Our teacher brought in a **quipu** today to show us how ancient Peruvians kept track of their accounts.*

Rr

raft•ers (raf´tərz) *noun, plural.* The sloping beams that support a roof. *Termites caused a lot of damage to the **rafters** in our house.*

ran•chos (ranch´ōs) *noun, plural.* The Spanish term for ranches. *The **ranchos** of Old California were known for their fertile land.*

ran•dom sam•ple (ran´dəm sam´pəl) *noun.* In statistics, a sampling technique where a group of subjects (sample) is selected by chance from a larger group (population) for study. Every possible sample that could be selected has the same probability of being selected. *We conducted a survey on Americans' opinions about recycling, so we used a **random sample** of men and women from the ages of 18 to 85.*

rav•aged (rav´ijd) *verb.* Laid waste to, destroyed. *The flooding caused by the heavy rains **ravaged** the town.*

rec•om•mend (rek´ə mend´) *verb.* To suggest or advise favorably. *I would **recommend** pizza if you go to that restaurant.*

reg•u•late (reg´yə lāt´) *verb.* To control, manage, or set. *The mayor wanted to **regulate** the amount of traffic on some streets.*

reg•u•la•tion (reg´yə lā´shən) *adjective.* Required by law or rule. *The teacher issued **regulation** PE uniforms to the students.* —*noun.* A rule or order prescribed by authority. *There was a **regulation** dealing with excessive lateness at the elite prep school.*

rem•e•dies (rem´i dēz) *noun, plural.* Things that relieve, heal, or improve a disease, disorder, or other ailment. *The village doctor had many jars of **remedies**.*

re•mote (ri mōt´) *adjective.* Located out of the way, secluded. *It was a **remote** part of the mountains where few ever go.*

Ren•ais•sance (ren´ə säns´) *noun.* A revival of art, intellectual, and scientific learning that took place in Europe from the fourteenth through the sixteenth centuries. *This weekend I need to finish my paper on the Italian **Renaissance**.*

at; āpe; fär; câre; end; mē; it; īce; pîerce; hot; ōld; sông; fôrk; oil; out; up; ūse; rüle; pull; tûrn; chin; sing; shop; thin; <u>th</u>is; hw in white; zh in treasure.

The symbol ə stands for the unstressed vowel sound in about, taken, pencil, lemon, and circus.

ren·dez·vous (rän′də vü′) *adjective.* Of or relating to an appointment to meet at a fixed place or time; the place chosen for such a meeting. *The **rendezvous** point for the members of the sewing club was set for the local café.*

Word History

Rendezvous comes directly from the French *rendezvous* which also means "appointment" or "place of meeting."

re·new·a·ble (ri nü′ə bəl) *adjective.* Able to be replaced or restored. *The lease to the apartment was **renewable** after three years.*

rep·re·sent·a·tive sam·ple (rep′ri zen′tə tiv sam′pəl) *noun.* In statistics, when the group sampled represents a typical example or specimen. *Our survey was about school activities, so we chose a **representative sample** from all grades.*

rep·u·ta·tion (rep′yə tā′shən) *noun.* The public's opinion or reception of something or someone. *The scholar's **reputation** was ruined when he was caught cheating.*

re·sem·blance (ri zem′bləns) *noun.* A similarity, as of physical appearance; likeness. *There is often a close physical **resemblance** among members of the same family.*

res·o·nat·ed (rez′ə nā′tid) *verb.* Exhibited or produced fullness and richness of sound. *The actor's voice **resonated** throughout the large theater.*

re·vived (ri vīvd′) *verb.* Gave new strength or freshness. *It was so humid that I felt **revived** when I drank the glass of iced-tea.*

rev·o·lu·tion (rev′ə lü′shən) *noun.* In astronomy, the turning of a celestial body on its axis. *Earth makes one complete **revolution** every 24 hours.*

ric·o·chet·ing (rik′ə shā′ing, rik′ə shā′ing) *verb.* Bouncing of an object off the surface that it strikes at an angle. *The hail stones were **ricocheting** off cars during the storm.*

rum·maged (rum′ijd) *verb.* Having searched through (something) thoroughly by moving about its contents. *We **rummaged** around the attic until we found Grandma's old toys.*

rup·tured (rup′chərd) *verb.* To break open or apart. *The pipe **ruptured** in the basement and caused a flood that ruined the carpet.*

Ss

sat·el·lites (sat′ə līts′) *noun, plural.* **1.** In astronomy, celestial bodies that revolve around planets; moons. *Jupiter has many **satellites**.* **2.** Persons or things that depend on, accompany, or serve someone or something else. *The king's **satellites** were so numerous that they had to have separate lodgings.*

scribes (skrībz) *noun.* Before the invention of the printing press, the people whose profession was writing down or copying letters, manuscripts, contracts, or other documents. *The **scribes** spent several months copying the Athenian bylaws.*

scroung·ing (skroun′jing) *verb.* Gathering or collecting with effort or difficulty. *After school, I found my brother **scrounging** around the cupboards for something to eat.*

se·dat·ed (si dā′tid) *verb.* Made calm. *The nervous patient was **sedated** so she could sleep.*

sen·sa·tion·al (sen sā′shə nəl) *adjective.* Arousing or intending to arouse great excitement or interest; outstanding or extraordinary. *The **sensational** news story was, in fact, an exaggeration.*

sev·ered (sev′ərd) *verb.* Separated by cutting or breaking. *The hose was **severed** when the gardener hit it by accident.*

shak•i•ly (shāk´i lē) *adverb.* Moving quickly to and fro, up and down, or side to side. *The little boy **shakily** picked up the heavy box.*

sheep•ish•ly (shē´pish lē) *adverb.* In an awkward, shy, or embarrassed way. *After slipping on the floor, the man **sheepishly** got up and left the room.*

sig•nif•i•cance (sig nif´i kəns) *noun.* Of special value or importance. *The flag of any nation holds **significance** for its people.*

sleuth•ing (slü´thing) *verb.* The act of detecting or investigating. *Ramona's **sleuthing** led her to solve the mystery.*

sou•ve•nir (sü´və nîr´, sü´və nîr´) *adjective.* Reminder of a person, place, or event; keepsake. *Mom kept the **souvenir** baseball we bought at the championship game.*

spe•cial•ists (spesh´ə lists) *noun, plural.* Persons who focus on or specialize in a particular branch of a profession or field of study. *When faced with a disease, it is helpful to consult **specialists**.*

spec•ta•tors (spek´tā tərz) *noun, plural.* People who observe. *The spectators cheered for their team.*

spec•u•lat•ed (spek´yə lā´tid) *verb.* Thought carefully or seriously about; thought of reasons or answers for. *Because there were so few fish in the lake, the community **speculated** on the possibility of pollution.*

spic•y (spī´sē) *adjective.* Seasoned with a spice or spices, such as pepper or cinnamon. *At first Mia was afraid to try the **spicy** food, but when she did, she loved it.*

spon•sor•ing (spon´sə ring) *verb.* Assuming responsibility for or support of another person or thing. *Ms. Kaplan will be **sponsoring** the newspaper next year.*

spon•ta•ne•ous (spon tā´nē əs) *adjective.* On the spur of the moment; unplanned. *Since I like to control everything, I am not a **spontaneous** person.*

starch (stärch) *noun.* A carbohydrate used for stiffening cloth. *Stiffen that tablecloth with **starch**.*

sta•tis•tics (stə tis´tiks) *noun.* Numerical facts or data or the study of such. ***Statistics** show that American women vote in greater numbers than do American men.*

stead•fast•ly (sted´fast´lē) *adverb.* In an unchanging, unwavering way; faithfully. *The crew was **steadfastly** loyal to their captain.*

sum•mit (sum´it) *noun.* The highest part or point. *The climbers reached the **summit** of the mountain and had a fabulous view.*

sump•tu•ous (sum´chü əs) *adjective.* Expensive and lavish, richly done. *The castle had **sumptuous** furnishings.*

su•per•sti•tious (sü´pər stish´əs) *adjective.* Having beliefs based on an unreasoning fear of the unknown. *Many architects of tall buildings are **superstitious** and never include a thirteenth floor.*

sweet•en (swē´tən) *verb.* To make or become sweet or sweeter. *Because the batter was bitter, the cook had to **sweeten** it with honey.*

---

at; āpe; fär; câre; end; mē; it; īce; pîerce; hot; ōld; sông; fôrk; oil; out; up; ūse; rüle; pùll; tûrn; chin; sing; shop; thin; <u>th</u>is; hw in white; zh in treasure.

The symbol ə stands for the unstressed vowel sound in about, taken, pencil, lemon, and circus.

swiv•eled (swiv´əld) *verb.* Turned something on a base. *The principal swiveled around in her chair when she heard me enter her office.*

sym•me•try (sim´i trē) *noun.* An arrangement of parts that are alike on either side of a central line; beauty, proportion, and harmony of form. *The starfish shows a lovely symmetry in its shape.*

Tt

tech•nol•o•gy (tek nol´ə jē) *noun.* Methods and machines used in doing things in science or industry. *The surgeons used the newest technology during the operation.*

ter•rac•ing (ter´i sing) *verb.* To form raised, level platforms of earth with vertical or sloping fronts or sides. *The farmers were terracing their land to conserve the soil.*

ter•rain (tə rān´) *noun.* A region or tract of land. *The terrain was not easy to climb; it was muddy and very steep.*

tink•er•ing (ting´kə ring) *verb.* To busy oneself in a trifling or aimless way; putter. *The farmer had been tinkering with the engine of his tractor all morning.*

trench•es (trench´əz) *noun, plural.* Long, narrow ditches. *We dug trenches around the road to put in new sewer lines.*

tri•ples (trip´əlz) *noun, plural.* Hits in baseball when a batter reaches third base. *Sara hit two triples during the game.*

tur•bu•lence (tûr´byə ləns) *noun.* Violent disorder or commotion. *There was so much turbulence on the flight that the attendants had to walk carefully in the aisles.*

typ•i•cal (tip´i kəl) *adjective.* Showing the qualities of a particular type; usual. *Jake's joking response was typical; he likes to get me to laugh about my problems.*

Uu

un•bear•a•ble (un bâr´ə bəl) *adjective.* That which cannot be endured or tolerated. *When there are presents to open, the wait can be unbearable!*

un•der•growth (un´dər grōth´) *noun.* The growth of small plants beneath the large trees of a forest. *The hikers had to make a trail in the woods by cutting down the undergrowth.*

un•de•tec•ted (un´di tek´tid) *verb.* Not being noticed or discovered. *The secret plot was undetected for some time, but the police soon learned the truth.*

un•done (un dun´) *adjective.* Unfastened; untied; open. *The ribbon on the package came undone, and Chris was tempted to open it!*

un•i•mag•i•na•ble (un´i maj´ə nə bəl) *adjective.* Unable to be imagined; hard to imagine. *That the whole class could fail the test was unimaginable.*

u•ni•ver•sal•ly (ū´nə vûr´sə lē) *adverb.* In every instance or place; without exception. *The movie was universally criticized for its horrible acting and ridiculous plot.*

un•sat•is•fac•to•ry (un´sat is fak´tə rē) *adjective.* Not good enough to meet a need or desire; not satisfactory. *Builders cannot risk doing unsatisfactory work because the safety of many is in their hands.*

un•stead•y (un sted´ē) *adjective.* Shaky or not firm. *Everyone was nervous when Michael climbed up the **unsteady** ladder to get on the roof.*

u•ten•sils (ū ten´səlz) *noun, plural.* An object that is useful in doing or making something. *One third of the world eats with its fingers, one third with chopsticks, and one third with metal **utensils**.*

ut•tered (ut´ərd) *verb.* To express aloud. *The teacher got very angry when someone **uttered** the answer during the test.*

Vv

va•pors (vā´pərz) *noun, plural.* Visible particles of matter suspended in the air, such as mist or smoke. *Our teacher told us that some of the **vapors** from the science experiment were harmful.*

veg•e•ta•tion (vej´i tā´shən) *noun.* Plant life. *The fields and forests are full of **vegetation**.*

ven•om•ous (ven´ə məs) *adjective.* Able to inflict a poisonous wound, especially by biting or stinging. *Some snakes are **venomous**, so be careful not to get too close!*

vic•to•ri•ous (vik tôr´ē əs) *adjective.* Having won a contest or conflict. *The **victorious** team was given a parade when they returned home.*

vig•il (vij´əl) *noun.* The act or period of remaining awake to guard or observe something. *Ka-Po's mom kept a **vigil** all night to be sure the fever came down.*

vig•or•ous•ly (vig´ər əs lē) *adverb.* Done in a powerful or forceful way; with healthy strength. *The lawyer **vigorously** defended the U.S. Constitution.*

vi•tal (vī´təl) *adjective.* Of greatest importance. *The information was **vital** to everyone who wanted the project to succeed.*

Word History

Vital comes from the old French *vital* meaning "having or supporting life."

Ww

with•stood (with stu̇d´) *verb.* Held out against or fought against successfully. *The beach house **withstood** the force of the hurricane.*

wrath (rath) *noun.* Extreme or violent anger. *The football player tried extra hard in the game to avoid the **wrath** of his coach.*

wreck•age (rek´ij) *noun.* The remains of anything that has been destroyed. *A lot of **wreckage** from the sunken ship washed up on the beach.*

at; āpe; fär; câre; end; mē; it; īce; pîerce; hot; ōld; sông; fôrk; oil; out; up; ūse; rüle; pu̇ll; tûrn; chin; sing; shop; thin; **th**is; hw in white; zh in treasure.

The symbol ə stands for the unstressed vowel sound in about, taken, pencil, lemon, and circus.

Acknowledgments

The publisher gratefully acknowledges permission to reprint the following copyrighted material:

"After Apple Picking" by Robert Frost is from NORTH OF BOSTON. Copyright © 1915. Reprinted by permission of Henry Holt and Company.

"Amazing Artificial Limbs" includes information from "Bionic Arms for 11-Year-Old." BBC News. March 15, 2001. http://news.bbc.co.uk/1/hi/health/1222642.stm.

"Baseball by the Numbers" chart is from THE NEW YORK TIMES 2004 ALMANAC edited by John W. Wright. Copyright © 2003 by The New York Times Company. Used by permission of the Penguin Group Penguin Putnam Inc.

"Bicycle Riding" is from CRICKET by Sandra Liatsos. Copyright © 1984 by Sandra Liatsos. Reprinted by permission of Marion Reiner for the Author.

"Birdfoot's Grampa" is from NATIVE AMERICAN STORIES by Joseph Bruchac, illustrated by John Kahionhes Fadden. Text copyright © 1991 by Joseph Bruchac. Illustrations copyright © 1991 by John Kahionhes Fadden.

"Breaking into Print: Before and After the Invention of the Printing the Press" is from BREAKING INTO PRINT: BEFORE AND AFTER THE INVENTION OF THE PRINTING PRESS by Stephen Krensky, illustrations by Bonnie Christensen. Text copyright © 1996 by Stephen Krensky. Illustrations copyright © 1996 by Bonnie Christensen. Published simultaneously in Canada by Little, Brown & Company (Canada) Limited.

"Breaking Through" is from BREAKING THROUGH by Francisco Jiménez. Copyright © 2001 by Francisco Jiménez. Reprinted by permission of Houghton Mifflin Company.

"Caged Bird" is from MAYA ANGELOU: POEMS by Maya Angelou. Copyright © 1986 by Bantam Books. Reprinted by permission of Random House, Inc.

"Cool Collections" from "Smithsonian Kids Collecting." http://smithsonianeducation.org//students/idealabs/amazing_collections.html.

"The Crow and the Pitcher" is from AESOP'S FABLES by Jerry Pinkney. Copyright © 2000 by Jerry Pinkney. Reprinted by permission of SeaStar Books, a division of North-South Books, Inc.

"The Dog of Pompeii" is from THE DONKEY OF GOD by Louis Untermeyer, illustrated by James MacDonald. Text copyright © 1999 The Estate of Louis Untermeyer. This permission is expressly granted by Laurence S. Untermeyer.

"Earth and the Sun" includes information from McGRAW-HILL SCIENCE. Copyright © 2002 by Macmillan/McGraw-Hill. Illustration credits: p. C20: Art Thompson.

"The Emperor's Silent Army: Terracotta Warriors of Ancient China" is from THE EMPEROR'S SILENT ARMY: TERRACOTTA WARRIORS OF ANCIENT CHINA by Jane O'Connor. Copyright © Jane O'Connor, 2002. Reprinted by permission of Viking, a division of Penguin Putnam Books for Young Readers.

"Empire in the Andes" includes information from LOST CITY OF THE INCAS by Hiram Bingham and New World News. Copyright © 2001 by Labyrinthina.

"Exploring the Titanic" is from EXPLORING THE TITANIC by Robert D. Ballard, cover illustration by Ken Marshall. Text copyright © Odyssey Corporation 1998. Illustration copyright © 1988 Madison Publishing Inc. Used by permission of Scholastic Inc.

"The Golden Touch: The Story of Bacchus and King Midas" is from FAVORITE GREEK MYTHS by Mary Pope Osborne. Copyright © 1989 by Mary Pope Osborne. Reprinted by permission of Scholastic Inc.

"The Great Serum Race: Blazing the Iditarod Trail" is from THE GREAT SERUM RACE: BLAZING THE IDITAROD TRAIL by Debbie S. Miller, illustrations by Jon Van Zyle. Text copyright © 2002 by Debbie S. Miller. Illustrations copyright © 2002 by Jon Van Zyle. Used by permission of Walker & Company.

"Haiku" is from JAPANESE HAIKU by Boncho. Translated by Peter Beilenson. Copyright © 1955, 1956 by Peter Pauper Press. Reprinted by permission of Peter Pauper Press.

"Honus and Me" is from HONUS AND ME by Dan Gutman. Copyright © 1997 by Dan Gutman. Used by permission of HarperCollins Children's Books.

"How Tía Lola Came to Visit Stay" is from HOW TÍA LOLA CAME TO VISIT STAY by Julia Alvarez. Text copyright © 2001 by Julia Alvarez. Jacket Illustration copyright © by Sally Wern Comport. Reprinted by permission of Alfred A. Knopf, a division of Random House.

"How to Conduct a Survey" is from MACMILLAN/McGRAW-HILL MATH. Copyright © 2005 by Macmillan/McGraw-Hill. Illustration credits: p. 140: Brian Dugan.

"Interrupted Journey: Saving Endangered Sea Turtles" is from INTERRUPTED JOURNEY: SAVING ENDANGERED SEA TURTLES by Kathryn Lasky. Copyright © 2001 by Kathryn Lasky. Used by permission of Candlewick Press.

"I Dream a World" by Langston Hughes is from THE COLLECTED POEMS OF LANGSTON HUGHES edited by Arnold Rampersad and David Roessel. Copyright © 1994 by the Estate of Langston Hughes.

"In the Days of the Vaqueros: America's First True Cowboys" is from IN THE DAYS OF THE VAQUEROS: AMERICA'S FIRST TRUE COWBOYS by Russell Freedman. Text copyright © 2001 by Russell Freedman. Reprinted by permission of Houghton Mifflin Company.

"Juan Verdades: The Man Who Couldn't Tell a Lie" is from JUAN VERDADES: THE MAN WHO COULDN'T TELL A LIE by Joe Hayes, illustrated by Joseph Daniel Fiedler. Text copyright © 2001 by Joe Hayes. Illustrations copyright © 2001 by Joseph Daniel Fiedler. Used by permission of Orchard Books, an imprint of Scholastic Inc.

"LAFFF" is from LAFFF by Lensey Namioka, illustrations by Raúl Colón. Copyright © 1993 by Lensey Namioka. Used by permission.

"Leonardo da Vinci" is from LEONARDO DA VINCI by Diane Stanley. Copyright © 1996 by Diane Stanley. Used by permission of William Morrow and Company, Inc.

"Leonardo da Vinci" caption from http://www.museoscienza.org/english/leonardo/vitc.html.

"Leonardo's Horse" is from LEONARDO'S HORSE by Jean Fritz, illustrated by Hudson Talbott. Text copyright © 2001 by Jean Fritz. Illustrations copyright © 2001 by Hudson Talbott. Reprinted by permission of G.P. Putnam's Sons, a division of Penguin Putnam Books for Young Readers.

"Let It Shine" is from LET IT SHINE by Andrea Davis Pinkney, illustrated by Stephen Alcorn. Text copyright © by Andrea Davis Pinkney. Illustrations copyright © 2000 by Stephen Alcorn. Used by permission of Harcourt.

"Lost City: The Discovery of Machu Picchu" is from LOST CITY: THE DISCOVERY OF MACHU PICCHU by Ted Lewin. Copyright © 2003 by Ted Lewin. Reprinted by permission of Philomel Books, a division of Penguin Putnam Books for Young Readers.

"The Magic Gourd" is from THE MAGIC GOURD by Baba Wagué Diakité. Text and art copyright © 2003 by Baba Wagué Diakité. Used by permission of Scholastic Press, a division of Scholastic Inc.

"Major Taylor: Champion Cyclist" is from MAJOR TAYLOR: CHAMPION CYCLIST by Lesa Cline-Ransome, illustrated by James E. Ransome. Text copyright © 2004 by Lesa Cline-Ransome. Illustrations copyright © 2004 by James E. Ransome. Reprinted by permission of Atheneum Books for Young Readers, an Imprint of Simon & Schuster Children's Publishing Division.

"The Night of the Pomegranate" is from SOME OF THE KINDER PLANETS by Tim Wynne-Jones. Copyright © 1993 by Tim Wynne-Jones. Used by permission of Puffin Books.

"Nothing Ever Happens on 90th Street" is from NOTHING EVER HAPPENS ON 90TH STREET by Roni Schotter, illustrated by Kyrsten Brooker. Text copyright © 1997 by Roni Schotter. Illustrations copyright © 1997 by Kyrsten Brooker. Reprinted by permission of Orchard Books.

"Old Stormalong Finds a Man-Sized Ship" is from BIG MEN, BIG COUNTRY by Paul Robert Walker, illustrations by James Bernardin. Text copyright © 1993 by Paul Robert Walker. Illustration copyright © 1993 by James Bernardin. Reprinted by permission of Harcourt, Inc.

ILLUSTRATIONS

Cover Illustration: Anton Petrov

PHOTOGRAPHY

All photographs by Macmillan/McGraw-Hill except where noted below.